BRUCE

BRUCE

PETER AMES CARLIN

SIMON &
SCHUSTER

London · New York · Sydney · Toronto · New Delhi

A CBS COMPANY

First published in Great Britain by Simon & Schuster UK Ltd, 2012
This paperback edition published by Simon & Schuster UK Ltd, 2013
A CBS COMPANY

Copyright © 2012 by Peter Ames Carlin

1 3 5 7 9 10 8 6 4 2

Simon & Schuster UK Ltd
1st Floor
222 Gray's Inn Road
London WC1X 8HB

www.simonandschuster.co.uk

Simon & Schuster Australia, Sydney
Simon & Schuster India, New Delhi

A CIP catalogue record for this book is available from the British Library

ISBN: 978-1-47114-193-5
ISBN: 978-1-47111-235-5 (ebook)

Designed by Ruth Lee-Mui

Printed and bound by CPI Group (UK) Ltd, Croydon, CR0 4YY

For Sarah Carlin Ames—"This is not a dark ride."

CONTENTS

PROLOGUE:
THE GUT BOMB KING

THE FIRST TIME ANYONE CALLED Bruce Springsteen the Boss was in the early weeks of 1971, in the dining room of a chilly apartment on the edge of downtown Asbury Park. Once a beauty parlor, the ground-floor flat was then the home for Steven Van Zandt, Albee Tellone, and John Lyon, all musicians in their early twenties and already veterans of the club circuit on the Jersey Shore. Their house became a nexus in Asbury Park's rock scene. When they threw open the door for their weekly Monopoly games the place filled quickly. Garry was a regular, so was Big Bad Bobby, Danny, Davey, and a dozen others.

Bruce had a particular talent for the rogue brand of Monopoly they played. In this version, the game's actual rules barely figured in the action. The real gaming took place between the players' turns, when they could build alliances, negotiate settlements, offer bribes, and resort to trickery, coercion, and what an outsider might think of as cheating. And this was where Bruce excelled, due both to his shifty powers of persuasion and the leverage provided by the sacks of candy bars, Ring Dings, and Pepsis he brought with him. Funny what a young man, when hungry and presented with two cream-filled cupcakes of sheer chemical deliciousness, will agree to when it's 2 a.m. and he's really, really hungry.

And so Bruce won enough Monopoly games to inspire the others to dub him the Gut Bomb King. This lasted only until Bruce, who also had a talent for inventing nicknames, came up with a new one for himself: the Boss.

That stuck. "I remember people calling him that and not taking it seriously," recalls fellow bandleader Steve Van Zandt. "Not 'til I started calling him the Boss. Then they took it seriously because I was a boss, too. So when I started calling him the Boss the vibe was, 'If Stevie's doing it, there's something to this!'"

Hearing this now, Bruce cackles cheerily. "I'll leave you with that," is all he says.

For three years, Bruce's semi-secret nickname didn't leave the tiny loop of his band and their friends. All of whom understood how seriously Bruce took such things. Because one of the privileges of being a Boss is controlling who can and can't call you that. Definitely the band and the roadies. Also some friends, but only the ones who bore their own Bruce-bestowed nicknames. Southside, Miami, Albany Al, and so on. Which made it all the more outrageous when the Boss got wrenched into the public domain.

It happened in 1974, when the crowds got bigger and the records began to sell. Bruce's Jersey Shore mystique grew into a point of journalistic intrigue, and when one writer heard a crew member drop a casual "Hey, Boss!" into a conversation the game was up. By the time *Born to Run* broke through in 1975 the Boss had become something else entirely. An honorific. A championship title. Another piece of Bruce sacrificed to his own ambition.

Bruce didn't complain in public but he made his feelings clear as early as the mid-1970s by revising the lyrics of his best-loved party song, "Rosalita": "You don't have to call me lieutenant, Rosie/Just don't ever call me *Boss*!"

Because there were rules. Including the crucial one about not acknowledging the existence of the rules. Because the Boss isn't supposed to be seen compelling others to put him on a pedestal. As far as you know he's just there, his power and authority as inevitable as the tides. So don't even ask, because that's when Bruce will cock his head and give you that vaguely annoyed look.

"Rules? I don't have any particular strict rules about it."

Ask again in a slightly different way and his vaguely annoyed expression gains clarity.

"There was no exalted reasoning behind it," Bruce says with purposeful evenness. "That was just because I paid people's salary and it was literally like, 'What are we going to do? Hmm, I don't know, somebody better ask the Boss.' So really, it was just a name you would use wherever you were working."

So the Boss is a generic term? With no larger significance or accompanying ethic? Meaning that anyone, present company included, can call him Boss whenever and wherever?

For a moment Bruce just stares.

"Well, for you to call me that would be *ridiculous*," he says. "Besides that, it wouldn't necessarily be *right*."

He throws back a little tequila and shrugs again.

"And this is still the first I've heard about rules."

Call him Bruce.

BRUCE

ONE

THE PLACE I LOVED
THE MOST

THE TRUCK COULDN'T HAVE BEEN moving fast. Not down a sleepy residential street like McLean. If it had just turned in from Route 79—
known in Freehold, New Jersey, as South Street—it would have been
going even more slowly, since no seven-ton truck could round a
90-degree corner at a fast clip. But the truck had the height and breadth
to all but fill the side road and sweep the other cars, bikes, and pedestri-
ans to the side until it grumbled past. Assuming the other folks were paying attention to the road ahead.

The five-year-old girl on the tricycle had other things on her mind.
She might have been racing her friend to the Lewis Oil gas station on the
corner. Or maybe she was simply a child at play, feeling the spring in the
air on a late afternoon in April 1927.

Either way, Virginia Springsteen didn't see the truck coming. If she
heard the driver's panicked honk when she veered into the road, she
didn't have time to react. The driver stomped hard on the brakes, but

by then it didn't matter. He heard, and felt, a terrible thump. Alerted by the screams of the neighbors, the girl's parents rushed outside and found their little daughter unconscious but still breathing, They rushed her first to the office of Dr. George G. Reynolds, then to Long Branch Hospital, more than thirty minutes east of Freehold. And that's where Virginia Springsteen died.

The mourning began immediately. Family members, friends, and neighbors streamed to the little house on Randolph Street to comfort the girl's parents. Fred Springsteen, a twenty-seven-year-old technician at the Freehold Electrical Shop downtown, kept his hands in his pockets and spoke quietly. But his twenty-eight-year-old wife, Alice, could not contain herself. Hair frazzled and eyes veined by grief, she sat helplessly as her body clutched with sobs. She could barely look at Virginia's toddler brother, Douglas. The boy's father couldn't be much help either, given the pall of his own mourning and the overwhelming needs of his distraught wife. So in the immediate aftermath of the tragedy virtually all of the care and feeding of the twenty-month-old boy fell to Alice's sisters, Anna and Jane. Eventually the others eased back into their ordinary lives. But the approach and passing of summer did nothing to ease Alice's grief.

She could take no comfort in the clutching arms of her small son. Nearing his second birthday in August the boy grew dirty and scrawny enough to require an intervention. Alice's sisters came to gather his clothes, crib, and toys and took the toddler to live with his aunt Jane Cashion and her family until his parents were well enough to care for him again. Two to three years passed before Alice and Fred asked to be re-united with their son. He went home soon afterward, but Virginia's spirit continued to hover in Alice's vision. When Alice gazed at her son, she always seemed to be seeing something else; the absence of the one thing she had loved the most and lost so heedlessly.

A semblance of family structure restored, the Springsteen home still ran according to its residents' imprecise sense of reality. No longer employed by the Freehold Electrical Shop, Fred worked at home, sifting through mountains of abandoned electronics in order to repair or build radios he would later sell to the migrant farmworkers camped on the fringe of town. Alice, who never worked, moved according to her internal currents. If she didn't feel like getting up in the morning, she didn't. If Doug didn't want to go to school in the morning, she let him stay in bed. Cleaning and home repair ceased to be priorities. The walls shed curls of paint. The plastered kitchen ceiling fell off in chunks. With a single kerosene burner to heat the entire house, winters inside were Siberian. For Douglas, whose DNA came richly entwined with darker threads, the peeling wallpaper and crumbling windowsills framed his growing sense of life and the world. No matter where he was, no matter what he was doing, he would always be looking out through the fractured windows of 87 Randolph Street.

Doug Springsteen grew to be a shy but spirited teenager matriculating at Freehold High School. He loved baseball, especially when he was with his first cousin and best friend, Dave "Dim" Cashion, an ace pitcher and first baseman. Cashion was already considered one of the best players to ever emerge from Freehold. Off the diamond, the cousins passed the hours shooting pool at the small game rooms tucked between the stores, barbershops, and news stores clustering Freehold's central intersection at South and Main Streets. Cashion, who was seven years Doug's senior, launched his baseball career just after leaving school in 1936. He spent the next five years working his way from the local amateur and semipro leagues all the way into the major league farm system. He got there just in time for World War II to shutter the leagues and redirect him into the US Army.

Raised by parents for whom education amounted to a long distraction from real life, Doug quit his studies at Freehold Regional after his freshman year ended in 1941, taking an entry-level job as a bottom-rung laborer (his official title was *creel boy*) in Freehold's thriving Karagheusian rug mill. He kept that job until June 1943, when his eighteenth birthday made him eligible to join the army. Shipped to Europe in the midst of the war, Doug drove an equipment truck. Back in Freehold following the war's conclusion in 1945, Doug took it easy and lived off the $20 in veteran's pay he received from the government each month.

As Fred and Alice made clear, academic and professional ambition were not priorities, if only because of their absolute disinterest in achievement—to say nothing of books, culture, or anything that gestured beyond the here-and-now. So if Doug wanted to live in their house and slouch through his life, that suited them perfectly. He was, after all, his parents' child.

Doug barely made a gesture toward adult life until his cousin Ann Cashion (Dim's younger sister) came by offering a night out. She had a friend named Adele Zerilli he might like to meet. So how about a double date? Doug shrugged and said sure. A few nights later the foursome were sitting in a cafe together, making polite talk while Doug snuck glances at the bewitchingly talkative dark-haired girl sitting across the table. "I couldn't get rid of him after that," Adele says now. "Then he says he wants to marry me. I said, *'You don't have a job!'* He said 'Well, if you marry me, I'll get a job.'" She shakes her head and laughs.

"Oh, God. What I got into after that."

Married on February 22, 1947, Douglas and Adele Springsteen rented a small apartment in the Jerseyville neighborhood on the eastern edge of Freehold and experienced the postwar boom along with much of America. True to his word, Doug had landed a job on the factory floor of the Ford auto plant in nearby Edison. Adele already had a full-time job as a secretary for a real estate lawyer. A baby was on the way by the start of 1949, and the boy emerged at 10:50 p.m. on the evening of September 23, taking his first breath in Long Branch Hospital (since renamed Monmouth Medical Center), where his father's sister had breathed her last twenty-two years earlier. He had brown hair and brown eyes, weighed in at 6.6 pounds, and was declared healthy in every respect. His twenty-four-year-old parents named him Bruce Frederick Springsteen and though they had their own home, instructed the nurse to write into the birth certificate that their home address in Freehold was 87 Randolph Street.

When his wife and child were discharged from the hospital a week later, Doug took them to his parents' house and handed little Bruce to his mother. She held him close, cooing gently at the first new life that had entered their home since the long ago death of Virginia. When Alice peered into his eyes, her own tired face came alight. Almost as if she were seeing the glimmer that had once glowed from inside her own lost daughter. She clutched the boy to herself and for the longest time would not let him go.

She must have loved you to pieces, Bruce heard someone say not long ago. He laughed darkly. "To pieces," he said, "would be correct."

Spending his first months in his parents' small apartment, Bruce ate, slept, stirred, and cried like every other baby. And yet the blood in his veins carried traces of forebears whose lives describe American history going all the way back to the early seventeenth century, when Casper Springsteen and wife Geertje left Holland to build their future in the New World. Casper didn't survive very long,[1] but a son who had remained in Holland followed in 1652, and Joosten Springsteen launched generations of Springsteens, including a branch that drifted to the farmlands of Monmouth County, New Jersey, at some point in the mid-eighteenth century. After the Revolutionary War broke out in 1775, John Springsteen left his farm to serve as a private in the Monmouth County militia, fighting multiple battles during a three-year hitch that ended in 1779. Alexander Springsteen, also of Monmouth County, joined the Union army in 1862, serving as a private with the New Jersey Infantry until the end of the Civil War in 1865. Throughout, and into the twentieth century, the Springsteens worked as farm laborers and, with the growth of industrialization in Freehold, factory workers.

Alice Springsteen's family were Irish immigrants from Kildare who came to America in 1850, settling in the farmlands of Monmouth County, where they worked the fields and, in some cases, pushed their families up another rung or two on the economic ladder. Christopher Garrity, the patriarch of the family, sent for his wife and children in 1853. His daughter Ann met a neighbor, a laborer named John Fitzgibbon, soon after and married him in 1856. Two years later he invested the $127.50 it took to buy a family home at 87 Mulberry Street[2], a street in a growing neighborhood of working-class homes just south of Freehold's

---

[1] He may have died during the ocean crossing, or possibly before the boat even left Holland, depending on which genealogical record you consult.
[2] Renamed Randolph Street in the 1870s.

center. Ann Garrity marked their place by planting a beech tree seedling she had brought to America from Kildare. The tree flourished, as did Ann and John Fitzgibbon, who had two children in the years before John went to serve in the Civil War. As a sergeant in the Union army, John earned a chest full of ribbons for his courage on the battlefields of Fredericksburg and Charlottesville, Virginia, then returned home to father another seven children before dying in 1872. Remarried to a shoemaker named Patrick Farrell, Ann delivered a set of twins, including a girl named Jennie, whose own daughter, Alice, eventually married a young electronics worker named Fred Springsteen.

If only every member of the family could have grown as straight and strong as Ann Garrity's beech tree. But as fate and genetics must have it, both sides of Fred and Alice Springsteen's lineage came with a shadow history of fractured souls. The drinkers and the failures, the wild-eyed, the ones who crumbled inside of themselves until they vanished altogether. These were the relatives who lived in rooms you didn't enter. Their stories were the ones that mustn't be told. They inspired the silence that both secreted and concentrated the poison in the family blood. Doug could already sense the venom creeping within himself. Which may have had something to do with why he had fallen so deeply for Adele Zerilli, whose indomitable spirit would protect and nurture him for the rest of his life.

The youngest of the three daughters born to Anthony and Adelina, Italian immigrants who had arrived as teenagers (separately) at Ellis Island during the first years of the twentieth century, Adele spent her childhood in the Bay Ridge neighborhood at the southern tip of Brooklyn. The family's luxe home came courtesy of Anthony, who had learned English on the fly and quickly earned his American citizenship and a law school degree. Taking a job in a law firm his uncle had founded to specialize in real estate, investments, and the like, Anthony's bluster grew along with the firm's success in the 1920s. Short but broad chested, possessed of a big voice, stylish wardrobe, and charisma to match, the thriving attorney moved through the world like a weather front, altering the barometric pressure of any room he entered. Adelina, on the other hand, pursued the life of an old-fashioned Italian lady, wearing traditional dresses, surrounding herself with reminders of the Old World, and refusing to utter more than a small handful of English words even as her daughters grew to be modern American girls.

When the Depression hit in 1929, Anthony wished he could go back in time, too. Reduced to moving his family into an apartment, he borrowed some of his remaining clients' cash to keep his own investments afloat. Then he borrowed more. Then he borrowed too much. Meanwhile, Anthony had other indulgences, too, including an affair with a secretary who eventually claimed his heart. Anthony's marriage ended first, and then the federal agents came knocking. "I guess the word is *embezzlement*," Adele says.

Then the word was *convicted*, then *sentenced*. And as Anthony prepared to spend a few years away, he bought an inexpensive old farmhouse on sixty acres near the edge of Freehold and had it fixed up so his family could live as comfortably, if inexpensively, as possible while he did his bit in the grim caverns of Sing Sing prison. Only by then, Adelina's broken marriage and abrupt financial descent had unstrung the observant Catholic so thoroughly that she decided to let her daughters make their own household while she took refuge with relatives. Told to provide for her younger sisters, the recent high school grad Dora took a job as a waitress and kept her sisters on a short leash. Weekly visits from an aunt who always came bearing a suitcase full of spaghetti and tinned tuna helped make ends meet. The girls could also count on the help of the man their father had introduced as George Washington, an African-American day laborer he hired to serve as his daughters' chauffeur and handyman. And though his name wasn't really George Washington (that was apparently Anthony's invention), and he was a grown man in his thirties, he became a regular presence in the home. "All we knew about him was that he could dance," Adele says. According to middle sister Eda, the action heated up at seven o'clock when the nightly *Your Hit Parade* came on the radio. That's when they turned up the volume, pulled aside the living room rug, and kicked up their heels. "That's when we learned how to dance," she continues. "It sounds crazy, I know, but that's how it went." The vision makes Adele's son laugh out loud. "They used to go to the balls, and the soldiers were on leave, and they went to dance, dance, dance," Bruce says. "They had it all going on."

Dora and Eda had sided with their mother in the divorce, while Adele was officially neutral but sympathetic enough to heed her father's request to accompany his girlfriend on the journey to Ossining, New York, so she would have the right to participate in Sing Sing's family visiting hours. When Dora got wind of her sister's jailhouse visits, she filed papers with the Monmouth County courts to bring it to a stop. And when Anthony convinced Adele to join his beloved secretary on another trip anyway, Dora had her sister put on probation. "It was stupid, because I was a baby!" Adele says. So she must have been terribly aggrieved, yes? "Nope. I just couldn't go anymore, and that was that." When daughter Ginny contradicts her—"She never got over it"—Adele admits it instantly: "I still have the letter!"

Either way, the dancing never stopped. And even when the Zerilli girls became adults and took on jobs, careers, and husbands, were made to confront hardship, and even face down tragedy, the sound of music always got their spirits up, always pulled them to their feet, swept aside the carpet, and carried them away. "To this day," Bruce says. "You get the three of those girls, and they'll still dance. It was a big part of their lives. Still is."

Adele became pregnant again five months into Bruce's life, and when the Springsteens' second child—a girl they named Virginia in tribute to Doug's lost sister—arrived in early 1951, it didn't take long for Doug and Adele to realize that their apartment was no longer large enough to contain their growing family. Without the money to rent a larger place, they had no choice but to retreat to 87 Randolph Street, searching for space among the broken radio parts, the unsteady furniture, and the drafty corners of the living room. And then there was Alice, so joyous in having her beloved Bruce in the house she could barely contain her excitement. Virginia, on the other hand, barely registered in her vision. "They were sick people, but what do I know when I'm so young?" Adele says. "I thought I was doing the best thing calling her Virginia, but it wasn't." Besides, Alice and Fred had already settled on their favorite. "With Bruce, he could do no wrong."

From the day the family moved in, Alice catered to her young grandson like a sun king. She washed and folded his clothes, then laid out each morning's wardrobe on his freshly made bed. When Adele and Doug were out during the day, both Alice and Fred kept the toddler fed, warm, entertained, and always within reach. Ginny, on the other hand, was lucky to get much more than the occasional glance. Quickly frustrated by her grandparents' disinterest, two-year-old Ginny demanded to be left with other adults during the day. Adele: "She didn't want to stay with them, so she never did."

"That was very caught up with the role I was intended to play," Bruce says. "To replace the lost child. So that made it a very complicated sort of affection and one that wasn't completely mine. We [Ginny and Bruce] were very symbolic, which is an enormous burden on a young child. And that became a problem for everybody." Consumed by his grandparents' unyielding attention, Bruce assumed that they, and not his parents, were his primary caregivers. "It was very emotionally incestuous, and a lot of parental roles got crossed. Who you answered to and the different kind of responsibilities you had were very confusing for a young kid. Your allegiances were being pulled in different ways. Then we were beyond the point of no return."

Bruce remembers his grandparents' house as a strange, austere place, its cracked walls adding to an atmosphere already clotted with loss, memory, and regret. "The dead daughter was a big presence," he says. "Her portrait was on the wall, always front and center." Fred and Alice trooped everyone to the St. Rose of Lima cemetery each week to touch her stone and pick weeds and errant grass from the little girl's grave. "That graveyard," Ginny says, "was like our playground. We were there all the time." Death was a regular presence, particularly with so many older relatives on the block. "We went to a lot of wakes," Bruce says. "You got used to seeing dead people lying around."

Death was one thing. But for Alice, whose Old World Catholicism came larded with superstition and other terrors, eternal damnation was more difficult to confront. Grandma Alice sensed the presence of Satan in lightning and thunder, so the first flash would send her into the throes of panic. Within seconds she scooped up the children and sprinted the block to the home of her sister Jane, who kept bottles of holy water to protect her family against such attacks. "People would huddle together," Bruce recalls. "You'd have near hysteria."

When Fred lost the use of his left arm to a serious stroke in the late 1950s, he brought Bruce along to help troll for cast-off radios and electronic parts in the neighborhood trash cans. The time together deepened the bond between grandfather and grandson, and drew the young boy deeper into the eccentric rhythms of his grandparents' home. So while Adele's work as a secretary kept her on a normal schedule, the rest of the family—including Doug, already riding the currents of intermittent employment and long stretches at loose ends—abandoned clocks altogether. "There were no rules," Bruce says. "I was living life like I've never heard of another child living it, to be honest with you." At four years old, the boy took to staying up late into the night. Rising from his bed, padding out to the living room, flipping through his picture books, playing with his toys, and watching television. "At three thirty in the morning, the whole house was asleep and I'd be watching 'The Star-Spangled Banner' and then seeing the test pattern come on. And I'm talking *before* the first grade." Many years later, when Bruce finished school and took to living by the musician's up-all-night schedule, he had an epiphany: "I just returned to the life I'd had as a five-year-old. It was like, 'Hey! All that school stuff was a mistake!' It was a return to how I lived as a very small child, which was upside down, but that's the way it was."

When Adele read to him each night, Bruce made a nightly ritual of a picture book called *Brave Cowboy Bill*. Written by Kathryn and Byron Jackson, illustrated by Richard Scarry (in a style not the least bit reminiscent of his *Busy, Busy World* books), and published in 1950, *Brave Cowboy Bill* became such a fixation for Bruce that Adele could recite it from memory on her eightieth birthday in 2005. Central character Bill, who looks to be about six years old, storms gently across the frontier, rounding up cattle rustlers, killing deer and elk for his dinner, befriending Indians—albeit at gunpoint ("We'll be friends, he told them firmly . . .")—kills a bear, dominates every competition in a rodeo, and then stays up all night singing songs by his campfire before coming home to dream of the frontier where "No one *ever* argued with the daring Cowboy Bill." All of which serves as an intriguing glimpse into the aspirational fantasies of a boy from a home governed by such a skewed set of expectations.[3]

When Bruce became old enough to play outside with the other neighborhood kids, his visits to their well-kept family homes both confused and bothered him. Suddenly he realized that his friends' bedroom walls were freshly painted, their windows didn't rattle in the frames, and the ceilings in their kitchens stayed securely above their heads. All the adults seemed dependable; steady jobs, regular paychecks, and no edge of incipient hysteria. "I loved my grandparents so deeply, but they were very outsider," he says. "There was an element of guilt and shame, but then I felt bad about being embarrassed."

With Bruce moving toward school age in 1956, Adele signed her son up to start first grade at the St. Rose of Lima's parochial school in the fall. To the extent that Doug had an opinion, he kept it to himself. But Fred and particularly Alice had other plans for their grandson. Bruce, they declared, didn't have to go to school at all if he didn't want to go. Fred hadn't spent much time in school, and neither had Doug. So why make such a fuss getting an education Bruce wouldn't need? Adele, whose father had insisted his daughters all finish high school, at the very least, was having none of it. "He had to go to school," she says. "But [Fred and Alice] wouldn't let him." Already feeling shoved aside in her son's life, and more than tired of playing the dutiful wife in such a topsy-turvy environment, Adele made her stand. "I said to my husband, 'We've gotta get out of here,'" she says. If Doug argued about it, he didn't win. Hearing that a pair of cousins were about to leave their rented duplex apartment at 39 1/2 Institute Street, just three and a half blocks east of Fred and Alice's home, they took over the lease and moved in almost immediately.

It was, Bruce says now, the only way his mother could give her family

[3] And even more so when you count the number of songs he would write about frontier-wandering heroes bent on gaining control over their lives and the meaning of same. Asked to consider the connections between childhood fixation and lifelong creative vision, he laughs. "Rosebud! You found my Rosebud, man!" He does not appear to be serious.

anything like a normal life. But for Bruce, that realization was a long time in coming. As a six-year-old, he says, the abrupt change was devastating. "It was terrible for me at the time because my grandparents had become my de facto parents. So I was basically removed from my family home." The boy's anxiety eased a bit thanks to his daily visits to his grandparents for after-school supervision. It also didn't hurt that the two-bedroom, two-floor apartment on Institute marked a significant step up in the family's residential standards. "We had heat!" says Bruce, who shared the larger of the home's two bedrooms with Ginny. Doug and Adele made do in a cramped room that seemed closer to a closet than a real bedroom. Worse, the house had no water heater, which made dishwashing, and especially bathing in the upstairs tub, complex operations. As Bruce recalls, bathing was not one of his more regular habits.

Already shaken by the abrupt change in his family's home and parental structure, Bruce reported for school in an especially vulnerable, and angry, frame of mind. The nuns' strict rules and work requirements first confused, then enraged the boy. "If you grow up in a home where no one goes to work and no one is coming home, the clock is never relevant," he says. "And suddenly when someone asks you to do something, and says you have twenty minutes to do it, that's going to make you really angry. Because you don't know from twenty minutes." Just as Bruce also had no idea how to sit still in class, absorb the nuns' lessons, or see their pinched faces and ruler-wielding hands as anything more, or less, than earthly visions of a fuming God.

Bruce did what he could to fit in. He pulled on his uniform in the morning, then marched proudly to school with Adele clutching his hand. "He had his head held high when he walked in there, and I thought, 'Good,'" Adele says. But what was going on during the school day? To see for herself, Adele took a break from work and stood across from the playground to check on her son during recess. "And there he is, against the fence, all by himself, not playing with anybody. It was so sad." For Bruce, his tendency for social isolation came as naturally as his secret desire to be at the center of everything.

"Companionship is a natural human impulse, but I didn't make social connections easily," he says. "I was a loner, just to myself, and I had gotten used to it." No matter where he was, his mind was meandering somewhere else. "I had a very vibrant internal life. I seemed to be drawn to other things, different than what the subjects were supposed to be at a given moment. Like how the light was hitting a wall. Or how the stones felt under your feet. Someone might be talking about a normal subject, but I'm sort of zeroing in on that."

Bruce had his small circle of friends, mostly the boys he'd tossed balls and pushed trucks with in the yards around Randolph Street. His closest pal among them was Bobby Duncan, a slightly younger boy he'd befriended when they were both preschoolers. To Duncan, the young Bruce was a regular kid: passionate about baseball, content to spend an afternoon riding bikes to the candy store on Main Street, then pedaling back to his grandparents' house to watch the children's shows on TV, read *Archie* comics, or both. Duncan also noticed his friend's differences. "He was like the lone rebel back then. He didn't care what people thought." Which presented such a striking distinction from the typical grade school boys that the other kids in the neighborhood were often at a loss. Particularly when they grew up enough to battle for stature in the traditional arena of sandlot fistfights. "I grew up on a black block, but we were surrounded by blocks of white families," says David Blackwell, who lived a few blocks away from Bruce's street. "We all became friends because we were all fighting. I had fights with all my friends, white and black. But something about Bruce . . . I don't think you can find anyone at Freehold who tried to fight him." If only because, as David's brother, Richard, remembers, the Springsteen kid either ignored or was somehow immune to the childhood taunts that sparked battle. "You could be sayin' some shit about his mother, and he'd just shrug, say 'Okay!' and keep on walking," he says. "Nothin' you can do about that. You gotta respect it. Let that boy go about his business."

Bruce's odd yet stubborn ways made him a juicy target for the nuns and their vaguely medieval humiliations and for the classmates who tittered at the odd boy's hapless flailing. Bruce incited enough institutional fury to end more than a few of his school days in the principal's office, where he waited for hours before Adele could come claim him. Faced down by his parents at the end of the day, Bruce always had the same explanation for his behavior. "He didn't want to go back to Catholic school," Adele says. "But I made him do it, and now I'm sorry I did. I should have known he was different."[4]

Douglas Springsteen spent most of those years huddled inside himself, handsome in the brooding fashion of actor John Garfield, but too lost in his own thoughts to find a connection to the world humming just outside his kitchen window. Often unable to focus on workplace tasks, Doug drifted from the Ford factory to stints as a Pinkerton security guard and taxi driver, to a year or two stamping out obscure industrial doo-dads at the nearby M&Q Plastics factory, to a particularly unhappy few months as a guard at Freehold's small jail, to occasional spurts of truck driving. The jobs were often bracketed by long periods of unemployment, the days spent mostly alone at the kitchen table, smoking cigarettes and gazing into nothing.

Doug felt more comfortable with his cousin and closest friend, Dim Cashion, who had pivoted from his years in the farm system of Major League Baseball to a position as coach for Little League teams and a player-coach in New Jersey's semipro leagues. But even while Dim's talent and charisma helped him lead generations of Freehold boys to the joys of baseball, it also came with the spiraling undertow of manic depression. The seesaw of black-eyed despair into neon auroras of unhinged energy could trigger fits of often uncontrollable behavior. "Kitchen cabinets came off the wall, telephones came off the wall, state troopers were called," says Dim's youngest brother, Glenn Cashion. And while Doug and Dim didn't always get along, and sometimes went months without seeing each other (despite living within a block of each others' homes), the cousins still passed their empty hours together in the same pool halls, still drank beer together, always linked by the same history and the same genetic information.

Eager to feel connected to other kids—and maybe even create a bond

<hr>

[4] Adele surrendered to her son's pleas to leave the St. Rose schools in 1963, just in time for Bruce to matriculate at Freehold Regional High School, the public institution that then drew students from all of Freehold and some of the nearby small towns, too.

with his father at the same time—Bruce threw himself into the Indians, his team in Freehold's Little League, coming off the bench to play right field. Bruce was perhaps more enthusiastic about baseball than he was talented. Jimmy Leon (now Mavroleon), who shared teams with Bruce for years, still recalls the time when a high fly ball floated across the summer sky toward his teammate's outstretched glove. Money in the bank. "But then it just hit him in the head. So it was kind of like that." Still, Bruce was proud to be a part—no matter how small—of the Indians' undefeated season in 1961. Which became slightly less perfect when the team lost the championship series by coming up short in two straight games again the Cardinals, a team coached by Freehold barber Barney DiBenedetto.[5]

But no matter how sweet the boyhood moments, Bruce still had his old man's fragile psyche to deal with. "You couldn't access him, you couldn't get to him, period," says Bruce, recalling his many attempts to talk to his father. "You'd get forty seconds in, and you know that thing that happens when it's not happening? That would happen." When dinner was over and the dishes were done, the kitchen became Doug's

---

[5] This introduces a level of controversy to the tale, because the Indians actually came within a whisker of winning the second game, only to be undone in the bottom of the final inning by a very rare—and to many minds, highly questionable—catcher's balk call made by umpire Boots "Bootsy" Riddle. The ump's call, made with the score tied, two men out, and the bases loaded, advanced batter Jimmy Mavroleon to first, thereby granting the Cardinals the game- and title-winning run. Opposing coach DiBenedetto insists the game-winning call simply hastened the classic's inevitable outcome: "We beat 'em with half our team," he says a half century later. "If we'd have had our whole team, we would have massacred 'em." Mavroleon feels a bit more sheepish about the whole thing. "It was the silliest thing ever because umpires never call [catcher's balks]," he says. "We were lucky." He and Bruce had a chance to refresh their memories in 1976 when Bruce happened into Jimmy's parents' Monmouth Queen Diner late one night. Mavroleon was just finishing his late-night shift at the register, but Bruce lingered to catch up and reminisce about the old days and the dazzling speed of his old competitor's fastball, which proved powerful enough to take him to the farm system of the Cincinnati Reds for two seasons, 1970–71. But if you think that resolves the matter of exactly who could throw that speed ball by you, as described in the song "Glory Days," read Kevin Coyne's story about Joe DePugh (*New York Times*, July 9, 2011). Lance Rowe, son of the Indians' coach, also strikes former teammates as a possible candidate. Or maybe it's some combination of all three.

solitary kingdom. With the lights out and the table holding only a can of beer, a pack of cigarettes, a lighter, and an ashtray, Doug passed the hours alone in the darkness.

In February 1962 Adele gave birth to her and Douglas's third child, a daughter they named Pamela. The baby's arrival required the family to pick up stakes and move to a slightly larger duplex at 68 South Street, in a white house (equipped with both a furnace and running hot water) nestled up against a Sinclair filling station. Absent the burdens of history and expectation, baby Pam's sweet presence was strong enough to evaporate the gloomy fatalism that defined so much of Doug's family experience. The thirteen-year-old Bruce proved an especially doting big brother, so while it was officially Ginny's responsibility to keep the baby changed, fed, and peaceful, Bruce was, by all accounts, more attuned to the baby's needs. No matter what else Bruce was doing, the sound of his baby sister crying triggered immediate action. "I really took care of her," Bruce says. "I did everything, the diapers and all that. So we were very close when she was very young."

One day in 1962 Fred and Alice were chatting with Adele in her new South Street kitchen, visiting with the baby, and waiting for Doug to come home from his night shift at the plastics plant. Saying he felt a little under the weather, Fred went upstairs to take a nap. When Adele went up to check on him an hour later, the old man was cold and still; obviously dead. Running downstairs to tell Alice the terrible news, the older lady responded with a nod. Deciding to hold off from doing anything else until Doug came home, they sat together in the kitchen until the door opened. Doug responded with the same absence of emotion his mother had shown. He paused for a moment, said, "Oh, okay," checked his pockets for coins, and then went to a pay phone to call the funeral home and alert a few relatives. When Bruce heard the news after coming home from school, he became hysterical. "It was the end of the world," he says. "But we didn't talk about my grandfather's death. He was probably about sixty-two, sixty-three, or sixty-five when he went. I was quite close to him, but you never know how to react as a child. I remember the funeral, the wake, and all those things. But it wasn't like today. Everyone was still . . . just different."

With the Randolph Street house close to being condemned, the widowed Alice moved in with her son's family. She spent most of her days helping care for Pam and also took the opportunity to shower more adoration over her fourteen-year-old grandson. Once again, she took to laying out his clothes in the morning, making his favorite treats, and glowing at his every word and gesture. Then Adele was playing the game too, making certain that Bruce had the one bedroom that was actually a suite, given its attached sunroom. And when Bruce realized that the sunroom had enough space for a real pool table, Adele and Doug scrimped for the money, then drove to another town in a snowstorm in order to bring it home in time for Christmas morning.

Alice had been hiding it for weeks, maybe for months: something was wrong with her insides. But without a fortune to pay the bills, what was the point of asking anyone to help? Adele took her to the hospital, and when the doctors concluded that Alice had cancer, they took her into their ward and kept her for the next three months, running the older woman through a litany of treatments, all debilitating, and many of them experimental. "I think they treated her like a guinea pig because she had no money or insurance," Adele says.

When she finally came home, Alice was weak at first and then rallied. She seemed nearly back to her old self when Pam, then three years old, woke up in the middle of the night and asked her mother if it was okay for her to sleep in her Aggie's bed. Adele thought it a bit strange—Pam had never asked to do that before. But she nodded and saw her daughter pad down the hall and slip through the bedroom door at the end of the hall. "I remember going into her room, her moving over and lifting the covers to let me in," Pam says.

They both fell asleep that way, the little girl cuddled up against the older woman's body, just as little Virginia had done so many years ago. Whatever Alice thought or dreamed about the past during her drift toward sleep will never be known. "When I woke up the next morning, I shook her to get up, and she didn't move," Pam says. Bruce, headed to school, had no idea. Bruce: "I'm sure I went through the room when they were there, only about fifteen feet from my own bedroom. That was a life changer; the end of the world for me. I don't remember anyone making a huge deal about (my grandfather), but it was different when my grandmother died. My dad was really upset."

The untended 110-year-old house on Randolph Street trembled on its long-fractured foundation. Vacated by Alice in 1962, it stood for only a few more months before the bulldozers rolled in. The house's weathered framework fell into a cloud of dust, then became a chalky pile of detritus hauled away in a truck. Once cleared, the property was rolled flat and paved over, cast for eternity as a part of the St. Rose church's parking lot. Bruce refused to look. "I didn't go back for years after it was knocked down," he says. "I couldn't go back and see the space. It was very, very primal for me." The stillness in the air, the desperate love of his grandparents, the adoration he'd earned simply by being himself. This was the seat of his consciousness. His roots as deep and entangled as the ones anchoring the Irish beech still in the soil out front.

"I thought back," Bruce says of the warped house that never stopped feeling like home, "and realized it was the place I loved the most."

TWO

A NEW KIND OF MAN

WHAT BRUCE REMEMBERS MOST VIVIDLY is the way the man looked. The way his every step, gesture, smile, and sneer set him apart from everything you were supposed to think, feel, or know about modern America. "A child wants nothing but to upset the world, and so there it was being done. It's like sort of tearing your house apart and reconfiguring it according to your dreams and your imagination. You knew that this man was doing that."

He's talking about Elvis Presley, adding just a little retroactive analysis to the perspective of the grade schooler he was in 1957, gazing up from the rug just in front of his family's little black-and-white television. As Bruce recalls, he was eight years old[1] and completely unsuspecting, since

---

[1] Bruce says he was in third grade when he saw Presley on the *Sullivan* show, but this is difficult to square with Presley's TV appearance schedule. The rock idol's third and final appearance with Sullivan took place in January 1957, when Bruce was in first grade. Elvis

his main interest in *The Ed Sullivan Show* revolved around the comics, jugglers, and puppets who generally performed on CBS's Sunday night variety show. Adele Springsteen was a regular viewer and also, as it turned out, something of an Elvis fan. "In those days," she says, "we always danced when Elvis Presley came on." Nothing could keep the electric vision of Presley's wildly rebellious image from imprinting itself onto the boy's consciousness. "He was actually the forerunner for a new kind of man," Bruce says. "Everyone changed their ideas about *everything* after that. About race, about sex, about gender descriptions, what you could look like, what you could wear. It was outrageous. It's a fantastic thing to be.

"It was an early signal that you could just be different," Bruce continues. "And that the difference you may have already been feeling was not necessarily a handicap; was not necessarily inappropriate, wrong, or unsuitable. Suddenly there was some cachet just through your own uniqueness." Obviously a powerful message to a kid who had long since sensed the chasm between the other kids' families and the life he'd been born into. Better yet, Elvis said all that with an attitude that made it clear he wasn't about to entertain dissent, let alone complaints.

"He had this enormous, balls-out, unchallenged authority," Bruce says. And he did it with the insouciant joy of the world's naughtiest boy. "It looked like he was playing, like a child is drawn to play. It looked like so much fun. Imagine throwing out all the self-consciousness that's sort of like a blanket over you. What would happen if you threw all that off for two and a half minutes, three minutes, as a performer! It was an enormous key that unlocked your imagination and your heart and soul."[2]

---

entered the military in March 1958 and didn't make any TV appearances until 1960, when he starred in Frank Sinatra's "Welcome Home Elvis" episode of *Timex Special.* And that doesn't seem likely, given that the songs Elvis performed on that show did not include any of the truly explosive hits that might have signaled the dawn of anything beyond a trip to Miami Beach's Fontainebleau hotel, where the show was taped.

[2] Subsequent years of reading and experiencing cultural and political processes sparked an even deeper analysis of Elvis and the 1950s rock 'n' roll revolution. "There's an element of early rock star that was simultaneously democratic, myth-like, and majestic," Bruce says. "The King! Not the president of the United States. *The King of Rock and Roll!* So there was a fabulous sort of twisted aristocracy that said, This. Rules. *Now.* I'm the King! And you are all going to be subjected to the new rules that I have written."

Music always called to him, from the speaker of the radio Adele kept on top of the refrigerator in the family kitchen, and, even as a toddler, from the spinet piano his aunt Dora had in her living room. "He'd come running in and put his hands on the keys," she recalls. But once he glimpsed Elvis, Bruce needed a guitar. He went straight to Adele, who loved the idea of her son making music, and within days, she had Bruce in hand, walking him to Mike Diehl's music store to rent an acoustic instrument for her quivering son. She also signed him up for lessons. But Diehl's formal style of teaching—music theory first, then scales, then at some too-distant-for-an-eight-year-old point, chords and songs, required far more patience than he could muster. As Bruce told Steve Van Zandt many years later, being subjected to yet another set of strict rules was the last thing he was looking for. "I need to make a horrific noise right *now*." Stuck between that frustration and his own inability to coax anything resembling music out of the instrument by himself, Bruce's interest faltered quickly. The guitar went back to Diehl's music store, and that, it seemed, was that.

Except that now his ears were open. And it was easy to find and fall in love with new music, given Adele's appetite for pop and her ear for a danceable tune. Still in the thrall of Elvis, Bruce scraped together sixty-nine cents to buy a four-song EP (extended play 45) of Elvis's biggest hits, only performed by a guy named Dusty Rhodes. Who clearly wasn't Elvis but, as far as Bruce was concerned, that didn't matter. "I could put it on, and it made me *remember* Elvis," he says. "It was close enough to give me a piece of what I was looking for." That, and Adele's radio, held him for the next few years, although Bruce also had an ear for novelty records, particularly Sheb Wooley's 1958 smash "The Purple People Eater," which he played ceaselessly on the local luncheonette's jukebox, along with British skiffle[3] star Lonnie Donegan's "Does Your Chewing Gum Lose Its Flavor (On the Bedpost Overnight)." Both Bruce and Ginny were so crazy for Chubby Checker's "The Twist" that in July 1961 Adele piled them into the car and took them to Atlantic City to see him perform as

---

[3] A British variation on American rockabilly music, with washtub bass, harmonica, banjo, and other front-porch-style instruments.

part of a Dick Clark package tour that also included Freddy Cannon, the Shirelles, and Bobby Rydell. And while both kids were eager to see the Steel Pier's diving horse, they were, Adele recalls, both mesmerized by Checker's star turn. He could dance, he could sing, he could play their favorite song exactly the way it sounded on the radio. And the crowd stood up and cheered! What could be better than that?

Because he lived halfway between New York and Philadelphia, Bruce's transistor radio pulled in a wide array of radio stations, and when he tuned into the Philly rhythm and blues stations, a new horizon opened up. One of his favorites—thanks most immediately to his family's new address—was called "South Street," a doo-wop-style party tune by the Philadelphia-bred singing group the Orlons, whose male singer Stephen Caldwell boasted a tummy-rumbling double baritone voice. "Meet me on South Street," they sang, "the hippest street in town!" Did it matter to Bruce that Freehold's South Street was the furthest thing from the Orlons' minds? Of course not. "But it gave some magical cachet to the address, so I went out and bought it," Bruce reminisced with Van Zandt. Then came Dick Dale's proto-psychedelic surf guitar tune "Miserlou," the razored harmonies of the Four Seasons, the white-guys-on-a-front-porch folk groups on the TV show *Hootenanny*, and then the California vision of the Beach Boys, strolling the golden coast to the gorgeously wrought songs of Brian Wilson.

In early 1964 Bruce was riding in the front seat of his mother's car when "I Want to Hold Your Hand" beamed out of the radio. "It's those old stories, like when you hear something and your hair stands on end," Bruce reminisced to Van Zandt. "It's having some strange and voodoo-like effect on you." Leaping out of the car, Bruce sprinted to a nearby bowling alley that he knew had a telephone booth, slammed his way into the box, and spun the number of the girl he was dating. *"Have you heard of the Beatles? Have you heard this song?"*

"It stopped your day when it hit," he said on Van Zandt's syndicated *Underground Garage* radio show in 2011. "Just the sound of it. And you didn't even know what they looked like." Then the Beatles were shaking their astonishing mops on *The Ed Sullivan Show*, and then they were dominating the radio dial, with a wave of similarly tressed countrymen marching on their Cuban boot heels. When summer came, Bruce invested a few weeks painting his aunt Dora's house, then used $18 of his proceeds to buy an acoustic guitar he'd seen in the window of the Western Auto store[4] on Main Street. Next he bought himself a copy of the *100 Greatest American Folk Songs* songbook and committed himself to mastering the instrument.

It didn't come easily, even as a fourteen-year-old. It took a week or two for Bruce to figure out (thanks to his slightly older cousin Frankie Bruno) that the guitar was far enough out of tune to be a completely different instrument. And even when it was tuned correctly, the auto store guitar wasn't what you'd call user-friendly. "The neck," Bruce recalls, "was basically razor wire on a two-by-four." Something about its sound, or perhaps Bruce's deepening fixation on the instrument, abraded his father's fragile nerves.

"I'd be with Bruce up in his room, holding up the music book while he was learning chords," his friend Bobby Duncan says. "And we'd hear his father yelling upstairs, '*I don't wanna hear that goddamn thing!*'" Even the dull murmur of an acoustic guitar being played behind a closed door on a different floor of the house? "His dad hated that stuff," Duncan says. "But his mom would do anything for him." Which Bruce knew full well in December when he took Adele by the hand and led her to Caiazzo's Music, near the Karagheusian Rug Mill on the corner of Jackson and Center Streets, and showed her the wickedly thin black-and-gold electric guitar gleaming in the window. Built in Japan, Kent guitars didn't register on the professional musician's list of must-haves. But it had the shimmering look, the jagged edges, and the electrified volume this young rocker craved. So he knew it was expensive, but if it were possible, somehow, it was the only thing he could ever imagine wanting again.

Adele took another look at the $60 price tag, and a few days later made another visit to the Household Finance Company for one of the short-term loans she turned to when she needed help squeezing through a tight spot or making the holidays as merry as possible. If Doug had any objections, the family's main breadwinner wasn't listening to him. So

---

[4] Western Auto sold its own line of electric guitars.

when Christmas morning dawned in 1964, the precious instrument was
waiting right where Bruce knew it would be, just beneath the lights deco-
rating the lower boughs of the Springsteens' Christmas tree.

His room equipped with the Kent and a small amplifier, the fifteen-year-
old felt wired. When he got home from school, he ran upstairs to his
room, shut the door tight, strapped the guitar over his shoulder, snapped
the amp's power switch, hit a chord, and *boom*: instant glory. "It was just,
door closed, and you're in there, doing your jam," he says. "I had a pretty
decent ear, so that helped. And then I developed quick, so that helped
too, once I got just a little bit of the mechanics in." Working through the
chords, then the simple guitar solo from the Beatles' arrangement of the
Isley Brothers' "Twist and Shout." Mastering the twelve-bar basics of rock
'n' roll, then working into the pop realm, with its larger palette of chords
and melodic possibilities. Sometimes he played to the mirror, watching
his hands on the guitar's neck and reveling in the instrument's potential
to serve both as a shield against his shyness and a bridge to carry him to
the center of everything. As he told *Newsweek* writer Maureen Orth in
1975: "The first day I can remember lookin' in the mirror and standin'
what I was seein' was the day I had a guitar in my hand."

Other kids were so entranced by the rock band image—the blithe
rebelliousness magnified by the power of a group identity—they bypassed
the music altogether in order to move straight to hipness, giving themselves a cool name and creating a logo to set them apart from everyone
else. "It was magic in those days," Bruce says. "There was no greater cachet. It was so good, people lied about it. I knew guys that had band jackets printed up with no band." One guy Bruce didn't know yet, a classmate
at Freehold Regional High School named George Theiss, spent part of his
freshman year as a member of the Five Diamonds, a pretend band linked
by the matching green rain slickers they decorated with sporty black diamonds they hand-painted on their backs. As Theiss says, "One guy knew
something about a guitar, but no one played." Theiss bought himself a
guitar, and with the help of his pal Vinnie Roslin's older brother, learned
how to play chords in an open E tuning. Theiss, a handsome kid with
just the right facial structure to seem both menacing and mysterious at

the same time, also had a strong voice and a kind of indefinable presence. Soon he abandoned the Five Diamonds to form the Sierras, an actual instrument-wielding band that featured Vinnie Roslin on bass and a guy named Mike DeLuise, who came with a Gretsch guitar just like the one George Harrison played. When another friend, Bart Haynes, showed up with a drum set, they could count to four and make something that, in certain moments, sounded like real rock 'n' roll.

Still, the Sierras' momentum ebbed. Theiss and Haynes teamed up with another guitarist named Paul Popkin, settled on a new name—the Castiles, named in tribute to Castile shampoo, the brand local teens seemed to favor—and began rehearsing in the living room of Haynes's parents' house. Because the Hayneses lived in a two-family duplex, and their living room shared a wall with the neighbors', the constant thrum and pound of the guitars, bass, and drums soon got on the nerves of neighbors Gordon "Tex" Vinyard and his wife, Marion. Vinyard, then an unemployed factory worker, pounded on the Hayneses' door to get the noise shut down. But when he saw the boys peering back from the Hayneses' living room, his anger melted. Stepping inside to chat for a while, Vinyard got them to play another song or two, then started in on the questions, asking what the high schoolers were hoping to achieve with their music; whether it was just a goof or something they thought they could pursue with a professional attitude.

Whatever they said, or maybe the hopeful way they said it, charmed the older man. And whether the bluff thirty-two-year-old was looking for something to keep himself busy during his downtime or wanted to add some youthful energy to his and Marion's childless lives, he told the boys that he'd like to serve as their manager. They could use his living room as a rehearsal space, and he'd provide as much musical guidance as he could, while helping to keep them focused, improving, and, if everything went according to plan, working. "We were there all the time," Theiss says. "More there than home."

Back on South Street, Bruce threw himself into his guitar with a passion and determination far beyond anything he had ever experienced. "If I wasn't in school, I was either playing my guitar or listening to records," he says. Playing six, eight, sometimes ten hours a day, he improved quickly. "It's like science in the twentieth century, you know. Suddenly there it is, bang, and it's compounding itself on a daily basis. It was that kind of musical development—like the big bang, only twice as big." It took Bruce only a couple of months to gain enough confidence in his guitar skills to go looking for a band to join. A friend from the YMCA, where Freehold kids could play sports and attend dances on weekends, pointed him to a group called the Rogues, whose members were searching for a rhythm guitarist. Bruce brought his Kent and played through enough songs to win the job and then rehearsed with the group for just a week or two before he played his first-ever paid performance at a teenage dance held in the Freehold Elks Club. The band opened its set with "Twist and Shout," the first rock song Bruce had taught himself to play.[5] But it must not have gone very well, at least not for the new rhythm guitarist. The rest of the band rescinded his membership a few days later, declaring his Kent guitar "too crappy," and sent him back home. "I'm sure I was pissed," Bruce says, recalling his long trek from that last practice session back to 68 South Street. "I went home that night and taught myself the solo to a Stones tune, 'It's All Over Now.' And that was it."

But not for long, as it turned out. Because Bruce's de-Roguing took place at the same time that George Theiss started noticing this cute freshman girl in the halls of Freehold Regional. She had dark hair, a beguiling smile, and a wicked sense of humor. And once he came up and started chatting with her, Ginny Springsteen kind of liked Theiss, too. They started dating soon afterward. "So I knew Bruce well enough to say hi," Theiss says. "But it wasn't like we were friends." Whether Theiss had a role in recruiting Bruce for the Castiles is unclear. What's certain is that the band needed a lead guitarist, and one day Bruce knocked on Tex and Marion's door at 39 Center Street, just a few doors away from Caiazzo's Music, asking to audition. He plugged in with the band and knocked out two or three songs, only to be sent home for not knowing any others.

When he came back to the next rehearsal (which might have been the

5 And for decades a standby in the encore-to-end-all-encores slot of his shows.

next day), Bruce had not only mastered half a dozen other songs but also played them with such ease and precision that Theiss, standing just to the right of the new guitarist, felt stunned. "I just remember that Tex looked up at us and said, 'Well?' and we all said okay," Theiss says. "Then I went up to Tex and said, 'I'm still the lead singer, right?'" Vinyard nodded, Theiss let loose a sigh of relief—and the Castiles started a new chapter in their nascent career.

Once they were bandmates, Theiss and Bruce also became fast friends. Theiss, by then broken up with Ginny, now made a habit of dropping by 68 South Street in the mornings to roust Bruce and haul him off to school. Most days, this meant cooling his heels in the Springsteens' kitchen, waiting for Bruce to emerge from his room. "He was always late, or not dressed, or couldn't find his shoes," Theiss says. "Then I had to wait for him to eat his bowl of Cheerios."

When they finally got to school, Bruce went back into drift mode, floating in and out of classes as his interest and patience dictated. Some days he brought his guitar with him, and when his academic motivation ebbed, he headed toward the school's band room, where he set up in a remote hallway and worked through a song or riff for hours at a time. "He'd sit there with his guitar and play," says then music teacher Bill Starsinic. "Every once in a while, I'd have to say, 'Bruce, you've gotta go back to class now,' but he was very intense. Very focused. He wasn't interested in academics or participating in the school band, orchestra, or anything else. He was interested in his music and himself."

When Bruce did get swept up in a class, it had less to do with the subject than his feelings for the teacher, such as a relatively young English teacher named Robert Hussey, whose outsider perspective came to influence the stories and poems Bruce wrote. Hussey also projected an intellectual dedication and emotional empathy that made a deep impact on his bright but academically adrift student. In Hussey's yearbook one June, Bruce's admiration came through in a chain of superlatives: "This page is too small for me to write a fraction of the complimentary things I would like to say to you," he began. "You have taught me things I could not get from any book. You have helped me understand people so much more than I had previously. You have gained my utmost respect and appreciation."

When the Castiles' eventual line-up gathered for their regular rehearsal sessions in the Vinyards' living room, they made a distinctive collage of style. Clad in his button-up madras shirts and tight black pants tucked into calf-high Dingo boots, Bruce tiptoed the line between rah-rah and greaser. The glower-y Theiss dressed tougher, while clean-cut singer-guitarist Paul Popkin could have been a yell leader. Drummer Bart Haynes, a bit older at seventeen, existed somewhere in the shadows of Marlon Brando and an old-fashioned New Jersey wiseguy. "He was a classic sharkskin pants, pointy-toed, spit-shined Italian shoes with black socks guy," Bruce says. "He had a sloppy, casual cigarette hanging in the mouth, eyebrows up, hair kind of slicked back, but it would slip down as he was playing. He had a ton of attitude. And, looking back on it, a sweet sort of way."

Tex Vinyard did his part to make the teenaged Castiles even more diverse by recruiting Frank Marziotti, the twenty-eight-year-old owner of the Triangle Chevron station on Route 33 in Freehold, to play bass. As Vinyard learned when he had become a regular at the station soon after it opened in 1962, Marziotti moonlighted as the bass player for the Rolling Mountain Boys country band. "One day I was sitting in the backroom picking a guitar," Marziotti says. "Tex walked in and said, 'I got a group of kids, and I could use you to guide 'em.'" Marziotti agreed to do it, more as a favor to Vinyard than a career move, and when he turned up at the next rehearsal, he was surprised to discover that his pint-sized bandmates were actually pretty good. "I just slid right in with them," he recalls. "No problems at all, and I certainly wasn't feeling they were amateurs." Marziotti was (and remains, he insists) most impressed with Theiss, both for his strong vocals and his distinctive way with the rhythm guitar. "He'd use an open E tuning, and barre chord it. And he was so good at it; I never saw anyone as good as he was."

The lead guitarist, on the other hand, required more assistance, particularly when it came to chords. "Bruce was always a fast learner. You showed him one thing, and he came back the next day and showed you three." Credit the fact that Bruce had no ambitions that came close to rivaling the call of his guitar. "I guarantee you that once I had the job, I went home and started to woodshed like a mad dog," Bruce says. "I was in a band. I'd taken some, I'd gotten tossed out of [the Rogues]. But oh yeah, after I got in the band, I just listened and played all night. Every available hour and minute. And it was never work for me." As Marziotti recalls, the guitarist took enormous pride in his progress. "He'd come back and show off to Tex: 'Hey, look what I did!'"

Vinyard landed a job as a machine operator on the floor of the Peter Schweitzer cigarette paper factory, but full-time employment did nothing to dampen his enthusiasm for the Castiles. Together Tex and Marion became de facto parents to the boys in the band, with Tex guiding the rehearsals with a confidence that belied the fact that his own hands-on musical expertise extended as far as the knobs of his own radio. But he knew what sounded good to him, and if the boys weren't getting there, he'd hold up his hand and call for changes.

"He really did run the rehearsals when we played at his place," Theiss says. "He'd yell, *'Stop, that doesn't sound good! Do this, do that!'* Even when he didn't know what the hell he was talking about." What the Castiles knew was that Tex, unlike their own fathers, believed in what they were doing and wanted nothing more than to help. And if their own moms nagged endlessly about their hair, clothes, and grades, Marion was more than happy to be their uncritical den mother, busily whipping up platters of tuna fish and bologna-and-cheese sandwiches in her kitchen, laying out the spread with the case of Foodtown soda she kept on hand to ease the Castiles' thirst.

The group's growing repertoire leaned mostly on the AM radio hits of the day, with an emphasis on the harder-edged singles by the Rolling Stones ("[I Can't Get No] Satisfaction" and "The Last Time") the Kinks ("All Day and All of the Night"), Ray Charles ("What'd I Say"), and the Who (an instrumentally furious "My Generation," with Bruce taking the lead vocal). They mostly steered away from the Beatles, unless you count the British group's cover of "Twist and Shout," to differentiate themselves from all the other teenage bands trying to scratch their way out of their parents' garages and basements. Tex had his own commercial strategy, which was for the boys to master Glenn Miller's "In the Mood," Henry

Mancini's "Moon River," and other jazz-pop numbers that would give the Castiles a cross-generational appeal. "Tex wanted us to get as many paid jobs as we could," Bruce says. "But the [band's] cards said Rock 'n' Roll, Rhythm & Blues, so that was our image of ourselves."

Vinyard also created—and paid for—the group's onstage wardrobe, which began with black pants, shiny black vests, and white shirts buttoned up to the neck, then branched into frilly shirts and other showy garb. But it wasn't long before the uniforms chafed against the Castiles' rebellious skin.[6] Bruce: "At some point, we just said [to Tex], 'Yeah, we're doing it like this.' And the frilly shirts came off."

Vinyard managed to book the band at a few teen dances starting in the midsummer, and drafted Marziotti's gas station van to haul the amps and instruments while he drove the boys in his sky blue Cadillac. Tex monitored the sound from the back of the room during the set, using his thumb to signal "turn it up" or "turn it down" to each player. And when the show was over and the gear packed up, he piled everyone into the Caddy and took them downtown to Federici's for pizza and the presentation of the night's pay. Usually it came to about $5 a man, which was serious teenage money in those days. Vinyard took the same for himself, if only until the waitress came to pick up the bill for the boys' pizza and soda. "Damn straight, we were making a living," Bruce says. "Well, it was enough to not have to ask my folks for money anymore."

The steady, if unspectacular, flow of cash also helped the Castiles (often with an assist from Vinyard's wallet) to strengthen their sound with new amps, speakers, and microphones. They played about a dozen shows in the second half of 1965, the most memorable being a bizarre afternoon in a lockdown ward at the Marlboro State Hospital, where, according to Bruce, the master of ceremonies spent twenty minutes singing the group's praises to the heights of the Beatles and

---

[6] One promotional photo shot by Tex during the summer of 1965 shows Bruce slouched on a teeter-totter, his outstretched legs cloaked in skintight pants that were obviously several shades lighter than everyone else's, tucked into suede boots that didn't match the other guys' shiny black shoes.

beyond. "Then," Bruce recalled, "the doctors came up and took him away."[7]

But most of the shows were far more typical teen dance gigs held at the Woodhaven Swim Club, the Freehold Elks Club, the Farmingdale Mobile Home Park, and several weekend socials held for Bruce's old classmates at the St. Rose of Lima School around the corner from his house. One night that fall, Adele put on her coat to walk her son down the block and to the door of the St. Rose cafeteria, where she paused to kiss him, and then watched as he stepped inside the door and toward his bandmates on the stage. Recognizing Freehold police officer Lou Carotenuto holding down a security post near the door, she went up to say hello. "She said, 'Keep an eye out for Bruce, he's going to be famous someday!'," Carotenuto says. "I just thought, 'Thank God for mothers. They're the only ones who always believe in you.'" But then, Adele was a Zerilli, so her faith was automatically tripled by her sisters Dora and Eda, both of whom lined up with the high school kids to get tickets for the Castiles' set at the opening festivities for the new ShopRite supermarket in Freehold. "Oh, I loved it," Bruce's aunt Dora says. "But even then he was pretty famous. To us, he was."

And yet for Douglas Springsteen, it still sounded like noise. A screeching clamor from beyond the ceiling; the sound of his son's tumble into the same trap his own life had become. When it bore down on him, Doug took the kitchen broom and used the handle to pound the ceiling beneath Bruce's room to shut him up. "Because of the neighbors!" Ginny Springsteen says. "We lived in a duplex, and they were right next to us." For his sister, for Adele, for Theiss, and for all the other neighborhood kids who knew Mr. Springsteen well enough to bid him hello when they entered the kitchen, the father-son static seemed par for the generational course. "Nothing happened out of the ordinary. He wanted Bruce's hair short, and Bruce wanted it long," Ginny says. She thinks some more. "Maybe to us it wasn't that big of a deal, but obviously to Bruce it was."

[7] George Theiss also told the Brucebase website that one female patient worked intently to seduce the band members, while another guy ran around the floor screaming "Banzai!"

Doug may not have understood his son but he definitely feared for his future. He certainly didn't know how to protect the boy from the hard truths waiting to greet him once he got out of school and faced up to the working man's world. It had made sense for Doug to abandon his education to take up with the rug factory: the Karagheusian employee rolls touched nearly every family in town. But World War II had disrupted that career path, and nearly twenty-five years later, Doug still hadn't found a career he could stick with. Once the very picture of a prosperous working-class town, Freehold saw its fortunes take a dark turn when the Karagheusians, who had once employed more than four hundred residents, abandoned Freehold in 1961, moving their factory to North Carolina, where labor came cheap. With the town's other factories either gone or on their way out, and all the tertiary shops, restaurants, car dealerships, and so on collapsing in their wake, laborers like Doug were left to fight over the scraps. "It felt like the death of the town," says Freehold native, historian, and journalist Kevin Coyne, whose own grandfather's thirty-two-year commitment to Karagheusian ended with a pink slip and two weeks of severance pay. "There was a lot of bitterness. A sense of broken promises. Of loyalty unrewarded."

Douglas Springsteen eased his pains with his cigarettes and six-pack. For him to see his son come up the back-door steps, guitar in hand, his long hair so unkempt, his clothes so flashy, and his youthful face so untroubled, whispering "Hey, Pop" on his way up to his room grated against the open wounds in his psyche. Needing to prepare his son to confront the bleak grind that had claimed him, Doug stiffened in his chair and asked Bruce to come back and chat for a bit. The music and applause fast fading from his ears, Bruce would lay down his guitar, grit his teeth, and walk dutifully back into his father's charred vision of the world.

For years friends have wondered if Doug lashed out at his son with fists or an even more toxic form of psychological cruelty. The best-intentioned people whisper words like *abuse* and *brutality*. What got lost over the years is that Doug's gruff demeanor was the thinnest veneer over his own torment. And while he was ashamed of his weakness and desperate to keep his oldest child from suffering the fate he'd been dealt, it was all but impossible for Doug to connect with Bruce in a meaningful way. So it wasn't the lectures, criticisms, and occasionally heated arguments that cut into Bruce's skin. It was the vacancy that swam into his father's eyes whenever he came into the room. When Bruce turned toward his father hoping to see something—a spark of affection, pride, a glimmer of love, a nod of recognition, even—only emptiness stared back.

"It wasn't in the doing, it was in the *not* doing," Bruce says. "It was in the complete withholding of acknowledgment. It was in the vacantness." The air seems to crackle, and it's like no time has passed, as if the smoke and the alcohol fumes still clung to him. If only because Bruce has come to understand that the hurt in the room didn't begin or end with him. "My father, in truth, was a wonderful guy," he says. "I loved him. *Loved* him. But the drinking was a problem. On a nightly basis, every single day, an entire six-pack is not insignificant. I don't know if the withdrawal came from that, or . . ." He trails off, glances out the window, and then shrugs. "I've written about it a little bit myself. I don't know how much of it you don't get. You get the gist of it."

The Castiles rolled into 1966 at a good clip, playing a steady stream of teen dances, and then working into the battle-of-the-bands competitions that pitted local groups against one another in judged (if at times suspiciously) contests for cash and prizes that sometimes included opening spots for famous acts. Those bigger breaks didn't always materialize, even for the supposed winners. But the shows did allow the aspiring bands to meet, compare acts, and build a musical community that went beyond their own schools and towns. When Bruce met a skinny, quick-witted guitarist from the Shadows at Middletown, New Jersey's Hullabaloo Club one night, they didn't have to chat long before he realized he'd met a rock 'n' roll soul mate.

"The bottom line is that we were obsessed with the same levels of detail," Bruce recalls. "If someone cut their hair, if someone changed their shirt . . . it was about everything the performers were doing, thinking, breathing, eating, drinking, and seeing. And there was *one* other person who understood the significance of all these events in the same way that I did. And that person was Steve Van Zandt." And although

Van Zandt's mother and stepfather[8] lived a half hour and cultural world away in Middletown ("Freehold was the home of greasers and inlanders," Bruce says. "When you got closer to the coast, it was more upscale"), the boys still found a way to spend endless hours together listening to records, stripping them down to components, and analyzing what made each part distinctive, from the lead vocal, to the rhythm guitarist's chord inversions, to the drummer's contrasting hi-hat patterns. "Steve was the guy you went to—every deep rock fan has one—who you don't have to explain yourself to," Bruce says. "You don't have to explain why you're so worked up that on this record the guy used a different guitar than on the last one, and it's a *betrayal of all that is good!* All that is *righteous* in the world! And why did he comb his hair this way, then comb it that way? *No! No!* The wonderful argumentative minutiae of rock 'n' roll came alive and on fire when we sat down together, and that continues to this day. If I ever want to revel in the oversignificance of anything that's going on or we're trying to do, Steve is my man. He'll explain it all to me. And the worst part is that even if I disagree, I know exactly what he's talking about. I can't dismiss his argument out of hand, because I know exactly where he's coming from."

The Castiles developed a small but devoted following in and around Freehold, including a collection of exactly forty-two high schoolers, most of them girls, who wrote and signed a petition demanding the group "get some recognition." To wit: "The group has a sensational sound, and we protest against the fact that record companies and radio stations completely ignore these fantastic boys." Such girlish enthusiasm was already wearing on Marziotti's twenty-nine-year-old nerves, so when a moist-eyed fan cornered him after an early May gig at the Le Teen-dezvous club and asked "Are you Brucie's daddy?" the bass player had enough. "I told Tex they could stand on their own now," he says. Marziotti stuck around long enough to run the much more age-appropriate

[8] Born in Boston as Steven Lento, Steve's parents broke up when he was a toddler. His mother moved her family to New Jersey when her son was seven, and soon married William Van Zandt, who adopted her son and gave him his Dutch surname. Steve never contacted or saw his biological father again. "He was just some kinda lazy fuck, I guess," he explains.

bass player Curt Fluhr through the basics of their set, then bid the group farewell.

Fluhr had been a Castile for less than two weeks when he accompanied the others to the Mr. Music recording studio in Bricktown, New Jersey, to cut both sides of the Castiles' first single, a pair of original songs credited to Springsteen-Theiss. The A side, a high-spirited breakup song called "Baby I" with a distinct Carl Wilson[9] touch to the guitar work, makes light work of its romantic brush-off, breezily informing its femme fatale that her faithless services will no longer be required, as the singer, "Got somebody new / Somebody better than you / Somebody who'll be true." But while all's fair in adolescent love and pop songs, the flip side, "That's What You Get," anticipates a legion of Bruce's subsequent songs, with gloomy verses in which one man's lie of a life results somehow in the untimely death of his girlfriend, which shocks but doesn't surprise the narrator. "That's what you get for loving me," he concludes in the chorus.[10] What they got for recording the single added up to an impressive showpiece for friends, a calling card for bookers, and not much else.

The single also featured the band's new drummer, Vinny Maniello, tapped to replace Bart Haynes when the older boy, then completing his senior year at Freehold Regional, joined the US Marines, hoping to earn a better rank and assignment for having enlisted rather than waiting for the draft. Haynes knew he was destined to wind up in Vietnam with a rifle in his hands, but when he came home for a post–boot camp break, he made it all seem like just another goof, wearing his corporal's uniform with all the authority of a kid on Halloween. "He was a tough kid, kind of drawn by happenstance," Bruce says. "He was crazy, loose, and a very funny guy." Handed a map of the world, Bart Haynes had absolutely no idea where to locate the obscure country for whose jungles and mountains he would soon be risking his life.

[9] The lead guitarist of the Beach Boys, whose Chuck Berry–meets–Dick Dale sound helped define 1960s surf guitar (though Carl was channeling his brother Brian's directions, which often filtered through LA session guitarists first).

[10] Also note the line where the singer says, "I fall down on my knees and I cry," which would be repeated more or less word for word in Bruce's "Downbound Train" nearly two decades later.

The rest of the Castiles spent the next year struggling to hone their music and work their way up into the better beach clubs, teen clubs, and possibly a concert stage or two, even if at the bottom of a dozen-band lineup. The concert bookings never quite worked out, but Vinyard did manage to land them a semiregular series of shows at the Cafe Wha?, one of the best-known (and now iconic) rock 'n' roll venues in New York's Greenwich Village. Almost all of their sets at the club took place during the afternoon shows presented for the city's teenagers. But playing the same stage that helped launch both Bob Dylan and Jimi Hendrix, the latter of whom had played the club just months earlier, was no small thing. So while most of the area's other Beatlemania-bred bands had either surrendered their ambitions or broken up, the Castiles had evolved into a solidly professional unit, thanks equally to Bruce's ever-improving chops, Theiss's growing poise as a front man, and the strong three-way harmonies by Theiss, Popkin, and Bruce. The addition of organist Bob Alfano, who had mastered the swirling blues-meets-gospel favored by California's new breed of psychedelic rockers, gave the band an even more complex sound.

As 1966 gave way to 1967, and the once shaggy youth culture tipped toward full-blown psychedelia, the Castiles all kept pace. Bruce's wardrobe took on wild colors and flowery designs, while his black curls grew into a curtain over his eyes and a waterfall down his shoulders and neck. An eager student of the rock 'n' roll performances on TV—the Who's literally explosive (thanks to the firepower-hungry Keith Moon and guitar-splintering Pete Townshend) performance on *The Smothers Brothers Comedy Hour* was a huge eye-opener—Bruce took to starting the shows perched on a tall lifeguard chair, which he would leap from at some dramatic moment. He also added flash to the group's Catholic Youth Organization show at St. Rose of Lima in April by rigging the stage with a strobe light, smoke bombs, and more. When they got to their climactic number, Bruce nodded to a friend to switch on the strobe and then ignite the smoke bombs. When the smoke cleared, Bruce climbed on top of his amplifier and used his guitar to smash a specially purchased vase of flowers into petal-strewn rubble. The kids roared, and the smoke-sheathed Bruce felt like a visionary psychedelic artiste until a few minutes after the cafeteria lights came up. That's when his eighth-grade geometry teacher came up and patted him on the back. "Bruce!" he proclaimed, "that was very nice."

Such displays of intergenerational warmth were increasingly hard to come by. By the middle of 1967, Freehold, like virtually every other crossroads, town, and city in the nation, had spiraled into opposing camps: parents against kids, hawks against peaceniks, traditionalists against progressives, whites against blacks, and on and on. So maybe Bruce shouldn't have been surprised when he walked into Freehold Regional on June 19 to collect his cap and gown for the evening's graduation ceremonies, only to be told that he would be barred from the auditorium unless he got his shoulder-length hair cut. Bruce turned around and marched out the front door to catch a commuter bus up to New York so he could spend the afternoon checking out bands in the Greenwich Village clubs.[11]

The crowning irony, of course, was that Bruce's wild hair and clothes signified nothing about actual vices he might have had. Hobbled by his grandparents' odd ways and repulsed by his father's smoking and habitual drinking, Bruce treasured his sense of control too much to risk destabilizing himself with drugs, alcohol, and psychosocial anarchy. So while his hair made him seem freaky to his parents' generation, Bruce's stubbornly sober habits also set him apart from the hazy-eyed hippies he moved among. And while teenage Bruce could summon some energy for politics and the antiauthoritarian sentiments of the day, those interests were less philosophical than visceral. "It was very real," Bruce says. "Generationally, everything was politicized. I didn't know anybody who didn't at least feign interest. If you didn't, you had to adopt a pose of some sort." And in Freehold, a nontraditional haircut and an untucked, flowery shirt were

---

[11] Much to the aggravation of his mother, Adele, not just because she was so excited to see her son graduate but also because she took a half day off from work to prepare for the large house party she had planned. The party, at least, came off without a hitch, becoming especially festive later in the evening when Bruce showed up, just in time to claim the beginner's motorcycle Adele bought him as a graduation present. Still, she remains a bit peeved about Bruce's teenaged thoughtlessness. "I was crying and everything," she says. "Let *him* tell you that story."

enough to put a target on your back. Even now, Bruce's 1960s image is enough to reawaken suspicion among some former police officers. "He used to run the street with the rest of 'em!" says ex-patrolman (and subsequent chief of police) Bill Burlew. "He had the long hair; he used to hang out with [the] Street People [a known gang in Freehold]." When a chorus of disagreement rises around him in Joe's Barbershop, Burlew can only shrug. "Ahh, maybe he was just a typical kid."

As was the Castiles' founding drummer and US Marines corporal, Bart Haynes, who on October 22, 1967, was on patrol with his unit in the Quang Tri Province when North Vietnamese soldiers let loose a shower of mortar fire on the American troops. Haynes was killed in the barrage, and when word of his death hit Freehold a week later, Bruce and the other Castiles found it difficult to absorb the shock. Particularly George Theiss, who only a few days earlier had a vivid dream about his friend. As Theiss told Kevin Coyne, his subconscious had concocted a ringing telephone, which Theiss reached out to answer. The voice on the other end belonged to Bart Haynes, coming through the static with one eerie message: "I'm all right . . . I'm all right." [12]

---

[12] This entire paragraph is derived from Coyne's *Marching Home*, a history of Freehold and the soldiers it sent to American wars (Viking, 2003).

THREE

AS MY MIND BENDS CLOUDS
INTO DREAMS

A T THE START OF 1968, the Springsteens seemed to be on the upswing. Bruce was midway through his first year at Ocean County Community College (subsequently called Ocean County College), focusing his studies on English and earning good marks in his writing classes.[1] Doug settled into his new job at the Lilly cup factory, which gave the family more financial stability and his days a sense of structure. Doug could trudge through days, even weeks, dull eyed but determined. Then he'd wake up tangled in his own sheets and barely find the energy to pull on a shirt and coat and find the door. That would pass, and with another dawn, he'd wake up on the ceiling and pinball through the next week, frantic and unpredictable. "With everything going on, we had no idea what was mental and what wasn't mental," Ginny Springsteen says. Her

[1] While simultaneously keeping the military and the working world at bay with his college deferment.

mother nods sadly and then alludes to an event that makes them both cringe. Adele comes back with another cryptic "Oh, and remember when . . ." but all they'll share about that are rolled eyes and a few dark laughs. "He just wasn't right," Adele says finally. "That poor man."

Sometimes trouble came out of a clear blue sky. One evening that winter the family was settled into their postdinner routine—Doug in the kitchen; Ginny, Adele, and Pam watching TV in the living room; Bruce headed up the stairs to his room—when someone out on South Street pointed a gun at the Springsteens' front door and pulled the trigger. The bullet tore through the front door and smashed into the wooden bannister an arm's reach from where Bruce was climbing the stairs.

What the *hell*? They still don't know. Maybe it had something to do with the growing racial tension in town. Or maybe the work of a random madman or a joke gone terribly wrong. "I think the police came," Bruce says. Whatever it was, he certainly didn't take it personally. "I was a kid then, so I mostly thought it was exciting," he says. "It was just strange."

One Sunday morning a few weeks later Bruce fired up his motorcycle to give Ginny a ride to a friend's house, dropped her off, and turned for home, the soft spring air in his trailing curls. He was nearly home when a man driving his son home from church in a large sedan failed to see the motorcyclist headed his way on Jerseyville Avenue. Bruce got tossed over the hood and landed headfirst on the pavement. When patrolman Lou Carotenuto got to the scene, Bruce was on the sidewalk, conscious but dazed and cradling the knee that now poked through his torn and bloodied jeans. "He was rubbing his knee, but he kept saying, 'I'm fine! I'm fine!'" Carotenuto says. "Just like Doug would have done." With Bruce's eyes glazed, bloodied knee swelling visibly, and his responses fuzzy at best, Carotenuto called for an ambulance, which rushed the mostly unconscious teenager to a hospital near Asbury Park. There, the emergency room staff cut off his blood-soaked jeans and presented Bruce to an older doctor whose patience for beaten-up teenaged hippies had obviously run short.

Presented with a bloodied, semicoherent adolescent, the doctor glared at his patient's shoulder-length hair and muttered that maybe the hippie deserved what he got. The physician stayed long enough to diagnose a concussion, and ordered that Bruce be held for observation and more tests. Fretting both about her son and the astronomical cost of hospital care, and then presented with a police report that set the blame for his accident squarely on the other driver, Adele hired a lawyer to prepare for litigation in case the man's insurance company refused to pay. She learned quickly that their chances in civil court would improve dramatically if Bruce appeared on the stand looking like a clean-cut American. When Doug returned to the hospital with a barber in tow, Bruce screamed bloody murder. "Telling him that I hated him, and that I'd never forget," Bruce recalled onstage during the 1980s. Even now Adele seems horrified to recall the episode, though they were just trying to help keep the family—and particularly her son—afloat. "Everyone was making fun of him!" she says. "But we felt so terrible. I never thought that he would feel that bad." However, with three children to feed and all the regular bills to pay, the family needed the money more than Bruce needed his hair.

Then Ginny, in the midst of her senior year in high school, got pregnant. That her then boyfriend, Michael "Mickey" Shave, was a professional rodeo rider did not help her parents confront the social and religious stigmas attached to out-of-wedlock teen pregnancies. But Ginny's predicament was by no means a first in their corner of Freehold, or in the family itself, so Adele took a deep breath and did what had to be done. The young couple were married in a small ceremony, the family had a party to celebrate, and the youngsters braced themselves for a premature adulthood that would test them both in ways that no teenager could imagine.[2]

Back in Doug's midnight kitchen, one thought gripped him, then wouldn't let go: he'd had enough. Enough family history, enough probing eyes, enough Freehold. Imagining sunny skies and a shore as far from New Jersey as possible, his thoughts turned to California, the traditional destination for East Coast refugees in search of a fresh start. "He just wanted to get out," Adele says. "I didn't want to go. I didn't want to leave Ginny because she'd just had her baby, and I had worked for the same man for twenty-three years. But Douglas said, 'I'll just go without you, then.'" Sensing the desperation in his voice, Adele could not deny

---

[2] Ginny and Mickey are still married, forty-four years later, with three kids and three grandchildren.

her husband's need. So they agreed: it might take some time—probably several months—to save the money they'd need for such a big move. But they would go. And as Doug made clear, he was never coming back.

In late September 1968, Tex and Marion Vinyard invited the Castiles and their friends to what had become a regular party at their house: a joint celebration to mark the birthdays of Theiss and Bruce, born one day apart. On the surface, it was quasifamily business as usual: a big cake, sandwiches, chips, the usual array of Foodtown soda pop. The snapshots in Marion's scrapbook—the pages titled "19th Birthday Party for Our Boys, George and Bruce"—reveal a house full of skinny, long-haired boys, all freshly washed and (except for Theiss) shaved, dressed in their nicer pants, ironed shirts, and collegiate sweaters. In one picture, a heavily bearded Theiss is a vision in late-sixties rock glamour, his shirt unbuttoned to reveal his naked chest, the arms of a willowy blonde draped over his shoulders. In another, a shirt-and-sweater-vest-clad Bruce sits cross-legged on the floor, bent over an acoustic guitar while a young woman gazes raptly from a respectful distance. Reminded of the disparity between the photos of the Castiles' front man and lead guitarist, Theiss laughs. "Yeah, it's pretty telling. That's pretty much how it was."

What doesn't come through in the warm tableau is that the Castiles had broken up just weeks earlier. Perhaps the most surprising thing was that they had managed to stay together for so long. "We started out as little Freehold greasers, and we all ended up as long-haired hippies," Bruce says. "We were all just growing up and changing. I do remember we had some feelings between us, but I don't even remember what it was about. I was either starting to sing, or maybe we wanted to play different music." Probably both. Deep in the thrall of singer-songwriters Tim Buckley and Leonard Cohen, Bruce had spent the winter filling notebooks with his poems, such as the dreamy "Clouds" ("As my mind bends clouds into dreams / That I like as the sun disappears into / The night I look and you have gone") and the so-surreal-it's-real "Slum Sentiments" ("Golden horses ride down the city streets / Starving children clutter beneath their feet / 'Cause they haven't had enough to eat"). In "Until the Rain Comes," Apollo himself thunders across flaming clouds in service of a revelation: "Upon reaching the ancient age of 18 I have found / What is round isn't round at all, and what is up may be down." All very deep and romantic, and just the thing for a young troubadour with trouble in mind and a guitar in hand. Heading into the spring with a new repertoire of acoustic songs, he had played a few solo shows at the Off Broad Street Coffee House in Red Bank, and felt an entirely new charge standing alone with only his guitar, voice, and innermost thoughts to offer.

At the same time, the Castiles, all graduated from high school and moving into college or the professional world of entry-level jobs and training programs, were losing steam. According to the rock 'n' roll calendar, the split was more than due: teenage bands are supposed to be transient creatures. But even inevitable change can be jarring, and by the middle of July, Bruce and Theiss could barely speak to each other. Sometimes they bickered onstage. And at one mid-July show at the Off Broad Street, a fan took a picture that captured a pissed off-looking Bruce hoisting his middle finger to a visibly cranky, microphone-wielding Theiss. Things were clearly not well in the Castiles' world. And that was before the Freehold police got involved.

It happened in the first week of August 1968. And while not every eighteen-year-old Freeholder had become enraptured by the drugs and weirdness that had become the definitive mark of their generation, the Freehold Police Department had already concluded that the stream of drugs flowing into town, and the enthusiastic consumption of same by young Freeholders, had grown to disturbing proportions. They weren't exactly wrong. Marijuana had been remarkably easy to find since the summer of 1967, assuming you knew the right people. By 1968, those same people could also be relied upon to supply LSD, psychedelic mushrooms, amphetamines, downers, cocaine, DMT, crystal meth, heroin— the whole candy store. Naturally, the question of who was doing which drugs became a hot topic among the younger set. When some group of stoners started wearing necklaces strung with small, colorful discs (distributed originally as part of a cereal box game), you didn't have to look further than a kid's neck to figure out his or her drug of choice: green stood for grass, yellow was LSD, red for speed freaks, and so on. All good fun for the devil-may-care youth of Freehold until it turned out that one of their number was either a narcotics officer or someone yearning to become one. Once the cops knew the secret, the necklaces did the rest of their work for them. It took about a week for them to put together the names, addresses, and drugs of choice.

The police cars rolled at four in the morning. They hit virtually every neighborhood in town, the officers pounding on family doors in the middle of the night, flashing their warrants, conducting their searches, collecting what they already knew they would find, and hauling the young lawbreakers off to jail. By the time the sun rose, the entire town was scandalized. "They were all living with their mommies and daddies, and the police came and took them out of their mommies' and daddies' houses!" Bruce recalls with mock horror. "That's in the *middle of the night*! Who had ever *heard* of such a thing? There had been no busts before! That word, the act itself, was *unknown*. People were shocked! *Here in River City?*" The drama made a big impact on the Castiles, largely because Vinny Maniello, Paul Popkin, and Curt Fluhr got nabbed in the dragnet. "All I remember is that I woke up one morning and half the guys were gone," Bruce says. "George and I were on the outside and said, 'Well, this seems like a good moment to call it a day.'"

A day or two later, Bruce happened upon John Graham and Mike Burke, a pair of slightly younger musicians (they were sixteen or seventeen) from New Shrewsbury. Just finishing an unsatisfying run with a blues-and-Stones cover band called Something Blue, the bassist and drummer were on the hunt for a singer-guitarist when they overheard Bruce talking about the big drug bust in Freehold. The three musicians chatted for a while, and when they got to their mutual love for Cream and the Jimi Hendrix Experience—the best of the psychedelic blues bands, and both three-piece groups—*and* with a replacement band needed for the Castiles' gig at the Le Teendezvous club on August 10, it all clicked together. "I was ready to power trio, you know," Bruce says. "I think we rehearsed a night or two and played that weekend. And then there was no looking back."

Calling themselves Earth (shortened from the original the Earth Band), the trio—which performed as a quartet whenever the Castiles' gifted organist Bob Alfano hauled his Hammond to a show—built a repertoire from the most popular works of Cream, Hendrix, Traffic, the Yardbirds, and Steppenwolf, whose just-released single "Born to Be Wild" became one of Earth's big set closers. Specializing in such jam-heavy songs made it easy to play long shows, particularly given Bruce's increasingly dynamic guitar work. Soon a pair of aspiring young managers named Fran Duffy and Rick Spachner convinced Bruce, Burke, and Graham to let them guide their nascent career and booked an assortment of shows to keep the band busy through the fall.

At the same time, Bruce, who still felt out of place in academic surroundings, surrendered to his parents' pleas and registered for another fall term at Ocean County Community College. His new bandmates, both of whom grew up in a well-to-do town where education was taken seriously, helped keep him motivated. "They were smart, they seemed educated, and they had families that seemed educated," Bruce says. "Those kids were going to college, which made them different than my Freehold buddies, who were going to Vietnam." Crashing in the Graham family's basement (where the band rehearsed), Bruce absorbed the leafy suburban zeitgeist of New Shrewsbury, and for a time tried on its expectations. Both Graham and Burke were enthusiastic readers and writers, so when they ran out of music talk, the three boys considered their literary futures. Temporarily fired up about his academic prospects, Bruce told his bandmates that he now planned to pivot from his two years at Ocean County and jump into the journalism school at Columbia University. Graham and Burke had no doubt that he could do exactly that. "He was very impressive and likable," Burke says. "A very nice guy, funny, smart, and knowledgeable about music," Graham says. "And onstage he was fearless."

The administrators at Ocean County Community College felt less confident of their own futures. With so many other colleges and universities becoming battlegrounds of protest, dissent, and, sometimes, pitched riots, they feared the same thing happening at their own as-yet-unaccredited institution (those formalities were concluded in 1969), a prospect the school seemed far too fragile to survive. Hoping to stave off that calamity, the administrators decided to be proactive: they'd look for kids who seemed not to fit in with their peers, and then keep an eye on them. Not to control them or concoct reasons to eject them, of course. Just to make sure everyone was happy. And not planning to blow anything, or anyone, to smithereens.

Instantly, Bruce was on the school's radar. "There were only a handful of us with long hair, and he was one of them," says classmate Bo Ross. "We all sat together at one table in the student union, hanging around and talking." Bruce, he recalls, didn't say very much and wore metal-framed sunglasses with yellow lenses that made him look like an assassin. Usually absorbed in his own thoughts. Bruce impressed, or perhaps unsettled, the other students by abruptly filling a silent hallway with a burst of hoarse-voiced melody. Once again, he seemed so far out on his own wavelength that even the aggro jocks who so enjoyed bullying the hippie kids kept their distance. "He just seemed too weird to mess with, I guess," Ross says.

Perhaps all that public strangeness was another performance—an encore of the routine that kept him so comfortably distant during his boyhood. But in the confines of his Advanced Composition class, Bruce felt free enough to throw open the doors to his hidden depths. Written neatly on college-ruled paper, Bruce's short stories read like dark meditations on a world leeched of humanity. In one piece, the narrator spies a woman alone at night, "caressed only by the icy hands of the moon. She shared her love and was crushed by the greediness of those to whom she gave." His teacher awarded the story an A and scrawled his praises in the paper's margins: "Oh, Bruce, you have a lovely mind . . . at least what shows on paper." Another paper earned another A, and praise for his use of imagery and metaphor but ends with a plea for more information: "Where do you want to go? Until I know your direction, I can't help you at all."

But Bruce's most striking composition is also his most disturbing. Even his admiring teacher appended his/her A grade with a note admitting "I can't pretend I enjoyed the story," and for good reason. Starkly composed and washed in misery, the story describes a young girl, clad in a thin white party dress, attacked by a "faceless creature" that "beat her fragile body down upon the hard pavement." Vivid descriptions of the girl's wounds and the bloody shreds of her dress lead to a final image of the mangled girl dying slowly on the pavement, "[c]rucified upon the cross of night by the violence of man."[3]

---

[3] Obviously, the details have been changed. But anyone familiar with the Springsteens' family story must think immediately of Virginia Springsteen, another little girl whose death came at the hands of a (faceless) truck on the pavement of McLean Street.

At some point during Bruce's third semester at OCCC, he got a message in his mailbox: Could he make an appointment to speak with the school counselor? He did as asked, and as Bruce remembers, the conversation was extraordinarily personal and hurtful. "I was told people were complaining about me," he says. "And to be honest with you, that's all they said. It was weird. I said, 'What about?' but it was nothing." In earlier tellings, Bruce recalled that his fellow students had gone so far as to circulate a petition demanding that he be ejected from school, on account of being too odd to countenance. But Bo Ross finds that story far fetched at best, if only because Bruce wasn't the only student who received a referral to the counselor's office. Determined to head off that dreaded student riot, the administration had sent the same request to all of the kids who spent their lunch hours at the cafeteria's long-hair table.

"We *all* had an appointment," Ross says. "And the guy was cool. He'd ask for our thoughts on certain things, and I kind of liked it, actually." But for Bruce, who still swears the counselor described the petition calling for his ouster, it was another in a long line of school-based humiliations. "It kind of cemented my feelings that I was someplace I didn't really belong," he says. "And, really, I had the one [Advanced Composition] class that I was enjoying, and I did get some value out of it, because it did encourage me. And the rest was just another instance of, you know, it's just not your time."

Earth played a series of shows in the usual Monmouth County spots—Le Teendezvous, the Off Broad Street Coffee House, the Hullabaloo—through the fall, building enough of a reputation to draw crowds throughout the region. But although the group had played a semester-starting concert at Ocean County Community College in September, Bruce kept his musical life separate from his academic identity. Even his pals at the hippie table knew nothing about Earth, or Bruce's ability to play guitar, until a friend of Bo Ross's came in talking about this hot new band he'd just seen. "He was saying, 'Holy shit, this guy is *good*,'" Ross recalls. And he wasn't just talking about Bruce's prowess on guitar. "What impressed him the most was that this guy got onstage and just *activated* everyone. He just had a presence." A few days later another friend from the hippie table brought in a picture of

Bruce playing with Earth onstage. "He *looked* great up there, too. And we thought he was weird, right? So we were like . . . wow."

At the same time, managers Spachner and Duffy had secured Earth a gig at the famous Fillmore East theater, then the New York showcase for virtually every significant hippie/psychedelic band coming through the city. Bruce was already a regular concertgoer at the Fillmore—going alone, generally, to check out whoever was in town and absorb what he could from the bands' musical and stage performances for subsequent adaptation and use—but on this day, the Fillmore was officially closed. The audience, such as it was, would be the cast of *NYPD: Now You're Practically Dead*, an arty, albeit porny film that included a wild party scene set at a rock concert. Earth's job was to play the band onstage, lip-syncing to a song recorded by a group called Rhinoceros[4] while the actors and extras danced, tore off their clothes, and tussled and rolled across the stage around them. "So while we're lip-syncing, the director's giving direction to this hot babe to take off her top," Burke says. "Bruce had this *look* on his face." Later in the evening, the director took to the catwalk above the stage to film a midair sex scene punctuated at one crucial moment by a shot of panties tumbling through the spotlights to drape elegantly across the tuning pegs on Bruce's guitar. The film was never released, but Earth still collected their enormous (to them) fee of $350 for the day's work.

The band's next (and last) New York gig was as half the bill in a December 28 show booked into the Crystal Ballroom, an 1,800-capacity hall in the Diplomat Hotel on West Forty-third Street. It didn't take long for the promoters to realize they'd made a serious error: Earth was completely unknown in New York, and the fans it did have lived on the Jersey Shore. Facing economic disaster, the promoters came up with the brilliant solution of renting some buses and offering to transport Jersey fans to and from the show for free. When the OCCC activities committee agreed to help promote the shows, the tickets began to move. By the time Earth hit the stage on the twenty-eighth, the hall was nearly sold out, giving the trio the largest audience it would ever have.

[4] Then an up-and-coming hard rock band signed to Elektra Records whose structure and sound would soon become a significant influence on Bruce's writing and performing.

And there were some special guests in the seats. As Spachner told Bruce, Graham, and Burke the next day, two executives from different major labels[5] had buttonholed him after the show, both eager to sign the group to a recording contract. But nothing that serious could happen, Spachner added, until each member of the band signed a contract designating Spachner and Duffy as the band's official managers. The only problem was that Graham and Burke were still young enough to require their parents to countersign their legal agreements. And neither set of parents was happy about the amount of time and energy their sons were investing in their music hobby. Spachner and Duffy put together a presentation to appeal to the boys' parents. "But even going in, I had a feeling of doom because my situation at home was tenuous at best," Burke says. "I had an absolutely terrible relationship with my parents, and John was even worse off." The contracts did not get signed.

Earth played a small handful of shows in the first weeks of 1969, including a dance in the Ocean County Community College student union[6] and a pair of nights at the Le Teendezvous club. A February 14 show scheduled originally for the Paddock Lounge in Long Branch sold out so quickly that the promoters rebooked the "St. Valentines Day Massacre," as they called it, for a larger room at the town's Italian American Men's Association Clubhouse. The show was another good night for Earth, and a great one for Bruce, whose screaming guitar and catalytic presence as a front man riveted one tall onlooker at the back of the room. Vini Lopez had known of Bruce since his days as the drummer in local guitar hero Sonny Kenn's band, Sonny and the Starfighters, when they shared concert bills with the Castiles. When Lopez learned that the teenage guitar player was the same guy his Asbury Park music pals were talking about, he drove up to Long Branch to see what was going on. He was not disappointed. "Imagine your rock star, and there he was, right in front of you, when he was a kid," Lopez says. "I didn't need any more convincing."

Earth would never play in public again.

---

[5] Burke and Graham recall that the labels were Columbia and Elektra.
[6] How Bruce could continue to be ridiculed by a student body that had so many opportunities to see him playing lead guitar and singing with an increasingly popular rock band is anyone's guess.

FOUR

OH GEEZ, LET'S MAKE A BAND

ON THE MORNING OF SUNDAY, February 23, 1969, sometime after three o'clock, Bruce climbed the stairs to the Upstage Club's third-floor entrance. Sitting on a stool at the top of the steps, Margaret Potter, who owned the Asbury Park club with her husband, Tom, watched him coming. He seemed underfed and, given his worn-out clothes, dangling black curls, and beat-up guitar case, even more ragamuffin than most of the rest of the Upstage's waifish clientele.

"Is it okay if I play my guitar here tonight?"

The Upstage had been around almost exactly one year, so a lot of unknown guitar slingers had already climbed those very steps to ask that very question, all hoping to join the club's after-midnight jam sessions. Ordinarily, she'd have a kid sign in on the clipboard and tell him to hang out until he heard his name called over the PA. But the musicians were taking a break, and something in Bruce's voice, or maybe the way he couldn't seem to hold eye contact, made her warm to him.

"That's why it's there," she said, gesturing to the microphones and amps on the stage. "Go ahead and plug in."

It wasn't Bruce's first visit to the Upstage. As coincidence would have it, he'd come in a month or two earlier to see the Downtown Tangiers Band, an Asbury Park group made up of singer-guitarist Billy Chinnock, bassist Wendell John, keyboardist Danny Federici, and Vini Lopez on drums. Bruce was impressed: "I thought that Vini and them were superstars. They just all seemed great," he says. But the after-hours, jam-happy club—its floor teeming with musicians, serious fans, and musician-eyed girls—made him fall in love. "I just thought, 'This is the coolest place I've ever seen in my life.'"

Exactly a week after Earth's Valentine's Day show, Bruce went back to the Upstage, guitar in hand. Given Margaret Potter's approval, he climbed the steps to the stage, opened his case to retrieve his new gold-top Les Paul, and slung the strap over his head. Feeling the instrument's weight on his shoulder, he cranked the volume and took a breath. "I came to stun, you know," he says now.

At the start of 1969, the Upstage was the place to do it. Opened in March 1968 as a coffee house with live music, the club—located above a Thom McAn shoe store in downtown Asbury Park—was for musicians and serious music fans excited by the postmidnight jam sessions that kept the place thumping until dawn. Potter took a lease on the building's third floor that fall, building a larger stage equipped with a powerful PA system, lights, and a closet full of instruments to keep the jams going at full throttle. Drifting into the dawn above Cookman Avenue, the Upstage was like an ark for the Jersey Shore's musicians and other young renegades—a world bathed in black light and strobes, where the rhythm of life revolved around the club's day-for-night schedule.

Without looking up, Bruce let loose a long, soaring run up the neck of his guitar. The sound razored the smoky air. He kept going, his fingers spidering across the frets, chasing melodies, doubling into harmonies, reversing direction, and then leaping skyward again. Heads swiveled. Conversations stuttered to a stop. Within moments, all eyes turned to the guitarist, his face still hidden behind the curls draped over his face.

"That quickly, he took over the room."

Geoff Potter, Tom Potter's nineteen-year-old son, was working along-side his stepmother at the door. "Ordinarily, you had all kinds of hubbub and noise between sets," he says. "But he's up there, playing free-form riffs. And within five minutes, you couldn't hear a sound except for his guitar."

A few of the musicians recognized Bruce from the Castiles' days on the high school band circuit in the midsixties. Others had mentioned seeing an unfamiliar guitarist playing miraculously accurate renditions of Eric Clapton and Jeff Beck tunes around Ocean County Community College. But no one in the room expected this fusillade of power and finesse, especially with the visceral intensity he projected across the room.

After watching from the doorway for a few minutes, Margaret went down to the Upstage's second floor Green Mermaid coffee-house look-ing for Sonny Kenn. "You've gotta get up here!" she told him. "There's a guy playing guitar onstage, and he sounds just like Clapton!" Kenn followed her up the stairs, and although the sharp-dressed guitar hero looked doubtfully at the new guy's rope belt and torn jeans ("He looked like fuckin' Tiny Tim,"[1] Kenn says), he kept watching and listening. And when Upstage regular Big Bad Bobby Williams hit the drums, with the Motifs' former bassist, Vinnie Roslin, on his heels, the trio's rollicking blues cut right through Kenn's skepticism. "It was kinda cool," he says. "I remember thinking, 'Oh my God, he's got it!' Somehow that skinny kid was larger than life!"

Indeed, the knots of chatterers from a few minutes earlier now crowded the stage, with a steady stream from the Green Mermaid and Cookman Avenue rumbling up the stairs to press against their backs. Watching from another corner of the room as the blues jam they called "Heavy Bertha" evolved into Iron Butterfly's "In-A-Gadda-Da-Vida," Pot-ter's right-hand man, Jim Fainer, was starstruck. "You couldn't take your eyes off of him," Fainer says. "Bruce had this *presence*. The hairs on the back of your neck would tingle. He had an instinct, a gift."

[1] He's talking about Charles Dickens's *A Christmas Carol*'s Tiny Tim, not the ukulele-playing, late-sixties curiosity.

Vini Lopez knew that already, thanks to his trip to Long Branch the previous Saturday night. The drummer sang Bruce's praises to Danny Federici, the Downtown Tangiers Band keyboardist who had already agreed to team with Lopez in a new band. But neither of them heard another whisper about Bruce until they got to the Upstage a week later. When Lopez caught a glimpse of him leading a jam on the bandstand, he nudged Federici: "*That's* the guy!" They double-timed it to the edge of the stage, where the set had just come to an end. Lopez waved at Bruce and climbed up to invite him to stick around for another set. Bruce, just getting warm, smiled. "Let's go!" So Lopez climbed behind the drums. Bruce called for a twelve-bar blues and Lopez, with Federici perched behind the keyboard and Roslin hanging in on bass, launched into another improv. The guitarist made up some words to fill in the verses, and when his fingers stretched up the Les Paul's neck, the other three followed into a more intense instrumental passage. Almost instantly they were playing in unison, Bruce's ardent leads weaving with Federici's elaborate organ parts, Roslin's steady bass thrum, and Lopez's wild drum attack. It went on for forty-five nonstop minutes, drifting through songs, styles, and rhythms. The crowd members who weren't pasted against the stage were dancing and spinning across the floor. When Bruce sweated through his T-shirt, he peeled it off and tossed it, *splat*, into the corner of the stage.

When they finished an hour later, the drained musicians went downstairs to the Green Mermaid, where they sat around a red-and-white-checked table and beamed happily, fingertips still vibrating. Finally, Lopez voiced the thought that first occurred to him when he saw Bruce playing with Earth.

"Oh geez, let's make a band."

Bruce could sense that something big had pulled into the station. He'd wanted to play with guys as committed to their music as he was, and here they were. Better yet, Lopez had already met a local entrepreneur eager to serve as the group's patron and manager. Lopez took Bruce to meet the guy, a surfboard manufacturer named Carl "Tinker" West, and invited him to check out their next informal performance, scheduled to be the main attraction at the Upstage's after-midnight jam session the next Saturday night.

West showed up as promised, and after getting a firsthand look and listen at Bruce's guitar playing, and the way the young musician injected his own high-octane mix of fury and joy into every note, he realized Lopez hadn't been exaggerating. "That guy's got it," he said after the set. "That's someone I want to watch; he's the real thing."

No small compliment coming from the twenty-eight-year-old West, an Asbury Park newcomer who knew a lot about a surprising number of things and took obvious pleasure in sharing his unvarnished opinions. Also, West had a charisma that called out to young men with more ambition than they knew what to do with. "Once I met him, I realized he was someone to learn from," says Billy Alexander, who became one of West's top lieutenants. "What can't he do? Not a lot. So whatever I could do to get in his company, I did." And Alexander always knew how to back down anyone tempted to challenge his boss's decisions. "I'd say, 'Look, I know you've got your opinion. But don't go in there half-cocked, because Tinker really *is* a rocket scientist.'"

Indeed, West had worked as an aerospace engineer for the Wyle Laboratories in El Segundo, California. But no amount of military starch could stiffen West's enthusiasm for hanging out with beatniks, musicians, and other beach-dwelling members of LA's surfing demimonde. West liked his fun. He surfed, played guitar, and followed a rigorous course of study in order to master the conga drums. He built amplifiers and then became expert at acoustic design. At the same time, West channeled his aeronautics expertise into the world of surfing, designing and building a series of fast, lightweight boards most striking for their adjustable, removable skegs, or fins.

Thus began the Challenger Surfboard Company, which followed its creator to San Francisco in 1965, where West witnessed the growth of the city's hippiefied music scene. So in 1968, when he decided to expand the Challenger brand's grasp of the East Coast market by building a factory on the Jersey Shore, West had no doubt that he would find a similar scene around Asbury Park's boardwalk. Instead he found touristy bars, cover bands, and a scene that, in his hawk-sharp eyes, amounted to "total bullshit. No creativity. No original songs. I was bored as shit."

A visit to the Upstage, along with a good chat with Tom Potter, made him more hopeful. And when Potter introduced West to Lopez at the Green Mermaid one night, West made a proposition: if Lopez could put together a band that could play original songs in an interesting way, he would not only manage the group and build it a top-notch amplification system but also give it a permanent rehearsal space in the back of the Challenger factory.

He formalized the offer when Lopez brought Bruce to the factory a day or two after West saw the Upstage jam. All they had to do now, he declared, was become the best fucking band anyone had ever heard. "You guys can do the music," West declared. "I'll take care of the bullshit."

They all shook hands and set to work.

Bruce, Vini Lopez, Danny Federici, and Vinnie Roslin moved their amps into an unused room in the Challenger East factory, a low-slung concrete bunker plunked into a strip of utilitarian factories and warehouses on a hill in Wanamassa, just west of Asbury Park, and formal rehearsals started first thing in the morning. And they would continue, West decreed, until the end of the factory's workday. He didn't care how good they thought they were or how important they thought it was to spend hours staring at the horizon while dreaming up godly riffs. That was shit they could do on their own time. "If I've gotta work, you've gotta work," he told the four musicians. "So if I'm out there sanding a surfboard, I *better* be hearing you guys making music in here."

Billy Alexander helped enforce the policy. "If the music stopped for too long, either Tinker or I would go crack the whip. I'd knock on the door and poke my head inside. 'What are you guys up to? We're still making surfboards out there!' And none of them ever complained. They loved it."

So the group members kept office hours, learning Bruce's songs, putting their heads together to work out arrangements (the classically trained Federici proved especially helpful here), and then playing the tunes over and over until the chord progressions, abrupt stops, and surprise starts were tattooed into their fingertips. And when the formal practice was done, they spent hours blazing through the blues and rock standards they knew from other local bands or learned off the radio. Often these would inspire some other chord pattern, which proposed its own melody that Bruce established on his guitar before belting out a phrase or two he'd been carrying in his imagination for the last few days.

The long days and nights spent thinking the same thoughts and breathing the same air became a crucial part in weaving the players' individual tastes and personalities into a dense, unified sound that was equal parts Cream, Steppenwolf, and especially Rhinoceros, the little-known group that Earth had pretended to be during the filming of *NYPD: Now You're Practically Dead*. A sort of supergroup featuring veterans from Iron Butterfly, the Electric Flag, and the Mothers of Invention, Rhinoceros didn't sell a lot of records following its 1968 debut, but its combination of heavy guitars, gospel organ, and soul-influenced vocals turned more than a few shaggy heads on the East Coast music scene. Including Bruce and his friends.

Bruce's new band wore its influences as vividly as any other set of not-quite-formed adults. But the four had the chops to pull it off and the personalities to make it their own. The tall, muscular Lopez radiated a restless energy that made him a magnetic presence onstage, where he attacked the drums with power and panache, doubled on recorder, and belted note-perfect high harmonies. Lopez also came with an aggressive, at times explosive, temper that made him something of a menace everywhere else. "But the only reason I ever got into fights was to protect my friends," he says. "And I wouldn't back down for anyone."

Federici, on the other hand, was a cherub-cheeked prodigy who escaped the discipline of his classical training in a haze of pot smoke and occasionally dangerous pranks that became all the more explosive when he developed a fascination for electronics. Not that he needed external power to spark his sillier moments. Consider the afternoon Federici tried to move from one house to another, with the backseat of his car crammed full of clothes and the front seat weighed down with a large planter holding the bristling marijuana plant he'd been tending all summer. Realizing that he had some clothes waiting at a dry cleaner in downtown Asbury, Federici skidded into the nearest empty stretch of curb and dashed out to collect his shirts. Back on the sidewalk a few minutes later with wire hangers hooked over his thumb, Federici discovered that his car had vanished. Thieves, he reasoned. And now that they had not only his car but also his shirts, jeans, underpants, and socks, he had no choice but to dial the police.

As it turned out, the authorities had already located Federici's car. In fact, they'd found it right where he had left it, parked smack in front of a fire hydrant. With an enormous marijuana bush perched in the passenger seat. No matter. Federici marched right into the police station, only to be promptly arrested. When his mom bailed him out a day or two later, he came away with his car and his clothes. And he always knew where he could find more pot.

Roslin had been part of the Freehold music scene longer than Bruce. An original member of George Theiss's pre-Castiles band, the Sierras, Roslin moved into the Motifs, the band that often bested the Castiles in the midsixties battles of the bands. Whether the Motifs were actually better—or simply profited from having Jersey Shore musician and frequent battle-of-bands promoter Norman Seldin as their manager—was a bit of a controversy back in the day, but Bruce never doubted the Motifs' primacy in Freehold. "They were jaw dropping," he says. "I'd never stood near or seen anything up close that good." A bit older and more established in adulthood, Roslin preferred to keep his own place outside the factory. But he had the right look and feel for the band.

The group spent a month working on its small repertoire of Springsteen originals, with a few choice covers, including Hendrix's "Voodoo Chile," and "Crown Liquor," a Billy Chinnock tune that Lopez and Federici had played in another previous band, the Moment of Truth. Musing on a name for their new group, they came up with Child, signifying a new beginning; a band whose music would sound fresh and unspoiled.

Now all they needed was a gig. West walked the few blocks down Sunset Avenue to the Pandemonium club, a new addition to the Shore Motel on Route 35, returning with a contract for a three-night stand starting on Wednesday, April 2. The group would be the only act on the bill and thus responsible for three or four sets of music. But stretching tunes to the thirty-minute mark and beyond was second nature to experienced jammers, so no problems there.

When it came to preshow anxiety, they simply focused on the individual successes they'd had already. "We were like an all-star band," Lopez says, and when it came to the Jersey Shore in 1969, he wasn't wrong. So April 2 arrived, and while no one can recall exactly what the band played during that first show, it did draw a respectable crowd, many of whom went away feeling excited enough to come back the next night with their friends in tow. By Friday night, the crowd flowed into the street and around the corner. Club owner Mickey Eisenberg didn't let West leave that night until he agreed to bring his band back for a five-night stand the week after, with an encore show on April 20.

A booking at Le Teendezvous followed in early May, and served as a precursor to the pair of larger, outdoor shows that West figured would launch them into a career orbit well beyond the seaside bars and teen clubs of central New Jersey. "The strategy was to play big shows in parks, San Francisco–style," he says. West had already built the group a sound system designed to take on park-sized venues, and with a vibrant performer like Bruce going off like a Roman candle at center stage, Child would make all of those laid-back California bands seem translucent.

They started on Saturday, May 3, with an afternoon-long minifestival in Long Branch's West End Park. West hired a couple of other bands to play opening sets, and given a warm afternoon and a $1 ticket, the show attracted something like a thousand music fans. Child cleared $1,000—amounting to several nights of club work—but even more important to West, however, was giving the band a chance to feel and hear itself in front of such a large crowd.

"Bruce was a little insecure at first," West says of his star's first steps on the bigger stages. "Then once he started playing these shows, you could see something going on. He fed off the buzz. And once you've got people screaming at you, you begin to think you can do anything." Bruce got another dose of crowd worship on May 11 when the band went back to Long Branch to close a daylong music festival held on the great lawn at Monmouth College. The school set up the bands on a concrete patio outside the doors to Wilson Hall, about thirty concrete steps above the sunny lawn where the audience sat, danced, and tossed frisbees. But when West and the group set up their gear on the patio, the warm, sun-splashed afternoon took on a new charge. "I just went up to sit by the stage," says Barry Rebo, a Monmouth student who had heard about Bruce from a friend who'd seen an Earth show the year before. "Suddenly all these kids came running up and flooded the stage."

Surrounded by a mob of stomping, cheering fans, the patio unexpectedly broke out into a scene of Beatlemania-like proportions. But as viewed in the post-1968 era of riots and public violence, the scruffy, underfed teenagers at its core all experienced the same dread sense that the scene could career out of control. Lopez, Federici, Roslin, and Bruce backed away from their instruments and, as one, charged into the entrance to Wilson Hall, slamming the door behind them. They had only a minute to stammer at one another until the door flew open again and an incredulous Tinker West stepped inside. "Showtime!" he barked. "So why don't you assholes get out there and make some music?"

Off they went. A great cheer went up, and with instruments in hand, they kicked off a blast of high-volume rock 'n' roll. The songs were largely unfamiliar: Many were Springsteen originals, some less than a week old. But it was impossible for a campus full of church-raised small-town kids to miss the unholy outrage fueling "Resurrection"'s alternating currents of cathedral organ and full-band attack. "Special low price on three Hail Marys!" Bruce shouted between the end of one verse and the launch of another solo. "My soul is clean again. *Hey!*"

The crowd danced and leaped to the rhythm, and they called Child back for three encores, all of which put the icing on a "wild, mind-bending show," according to the Monmouth College's newspaper review. "They literally rocked and blasted out the entire area." Better still, the story continued, complaints about the noise came from homes as far away as Norwood Avenue nearly a quarter of a mile away. Afterward, Rebo walked over to where the band was unhooking the amps and looping up the electrical cords and introduced himself to Bruce, who seemed, Rebo recalls, entirely stunned. "He was obviously shocked by the response. And when we talked, he couldn't look me in the eye, which was weird because he'd just been so dynamic on the stage. I'd never seen someone become an entirely different animal like that."

The band did nearly as well at a free outdoor show mounted 350 miles south of Asbury Park, in Richmond, Virginia. The gig had been set up by Billy Alexander, West's once-and-future lieutenant, who had moved down to go to college. Quickly expert in the ways and means of the college town's clubs, bars, and frat parties, Alexander convinced West to let him set up a free show in a park—ostensibly to help celebrate the end of the school year but mostly to prime the Richmond market for a series of paying gigs he'd set up for the start of the new school year. The free afternoon show attracted between four hundred and five hundred rock 'n' roll fans, impressing them enough to lay the foundation for a rock-loving market that would help sustain the group, and Bruce, for years to come.

In mid-June Bruce's parents quit their jobs, packed their belongings and youngest daughter, Pamela, into their car, and left Freehold for what Doug swore would be the last time. The departure hadn't been easy. Doug's moods had been cycling into the red zone that spring, and for a time, Adele worried that something terrible might happen on the long drive to the opposite coast. "He was thinking things that just weren't true," she says. "Now everybody's bipolar. But then . . ." she trails off. "Let's just say there are a lot of stories," Ginny says.

Finding himself alone in the South Street house, Bruce felt as relieved as he was sorry to see them go. "It was tough because I'd been so close to my little sister," he says. But just as he understood the ferocity in his father's need to get himself away from the family ghosts in Freehold, Bruce felt just as eager to shake off his parents' expectations—particularly the ones that had sent him to community college—and see where his own ambition, and the internal currents that fed it, would take him.

Only a few weeks later, Bruce saw Pam Bracken sitting at the bar of the Student Prince club in Asbury Park. Just home from her freshman year at Kent State University, Bracken noticed Bruce drinking a soda pop at the bar and felt smitten by the sweet, flirtatious young musician. Bracken was particularly charmed by the contrast between his notoriously decadent profession and his relatively reined-in habits. As Bruce made clear when they spoke, he didn't curse, drink, or take drugs. He just seemed so *nice*. So when Bruce invited Bracken up to Freehold for lunch the next day, she said she'd be there.

She knocked on his door almost exactly on time. Then Bracken knocked again. No sounds emerged from inside. Finally, a dream-dazed Bruce came out and sat down on the stairs. He was really happy to see her, he said. He was a little sleepy but knew what would fix that: a quick walk to the bakery to pick up a crumb cake and bring it back home for the guys. So off they went, the picture of young romance, strolling through a bright summer day. "Years later," she says, "Bruce told me that the real reason we had to go out was so the other woman he met that night could get out of his room." And yet they grew close, and then serious enough to take them through most of the next two years, with long spells of separation due both to her collegiate schedule, his footloose career, and the emotional trip wires hidden behind Bruce's dark if always hopeful eyes.

Given two months of prepaid rent in his family's deserted home, Bruce opened the bedrooms, sofas, and floors to his bandmates. Both Lopez and Federici moved in for the summer, and they commuted to the Challenger factory to rehearse for their upcoming shows. Meanwhile, the group's summer schedule became a pattern of packed, sweaty performances at the Pandemonium and a handful of other clubs on the sandy stretch between Sea Bright and Asbury Park. Which meant that Child could generate income, even before it became the festival circuit fixture that West intended it to become. But West still had his master plan, so when his old California electronics compadre Doug "Goph" Albitz sent over a pass to the three-day music-and-arts fair scheduled for mid-August in White Lake, New York, he also passed along an open invitation for West to bring his new band to play on the side stage the clown/activist Wavy Gravy would manage with the members of his Hog Farm Collective. Unfortunately, Child already had a booking for the same three nights at the Student Prince on Kingsley Street. Knowing it would be a mistake to alienate the club's owner—and, like everyone else, having no idea exactly how big an event Woodstock would turn out to be—West left the band in Asbury Park and drove up to the festival by himself.

"And they had such crap up there," he grumbles. "I was walking around thinking, 'Fuck! I'm an idiot! Why'd I leave the band in New Jersey?' And I was right about that, of course, because if I could have had Springsteen at Woodstock, it would have been all over. Years of bullshit totally avoided. But the band was booked, we needed the money, and that was that."

It's impossible to say how the Aquarian-spirited, mud-and-acid-soaked crowd at Woodstock would have responded to the full-throttle rock 'n' roll by Bruce and Child. But it took only a week for one of the festival's biggest stars to register her overwhelming approval of the aspiring young musician. Not that Janis Joplin ever heard Bruce play a note of music. But when the psychedelic blues singer came to perform at the Asbury Park Convention Hall on August 23 and glimpsed the nineteen-year-old guitar player watching from the wings with Lopez, Roslin, and West, she didn't hide her enthusiasm. "When she finished her set, she came offstage, saw him, and gave one of these, 'Where have *you* been all my life' looks," Lopez says.

"Some whispering attention was paid, I guess," Bruce recalls. "I was nineteen, had hair to my shoulders, was a big local star and carried myself like that." But Joplin didn't have a chance to say anything before her road manager grabbed her by the shoulders and steered her back to the stage to perform her encore. At which point Bruce turned to his friends with what West describes as "that deer in the headlights look." According to West and Lopez, Bruce had no intention of getting to know the San Francisco–based blues singer any better. Instead, they both recall him stage-whispering, "I'm gettin' the fuck out of here!" and jogging down the hall to a fire door, through which he shoved his way out onto the boardwalk and beyond.

When Joplin finished her last song, she beelined back to where Bruce had been standing. Finding him gone, her brow knit in a combination of surprise and disappointment. "Where'd he go!?" she shouted to West, Lopez, and Roslin. Lopez pointed to the fire door down the hall: "He went *thataway*!" Joplin clattered off to her dressing room. A few minutes later, the manager of her coheadliner, James Cotton, approached West in the hallway. "C'mon, Tinker," he said. "Janis really wants to fuck Bruce." West shrugged. "What could I do? I just said, 'Sorry, he's outta here.'"

With Federici and Lopez stationed across the hall from his own room, the Springsteen house became a kind of all-musicians frat house, with endless hours invested in spinning records, fiddling with Federici's CB radios, and tearing off for impromptu journeys to the shore to surf, check out the boardwalk, or catch someone else play at one of the seaside bars. Bruce, meanwhile, had the gastronomic sophistication of a feral dog, feasting on Velveeta-and-mayonnaise sandwiches, or the glistening fried chicken at the Tasty Dee-lite drive-through. Vegetables rarely made an appearance, and dessert was often a heaping bowl of what Pam Bracken recalls as "this disgusting strawberry-flavored goop" that Bruce enjoyed with generous *shplorts* of Reddi-wip. When Bracken surprised him one night with a bowl of fresh-cut strawberries and cream, he took one bite, recoiled, and pronounced it "terrible."

Introduced to the rest of Child's extended family of helpers, friends, and hangers-on, Bracken felt increasingly at home with her dashing boyfriend's circle. West was particularly friendly, telling Bracken to consider herself part of the organization, welcome anywhere they played. Bracken felt delighted until Bruce stalked over, eyes ablaze. Why had she been talking to Tinker for so long? Why did she look so happy when she was with him? Even a glimmer of warmth passing between Bracken and another man was enough to send him into a rage.

"Bruce really didn't like having anyone else pay attention to me," she says. "If he thought I was having fun talking to some guy, he wouldn't even talk to me about it. He'd say, 'This relationship is over!' and I'd get the cold treatment for the next day or two."

The rent on the South Street house ran out in September, and the guys moved their stuff back into the Challenger factory, where West had installed new bathrooms and a few portable cots for their sleeping bags. Living rent-free with the band's gear immediately at hand was a close-to-perfect setup for a young man so eager to build his future. Then Bruce remembered the toy trains that Fred and Alice had given to him when he was a small boy.

Bruce hadn't played with them for years. But that was the one relic that meant the most to him; something he could pass along to his own son, if he ever had one. He'd stored them in the South Street house's attic for safekeeping, then forgotten them. He called the landlord asking to pick up his old toy, but the guy gave him a flat no. The house was *his* property, he snapped. And now that the Springsteens had stopped paying rent, everything *in* the house was his property too.

Stymied and furious, Bruce drafted Lopez to accompany him on a guerrilla-style rescue operation. The house was empty, the doors locked and windows shut tight. Bruce tried all of his usual tricks: shimmying up to his second-floor bedroom window, climbing across the roof— searching everywhere for a point of entry and finding nothing. Unwilling to break a window, Bruce sat in the darkness for a while, got back into Lopez's car, and rode stonily down Route 35, the road leading back to the Challenger factory, his guitar, and whatever else lay in his future.

Living (mostly) and rehearsing in the factory, the band worked constantly. And not always on music, if the surfboard shop got overwhelmed by orders. Conscripted to the factory floor, the musicians, including Bruce, would spend the next few hours pulling, sanding, and applying epoxy to Challenger boards. Mostly, though, West left the band to pursue its music with no distractions. And when the occasional hassle did emerge—such as the abrupt discovery that a band from Long Island, New York, named Child had also produced an original album under that name—they went to the Inkwell Coffee House in Long Branch, ordered some beers (Pepsi for Bruce) and burgers, and dispensed with a series of imperfect names, including Moose Meat, Locomotive, and the Intergalactic Pubic Band. Mercifully, Lopez's longtime pal Chuck Dillon came up with a tougher, cooler name, Steel Mill.

Down in Virginia, Billy Alexander took time away from his studies to spearhead the group's popular campaign in Richmond, setting up a series of bookings that took them to venues including multiple shows at the City's Free University and Virginia Commonwealth University, and then to a pair of late-November gigs at the 3,500-seat gymnasium, opening one night for a group of ambitious jazz rockers called Chicago Transit Authority and the next for heavy-metal heroes Iron Butterfly.

Steel Mill's ascent in the college towns of central Virginia gave the group another boost. In fact, its reputation in Richmond was so strong that it ended up playing after the headliners from Chicago. But for Alexander, who had helped build the band's sound system and had been present for its rehearsals and shows, the moment of clarity came at the Free University gig on November 20. It was early in the set, just as the band kicked into "Goin' Back to Georgia," a bluesy southern rocker Bruce wrote while in an Allman Brothers state of mind. Launching on a thunderously deep E chord, "Georgia" built into a full-throated Springsteen vocal, punctuated with spiky guitar riffs that touched off more rumbling fills from Lopez's drums, answered by organ riffs played out above Roslin's rumbling low end. Then the entire outfit pivoted back to the chorus, sung in three-part harmonies every bit as precise as the instruments had been anarchic.

"I swear the hair stood up on the back of my neck," Alexander says. "Everything just connected. The crowd was berserk, and Bruce was just beaming. It was like he *knew*. He'd taken a massive step. And the next step would take him into outer space."

FIVE

BREAK OUT THE GUNS AND AMMO, EVERYTHING'S GONNA BE JUST FINE

BRUCE'S VERSE WRITING HAD ALREADY come a long way from the romantic poems and singer-songwriter experiments he'd crafted in his high school and college years. No longer splayed among the diaphanous ladies, drifting birds, and starving children of his post–high school imaginings, Bruce looked to his own boyhood and the plague of draft notices, cops, teachers, and priests that haunted his adolescence.

And while most of his late-sixties lyrics seem less than fully formed, the visceral crunch of the music throttled the listener. "Sister Theresa," performed with a lone guitar and Lopez's bell-clear recorder, projects the passion of faith into unabashed eroticism. "You say you're married to Jesus Christ / And that he's in your bedroom every night," Bruce sings. "Come with me for a while / I promise I'll make you smile." The tune often served as a bookend with "Resurrection," a fan favorite thanks to its fire-and-brimstone attack on Catholicism. Yet neither of those songs packed the wallop of "The Wind and the Rain," an outraged breakup tune with a hurricanic climax that had the unsettling habit of coinciding with large-scale police busts, unexpected cloud bursts, and, on one breathtaking night, a lightning strike on the building they were playing. "Whoosh! It just exploded through the room," Lopez says. "It caused this chain reaction of sparks . . . like lighting a chain of sparklers."

Bruce also wrote a litany of antiwar songs: "We'll All Man the Guns," "The War Is Over," "The War Song," and more. But the lyrics were often undermined by their author's righteous indignation. "America Under Fire," for instance, describes the home front as a circle of hell populated by "conquered freak soldiers," lovers "all turned to whores," and streets chockablock with men who are both blind and "viciously insane." And if those horrors hadn't driven home the world-gone-wrong idea, the song's climactic coda of "America the Beautiful" includes a sarcastic recitation of the chorus to the *Mickey Mouse Club* theme song.

Clearly, Bruce's lyrics lagged behind the power of his music. But even at this awkward age, his authorial ambition is striking, particularly when it came to defying the conventions of rock 'n' roll songcraft. "Bruce started writing these . . . odd combinations of things," Steve Van Zandt says. "Epic, long songs. I don't remember anyone else going through all those chord changes. Maybe the Mothers of Invention, but I don't think he was a big fan of theirs." Bruce remembers being swept up in the Allman Brothers. "It was almost southern rock, some of them," he says. "Prog rock, southern rock. There was an amalgam of things, I think, at the time, Allman Brothers were very influential. But the interesting thing about those songs is that the arrangements were quite complex."

The sprawling "Garden State Parkway Blues," for instance, aggregates three or four distinct songs—different sounds, different styles, different voices—all knit together by instrumental pieces and various solos. Often stretching to thirty minutes or more in performance, "Garden" begins with a pleasant, midtempo rock groove accompanying a wry portrait of one working man's journey from his bed to breakfast ("Whoa, my Kellogg's Corn Flakes are my very best friend!"), to the driver's seat of a cheap used car that refuses to respond to the ignition key. "But I don't care . . . it's really got a heart!"[1]

The chorus introduces an increasingly frantic chant of "Punch in at nine, punch out at five," which transitions into double-speed guitar solos, and then back to a spoken-word segment about unpaid bills and unful-filled obligations. From there it is back to a full-throttle guitar-and-drums vignette describing an endless highway packed with "two-eyed monsters," to a dreamy, voice-and-recorder fantasy featuring Douglas Fairbanks, Peter Pan, the guards at Buckingham Palace, and the Hell's Angels' notorious leader, Sonny Barger. Then come the clipper ships, chariots, sunlight soldiers, and an unnamed guy who refuses to steer his car up the on-ramp. The band eases into a three-chord vamp (repurposed three years later as the coda of "Kitty's Back") and the dream world finds form in a musician who skips away, instrument in hand: "playing with his guitar singing, he goes down upon the green hillside . . . and sunlight soldiers dance and sing before your very eyes."

"Garden State Parkway Blues" may not be Springsteen's most suc-cessful attempt at picaresque writing, but even *Born to Run*'s ten-minute mini-epic "Jungleland," with its superior sense of narrative and restraint, can't touch the daring that went into "Parkway"'s twisty, modular struc-ture. Bruce dismissed his Steel Mill songs not long after, and hasn't played a note of them in public in more than forty years.[2] Now he concedes the songs were "fun," and he still hears the connections to the work that would come. "I ended up tightening things, like in 'Rosalita' and some of those early things that really had twists and turns," Bruce says. "I was always interested in that a little bit, you know. But I tell you what, Steel Mill played it for a long time and people liked it."

Tinker West certainly did. Bruce was just on the threshold of his songwriting career, no one could say how far he and Steel Mill might go. And with the Grateful Dead, Jefferson Airplane, Santana, and a paisley

---

[1] Bruce speaks often about watching his father struggle to get his car moving in the morn-ings. One Springsteen car wouldn't shift into reverse, so if Doug had left the car in the driveway, it had to be pushed into the street before he could go anywhere else.

[2] Although certain melodies, chord progressions, and a few phrases of lyrics would be recycled over the years.

cloud of other bands adrift in San Francisco, with music industry types giving laid-back chase, Tinker knew exactly where to find the most reliable launching pad.

West's first call went to Doug "Goph" Albitz, last seen working with Wavy Gravy at the Woodstock festival in August. He spent most of his time running the kitchens at the oceanside Esalen Institute a couple hours' south of San Francisco in Big Sur. A favorite meditation/getaway spot for California's most gilded hippies, Esalen's mix of exclusivity and aquarian ideals attracted some of the era's most popular artists and musicians. The Beatles, minus Paul McCartney, had meditated in Esalen's emerald hills. Bob Dylan also came through, blazing the way for Simon and Garfunkel, Arlo Guthrie, and Joan Baez. Most ended up performing in the institute's ocean-view art barn. And when Goph noted that the institute still needed a band for its End-of-the-Sixties New Year's Eve party, it all came together.

They set out the day after Christmas in a two-car flotilla, West and Bruce in West's reconditioned 1948 Ford pickup, while Roslin, Lopez, and Federici rode in a station wagon. They traveled to Memphis, then got separated when an exhausted West, who had been piloting the truck for fifteen hours, hit his limit. He wheeled to the shoulder and told Bruce it was his turn to take the wheel.

Bruce knew this moment would come but still had no real idea how to pilot an automobile. He'd avoided steering wheels ever since his sole attempt to learn from Doug had left him feeling humiliated. "It sort of was like one shot, you're not doing it, you're done," Bruce says. The few hours he'd spent piloting Pam Bracken's automatic transmission sedan around the Challenger factory's parking lot hadn't prepared him to work the aged pickup's herky-jerky manual transmission.

"So I'd have to tell him, 'Push that pedal! Move the gearshift over there and now let out the pedal,'" West recalls. "Then the truck is grinding, and we're lurching around the highway. But he got it going eventually, and as long as he didn't have to stop, he was fine."

Bruce and West pulled into Esalen on December 30, not long after the other guys had driven through the gates. They dropped their luggage at the main lodge, then headed straight to the art barn to spend the next few hours shaking road dust off their fingers and toes. Then a smiling woman arrived with a steaming loaf of just-baked bread, presented on a cutting board with a crockery cup full of hand-churned butter. The group members made straight for the cutting board, eagerly consuming two-inch-thick slabs of the warm, herbal-scented loaf. Just beyond the open barn doors, they could see fluffy clouds drifting across the sky and rays of sun dancing on the surface of the Pacific. All so beautiful that no one in the group, not even the experienced potheads (everyone but Bruce) thought to wonder exactly what had given the bread's aroma such a sweet, herbal undertone.

"Big Sur pot was some of the best in the nation back then," Albitz says. "And it was everywhere, so we used it for a lot of things."

It's unclear how much the perpetually starved Bruce gobbled up, or what the rigidly self-controlled young man thought of his unexpected ascent through the leafy doors of perception. "All I know is that we all ate it," Lopez says. "And things got a little strange."

That was it for the rehearsal. Lopez, Federici, Roslin, and Bruce put down their instruments in order to take a closer look at the hippie paradise they'd heard so much about. Bruce and Lopez drifted together across the institute's main lawn, almost stumbling over a class of spiritual seekers wrapped in white sheets and squirming across the lawn. "Someone told us they were being amoebas, going through phagocytosis," Lopez remembers. "So we're walking away saying, 'Aha! So *that's* how you get to your inner self. How could we have missed that?'" The two musicians found a trail leading up toward the desert canyons in the hills above. They climbed through the brush and rocks for a while, feeling the silence in the air and the sun on their T-shirted backs. And it was all so strange and beautiful that when Lopez saw something wriggling in the weeds, he reached down, turned over a rock and found "this *huge* fucking Gila monster. That's when Bruce and I freaked out and ran back down to Esalen."

Steel Mill played a second show at Esalen's art barn on January 2, then drove up to San Francisco to audition for Bill Graham's bookers—one of twenty bands competing for a place on the city's reigning promoter's list of opening acts. These off-night cattle calls were regular events at the Fillmore West Ballroom, a low-cost evening ($2 a ticket) that came with instructions for the audience: drink, laugh, or enjoy. Bruce had an attack of nerves when he caught sight of the band Grin, led by a teenage phenom of a guitarist named Nils Lofgren.

A Maryland boy, Lofgren dropped out of high school to pursue a music career in California, and was more shocked than anyone when Neil Young tapped him to play on his 1970 *After the Goldrush* album, and as a member of his touring band.[3] At first Bruce was intimidated by the younger guitarist's prowess. "No way am I playing after that guy," he muttered after watching Lofgren toss off yet another nimble-fingered solo. He regained his composure in time for Steel Mill's set, and once they met in person, Bruce felt instantly at ease. "When I met Nils, we kinda already knew each other," he said. "We looked at music in the same way and cared about the same things."

Graham's bookers were encouraging but noncommittal. No matter, as West had already booked a show at the College of Marin on January 10, and three days after that, they got a spot at the Matrix club, opening for Boz Scaggs. The *San Francisco Examiner* sent a critic named Phillip Elwood to cover the headline act. Instead Elwood devoted 90 percent of his review to Steel Mill's set. "I have never been so overwhelmed by an unknown band," he wrote, calling Steel Mill's set "one of the most memorable evenings of rock in a long time." The critic went on to praise Bruce's songwriting, particularly the dramatic stops and starts, and gave special mention to Bruce's "Lady Walking Down by the River," for its compelling lyrics and a guitar-fired coda that Elwood described as "very, very heavy."

Bill Graham called the next day, reaching Lopez at the Oakland home of Linda Mendez, a friend of West's who had agreed to put up the band. Graham congratulated Lopez on the *Examiner* review and then offered the group a gig opening for blues guitarist Elvin Bishop at the Matrix.

---

[3] Lofgren also joined the Young-less iteration of Crazy Horse for a short stint, and played on the drug-fueled sessions for Young's *Tonight's the Night* album and accompanying tour.

The gig came with a slight hitch: they'd have to get their shit together and be onstage playing in, let's see, three hours. Or slightly less. Three hours and one frantic journey across the Bay Bridge later, Bruce counted off the first song, and Steel Mill was back onstage, playing with all its might.

The pay didn't amount to much: Roslin recalled earning a hefty $5. But the electric feel of playing at the epicenter of America's rock scene kept them going, while the burgeoning following they could command at one or two of the nearby colleges kept their hopes up. Who knew where all of this might lead? As long as the group could up its game while also establishing a foothold in the West Coast's most important rock 'n' roll city, it all made sense.

Except for the increasingly pinched mood within the band. Most of the problem seemed to stem from Roslin, who had been spirited off by a pair of limpid-eyed girls who offered to share their apartment, their drugs, and (it would seem) themselves with the handsome bassist. Roslin didn't hesitate, and found his new setup to be so diverting that he frequently spaced on band rehearsals, meetings, and even the occasional pre-show sound check. None of this made his bandmates happy. And front man Bruce, with all of his endless, obsessive energy, was particularly irate.

If Bruce seemed especially moody in California, it often had something to do with his semiregular journeys to see his parents and baby sister in their new home in San Mateo. Doug, Adele, and Pam had arrived in the Bay Area the previous summer, and after a frustrating day or two exploring neighborhoods around the city, Adele found a real estate office that looked similar to the one where she had worked for so long in Freehold. Asking the first realtor she saw to point them to where "people like us live," she followed directions to the blue-collar suburb on the peninsula south of San Francisco, where they rented a small apartment. Doug found a job driving an airport shuttle bus, and though his darker visions continued to resist the endless sunlight of their new home, a kind of optimism drifted in. "It did seem better," Bruce says. "They had a better life, to my eye." And yet Doug's days still ended in the dark, smoky isolation of his lightless kitchen. "We became very close by our standards, but he never really changed," Bruce says. "It was just his lay of the land." And yet Bruce had to reach out. "I do remember the one time Bruce gave my dad a hug," Pam Springsteen says. "I think he was leaving after a visit. And that was a real moment."

Weeks turned into a month. Then it was mid-February, and Steel Mill was still in the Bay Area, hustling from one low-paying gig to another, still hoping to find a serious break. Which seemed to beckon when Bill Graham asked Steel Mill to perform an in-studio audition for his new Fillmore Records label. The band ripped through onstage favorites "Goin' Back to Georgia" and "He's Guilty," with "Cherokee Queen" representing the newer stuff and the piano-led, harmony-filled country ballad "The Train Song" to show off the band's musical diversity. Graham came into the studio beaming, saying he'd heard enough to offer Steel Mill a full recording contract. Which sounded dreamy until it turned out that the advance Graham had in mind was only $1,000. For which Graham also expected to claim the publishing rights to Bruce's songs, thereby controlling how they would be used and claiming the lion's share of money they generated in perpetuity. West gave the band members a chance to kick it around for themselves, but his opinion of the offer was obvious. "Graham wants Bruce's publishing? No way I'm letting anyone have that. That's Bruce's fuckin' pension plan, right? And it's not mine to sell."

West's argument swayed Bruce, although he certainly did like the sound of coming home with a record deal. Lopez didn't feel right about trying to talk his bandmate out of his song publishing, though he was also eager for the band to be stamped with Bill Graham's approval. But it fell to Roslin to try to argue his bandmates and manager into accepting Graham's proposal, no matter how stingy. "Let's just take the deal and go from there," the bassist said, speculating on how Graham's imprimatur would enhance their price for gigs, which would in turn enhance the value of the songs Bruce would write even after they scored a better deal somewhere else. But Bruce had already made up his mind. After the meeting, he called Lopez aside to tell him the news: Vinnie Roslin had to go.

He'd always been an odd man out. For all the dynamism Federici and Lopez put into their playing, Roslin struck Bruce increasingly as a bystander. He had a steady hand on the bass but, to Bruce's ears, not much more. Meanwhile, Roslin's stoic demeanor onstage added nothing to the band's energy. And he'd been even less on point since he'd taken up with Bambi and Thumper over there in San Francisco. All those missed rehearsals and sound checks had taken their toll: blown cues, forgotten riffs, and, sometimes, entire songs performed with bass lines that bore no relationship to what everyone else played. Given his role as protector/hatchet man for Bruce, Lopez knew it fell to him to give the bass player the bad news. "Bruce didn't do stuff like that," he says ruefully. "He relied on me for certain things, so I'd just do it." Lopez peers at his shoes as he recalls the rest of the episode: How the news pinned Roslin to the back of his chair, and how he wept and begged for another chance. "But there was no going back," Lopez says. "There never is any going back."

Nearly two months into their West Coast residency, West, Bruce, Lopez, and Federici agreed that their momentum in San Francisco had sputtered. With cash running perilously short, they booked a two-night gig in Richmond, Virginia, at the Free University's student center. But who would hold down the bass end of the music when they got there? At first Bruce made like he hadn't given it any thought at all. But when Lopez suggested pulling in Bruce's frequent wingman Steve Van Zandt, the guitarist nodded happily. They called back to New Jersey, and Van Zandt didn't have to think about it. He would meet them in Virginia, where he might get an hour or two to rehearse with the rest of the band before the first set began on February 27. "I figured, yeah, sure, why not?" Van Zandt remembers. The prospect of switching to bass, an instrument he'd rarely if ever played, didn't slow him down for an instant. "It's just not that big a deal with a hard rock band, you know."

Back on its usual circuit of clubs, universities, and opening slots, Steel Mill continued to fill the nightclubs and draw well at the schools, particularly at Monmouth College and Free University, where the group could attract crowds in the thousands. Local media attention started to flow too, especially after West invited a handful of writers, critics, disc jockeys, and other music industry insiders to an open rehearsal at the Challenger factory on April 11. Joan Pikula, an *Asbury Park Press* feature writer, came through four days later with a lengthy profile ("The Steel Mill Blazes Trail for New, Talented Musicians") describing them as musically innovative pioneers. "They've proven there is a following here for people with skills," Pikula wrote, concluding that Steel Mill might even make the Jersey Shore the country's next rock 'n' roll mecca.

For a time, Bruce took for granted that Steel Mill could take him as far as he wanted to go. The band was his future. "We played to thousands of people, with no record out," he says. "It was incredible. Auditoriums and gymnasiums filled. We didn't play a lot, but those were shows where you would come home with five hundred dollars in your pocket, and you could live on that for months. For a local band, that was big success. And in the area, we were big local stars."

Pikula wrote an even more impassioned story in mid-June when Steel Mill opened for the successful rockers Grand Funk Railroad. The Detroit band would soon set a new record for selling out New York City's Shea Stadium: what took the Beatles eighty days to do in 1965 took GFR seventy-two hours in 1971. For now, though, Grand Funk was still playing local arenas. When its scheduled openers the MC5 (the Detroit-based protopunkers whose just-released second album had been produced by a recent Brandeis University graduate named Jon Landau) had to cancel, Steel Mill took the last-minute invitation to fill in at Bricktown's Ocean Ice Palace.

According to Pikula's impassioned review, headlined "Rock and Inequity," Steel Mill blew the bigger band off the stage. To drive home her point, Pikula focused her critical microscope on the bands' respective leaders. "[Grand Funk's Mark] Farner is slick; what he writes is solidly mediocre, as is his playing," she wrote. "Springsteen is neither slick nor mediocre. His music is fine, diverse stuff which blends an infinite variety of musical idioms . . . and his playing, inventive, finely shaded, and clean, is superb."

Granted, Pikula's sense of the evening might have been influenced by her loyalty to the guys she had just gotten to know. She also took care to delineate Farner's ability to inspire an arena full of fans to raise their fists and make other quasi-revolutionary gestures. However, Grand Funk's rhetoric struck her ears as hollow, whereas the passion in Steel Mill's music prompted the crowd to not just dance off its frustrations but also to focus on the ideas and images in the lyrics. "Steel Mill made the music," she wrote. "Grand Funk got the money. Therein lies the inequity."

Bruce marveled at the story. "That was a biggie," remembers his long-time friend Lance Larson, a stalwart Asbury Park musician. "He dusted their fuckin' doors, and when the newspaper said he was way better than this big, established star, well, Bruce was incredibly proud of that."

He had more to be proud of during the summer of 1970. Steel Mill drew four thousand fans to an outdoor show held at the Clearwater Swim Club in Atlantic Highlands, New Jersey, and then scored a few big paydays at a series of end-of-term events at the usual Virginia colleges. They returned to Richmond for a huge summertime blowout held on the top deck of the Seventh and Marshall Streets parking garage in downtown Richmond, supported again by Mercy Flight, a local band whose entire lineup, from manager Russell Clem to drummer "Hazy" Dave Hazlett, had become friendly with the Steel Mill crowd. The group's lead singer, Robbin Thompson, developed a friendship with Bruce, who often slept in his apartment when Steel Mill came back to play another series of shows in Richmond. So when the garage show ended, they went off together and, as usual, talked about music deep into the night.

Bruce admired Thompson's vocal power and onstage charisma, and as he began to feel overburdened by the many demands he faced in Steel Mill, he asked his friend if he might consider auditioning for a spot as co-singer and front man for Steel Mill. Thompson absorbed the invitation in shades of disbelief. "Bruce was obviously the group's front man, so why did he need me?" The rest of the group shared his confusion. If all the crowds and critics declared themselves transfixed by Bruce's singular skills as a guitarist, performer, and lead singer, why bring in another front man to crowd him out? "It was an odd move," says Van Zandt. And yet, he continues, not surprising, given the number of options the group's chief writer, singer, lead guitarist, and music director could claim. "Bruce didn't know what kind of role he wanted to play. Because it's annoying to be that multitalented. So he was the front man, and the guitar hero, and the writer. And sometimes you're better off doing one fuckin' thing right."

After a week of rehearsals, Lopez, Federici, and Van Zandt could see his point. On the last day of Thompson's tryout, Bruce gathered his three partners in one of the factory's storage rooms to talk it all over. It took only a few minutes for the band to stream back into the band room and tell Thompson he could join up immediately if he still felt like it. Thompson did. He quit school the next week, packed up his belongings, and drove back to New Jersey.

The group returned to Richmond in late August, then drove overnight to Tennessee to play a set at the Nashville Music Festival, where the crowd of fifty thousand fans included more than a handful of record company executives. The promoters had also tapped Steel Mill to serve as the backup band for Roy Orbison's headline set, much to Bruce's and Van Zandt's fan-boy delight. When the executives swooped into the group's dressing area to shake hands and congratulate everyone for their good showing, Thompson noticed something the others either didn't see or simply didn't acknowledge.

"These people were saying, 'Hey, so-and-so record company is here, that's the guy talking to Tinker and Bruce,'" he recalls. "And as I was watching that go down, I realized that the guy—and all the other people talking about Steel Mill—were really there to see Bruce. And that was a little flag to me. 'Ah, I get what's going on here.'" For all that Steel Mill presented itself as a band consisting of five equal members, everyone could recognize the one guy who mattered more than everyone else. "And I never forgot it."

Back in Richmond, the group played another few shows before Lopez wandered off with the wrong girl, only to be roused at four in the morning by gun-wielding cops. Someone in her house had six pounds of marijuana hidden in his room, and now everyone in sight faced felony drug trafficking charges. Given the seriousness of the drug dealing charges, the only way Lopez would see the light of day in the next five or ten years would involve the labors of professional legal representation. Steel Mill didn't have immediate access to that kind of money, but the members knew where they could get it. With a summer-ending show set up for Friday, September 11, they could declare the evening a benefit and send their proceeds down to Vini in Virginia. Thompson's former bandmate Dave "Hazy" Hazlett could play Lopez's drums. To make matters all the more promising, they'd be performing at the same venue where they had drawn four thousand fans in mid-June: the Clearwater Swim Club in Atlantic Highlands.

It began as a dreamy, late-summer afternoon. Warm, but with a breeze off the ocean and acres of New Jersey kids splayed across the sloping lawn. The show started at five o'clock with sets by two local bands, Task and Sid's Farm, and then a final warm-up set by Jeannie Clark, who juiced up her usual folk repertoire with the help of Van Zandt on lead guitar, bassist Garry Tallent, and an Asbury Park blues singer-musician named John Lyon. The police presence outside seemed thicker than usual, but welcome to the Middletown Police Department's jurisdiction. "Middletown was famous for having no crime," says native boy Van Zandt. "And having no black people. And having the classic sort of suburban/authoritarian order." Eager to be forearmed in the event of a revolution, Middletown police chief Joseph McCarthy bought an inventory of riot helmets, clubs, shields, and other weapons for his force. And after receiving a few complaints from neighbors upset about the noise rising above the trees from Clearwater's summer concerts, McCarthy figured this end-of-summer music fest would be an excellent opportunity to try out the new gear. "Like Halloween, I guess," Van Zandt continues. "They had no use for it. But here they are."

Just like the Democratic convention in Chicago in 1968. Like the May 1970 Kent State University demonstration that Bruce's girlfriend Pam Bracken, a sophomore at the school, had ventured into moments before the National Guard opened fire and killed four unarmed students. Bracken ran for her life that awful day, and now, just four months later, nearly five thousand rock 'n' roll fans had herded together to hear loud music, suck up their secret stashes of whatever they had, and forget all about Middletown's just-imposed ten o'clock p.m. curfew. "It was the playing out of the generation gap," Van Zandt says of what transpired that night. "In a physical way."

Steel Mill, with Hazlett perched at Lopez's drums, hit the stage close to eight and launched into its usual set, alternating exhortations to fun, sex, heartbreak, runaway trains, and dancing in the streets with the feverishly subversive tunes Bruce had been writing for more than a year. The party packed tight across the hillside and tighter still on the patio near the stage, ecstatic with the music and comradeship. Maybe a few kids got busted for flagrant pot smoking or wine guzzling. So it goes. And if the crowd's temperature spiked at all, it had more to do with Bruce's intense performance. Dressed in a sleeveless white T-shirt and his usual rope-belted jeans, he fed off the crowd's energy, his voice entwined with Thompson's, his guitar leads pinwheeling from one verse to the next.

"Bruce was always set apart by that magic he had," says Joe Petillo, the Upstage guitarist who had come out to see his Steel Mill pals do their thing. He'd seen Bruce play; he'd traded solos with him at the Upstage. But from the middle of the crowd, Petillo felt the awe rising in him. "When he stepped onstage, he took charge. You knew something special was happening."

And it did. Right up until the second hand on Chief McCarthy's watch swept the hour past ten o'clock. Singing and playing at center stage, Bruce knew he was pushing the limits. "There was this '*If you play one minute past*' . . . thing," he says. "And, of course, we played one minute past, because that's what we did." In moments, the Middletown police, in full riot regalia, appeared at the top of the hills surrounding the Clearwater pool. "It was like a classic Western," Van Zandt recalls. "You look up and see all this riot gear all around the place. And at some point, they just descended." They came in, batons swinging, headed for the stage where Bruce and band were ripping into the first chords of the night's closer, "He's Guilty." Of all songs.

"My recollection is that people were smoking dope in the crowd, and somebody tried to make a bust," Bruce says. "They threw the cop into the pool, and that's what started the whole thing off."

All of which took place just as Bruce and Thompson were getting into the first verse: "We're here to try this boy for his crime," they shouted. "Jury all got up in their chairs / He's guilty! He's guilty! Send that boy to jail!"

"The band was rocking! The people were rocking!" recalls Bill Alexander, back to running Steel Mill's stage crew during the summer break from college. Then the PA system went dead: the cops had pulled the plug, thereby cutting the amps and the internal fans that kept the overheated electronics from melting. An enterprising crew member snuck behind the police to reconnect the wires, spurring a wild roar from Bruce as he kicked the band back into gear.

Chief McCarthy, realizing that the hippies had shoved his officers aside and defied his own chiefly orders, leaped with outrage. The obvious solution: arrest everyone in sight. Within seconds, every member of Alexander's stage crew had been shackled and shoved, hard, toward the riot vans idling in the center of Route 36. Alexander, who had somehow avoided the many arms of the law, ran to the back of the stage, only to be confronted by a fire-cheeked cop who grabbed a fistful of Alexander's shirt and pointed to the amps.

"Chief McCarthy wants that stuff offa there!"

"How am I gonna do that?" Alexander shouted back. "You just arrested all my guys!"

"I don't give a crap!"

"You're being an ass!"

This last observation, while arguably correct, also proved to be a strategic error. An instant later, Alexander wore shackles around his wrists, while a meaty forearm pinned him to the wall. "You're under arrest!" the cop shouted.

"What are the charges?"

A six-battery flashlight cracked against Alexander's forehead.

"*There's* your charges!"

Back onstage, Bruce, Van Zandt, Thompson, and Hazlett held on to the groove until the police regained control of the plugs, stopping the music cold. Which, amazingly, did nothing to loosen Bruce's grip on the crowd as he stood alone at center stage, clapping his hands over his head and bellowing into the air, "He's guilty! He's guilty! Send that boy to jail!"

Tom Cohen, who played guitar in a West-managed group called Odin, saw it all from the midst of the crowd. "It went very quickly to being total chaos. We thought the revolution was gonna happen right there and then." Except for one thing: no one could take their eyes off of Bruce, still clapping and shouting at center stage. "There's no music. There's no power," Joe Petillo says. "And he *still* has thousands of people in the palm of his hand."

From the stage, that realization was both thrilling and terrifying. "That was the first time we realized how much influence the band had over the audience," Thompson says. "People were really getting hurt, our equipment got damaged. But that audience looked like they would have done anything we asked." In Bruce's eyes, they were already doing it. "We were young rock 'n' roll punks," he says. "All the other stuff was in the air, but, really, we were just interested in music . . . Literally, I just wanted to keep playing. There wasn't anything beyond that, you know."

Except for the Middletown Police Department. "The police jumped up on the front of the stage," Bruce says. "And they were yelling at everybody and swinging the clubs and stuff. There was a lot of chaos going on in the front. I turned around, and it was all going on behind me too. And Danny was in a mess." Indeed, a few cops decided to clamber up the back side of the stage, but when they grabbed onto the amplifiers and started to climb, a stack of speakers came tumbling down, smacking Chief McCarthy in the head before pinning the climbers to the ground. Looking up to see Federici at his Hammond B3, the cops reached the obvious conclusion: "*That blond hippie just threw the speakers on us!*" But would the baby-faced organist even think of doing such a thing? Many onlookers don't remember it that way. But Van Zandt has no doubt. "Oh, Danny did that," he says. "How do I know? Because I *saw* him do it. I was standing right next to him. It was the PA stack, and he elbowed it right over on them."

No wonder the cops were so angry.

"*Arrest that asshole!*"

When Federici glanced down to see a wave of bruised, furious policemen hurtling at him, he launched himself across the stage, hit the ground at a sprint, and didn't stop until he was lying beneath a blanket in a car belonging to Steel Mill crewman Greg Dickinson, who drove the panicked organist to hide out at his place, with his wife, Flo, and their infant son, Jason.

Meanwhile, Bruce and the others hid under the stage, hoping to avoid the brunt of the police attack. Hearing that the cops planned to confiscate their gear, they leaped into action, hurling amps, instruments, wires, and the sound mix board into the back of West's truck. Bruce and

Hazlett jumped into the front seat, and the three guys rolled out the back entrance. Once they got to the open road, they trailed into silence, trying to work out what had just happened and what they could do next. They avoided the Challenger factory, thinking that it would be destination number one for any Middletown cop intent on locking up the band or its gear.

Thankfully, the postshow raids didn't happen. Instead the police cleared the area and filed an arrest warrant for Federici, who had vanished so completely that he earned the nickname he'd carry for the rest of his life: the Phantom. Poor Alexander—battered beyond recognition by the time Middletown's peace officers hurled him in the back of their riot van—filed a civil suit against the city's police force, while the American Civil Liberties Union launched an investigation into the circumstances of the two dozen arrests made for drugs, alcohol, and what the police called "assaults."

Alexander's plight enraged the rest of Steel Mill, and the entire organization held emergency meetings to talk through what had happened and put together a list of witnesses and evidence. But when Alexander, accompanied by his attorney (who doubled as his uncle) met with the Middletown police, he limped away with nothing but threats and warnings. "I heard McCarthy say, 'If your client doesn't drop these charges, we'll produce guns, knives, whatever it takes. And we'll put him away for a long time!'" Alexander says. True to their word, the police leaked news that their postconcert search beneath the stage had led to the discovery of a sack full of drugs and weapons, apparently stashed by a band that had forgotten the many available hiding places in the nooks of their own vehicles and packing crates. Given a stern warning from his uncle lawyer ("Do you really wanna go to jail for the rest of your life?"), Alexander dropped the civil case, to his everlasting regret.

For Bruce, just days away from his twenty-first birthday, the show left an indelible mark. He'd spent most of the evening reveling in the energy of another large and excited audience. But the show's ugly end, and the eager brutality of the Middletown police, hit him hard. "This political thing with Steel Mill," he said to Tom Cohen a few days later, ticking off the many tunes he'd written about stopping the war, bucking the authorities, and changing the world. "We always talk about the revolution, but nobody really cares. Nobody *does* anything. They just wanna *talk* about it." The next revolution song Springsteen wrote—probably with Robbin Thompson's help—was called "Change It." Only this time the cry for social revolution came drenched with sarcasm.

"Everybody's saying their favorite sayings, everybody's singing their favorite songs," the tune began. "Everybody's got a favorite game they're playing, well, ha, we're all right, but I guess we're all wrong." Moving on, the lyrics became increasingly acerbic. "So take LSD and off the pigs . . . Break out the guns and ammo, everything's gonna be just fine . . . all you gotta do is hang around."

Bruce's enthusiasm for fist-in-the-air rhetoric had vanished. It was time to think again about Steel Mill's strengths, limitations, and the wide-open future. So while the band continued performing throughout the fall, Bruce also renewed his trade in solo coffeehouse gigs. He'd toss the money back to the band's central kitty, but his mind was drifting in another direction.

SIX

FOR PERSONAL REASONS THIS HAS TO BE MY LAST SONG

BRUCE AND STEEL MILL STAYED off the stage for nearly a month after the Clearwater disaster—a break that had as much to do with Lopez's ongoing residence in the Richmond jail as it did with the group's smashed equipment and the sting of real and psychic wounds. Reemerging from the Challenger factory in early October, the band bolted to Richmond to play a lukewarm opening set for the Ike and Tina Turner Revue. On the plus side, they reconnected with Lopez, just released from jail, and that made the trip worthwhile.

Back on the Jersey Shore a couple of days later, Steel Mill played another sold-out show at the Monmouth College gymnasium, where the still-at-large Danny Federici nearly got nabbed by marauding Middle-town police at the end of the set. Fortunately, the cops underestimated the group's canniness when it came to evading the law. As Lopez remembers: "Bruce got everyone [at the front of the crowd] to come up onstage, then fellow Asbury Park musician Davey Sancious took over the keys, and Danny disappeared." The Phantom strikes again. Next, they went back to Richmond for a pair of shows in late October, and then waited a month for a headline set at Newark State College on November 25. Two days later, Steel Mill opened for Black Sabbath and Cactus at the Sunshine In, a new addition to the circuit near the Asbury Park boardwalk.

At first the lags between shows puzzled new member Robbin Thompson. But the concerts they did perform often drew crowds many times larger than most Jersey Shore bands would face in a week of nightclub shows. The Monmouth College show brought in four thousand Steel Mill fans, many of whom spent two or more hours waiting in a heavy rain to get as close to the stage as possible. When Thompson saw the stack of cash waiting for them after the show, he was flabbergasted. "We'd made more than three thousand dollars, and it was literally, 'Here's ten for you, ten for you, ten for me, ten for you . . . '" he says. "I made five hundred dollars and it was shocking. I'd never made as much money with a band before. The only problem was that we probably wouldn't work again for a month."

Indeed, the Thanksgiving gigs at the end of November were the group's final shows of 1970. Not long after, Springsteen traveled west to spend the Christmas holidays with his parents and sister in San Mateo. There he spent his time doting on his kid sister, consuming Adele's pasta and roasted chicken, and sharing the late-night silence with Doug.

Away from the usual faces and sounds, Bruce's rock-burned ears yearned for new music. Picking up on the FM radio stations in the South Bay, he felt enraptured by Van Morrison's new *His Band and the Street Choir*, and then fell hard for Joe Cocker's *Mad Dogs & Englishmen*, a live recording of the two-dozen-strong band Cocker had hauled around the United States the previous winter and spring. And while they were very different artists, with Morrison's exacting yet spiritual soul music contrasting with Cocker's shambolic gospel-soul, the two had similarly expansive visions, crowding their songs with horns, gospel singers, and multiple soloists. More than anything, both bands went at their music like evangelical preachers, throwing every fiber of themselves in the air knowing that music's righteousness would carry them up into the realm of the sacred. And after all the thump-and-snarl of Steel Mill, all the fist-in-the-air lyrics and guitar-bass-drums-organ, these new records presented entirely new possibilities.

The swing of old-fashioned rhythm and blues; the lockstep funkiness of James Brown; the seemingly endless possibilities that went along with a larger lineup of musicians, sounds, and inspirations. Asbury Park overflowed with musicians capable of playing all of it—including, of course, the members of Steel Mill. But with so much change already flowing through him, Bruce couldn't imagine building a new band around Steel Mill's name and the expectations it evoked. So when the first light of 1971 fell on California, Bruce had already decided it for himself: Steel Mill was finished.

Bruce broke the news a day or two after his return to New Jersey in early January. Back at the Challenger factory, he found Lopez and Federici in their rooms and told them directly: Steel Mill would grind and roar no longer. Lopez recalls being "surprised and dismayed" by Bruce's abrupt (and undiscussed) decision, but before he could respond, Bruce held up a hand and told him not to worry: "He said, 'I'm going in a new direction, and I want you to be my drummer,'" Lopez says. Federici received no such guarantee; he wouldn't play in a Springsteen-led band for nearly two years, much to his frustration. Thompson, who only months earlier had ditched his pals in Mercy Flight to join Springsteen's band, felt shocked by the news yet unsurprised to hear it. "It wasn't like our momentum was fading," he says. But he'd seen it coming since he watched the record company execs flocking around Springsteen at the daylong showcase in Nashville.

Tinker West, who had invested so much of his own money into building Steel Mill's career and reputation, took it the hardest. "I figured, look, we've been doing this for two and a half years, now we've finally got it to where guys are starting to make offers, it's going the way it's supposed to be," he says. "We're starting to pull down four thousand or five thousand a show. But then I thought, 'Well, I'll always be able to find another way to make money.' And Springsteen's a talent. He wanted to be able to write stuff for a ten-piece band. What the hell are you gonna do? I'm not gonna start screaming at him."

Steel Mill had one more scheduled gig to play, a club show at South Amboy's D'Scene on January 18 and then booked a pair of farewell shows at the Upstage on January 22 and 23. Both of the Upstage concerts sold out instantly, and given the litany of friends, neighbors, and compatriots who got through the doors, the floor became a solid mass of shoulders and upturned faces, all dripping sweat in the triple-digit temperatures. The encores went on for nearly forty minutes, climaxing with a wall-shaking "Resurrection" that still didn't satisfy the stomping, cheering audience. When they came out for the last time, Bruce stepped to the mic to introduce what would be the band's final encore. "For personal reasons," he declared, "this has to be my last song." He counted off the intro and launched once again into the song that described the twenty-one-year-old's own progress from Catholicism's darkest fantasies to the spotlit valhalla of the stage. "Hail, hail resurrection!" he sang. "I'll say my prayers to the earth and the sun / Hail, hail resurrection!"

Bruce's rock 'n' roll rebirth didn't end on the stage. An increasingly regular presence at the Upstage in early 1971, the shy young stranger who had marched up the stairs two years earlier had been replaced by a domineering presence. "He'd actually hog the spotlight," recalls Albee Tellone, a multi-instrumentalist who played regular folk sets at the Green Mermaid. "He'd do George Carlin routines he'd memorized, or perform movie scenes, doing all the dialogue himself. Bruce had this incredible charisma, and he loved joking around."

In his more personal moments with girlfriend Pam Bracken, Bruce could be every bit as engaging. "He told great stories, but he never gossiped," she says. "I thought that was sweet." But even as Bruce swept her up in his ambition and discipline, Bracken could also intuit the emotional turmoil fueling his determination. Something other than an early adopter of feminist principles, Bruce expected his girlfriend to tend to his (and sometimes his bandmates') laundry, and then sat impatiently while she produced the burgers, roasted chicken, and spaghetti-and-meatball dinners he required. When he broke a front tooth in the surf at Bradley Beach, Bruce called Bracken, commanding her to grab the bottle of Excedrin in her bathroom, and bring it *now!* "I guess he was in a lot of pain," she says, recalling the angry flash in her boyfriend's eyes when she found him bloodied and defeated on the boardwalk.

As desperate for the comforts of emotional intimacy as he was terrified by its requirements, Bruce veered between fits of jealousy and barely secret bouts of faithlessness. As Bracken recalls, Bruce could never resist a woman in need of help or succor. Robbin Thompson had been engaged to be married when he moved into the Challenger factory, but when his wife-to-be followed him to Asbury Park a week or two after he relocated, their already-unstable relationship shattered. Overwrought and confused, the young woman turned to her ex's friend-roommate-bandmate for comfort. "To my dismay," Thompson says. "But it wasn't like Bruce poached her or anything. We broke up, and someone else was there."

That nuance didn't do much for Bracken, who found it difficult to accept her boyfriend's sheepish story about lending Robbin's bereft girlfriend some emotional support in the midst of her trying time. In fact, Bracken reacted so heatedly to Bruce's news that their argument escalated into a screaming match that ended when Bruce slapped her hard across the face. Hurt and outraged, Bracken tore open the front door and took off down the street. She soon had Bruce running at her heels, wailing that he was sorry and had smacked her only because he feared she might become "hysterical."

Bruce's relationship with Thompson's ex-girlfriend ended within a week or two, which sent him back into Bracken's arms, albeit with a stern command that she stay away from his shows from that day forward: "Your mom didn't go to your dad's job, did he? Why do you need to watch me do my work?" Bracken shrugged. "My dad, obviously, wasn't a rock 'n' roll musician." She already knew what was bothering him, anyway. "I got in the way of his meeting other women."

Elusiveness came naturally, so Bruce felt comfortable ricocheting from one friend's sofa to another's disused bedroom, to a new girlfriend's apartment. He rarely stayed in one place for more than a month, so his friends and fellow musicians often had to struggle to track him down. And though Bracken knew when her on-again, off-again boyfriend was avoiding her, she found it impossible to stay angry at him. Not just for his talent and looks but also because she could sense the wounds he tried to keep hidden. He rarely mentioned his family to her, and although he doted on his young nephew (Ginny's son), Bracken met Ginny only once during the two-plus years she spent in Bruce's company.

Bruce did take Bracken to a family get-together at his grandfather Zerilli's home, still referred to as the House on the Hill, once the home of his mother, Adele, and her sisters, Dora and Eda, during their teenage years. Their wayward father, Anthony Zerilli, had made it his own when he got out of prison in the 1940s, and the Englishtown, New Jersey, farmhouse had served as his home ever since. No longer allowed to practice law, Anthony had built a new career in tax accountancy and enough other side businesses[1] to not only earn a comfortable living but also gain the eminence to work among foreign trade delegations and the like. Regarded among the family as a tycoon, Anthony played the role to the hilt, particularly when he was hosting a family function. Noticing the throngs of relatives clustered on his grandfather's lawn, Bruce rolled his eyes, recalling how some distant cousin had once paid a visit to the Zerilli patriarch and had come away with one of the old man's cars. "They're all hoping someone else gets lucky too," he grumbled.

Inside the house, Bracken noticed a formal dining room with a lavishly polished table that could easily seat a dozen. From there, Bruce took her into a small sitting room where an older lady perched in a creaky rocking chair, speaking rapidly in Italian, and introduced her to Adelina, Anthony's first wife, and Bruce's grandmother.[2] When she saw her grandson approaching, she waved him closer and took his face in her hands. "She kept pinching Bruce's cheeks and going, 'Sweet-ah! Sweet-ah!'" Bracken recalls.

When Anthony greeted his grandson, he took Bruce and Pam into a

---

[1] Details on Anthony's postprison work and life are a bit murky, due both to his estrangement from the rest of the family and to the fact that no one in the younger generations is quite sure exactly what he was up to.

[2] After decades of being divorced and distant from each other, the couple reconnected at a family wedding in the late 1960s. Anthony had just buried his third wife (the secretary for whom he had left Adela in the late 1930s had also died), and once they started talking again, the couple reestablished their bond. They never remarried but did live together in the House on the Hill for the final ten years of Anthony's life.

barn where he stored the treasures he'd gathered during his career. Opening a bureau drawer, he sifted the contents until he came up with a tin souvenir spoon that had been presented to him by some European dignitary. "It seemed silly to me," Bracken says. Bruce smiled, nodded a thank-you to his grandfather, and walked away without another word.

As the winter of 1971 bore down on Asbury Park, Bruce dug in with the circle of musicians he'd met through the late-night jam sessions at the Upstage. Most of the Steel Mill gang stayed close, particularly Van Zandt. But now Bruce's orbit also included Big Bad Bobby Williams, folk-rocker Albee Tellone, the blues singer-bassist-harp player John Lyon, Irish bluesman Big Danny Gallagher, Upstage bouncer Black Tiny (built "like a Pepsi machine with arms and legs," according to his Upstage colleague Jim Fainer), and feral orphans-turned-Upstage regulars John and Eddie Luraschi. Also, bassist and walking rock 'n' roll encyclopedia Garry Tallent and the classically trained David Sancious. And more, too, each toting his own small legend and oddities. And as beachside musicians hunkering down in the chill of the off-season, hardly any of them had two $10 bills to rub together. "We couldn't go out to the bars, we could barely buy a six-pack, let alone drugs," says Tellone, whose Sewall Avenue apartment (shared with Van Zandt and Lyon) became a gathering place for the scruffy young longhairs, particularly on the nights they hosted their weekly Monopoly games. Dubbed Cutthroat Monopoly, the game they played was as hotly competitive as it was spiked with absurdist rules, inside jokes, and enough improvised twists to render it a dice-driven satire of capitalism, authority, and random cruelty. Hand-drawn additions to the Community Chest and Chance cards assigned turns of fate cribbed straight from the headlines in the *Asbury Park Press*. Draw the Race Riot! card, and your little green houses and smart red hotels would be reduced to ashes. Pick another wrong card, and you'd be the victim of a police bust that would cost thousands in fines and legal fees. A luckier player would draw the Middletown police chief McCarthy card, thereby gaining the power to arrest and imprison any other player at any time.

But of course that's just where the fun began, since the most crucial gaming took place outside the boundaries of the Monopoly board. Few could rival Bruce's powers of persuasion, and he won more games than anyone else—although his dominance may have had just as much to do with the unique talent John Lyon described to *Time* writer Jay Cocks in 1975: "[Bruce] had no scruples."

Bruce also came to the games with his antic sense of humor and a romantic's eye for dramatic action. As he described it, the scene unfolded like a comic opera, populated with outsized characters and life-or-death struggles. Anyone who didn't already have a Bruce-generated nickname soon wore his own custom-tailored tag. "It was the formation of a group identity," Van Zandt says. "All the sudden we became a rock 'n' roll Rat Pack. It just kinda happened, and I very consciously encouraged it because I'm a band guy. A Rat Pack guy."

The emphasis on group identity made it easier for everyone to work in whatever pairings, groupings, and settings that might come up. For a time, Bruce seemed to turn up everywhere: acting as the center of electric jam sessions at the Upstage's third floor and serving in acoustic jams (most often as a part of Albee Tellone's Hired Hands) in the more laid-back Green Mermaid coffeehouse. Van Zandt and Williams formed a band known variously as Steve Van Zandt and Friends, the Big Bad Bobby Williams Band, and/or the Steve Van Zandt and Big Bad Bobby Williams Band. Whatever they were called, the band also boasted Garry Tallent on bass, David Sancious on keyboards, and the baby-faced blues nut Johnny Lyon on vocals and harp, with Springsteen occasionally showing up to add second guitar and vocal harmonies.

But as Bruce became serious about organizing his new band, virtually all of Williams's bandmates defected to the new enterprise. No surprise about Van Zandt, given the two guitarists' friendship. But then Garry Tallent took his bass to the Challenger factory, with Sancious fast on his heels, leaving a chagrined Williams to wonder what had just happened to his band. "He was hanging around in this bar going, 'Motherfucker!'" Tellone says. "When someone asked him what he played, he said, 'Second fiddle!'" But in the wake of Steel Mill, they all knew which bandleader had the best shot at actually hitting the big time. So when it came to hiring musicians in the winter of 1971, Bruce Springsteen was going to get what Bruce Springsteen wanted.

West put an ad in the *Asbury Park Press* in pursuit of female singers and horn players, and auditions started soon after. A stream of musicians came in to try out, including one flame-haired high schooler from Deal, New Jersey, who had already started sneaking into bars to sing with local bands. Bruce and West liked her chops but eventually had to break it to young Patti Scialfa that she needed to grow up a bit, maybe even graduate high school, before she'd be old enough to go on the road with them.

The candidates who made it further into the process heard Bruce's impassioned speeches about Van Morrison. The Irish bandleader's meld of rock, blues, jazz, Celtic, and gospel music should be this new band's musical north star, Bruce said. He ran saxophone player Bobby Feigenbaum through Morrison's songs, then sealed a deal with gospel singers Delores Holmes and Barbara Dinkins by putting on a Morrison album and asking them to improvise backing parts. Still, Dinkins thought that Bruce was most impressive for the power of his own compositions. "I was in awe of his original songs," she says. "He had all this wavy hair and these muttonchop sideburns, but he wrote those songs from his heart and spirit. I knew instantly that he was something special."

Once the singers had signed on, Bruce made certain that his gang of grungy young rock 'n' rollers treated them with the deference they deserved. "Bruce had met the women in a church, and when they first came by, he told me to be careful about what I said in their presence" says Tom Cohen, lead guitar player for the West-managed Odin. "So he'd say, 'Ah, these ladies, man. You don't wanna be caught cursing and swearing around 'em. They're *proper*.'"

Bruce ran some other musicians through a series of acoustic and electric jam sessions he played—sometimes booked and promoted as a Bruce Springsteen Jam Concert—at the Upstage and the Green Mermaid. Jazz trumpet player Harvey Cherlin signed on to join Feigenbaum in the horn section, and the entire band—Bruce, Van Zandt, Tallent, Sancious, Lopez, Feigenbaum, Dinkins, and Holmes, with occasional guest shots from West and his congas—took up a typical Bruce rehearsal schedule of four or five multihour sessions each week. "It was like a job," Feigenbaum says. "But when we performed live nobody was better rehearsed. We were *tight*."

In early March West got a call from the manager of the Sunshine In, hoping to book Steel Mill to open for the Allman Brothers on March 27. Undeterred by the news that Steel Mill had broken up in January, Fisher revised his offer: *"Just get me Springsteen, and I don't care who backs him up."* When Van Zandt, a huge Allmans fan, heard the news, he *insisted* that his friend take the gig, even if the real big band needed a few more months of work before attempting to claim Steel Mill's title. Bruce thought back to Joe Cocker's overflowing stages of *Mad Dogs & Englishmen*. If they didn't care who he played with, then he'd play with everyone he knew. Including the ones who couldn't play a note of music.

And so came the first stirrings of the band that would eventually be known as Dr. Zoom and the Sonic Boom. With the core of his still-forming band already rehearsed enough to play together, Springsteen fleshed out the party band—as he first called the project—by drafting John Lyon to sing and play harp, and then recruiting another band's worth of musicians (John Waasdorp on keyboards, Williams on drums, Tellone on shaky, schoolboy saxophone, and West on congas) to double the parts.

As usual, Bruce held regular rehearsals to make sure the outsized band would have some sense of the songs and arrangements. Even so, the group's real mission revolved around fun and just the right touch of strangeness. To make sure they looked the part, some of the musicians went to a secondhand clothing store in search of distinctive stage wear. When Lyon came back with the old pin-striped suit and vintage fedora of an old bluesman, Bruce howled with glee. "Hey, it's Johnny Chicago!" he said. "What are you doin' here, man?" Lyon, an expert in the legends of the great Chicago bluesmen, shot right back. "Don't just call me *Chicago*, man. I'm from the *south side*." And just like that, Lyon became Southside Johnny, and the blues vamp he led them through a few minutes later—a mainstay of the party band's brief career—became "Southside Shuffle." But what were they going to call their freak show of a band? At first they settled for West's offhand suggestion of Bruce Springsteen and the Friendly Enemies. Then the more memorable Dr. Zoom and the Sonic Boom came up but not quite soon enough to make it onto the Sunshine

In posters. So Friendly Enemies they were, at least for the March 27 gig.

The band's set at the Allmans' sold-out show delighted the Sunshine In crowd, all of whom seemed entirely enraptured by the spectacle of singing baton twirlers and skit players, the silent quartet of Monopoly players, and, near the front of the stage, the mechanic (Upstage bouncer Eddie Luraschi) who sprawled beneath a motorcycle while carefully adjusting and tightening the engine's spark plugs. Springsteen did his best to weird it up himself, dropping his guitar to dance with the backup chorus, donning a pair of heavy horn-rimmed glasses, and singing at least one song from a chair at the Monopoly board.

Watching from the wings, the night's headliners were both tickled and impressed. "The Allmans were so cool," remembers sax player Feigenbaum. "We were just local boys, but they were so welcoming. And Duane Allman was really into Steve's slide playing. I remember him saying that Steve was the best slide player in the country, except for him." After the show ended, Duane took Van Zandt aside to show him some more licks, and then set it up so the Friendly Enemies/Dr. Zoom would open for his group when its tour brought the Allmans back to Asbury Park in November. That show would never take place: the supremely talented but hard-living Duane Allman died in a motorcycle accident at the end of October.

When spring came, West transplanted the Challenger East factory to a funky wood-framed structure seventeen miles up the shore in Atlantic Highlands, so all of his electronics and the headquarters of Bruce's music career went along with it. Most of the other musicians worked day jobs to make ends meet: Lopez labored in a boatyard, Van Zandt worked construction, and so on. Bruce, on the other hand, remained steadfast in his determination to never, ever work outside the music industry. So he earned money by playing solo acoustic sets at coffeehouses up and down the shore, and by playing second guitar in Van Zandt's side project, the Sundance Blues Band, which also included Lopez, Tallent, Johnny Lyon, and, for a time, a guitarist named Joe Hagstrom. When the Upstage's Tom Potter booked him for an electric show, Bruce drafted the rhythm section from his new band and performed as Bruce Springsteen and the Hot Mammas. West did his part by booking a couple shows for the party band everyone now called Dr. Zoom and the Sonic Boom. Not that anyone mistook Dr. Zoom as an ongoing concern. The band made its official debut as the headliner of a triple bill at the Sunshine In on May 14 and then played a farewell gig the very next night at Newark State College.

Meanwhile, rehearsals continued for the big band, now dubbed the Bruce Springsteen Band as per Bruce's new determination to make himself the obvious leader and front man.

The nine-piece Bruce Springsteen Band made its long-prepared-for debut on the afternoon of July 10 at the Brookdale Community College's annual Nothings Festival. Three other West-managed bands (Sunny Jim, Odin, and Jeannie Clark) played warm-up sets. Anyone counting on the blistering sound of Steel Mill would have gone home disappointed (although the new band did cover "Goin' Back to Georgia"), but the jazzier sound of the big band still left plenty of room for Bruce's guitar explorations. The going got particularly hot during "You Mean So Much to Me," a new original that began in a Van Morrison mood, and then climaxed with an intricately rehearsed Allmans-style harmonized-guitar workout for Bruce and Van Zandt, before doubling back to the horns-and-singers-laced final verse.

The second show came a night later, with a featured slot at the Sunshine In opening for the UK's Humble Pie, an up-and-coming group featuring vocalist Steve Marriott, late of the Small Faces, and Peter Frampton on lead guitar. The British group had just played a massive show at New York's Shea Stadium (with Grand Funk Railroad topping the bill), but when it got to the Sunshine In during the midst of the BSB's set, the jet-engine roar of applause and cheers greeting the hometown heroes left the headliners feeling more than a little queasy. When the opening set ended, Marriott, Frampton, and company scampered back to the stretch limousines and slammed the doors behind them. How could they follow such a devastating warm-up band? Should they even try? "The club manager had to come out and talk them back inside," Feigenbaum says. "And I understood their problem. The audience didn't want us to leave. We absolutely tore the place apart."

Nevertheless, Humble Pie steadied its nerves and played a show hot enough to match the local band's ovation. Egos assuaged, they thought again about this Asbury Park outfit and its potential for enhancing their own tour. "We were sitting around afterwards, and Frampton was talking to me. 'We love you, we're gonna do a world tour, we want you to open for us!'" Cherlin remembers. "He said he'd get us a deal with A&M Records (Humble Pie's label) and help make us stars, but he was freaking out because he'd already said all that to Bruce, and he wouldn't listen to him."

Cherlin, who had never imagined hearing such talk being directed at him, marched up to West to find out what was going on. The manager shook his head and laughed. "He said, 'Oh yeah, a major label, eh? Good luck! They're gonna screw ya!' And in a way he was right. But I was twenty-two, and Humble Pie was a big name already."[3]

He wasn't the only band member who walked out of the Sunshine In that night questioning West's plans for the group. Still, the new band ripped through a string of shows in July, including a spectacular sixty-minute set at a daylong festival at the Guggenheim Band Shell in Lincoln Center's Damrosch Park in New York City. Kicking off with a gospel-blues arrangement of "C.C. Rider" which segued in and out of a jazzier reading of "Down the Road Apiece," the band swung into a half dozen new originals that revealed how far Bruce's musical vision had progressed in the previous six months. "You Mean So Much to Me," with its effortless blend of rhythm and blues and southern guitar boogie, came next, followed by the rocker "C'mon Billy," and then a Delores Holmes lead vocal on "I'm in Love Again," a joyous Springsteen song that bypassed a similarly titled song by Fats Domino to evoke the girl groups of late 1950s and early 1960s R&B.

The harder-rocking party song "Dance, Dance, Dance" (more like a rougher "Dancin' in the Street" than the Beach Boys song of the same name) roared in on waves of Bruce's spiky guitar and bebop-inspired horn solos. Then the last two songs upped the ante even more. Dinkin's composition (with an assist from Sancious) "You Don't Leave Me No Choice" began with a two-minute piano improv, and then bloomed into

[3] Bruce: "That doesn't sound completely plausible to me. If they offered us an opening slot we would have jumped at it."

a he-done-me-wrong tale that Dinkins sang over a double-fast minor chord progression propelled to mach speed by Lopez, all but beating his drums to death. From there the song grew wilder with a blistering Bruce guitar solo and then wilder still when Van Zandt, Feigenbaum, and Cherlin turned it into a four-way melee.

The band didn't pause for breath before diving into its climactic number: a thirteen-minute version of another original crowned with a familiar name. As per "Dance, Dance, Dance" and "I'm in Love Again," "Jambalaya" shared nothing with the Hank Williams song of the same name, other than its romantic vision of New Orleans. In fact, Bruce's handwritten set lists usually, if not always, called the song "Jumbeliah," either to clear up the confusion with Williams's song (although he obviously didn't care about doubling the Beach Boys, Fats Domino, and so on) or because he preferred the cruder spelling, or still showed the scars of his botched education. Built around a simple three-chord progression "Jambalaya/Jumbeliah" describes a girl who is "strong like a lion / Wild like a tiger," who loves you so hard, "all you can do is / Roll over, roll over, roll over." Once again, the music sings louder than the words, and the Van Zandt–written horn charts, combined with his slide guitar lines, the perfectly harmonized backing vocals, and Bruce's own fast, articulate guitar solos, transform the song into an epic. "That was the song everyone talked about," Cherlin remembers. "Our greatest hit. People asked for it, and we practiced it all the time."

Sadly, they had played the entire set to an audience consisting of a tiny handful of friends and one or two passersby. "Tinker said, 'Man, we're going to play at Lincoln Center!' And we thought like, yeah! The big time!" Bruce says. "But then there wasn't any audience there." The contrast between Bruce's glory-cloaked expectations for the Lincoln Center show and what actually happened still makes him cringe. "When I go to the city and see that place, I still say"—putting on his grimmest voice—"Oh. *There* it is."

SEVEN

SOMEBODY ELSE WHO WAS
A LITTLE CRAZY IN THE EYES

BRUCE REMEMBERS MEETING HER NEAR the beach during the summer of 1971. "She was working in a little stand on the Asbury boardwalk," he says. "She was great. Italian, you know. And funny! Just so funny." Diane Lozito describes it a bit differently, recalling that they first encountered each other at the Upstage's Green Mermaid coffeebar. Her boyfriend, Billy "Kale" Cahill, a law student who worked as an Asbury Park lifeguard during the summer, had met Bruce through some friends a few weeks earlier. Cahill, for all his law school smarts and squared-away lifeguard squint, spent his free time pursuing his interests as an enthusiastic beer drinker and fearless perpetrator of mayhem. Bruce took to calling him Wild Billy, and after he got to know Kale's sixteen-year-old girlfriend, he dubbed her Crazy Diane. Anyone who dated Kale, he said, *had* to be crazy.

Somewhere in the wee hours one night, Bruce, Cahill, Lozito, and one or two other friends skipped out of the moist heat of the Upstage and decided to take a predawn swim at one of the lakes scattered around Monmouth County. Whether they went to Freehold's Lake Topanemus—known popularly as Greasy Lake in honor of the suntan lotion slick that glinted on its surface during the summer—or the heavily wooded Lake Carasaljo on the edge of Brick Township, is no longer clear. Cahill leaped into the black water from the high rocks on the shore, and somewhere in the darkness, a magnetic charge sparked between the petite, dark-haired Diane and Bruce.

When Cahill went back to law school a few weeks later, Bruce called Diane and took her out to dinner. They spent the night together but quickly reined themselves in again, hoping to avoid hurting Cahill, their mutual friend. But as the next days and weeks unwound, the charge proved too powerful to ignore. "Bruce and I got together," Lozito says. "He was twenty-two[1] and when he wasn't onstage, he was shy and quiet. But it was cool to be introverted, and I thought he was perfect."

But as ever, no girlfriend could rival the pull of his music. When Tinker West moved the center of his surfboard and music productions up the shore to the Highlands[2] that spring, Bruce followed, moving into the front room of a house located right across the street, a bungalow occupied by friend Louie Longo and his fiancee, Dorothea "Fifi Vavavoom" Killian, who had been part of the Dr. Zoom chorus. "Bruce was such a good influence," Killian says. "He didn't drink or do any drugs; he just practiced all the time."

The long nights of rehearsing and playing in the clubs ate into Bruce's daylight hours, but, as Killian recalls, he still found the energy to bond with Dennis Palaia, a neighborhood kid who shared his older neighbor's love for baseball. "Bruce slept a lot during the day, but any time that boy knocked on our screen door, he'd drag himself outside, barefoot and in cutoffs, to have a catch. Literally, anytime Dennis asked, Bruce came out to play."

Bruce, for all his rock 'n' roll hair and muttonchops, not only bonded

---

[1] He celebrated his birthday on September 23.
[2] The Highlands is distinguished from nearby Atlantic Highlands by actually being on the Atlantic, and significantly lower than the AH.

with young Dennis but also became a local hero when Tinker rented Bruce a cheap spinet piano to play and write on at home. Bruce rode in the pickup truck to the music store, helped load it into the back, and when they got to the Highlands turnoff, he climbed into the back so that he could pound on the keys as they came rumbling to Locust Street. The carnival sound of music in motion called all the kids out of their houses, and they chased the musician all the way to his house, where the bigger kids helped push the instrument to its place in the enclosed sun porch.

The former social outcast now had friends and admirers up and down the Jersey Shore. But he lost the patience of Tinker West in the last few months when the manager's skepticism about the big band's future eclipsed his belief in its leader's talents. The going got especially tough in the fall when they booked some shows in the Springsteen-loving college town of Richmond, Virginia. Those trips were always a moneymaker during the lean, mean Steel Mill days, but now the same trip would cost multiples more in food, gas, and hotel room bills. How much sense would it make, Tinker wanted to know, to travel that far and work that hard just so everyone could clear $50 or at most $100?

By the start of the fall, Bruce and Tinker found a compromise: they'd play smaller shows with the five-piece core band, and then bring back the horns and singers for the more important gigs. But Tinker still didn't see the wisdom in saturating the market with a lot of small club dates, so when Bruce decided to take a long-term residency at the Student Prince, they reached an impasse. Tinker would stay on as the band's technical manager and sound designer. But his management days were over.

The five-piece Bruce Springsteen Band (Bruce, Van Zandt, Tallent, Sancious, and Lopez) held down the tiny Student Prince stage every Friday, Saturday, and Sunday night from the start of September through the middle of October, and then called in the horns and singers to take the full band to a headlining show at the University of Richmond. But the good cheer of the reunion soon collapsed beneath the weight of mini-disasters that began moments after the band got into town. Lopez, Cherlin, and a few other band members got menaced by a knife-wielding drug addict. When the trumpet player bitched too much about West, who had promised to get the band more ordinary (and less treacherous) digs, the superloyal Lopez socked the trumpet player in the lip, causing another abrupt resignation. Meanwhile, Delores Holmes got beaten up by her boyfriend, and when Bruce took her to the emergency room he wound up staying with her so long that they had to delay the show by hours.

So marked the beginning of the end of the big band. The five-piece Bruce Springsteen Band played regularly at the Student Prince through the middle of December, often airing out new Springsteen compositions. As ever, his songwriting pace seemed astonishing. But now the caliber of his work hit a new course, too. "I just started to drift back toward soul music, which was always very popular on the shore," he says. "I kind of had run through my guitar phase and was now interested in ensemble playing and interested in grooves and things that swung more. I'd studied all those soul band leaders, and for me it was a natural sort of progression. From that you can see where the E Street Band came out of."

Just give a listen to the songs that came to dominate the setlists of the Bruce Springsteen Band's shows during the last weeks of 1971 and early months of 1972. "Down to Mexico" rides a tide of Sancious's organ into a joyous groove that moves as smooth and fast as a car speeding southward on a cloud of dust. "All I Wanna Do Is Dance" rolls on chiming power chords, while other songs display Bruce's expanding range as a lyricist. "Look Toward the Land" describes a dream world of gypsies, sailors, and Mississippi boatmen imagined by an outsider determined to find his way to the center of the circle. "I wanna be / stealing diamonds from the rich men to throw in the sea," he sings. "Ballad of Jesse James," alternately known as "Don't You Want to Be an Outlaw," sounds even more striking, given its place among the first of the many songs that Bruce (still dreaming of Brave Cowboy Bill) would set in the mythic Western frontier.

Bruce built a stunning performance piece out of a mostly improvised two-chord vamp that came to be known as "I Remember." As captured in a club performance that winter, the tune comes off like an old-fashioned soul burner, rising from a whisper to a roar, only to fall back and then rise even higher as Bruce explores all the facets of passion, guilt, and hope. The song's climax comes in the midst of a recitation by an increasingly ardent Bruce, describing a chance encounter with an ex-girlfriend, as the band keeps pace with the swelling fire in his voice: "And I said, 'Darlin'

I *want* ya, I'm feelin' so *bad.*' An' she said, 'No, honey, I just can't make it' . . . But I *love* ya! 'I just can't make it!' *'I love ya!!' 'Won't you come on home?'* And she said, she said, 'Baby, I'm comin' home, I'm comin' home, I'm comin' home!'" Then he shouts it himself, his voice equal parts surprise and triumph. *"Baby's coming home!"*

The music rockets skyward again, Bruce's own guitar going off like fireworks across a murky summer night.

As Bruce strained toward some kind of glorious future, his life still took place in a dying city. Long segregated along racial lines—the African-American community and other nonwhites lived almost exclusively on the town's tumbledown west side—Asbury Park's beachside businesses were notorious for keeping African-Americans from all but the lowest-echelon jobs. Tensions had been on a low boil for years, but the combination of a heat wave, cutbacks in social programs, and a jobs shortage touched off days of on-and-off rioting that burned significant pieces of the west side before turning on the city's business district. The wave of destruction, and the racial and social conflicts that remained unresolved, reduced Asbury Park to a scorched shadow of its once-prosperous self. With retail businesses decamping for suburban malls and tourists content to stay on the turnpike until they found less troubled vacation spots, the town took on a scary, nihilistic chill.

By the fall of 1971, the gloom had taken root at the Upstage. "There were so many needles around, so much speed and heroin, that everyone I knew, except the guys with Bruce, had hepatitis C," says Upstage staffer Bobby Spillane. "We'd shoot anything we could get into a needle. Beer, wine, meth." The incursion of hard drugs, says Sonny Kenn, drained the club's once-electric atmosphere until it felt positively woozy. "People used to come and dance, or at least focus on the music," Kenn says. "But by the end, they were crashed out in front of the stage. The music was just a background to their own hallucinations."

Meanwhile, Tom Potter's drinking, and all the erratic behavior it inspired, had grown so corrosive that he lost interest in reining in staff weirdos such as Eddie Luraschi, who delighted in replacing the vintage cartoons Potter projected onto the wall between sets with a hardcore porn movie that centered around a helpless woman being raped by an escaped convict. "It was sick, and there were girls in the crowd," Albee Tellone says. "Guys would be going up to him, saying, 'Dude, what the fuck's wrong with you?' But he'd be laughing, running it backward and forward. That wasn't normal behavior, and Potter wasn't sober enough to stop him."

Potter let the Upstage's lease expire at the end of October, with enough warning to plan a few closing shows. Bruce and his band showed up to jam the night away on October 29, but they couldn't make it to the actual closing night on October 30: the Bruce Springsteen Band had already booked a show at Virginia Commonwealth University that night. Both of the band's backing singers (Delores Holmes and newcomer Francine Daniels) performed, but the horns were history, and the singers wouldn't return. Bruce's dream of leading his own R&B-style rock 'n' roll orchestra crumbled. "We had a lot of pretty good music," he reflects. "It was just something where I built up a big audience playing heavier riff rock, prog rock. And I realized that's what people like, and they didn't like rhythm and blues. So that was what *I* liked, but it tore my audience to pieces, and that was the end of that."

No one knew that Bruce had already established contact with a producer in New York who would soon devote himself, at the cost of virtually every other aspect of his life, to making this spindly guitar player from the most misbegotten stretch of New Jersey shoreline into the biggest rock 'n' roll star on the planet. Which is the sort of thing a lot of big-city hustlers say to a lot of starry-eyed small-town kids. But there was a big difference between all those guys and Mike Appel. Because Mike Appel meant every syllable of what he said.

Tinker West may have washed his hands of his management duties, but that didn't end his belief in his twenty-two-year-old ex-client, or his sense of responsibility for his well-being. Chatting with Pat Karwan, a music industry friend who played guitar with the critically reviled but popular bubblegum band the 1910 Fruitgum Company, West started talking about this incredible kid he'd been managing who needed to find a good, professional manager. Karwan mentioned a couple of industry pals who were, in fact, looking for a talented kid to take on. Mike Appel and Jimmy Cretecos were young contract songwriters at Wes Farrell's Pocketful of Tunes publishing company, he said. They had written a bunch of songs for Farrell's central project, the imaginary band at the center of ABC's popular *The Partridge Family* sitcom, and were looking to expand into production and management. It would certainly be worth setting up an introduction.

Given Karwan's endorsement, and then a call from West, Appel agreed to meet with the unknown songwriter in the early evening of November 4, 1971. Tinker collected Bruce in his pickup truck and drove him up the Garden State Parkway to the midtown Manhattan corner of Thirty-fourth Street and Madison Avenue, where Appel (Cretecos wasn't present for the first meeting) ushered the pair to the writer's room in Farrell's offices. They perched on chairs and talked while the ragamuffin musician propped an acoustic guitar across the thighs of his shredded jeans. West made his pitch to Appel, assuring Appel that Bruce wrote incredible songs, played a sizzling guitar, had a great voice, and exerted this kind of magical hold on audiences. And not just in his hometown; he'd seen it in cities all over the East Coast and in California too. Bruce, meanwhile, sat silently in his chair with West's acoustic Martin D-45 clutched to his chest. Baby faced but every bit as astringent as Tinker, Appel asked the guitar player what had brought him to his office in particular. Bruce shrugged. These days he felt like a big fish in a small pond, he said. Now he had to get himself into the ocean, or else he'd never earn a shot at the bigtime.

Bruce gazed at the guitar's fret board, hit a chord, and sang the first verse of "Baby Doll," a surreal ballad about a girl so isolated from society that everyone assumed she couldn't see, hear, or speak. "But I knew they were wrong," Bruce sang. "You were just a silent one." The next tune, "Song to the Orphans," offered a bit more verve, but neither song struck Appel's ears as anything close to a popular or critical hit. "There was no magic in them," he says now. "I think it was hard work for him to write those songs. He knew he had to get some kind of direction."

Bruce didn't play anything else for Appel, which seems surprising, given the vast catalog of tunes he had already composed for Steel Mill and the Bruce Springsteen Band. Still, Bruce kept all that to himself when Appel scolded him for not having more to share. "You're gonna need a lot more than two songs to get an album deal," he said. Still, Appel sensed something glimmering just beneath the skinny musician's hoodie sweat-shirt.

"That line about the deaf girl where they're dancing to a silent band, that hit me," he says. "And that other one ["Orphans"] had this line, 'The axis needs a stronger arm / Can't you feel your muscles play?' Those words stuck in my craw. I remember I asked Bruce what it was about, and he said, 'Hope! It's about hope!'"

Appel hadn't heard what he was after. But something in the things he didn't say—and Appel's suspicion that Bruce was holding back—intrigued him. And though he hated to drop his guard, Appel leavened his advice with a pep talk. "You've gotta keep writing," he told Bruce as he packed up Tinker's guitar and prepared to head home. Having a hot band would be fine if he wanted to stay on the New Jersey bar circuit. But in the big city, great bands were a dime a dozen. "If you want to break through," Appel decreed, "you've gotta make it as a singer-songwriter. Write great songs, and then you'll have yourself a real career."

Everyone shook hands. Bruce said he'd be in California for the holi-days and would concentrate on writing some songs during his break, then check back when he got back. "Terrific!" Appel said. "I'll be here."

Back on the Garden State Parkway, Tinker had one more piece of advice for his younger friend to consider. "The only thing I told him," Tinker says, "was that if he was gonna sign with them, or anyone, he needed to get his own accountant. Just make sure every piece of paper they send you goes into your accountant's file. But, of course, that wasn't how he was working back then."

In Asbury Park, the other members of the Bruce Springsteen Band won-dered if they still belonged to a functioning group. After investing the first half of 1971 in building the new band's sound and identity, the re-sponse had been underwhelming, to say the least. "Nothing was happen-ing at the shore," bassist Garry Tallent says. And maybe it had nothing to do with the group. The moribund, post-riot Asbury Park had killed off the club circuit for everyone, most of all for groups that played original material. The group booked another six-weekend residency at the Student Prince—a boon just in time for the Christmas gift season. But the band members had been scuffing their shoes on the Prince's stage since they were in high school. And now that they were adult professionals, the club paid them less than before. "Actually, the club owner didn't pay us anything—he just let us set up and play," Tallent says. "We had to put someone at the door and get a dollar apiece from the walk-ins. And that was the pay."

Heading into the depths of winter, the situation felt too dire to face. And that's when they decided to move, more or less in unison, to Richmond. The winter would be warmer there, and the town overflowed with music-loving college students, many of whom still remembered Steel Mill and its magnetic leader. The idea took root immediately, and the packing began within a few days.

At least that's what Tallent, Van Zandt, and Sancious thought. Lopez stayed north in order to work in a boatyard. And Bruce, still the linchpin in everyone else's career, had other things to do. "I don't remember ever planning to move to Richmond," he says. Not when he had this potential opportunity in New York. Though that wasn't his only option. With the holidays coming up, he would soon make his annual pilgrimage to his family's home in California. This time Bruce wasn't sure if he would come back. With no lease to an apartment or house, and no more clothes and books than he could fit into a rucksack, Bruce had grown accustomed to having a wide-open life. Which suited his own indecisive nature perfectly. "I was always ambivalent about whatever I was doing," he says. "Which is kind of funny to say because simultaneously I was the most committed person I'd ever run up against. But in the middle of that there was always this next thing. Always, if I'm *here*, I can't be *there*. If I'm making *this* music, I can't make *that*, you know."

So off he went. And when he said his good-byes to Lopez, Tallent, and Sancious, he guessed he'd see them when, or if, he got back. Days later Tallent got a call from a New Jersey manager named Peter Scherkeryk, best known for building the career of his wife, the folk singer Melanie, saying how much he loved the Bruce Springsteen Band and wondering if they'd be interested in his taking on their group. The bassist just laughed. "What group?" he said. "Our main guy just disappeared."

Once again Bruce drove west with Tinker, riding in the same pickup truck that had carried them two years earlier, when they came with the amps, mikes, and world-conquering hopes of Steel Mill. They'd been on a lot of roads since then. This time the highway seemed windblown, the passing towns a blur of shaded windows and closed doors. Arriving in San Mateo in the middle of the night, Bruce found the apartment locked and dark, so he tossed pebbles at the bedroom windows, eventually rousing nine-year-old Pam, who flew down the stairs to open the door for her big brother. He swept the wriggling girl into a bear hug, accepted his mother's moist-eyed hug, and his father's nod and handshake, then bid good-bye to West. He'd find his own way back, Bruce said.

The next few weeks were emotionally charged and creatively fertile. Some days Bruce sniffed around the clubs, searching for local musicians who might want to do some jamming with an out-of-towner. "I didn't have a lot of luck with that," he says. Possibly because Bruce had decided to get out of the rock 'n' roll band business. "I'm going, 'Okay, there's a lot of guitar players, a lot of pretty good bands out there, a lot of musicians, but not a lot of people with really their own voice and story,' and I had always been working in parallel through writing and other things, on this other voice. The solo voice. A guy, a story, some chords, some lyrics. And that was going to have to be enough."

He'd been writing poems and verse since before he got to Ocean County Community College, and the self-revelatory work he'd been encouraged to pursue in his Advanced Composition class helped Bruce open himself to that part of the creative process. "The college writing melded with the songwriting," he says. "It was about lyric writing, and I practiced my lyric writing very intensely. So it was something I continued to do, thinking that I wanted to be able to be completely independent and play completely on my own."

Bruce's new songs focused intently on the narrative, unexpected images, and metaphors that sometimes worked and sometimes didn't, but were always compelling to hear. "Cowboys of the Sea" wove Bruce's own childhood dreams of Brave Cowboy Bill (now grown into the outlaw Billy the Kid) into a eulogy for the vanishing frontier and the toll of an increasingly restrictive, money-obsessed society. "If I Was the Priest" takes place in a dusty corner of the west where blood and hypocrisy cut channels in the dirt. Jesus works as the sheriff, while the Virgin Mary runs the saloon by night, says Mass on Sundays, and works as a prostitute on Mondays.

Bruce turned to the roots of his own consciousness to fill "Randolph Street" with nostalgic glimpses back to his sweet, haunted boyhood with Fred and Alice. "Border Guard" addressed Doug directly, if not by name, describing an authority figure who suffers more than the people he shoos away from his sight. "The night is his master / And you know the dawn light brings his captor," he sang. Most of the other songs focused elsewhere, with a distinct tilt toward grandiose settings—the wild frontier, tarnished Hollywood royalty—and freakish characters who bear the mark of cruelty.

"I was starting to formulate the idea of myself: a guy and his guitar. And a group of songs that would just impress upon the bare basics," Bruce says. "This music was me in the early stages attempting to find that group of songs that one guy, a guitar with no case and a cracked neck, could take up to John Hammond."

A dozen songs emerged, then two dozen. They all seem like warm-up shots when compared to "It's Hard to Be a Saint in the City." Viewed from the surface, "Saint" seems an exercise in typical rock 'n' roll bravado: the singer declaring himself a modern inheritor of Casanova, *The Wild One*–era Marlon Brando, and the street fighters staking their turf in the alleys and on street corners. But about halfway through, the urban landscape comes into view in such hellish terms that the narrator fades into the background. Satan materializes from a manhole cover, showing off cards powerful enough to send the police—and the civic structure they represent—reeling. Escaping into the subway, the singer feels the fires of hell ("It's too hot in these tunnels / You get hit up by the heat!"). But then the train stops, and he fights his way back to the street, only to discover that he's back where he started: surrounded by the ubiquitous hookers, cripples, and street fighters. "It's so hard to be a saint," he cries, "when you're just a boy out in the city."

Unable to connect with simpatico musicians in California, Bruce went back to the Jersey Shore in mid-January 1972. He played a handful of shows as the rhythm guitarist with the Sundance Blues Band (Van Zandt, Lopez, Sancious, and Southside Johnny) before heading south to start the Bruce Springsteen Band's ten-show, monthlong residency at Richmond's Back Door club. But while he had a handful of new songs for the band to play and would continue to write more as the winter passed, Bruce had secretly committed himself to relaunching himself as a solo performer. "There was a moment when I had the band and a group of new songs, and I had my acoustic music, and I was sort of debating which way I was going," he says. "So I'm thinking, 'Okay, I played a lot of different genres that I put my own stamp on.' If someone had picked up Steel Mill at the time, we might have done well.

"But at the end of the day, I just thought what I was doing on my own was more interesting. There was more of an original voice in it."

When Bruce dialed the Wes Farrell offices in February 1972, Mike Appel had no idea who was on the line. Nearly three months had passed since the aspiring manager had greeted Tinker West and his skinny guitar player for that short visit. But when Bruce mentioned West's name, it all came back, and Appel invited him back to play his new batch of songs. Come on Monday, the fourteenth, after business hours, Appel said. And this time his production partner, Jimmy Cretecos, would be there to listen too.

Bruce took the bus from Asbury Park to the Port Authority on the westside of midtown Manhattan, then carried his guitar the mile or so to the Farrell office on Avenue of the Americas. He appeared at the front door just past eight thirty dressed up in his usual faded jeans, T-shirt, and hooded sweatshirt. Most of the offices in Farrell's suite were dark, but Appel and Cretecos, accompanied by Farrell's newly hired twenty-one-year-old song plugger Bob Spitz, ushered their guest to a chair in the reception room. Spitz might have been younger and less experienced than Appel and Cretecos, but he shared their determination to climb the showbiz ladder as quickly as possible. So while the songwriters stayed late trying to figure their way into their own production offices, Spitz clattered a typewriter, hoping to string together a usable script for the *Patridge Family* sitcom. But he'd try anything that seemed promising, so when Appel poked his head through the door and invited him to check out this new kid they had coming in, Spitz jumped up happily. "Bruce sat down, and I said, 'Hey, I'm gonna tape this!' I had this little reel-to-reel, so I came back and set it up, and Bruce pulled out his guitar and sang a song."

He started with "No Need," a yearning ballad about a beguiling rich girl who looks past the singer's awkwardness to see the beauty in his music. "And she knows I stumble when I talk," Bruce sang, "so she says, 'Don't talk at all babe, just sing.'" Something in the song—the combination of Bruce's vibrant verse, the melody, and the urgent belief in his voice—pushed the three men against the backs of their chairs. "Mike, Jimmy, and I were looking at each other, gaping," Spitz recalls. Then came "Cowboys of the Sea," "If I Was the Priest," and "It's Hard to Be a Saint in the City," which made Appel's pulse race. A handful of other songs followed, including early versions of "For You" and "The Angel," but Appel and Cretecos had already made up their minds. When Bruce finished, Appel talked at length about how these new songs were so much better than the ones he had played earlier: the lyrics more vivid; the chord changes so unexpected; the melodies so striking. These, Appel continued, were sophisticated songs that could turn the industry on its ear. So yes, he and Jimmy wanted to work with him. And if Bruce could find a more passionate manager—some guy who would sweat more, bleed more, and crawl over more glass for him—he'd better go sign with that guy right now.

In its way, Appel's performance had all the passion and fire the musician had just displayed. Flattered beyond belief, Bruce agreed to come back the next day to talk about contracts and other business matters. He said his good-byes and left Appel and Cretecos alone with Spitz, whose eyes had taken on a lemur-like shine. "I was fucking in love," Spitz says. "I would have sold my mother to go with those guys. And they knew it."

The trio closed down the offices and went to dinner at the nearby Burger Heaven, where they sat in a booth and schemed for hours, talking their way through the next few weeks and months. Their moment had arrived, Appel insisted. Farrell, best known for writing the smash "Hang On Sloopy," was then working almost exclusively on providing songs for the imaginary band at the core of ABC-TV's it sitcom *The Partridge Family*. They'd been searching for their way out of the *Partridge* factory, and now Appel had no doubt that Bruce Springsteen would kick open the door for them. Once they had that kid's name on a management contract, they'd have to leave everything else behind. He'd promised Bruce his sweat, his blood, his life. And if the kid kept giving his all to his music, they had to invest themselves completely. "By midnight we decided we were all leaving Farrell," Spitz says.

Not immediately, though. Recalling their contractual obligation to share all potential discoveries with Farrell, Appel dutifully brought Bruce to his boss's office to play a few songs just in case his boss heard an echo of the sound that had bowled over Appel. Whether he thought the man behind Keith Partridge (aka David Cassidy) would actually fall for such a rough-hewn artist is debatable. But Appel ushered his tangle-haired singer into Farrell's office. Two songs and ten minutes later, they were on their way. "It wasn't his cup of tea, so he passed on Bruce Springsteen," Appel says with more than a tinge of disbelief.

Cleared of their contractual obligations, Appel and Cretecos spent the next month making calls for their new artist and drafting agreements and contracts to serve as the foundation of their new entertainment concern. Most of this took place in the office of Farrell's office manager, Vel Thornton, who spent hours tending to business in other offices in other buildings. Spitz worked at a desk just outside Thornton's front door, and when he saw her marching in, he'd smack his elbow against the wall, signaling the songwriters to dash out of the office's rear door toward the small songwriter's office where they were supposed to be cranking out breezy pop tunes for the next Partridge Family album.

They quit their jobs in mid-March and formed a fifty-fifty partnership as co-owners of a management company they called Laurel Canyon, Ltd.[3] Spitz joined up too, serving as some combination of bookkeeper,

---

[3] Despite the popular assumption that Appel and Cretecos were hoping to piggyback on the then-overwhelming popularity of the artists based in Los Angeles's Laurel Canyon

office manager, demo recorder, and hotelier for Bruce, who took to crashing in the hammock Spitz had strung across the living room of his tiny downtown apartment. Still searching for a permanent address for their offices, the trio set up temporary residence in the West Fifty-fourth Street offices belonging to Jules Kurz, an old-time showbiz attorney Appel used, and with whom he had become friendly. When Appel needed a boilerplate set of contracts for his new client, Kurz cranked out the documents that defined the governance of Bruce's writing, performing, and recording careers. Whether Bruce—or Appel, for that matter—gave the documents a thorough reading is unclear. But both signed the management deal within a week of the February audition. And from that moment, Bruce's and Appel's lives would be linked through hard times, good times, and times that could be described only as truly awful.

The oldest of the five kids raised by Thomas and Marie Appel, Appel was born in the Bronx in 1942, and grew up in the wealthy village of Old Brookville, on the North Shore of Long Island. Appel's father worked obsessively to build his real estate business and expected his children, particularly his oldest son, to live up to his example. If they didn't, things got very bad, very quickly. "My father was dominant, domineering, and very restrictive," Mike's younger brother, Stephen, says. "It was tough for Mike. Very tough. Dad had a tough relationship with all of us, but Mike really bore the brunt of the physicality—the hitting."

Just like Adele Springsteen did for her son, Marie Appel nurtured Mike's artistic side. Once a singer and performer herself, she recognized and encouraged her oldest child's interest in music. When Michael first talked about playing the guitar, she bought him an acoustic and signed him up for lessons. When he tuned into New York City's Top 40 stations she bought him 45s by Elvis Presley, Chuck Berry, and Carl Perkins. When his love for rock 'n' roll grew into overwhelming desire to make music for himself, she bought him an electric Silvertone guitar and

---

(Joni Mitchell, Jackson Browne, Graham Nash, Carole King, and so on), Appel swears that his inspiration came from a weekend visit to a rural house that was surrounded by the most beautiful laurel bushes he'd ever seen.

amplifier, propelling her son into the work that would eventually define his life.

Appel's mother gave him the tools and encouragement, but when he got into a band and dug into the high school circuit around western Long Island, his father's hard-driving ambition took over. Perpetually striving, Appel put bands together, wrote their songs, and ran rehearsals with strict discipline. He also cultivated the professional connections that would gain his band a foothold in the music industry. He took his first group, the Humbugs, to record demos in a New York studio, and the outfit won a contract to one of 20th Century Fox's smaller rock 'n' roll labels. A couple of the group's instrumentals made the regional sales charts. Meanwhile, Appel earned a business degree at St. John's University, and when the army came calling, he sidestepped the draft by joining a reserve unit in the marines, which allowed him to avoid all but six months of boot camp and training before depositing him back in civilian life, save for a few years of monthly service on weekends. Still, the hard-ass marines training fed into Appel's already-growing reputation for being a taskmaster. "He was a real marine," Stephen Appel says. Indeed, Appel held on to a drill sergeant's hat he got at Parris Island, South Carolina, and perched it on his head when he went into ass-kicking mode.

Appel took over the roles of lead guitar, lead singer, and songwriter in a proto-hippie group called the Balloon Farm, writing one early psychedelic single, "A Question of Temperature," that rode its wild fuzz guitar and out-of-control lyrics (e.g., the "heat wave hurricane whirling in my head" that leaves Appel's narrator with a "cool disposition hangin' on a thread") into the Top 40 in 1968. Appel signed a songwriter deal with a production house and eventually encountered Jimmy Cretecos, a young songwriter who had just written a top 20 single, Robin McNamara's "Lay a Little Lovin' on Me," with the Brill Building icon Jeff Barry. Appel and Cretecos hit it off, and when Appel scored a staff songwriting job from Wes Farrell—already on his way to providing the songs and music production for the imaginary band portrayed in ABC's sitcom *The Partridge Family*—he asked to bring in Cretecos as his cowriter. Farrell offered both $250 weekly salaries, and their partnership began.

Tasked with writing snappy pop songs for AM radio, Appel and

Cretecos were productive but also eager to land their own groups and take responsibility for their success. Given more subterranean tastes than their employer, the pair signed a production deal with an early heavy-metal band called Sir Lord Baltimore. Excited by the band's prospects, Appel brought in the chummy Australian Dee Anthony to serve as the group's manager. Anthony shared Appel's enthusiasm, and was so grateful to be given the opportunity to work with the group that he convinced the musicians to ditch their producers and let him steer them to glory. Both furious and impressed (the *balls* on that guy!), Appel and Cretecos tried again with a country-rock outfit called Montana Flintlock, but the band failed to get any traction at all, and that was that. Except for the connection that Appel had established with the group's soundman, the guy everyone called Tinker.

Now that he had Bruce Springsteen in his life, Appel threw everything else away. His job, his health benefits, the financial security he'd built for his wife, Jo Anne, and their two small children, James and Germaine. "Mike had total devotion for Bruce Springsteen," says Peter Philbin, a writer turned publicist who would soon become an evangelist for the cause at Columbia Records. "I've never seen a manager as dedicated as Mike. He had complete belief in him. And he should be saluted for that."

Bruce still does. "Mike was for real," he says. "He loved music. His heart was in it, and everything else. That's part of what attracted me to him, because it was all or nothing. I needed somebody else who was a little crazy in the eyes because that was my approach to it all. It was not business. If business had to be a part of it, then it had to be a part of it. But it wasn't a business. It was an idea and an opportunity, and Mike understood that part of it very, very well. And that was important to me."

Back on the Jersey Shore, Bruce called his friend Howard Grant and arranged for another night at the movies. He'd met Grant back in the late Castiles–early Earth era, when they both hung out around the same Jersey Shore coffeehouses. Grant's family owned a few movie theaters around the shore, and when they bought the Cinema III in Red Bank, Howard managed the place. Soon his movie buff friend Bruce became a regular visitor—usually two or three nights a week, says Grant, who let the always underfinanced musician gorge on movies until the late show curtain fell. After Grant locked the doors, they swept up the scattered popcorn and candy wrappers and then rolled out a twenty-seven-inch television that Grant's father had hooked to an early-model VCR. Grant would turn off the lights, slap in one of the rock 'n' roll videotapes he had found, and the real focus of the evening began.

They'd been doing the same thing on and off since 1968. "We'd watch anything we could get: Elvis, the Beatles, the Rolling Stones, James Brown, and more," Grant says. "And he'd want to watch the same things over and over. Studying James Brown's dance moves, getting up, and doing it for himself." Bruce fixated just as much on the idols' personae—the way they spoke, moved, and behaved when they weren't onstage. "Bruce would be asking, 'What's it like to *be* Rod Stewart or Mick Jagger?' You could see he was already considering it as something that could—that definitely *would*—happen to him. He knew he could get there."

Desperate to become a successful musician, Bruce felt much less bedazzled by the prospect of fame and wealth. "It's like they don't have any friends," he said, watching footage of some rock 'n' roll superstars descending airplane stairs, interacting with the press, and then slipping into limousines, vanishing into a haze of polished chrome, glitter, and cigarette smoke. "Don't ever let me get like those guys. And if I ever *do* get like that—not remembering who my friends are—you gotta come right up onstage and smack me around."

To this end, Bruce devised a plan straight out of the Dr. Zoom playbook: if Grant ever caught him acting like a superstar onstage, he wanted his friend to climb onstage with another pal, perch next to his microphone stand, and start playing chess. "Then I'll figure it out, that I'm forgetting where I came from," he told Grant.

What struck Grant, beyond his friend's commitment to retaining his humility, was Bruce's confidence about where he was headed. "He already knew he was going to become one of those guys. His sights were that high. And good for him."

EIGHT

NOW I WANNA SEE IF YOU'VE GOT ANY EARS

BRUCE KEPT THE NEWS TO himself.

His meetings with Appel. The management contract he'd agreed to sign. The fact that his new career as a solo artist would soon torpedo the Bruce Springsteen Band his friends and partners had built their lives around. "I kept my own counsel, you know. That was just my nature," he says. Steve Van Zandt, for one, wasn't hurt or even all that surprised by his best friend's secrecy. "Bruce isn't exactly a blabbermouth," he says. And how deep did anyone's loyalty to the band run? Given the lukewarm reception they'd received and the grim succession of lightly attended bar shows they'd settled for in recent months, the enthusiasm had drained from the BSB. Virtually everyone had a day job and at least one other regular gig by the spring of 1972.

Still, they had a few gigs on the books, including a pair of high school shows that brought the Richmond-based members back to New Jersey in mid-March, right about the time that Tinker West put the final touches on the recording studio he'd built in the second-floor loft of the new Challenger factory. To help West work out the kinks in the setup, they put their gear on the studio floor and played some of their newer songs while Tinker ran tape, checked the balances, and twiddled his knobs and dials.

The tape captures a half dozen songs from the band's current set: four new Springsteen originals, a dirge-like cover of Bob Dylan's "It's All Over Now, Baby Blue," and a spirited take on the Jimmy Jones R&B rarity "I've Got to Have You, Baby." The most striking tunes are Bruce's new compositions. There's the frontier rocker, "Ballad of Jesse James," also known as "Don't You Want to Be an Outlaw," and the slower, piano-led "Look Toward the Land," while the nearly seventeen-minute "When You Dance" reveals the band's proficiency as an Allmans/Grateful Dead–style jam band. The instrumental "Funk Song," featuring bassist Garry Tallent (known variously as "Funk" or "Funky" or "Funky White Boy") growling "Right on!" at crucial points, showed the group's prowess in high-energy R&B workouts.

The between-song chatter revolves largely around mike levels and feedback but with a good amount of goofing and teasing. Both Bruce and Lopez address Tinker as "Stinky." Van Zandt sticks it to Bruce for his obsessive tinkering with his guitar strings: "Brucie gets in tune, take thirty-three!" And Bruce reminds his band that in a studio setting, a song is "a groove when ya move, but a take when ya shake!" When a microphone lets loose a shriek of feedback, he goes on a giggly, hipster rant denouncing electronics altogether. "I mean, what's dis electronic stuff, my boys play *acoustic!* My boys don't *dig* that electronic gadgetry . . . I mean, my boys play da roots. And they don't give two hoots."

The Bruce Springsteen Band played one last Richmond show on March 17, with a college gig in Hampden-Sydney, Virginia, the next day. A month passed before the band played the Rutgers College student union in mid-April. After that, the members went their separate ways until late June, when they performed at a private party held in a warehouse in Point Pleasant, New Jersey. Then the calendar went white. "All of the sudden there was nothing going on," Tallent says. "I'd pretty much given up on the whole thing."

With their group back in limbo, the five musicians drifted apart for the summer. Lopez stayed on the Jersey Shore, working at a Point Pleasant boatyard. Van Zandt, Garry Tallent, and David Sancious returned to the lives they were building in Richmond. Van Zandt formed a country-blues duo with John Lyon called Southside Johnny and the Kid and caught other club gigs where he could. Sancious worked at the just-opened Alpha Recording Corp. studio, while the freshly married Tallent took a job at a Richmond music store and contemplated opening his own music shop across town. Meanwhile, Sancious had been writing jazz-fusion tunes, and when Alpha had an empty studio to work in, he tapped Tallent and a jazz-and-rock drummer named Ernest "Boom" Carter to form a trio for the sessions.

In New York, and particularly in the Midtown offices of Columbia Records and the just-founded Laurel Canyon Ltd., the wheels of passion, hubris, and industry spun toward a series of events that would eventually seem so significant that virtually everyone involved would come to remember it in his or her own unique fashion. Particularly when the time came to divide the credit, the blame, and the subpoenas. All this for the underfed, undereducated guitar player standing at the Asbury Park bus stop, anxiously awaiting the bus that would carry him back to Manhattan.

While Bruce laid low on the Jersey Shore, Mike Appel, Jimmy Cretecos, and Bob Spitz worked their contacts in search of a friend or colleague who might help them unlock a record company's doors. They dialed. They charmed. They asked, asked again, and then implored. "You've never heard anything like him," Appel promised time and again. "And if you're too deaf to even give him a listen, that's gonna be *your* problem." Snake eyes.

Weeks went by. Pitch after pitch ignored or flat-out rejected. Unbowed, Appel opted for a more daring strategy. If the grinds in the small offices couldn't be bothered to even listen to Bruce, then he'd call Columbia Records president Clive Davis directly. Told that Davis was out of town, Appel scanned his memory for a Columbia executive—any executive—who might have the authority to hold an audition. Only one name flashed into his mind.

"All right, lemme talk to John Hammond."

The man who had brought Bob Dylan to Columbia in 1961. After he'd found, cultivated, and signed Billie Holiday, Count Basie, Benny Goodman, and Pete Seeger to exclusive contracts. Recognized roundly as one of the true visionaries in the history of the American music industry, Hammond's reputation was not to be taken lightly or approached with anything beyond complete respect and deference. Most people thought so, anyway. So when Hammond's secretary, Mickey Harris, picked up the line and heard Appel request a personal audition for his unknown singer-songwriter, she shot him down instantly. Mr. Hammond simply didn't have the time, she explained. Just send in a demo tape, and she'd let her boss know it was waiting for his perusal. So thanks again for calling, and Mr. Hammond will be in touch if he's interested, so . . .

Appel kept talking, only now in a sharper tone. Wasn't Columbia the label that was so committed to signing the most talented musicians and building them long-term, even decades-long, careers? Because if that was true, she was making a mistake—a *huge* mistake—in keeping her boss away from Bruce Springsteen.

"I'm just trying to figure out if anyone there has a clue about music," Appel barked into the receiver. Meanwhile, Cretecos and Spitz, listening from just a few feet away, felt their eyes widening with rapidly growing alarm. "We were waving our hands and hissing at him, 'Don't *do* this, man! *Don't fucking do this!*'" Spitz says. But Appel's righteous fury had flown into overdrive, and no man, let alone a record company reception-ist, was powerful enough to hold him back. Harris sputtered something else, but Appel's fusillade had the secretary so flustered and/or aggravated that she had lost the will to argue with him. When Appel hung up, he turned to his aghast compatriots and smiled. "I got Hammond," he said.

Cretecos and Spitz gaped at each other. Finally, Cretecos spoke. "Did you book an actual appointment?" Appel waved off the question. "They're gonna call back in ten minutes." Now Cretecos and Spitz were even more incredulous than they'd been a moment earlier. "We thought, 'No way!' No way in hell is anyone calling back in ten minutes." And yet the tele-phone rang almost exactly ten minutes later. Appel snatched the receiver and started scribbling in his date book. "It was Mickey in Hammond's office," Spitz says. "Mike had his audition."

When Hammond got back to work a week or two later, he glanced at his calendar for May 2 and drew a blank. *Mike Appel?* Who was this Mike Appel they had coming in at eleven o'clock? Just some manager who wouldn't take no for an answer, Harris explained. Other record executives might have been outraged. Their time is valuable, they have no intention of wasting it with some pushy manager and his completely unknown kid-with-guitar. Hammond, by contrast, was intrigued. As he'd learned decades earlier, the pursuit of interesting, and occasionally great, artists required a sharp eye for clues that might have nothing to do with music. The way Mickey described him, this Appel fellow seemed bonkers. But maybe something truly extraordinary had pushed him there. "Sometimes," Hammond wrote later, "that's just the way it is."

Born into the social and economic privilege reserved for descendants of the Vanderbilt family, the prep-school-and-Yale-educated Hammond re-created himself as a stalwart advocate of civil rights and every other form of populism. A rail-thin, tremulous fellow—the toll of a childhood bout with scarlet fever that had weakened his heart—Hammond had been a jazz obsessive since the 1920s when he scaled the walls of the exclusive Hotchkiss School to take a commuter train to Harlem's jazz and blues clubs. His fixation led to an early career as a music critic, which ultimately landed him his dream job as a talent scout and artists-and-repertoire executive, the artists' in-house advocate, advisor, and controller, for Columbia Records.

Unfailingly polite, particularly to musicians and their ilk, Hammond still spoke his mind when he smelled mediocrity or cynicism. "I'd sit next to him [at company meetings], and when they played a record he didn't like, he'd whisper to me, loudly, '*What a piece of fuckin' shit* that *is*!'" says then junior executive (later Columbia president) Al Teller. "But he was truly democratic, a music junkie, and he'd listen to anything that was presented to him." And if what he heard appealed to him, Hammond wouldn't hesitate to take it on as his next crusade.

But he still hadn't quite encountered a force as relentless as Appel, who led his client into Hammond's cluttered realm at precisely eleven o'clock on the chosen day. They all shook hands, and Hammond gestured to the album-stacked chairs in his office. When they were seated, Appel launched into his blistering sales spiel. "So you're the man who is supposed to have discovered Bob Dylan," he said by way of hello. "Now, I wanna see if you've got any ears, 'cause I've got somebody better than Dylan."

"This," Hammond wrote in his 1977 autobiography, "was rather more belligerent than the situation seemed to call for." Bruce, while thoroughly aghast, could only listen. "I went into a state of shock," he told writer, biographer, and friend Dave Marsh a few years later. "I'm shrivelin' up and thinkin', 'Mike, please give me a break. Let me play a damn song!'" When Appel paused for a breath, Hammond shot back. "I don't know what you're trying to prove, but you're succeeding in making me dislike you," he said. Then he turned to Bruce and asked him to play a song. Bruce snatched his guitar and launched into the opening bars of "It's Hard to Be a Saint in the City." Instantly, Hammond took note of the young man's powerful way with a guitar. Then he tuned into the lyrics. "I heard immediately that he was a born poet," he wrote. "I kept a lid on my excitement."

Bruce played a few others—"Growin' Up," "Mary Queen of Arkansas," and "If I Was the Priest"—and Hammond's enthusiasm surged. "I didn't want Appel to see how impressed I was," he wrote, recalling how he nodded at the young guitarist and asked him to keep playing. The listening session went on for what Hammond recalled as two full hours. Afterward, Hammond nodded and asked Bruce if he'd be interested in playing a showcase set in a New York club that night, to show how he worked with an audience. Mike and Bruce said that wouldn't be a problem, so Hammond picked up his phone and booked an early-evening slot at the Gaslight AuGoGo club in Greenwich Village, somewhere in the dead time between Happy Hour and blues singer Charlie Musselwhite's show set to start at nine o'clock.

Bruce and Appel floated back to the producer's temporary office on West Fifty-fifth, where Appel, Cretecos, and Spitz worked their phones to spread the news of the evening's show, hoping to attract as many friends, fans, and sympathizers as possible. Meanwhile, Bruce went to Spitz's

Greenwich Village pad to catch a nap in the living room hammock. When Spitz got home at five o'clock he loaned Bruce his handmade Martin D-35 acoustic and escorted him to the Gaslight, where a small crowd watched the unknown singer-songwriter climb onto the stage and crack a few jokes while he tuned up.

Playing solo on the same stage that helped propel Bob Dylan a decade earlier, he went back to the songs that had lit up Hammond's eyes that morning—"It's Hard to Be a Saint" and "If I Was the Priest," to name a couple—only now invested with the energy and charisma that always flowed through him on the stage. Even without his electric guitar and the forum for the lightning-fingered riffs with which he filigreed his band songs, Bruce's instrumental skill shone through. After a half hour, Hammond gave Appel the signal. "Get him off," he said, "and let's go."

Standing outside the club, Hammond told Bruce that his life was about to change. "You're going to be a Columbia recording artist," Spitz remembers Hammond saying. There would be a few steps between here and there—an audition with Columbia president Clive Davis, for instance—but Hammond promised to guide Bruce through the entire process, employing all of his juice and experience into making sure that the entire company would be aware of who he was and what he could do. They'd take the next step at the CBS building the following afternoon, when Hammond, with Appel serving as coproducer, would record enough demos to fill an acetate demonstration record he could circulate around the company. When Bruce walked into the studio with his guitar around his neck, the session flowed easily. "I just stood up and sang the best songs I had," Bruce recalled in 1998. "I felt very confident about what I was doing . . . and nervous at the same time." When Davis returned to the office a day or two later, Hammond appeared at his door holding a freshly cut acetate disc of the audition, laid it on his office turntable, and dropped the needle. Impressed enough to ask Hammond to schedule a face-to-face audition, Davis greeted Bruce warmly a few days later and asked him to take out his guitar.

Davis sat up in his chair before the first song was over. "I thought he was very special," he says. "I was very impressed with his writing and imagery." For while he could hear parallels between the young singer-songwriter and Dylan, Columbia's president was even more excited to hear how Springsteen stood apart from the other songwriter. And as Bruce's songs visited the gritty scenes from his real and imagined worlds in New Jersey and New York City, Davis felt drawn into a tableau that was as exciting as it was unexplored. "The subjects he was writing about, the poetry that made up his work, was very different from Dylan," he says. When it was over, Davis told Hammond to sign young Mr. Springsteen to Columbia Records as quickly as possible.

The finished contract arrived at Appel's office a few days later. Bruce took his copy back to Asbury Park to give it a thorough reading. Unable to parse the legalese on his own, he sat on the floor of his unfurnished apartment with Robin Nash, a friend from the Jersey Shore music circles, reading the vital document by candlelight, because he couldn't afford to pay his electric bill. "We went through it word by word," she wrote in a memoir published on a fan page. "I was looking up all of the big words in a dictionary."

The next day, Bruce called his parents' home in San Mateo and told his mother the good news. Pam Springsteen, just finishing fifth grade, recalls hearing the exchange from Adele's perspective. "Mom was saying, 'Uh-huh, uh-huh . . . really? *Really?* Well, what are you going to change your name to?' Silence. Then: 'You're *not* changing your name?'

"My mom was very excited," Pam says. "And I think my dad was pretty excited too."

More than that, Bruce's move into the big time (in Doug's estimation) prompted the start of a gradual but distinct shift in his conception of the world and its possibilities. "That," she remembers, "was when he began to say, 'From now on, I'm never going to tell anyone what they should or shouldn't do with their lives.'"

Now Bruce had a new set of advisors and helpers, all of them full of their own expectations and rock-solid advice. They didn't always agree, and it soon became clear that the brawl-ready Appel honed a growing rivalry with the courtly insider who had given them the break he and Bruce had craved so desperately. And not because he and Hammond had different ideas about Bruce's work and career. Still stung by his experience with

Dee Anthony and Sir Lord Baltimore, Appel couldn't help but be suspicious of anyone who might threaten his own primacy in Bruce's career.

The contracts that Appel produced for Bruce to sign in the next weeks and months all established Appel and/or Laurel Canyon Ltd. as full partners in the artist's creative and financial careers. The first set of papers outlined a recording contract that committed Bruce to work exclusively with the production team of Appel and Cretecos. So when the time came to sign with a record label, that deal would be between the record company and Laurel Canyon, in exchange for exclusive rights to Bruce's recorded music. The next contract made Laurel Canyon and its music publishing branch, Sioux City Ltd., 100 percent owners of the songs Bruce wrote. Which sounds outrageous, particularly for that era in the recording industry. But statutes and industry standards funneled about half of a song's proceeds back to its writer-performer, which would then divide Bruce's and Appel's share to something closer to fifty-fifty. Still, a generous percentage for Appel, who would also retain control over how and where the songs would be reprinted and reperformed.

The management contract, which Bruce stopped short of signing for several months, also entitled Appel to 50 percent of Bruce's earnings. "I was under the impression that Elvis Presley and Colonel Tom Parker had a fifty-fifty management arrangement," Appel explained later. When his lawyer, Jules Kurz, noted that Parker's share of Presley's career was actually closer to 25 percent, Appel revised the contract to give Bruce the heavier half of a 75-25 split.

Even given his foot-dragging, Bruce signed all of the contracts without even a glance from an independent lawyer. Which seems ridiculous, but from Bruce's perspective, trusting Appel's word that these were fair and equitable contracts was a matter of honor. They had already shaken hands, and Mike had been the first to leap, making his commitment in blood by quitting his job, going deeply into debt, and throwing his young family's security into limbo. All because he believed in Bruce and his music. So as far as Bruce was concerned, he had to extend the same faith to Appel. If he didn't, he wouldn't deserve to be treated fairly.

For now they were all in it together: Appel, Bruce, and Cretecos. Brothers united to give Bruce and his music the audience, acclaim, and rewards it, and they, deserved. Everyone had his own job to do and judgments to make, so Bruce didn't raise an eyebrow when the first wave of record company money fueled Laurel Canyon's move to its own suite of offices just around the corner on East Fifty-fifth—in the same building that housed Dylan's eccentric but notoriously effective manager, Albert Grossman. And if Appel wanted to spend a chunk of the advance on an office-furniture-shopping jaunt to Macy's, Bruce had no problem with that either. He also didn't care (or notice) how much an office suite's wall-to-wall carpeting, desks, chairs, sofas, and coffee tables might cost. And if his blood-oath manager felt like following Grossman's bizarro example by installing a King Arthur–style throne in order to peer down at anyone who entered his personal sanctum, well, that just seemed cool.

More than cool. Closer to life-affirming. Because for Bruce, after so many years of playing to the same fans in the same small circuit of New Jersey and Virginia clubs and colleges—rarely trying to break into the more competitive New York market—Appel had swept him up like a showbiz superhero. He kicked down doors. He turned naysayers into fools and made the powerful lick his hand. When Bruce looked at Appel, he saw an alter ego: a relentless fighter with music in his soul and the whole world in his sights. The $35 a week in salary, rent, and money for a new guitar and other occasional indulgences seemed like more than enough. He was on his way.

Now everything Bruce did mattered. Directed to list all the songs he'd written, Cretecos and Spitz spent weeks helping Bruce record professional-caliber demos that they could use to copyright all of his work. Most of these songs were never released in original form, although some (such as "Circus Town" and "Vibes Man") would lend components to, or evolve into, other completed songs. In the titles alone, Bruce's fascination for outsized characters and gothic imagery fairly explodes from the page. From "Balboa vs. the Earthslayer" to "Calvin Jones & the 13th Apostle" to "Black Night in Babylon," the allusions are as explosive as the daring of their author: a twenty-two-year-old already addressing the fundamental riddles of faith, war, God, life, and death.

And as Bruce confronted the darker currents guiding his artistry, the memories and visions felt just as piercing as when they had first abraded his skin. The writing process afforded some comfort—the rush of catharsis and then a sense of mastery over the tumult. But the work was always harrowing, the pleasures fleeting. And still Bruce craved connection, needed the balm of the lights and the energy that flooded from beyond the rim of the stage.

In mid-April Freehold record store owner Victor "Igor" Wasylczenko hired Bruce to play an acoustic set at a concert he was staging at Freehold Township High School, a crosstown rival to the Freehold Regional High School Bruce had attended. Visiting with Wasylczenko a few days before the show, Bruce walked the streets of his old neighborhood for the first time in months. He'd already been gone for three years. A long stretch for such a young man. But back on those same sidewalks, stepping gingerly up Randolph Street, taking a moment to lay a hand on the rough bark of the beech tree that still marked the place of his first childhood home, it was like he'd never left. Like he never would, no matter where he was or how long he stayed away.

Appearing unannounced at the concert (Steel Mill's regular opening act Sunny Jim had signed on as the headlining act, and he had no intention of stealing their glory), Bruce switched off between guitar and piano, working through an array of new songs, including several destined to become mainstays in his recording and performing career. But the one song that hit the audience the hardest—that left them with mouths hanging open and arms limp at their sides—would never be heard again.

"Bruce started doing this song with mommy-daddy words, like he was singing in a little kid's voice," Wasylczenko recalls. The lyrics describe a man and boy walking hand in hand to fish in a lake, but they could just as easily have been on one of Fred Springsteen's regular hunts for radio parts in the neighborhood trash cans. "You felt this incredible love the boy has for his grandfather, all in his description of this little fishing trip." The audience nodded along with Bruce's gently strummed vision right up until the song's final verse, which follows the boy walking home from school a few days later. "He describes coming to their family home," Wasylczenko continues. "He's walking across the porch and being stunned by something he sees in the living room." When the boy finally reaches his mother, his question serves as the song's crushing climax.

"He asks, 'Mommy, why is Grandpa sleeping in a box?' And it stunned the audience," Wasylczenko says. "I mean, the room was silent. No one applauded. They were just . . . breathless. Bruce turned away quickly, and I could see tears running down his face. I don't think he ever played that song again."

Bruce played a handful of solo shows that spring and summer, the most prominent of them being a July benefit old friend Howard Grant gave at his three-hundred-seat Cinema III theater in Red Bank to raise money for Democratic presidential candidate George McGovern, the liberal senator from South Dakota. The show sold out quickly, with overflow seating in the back and the aisles. And yet, Grant says, Bruce grew visibly impatient during the political speechifying. "He was entirely apolitical," Grant says. "He didn't believe that anything would be better or worse at the end of the day because of politicians. But remember who McGovern was running against. And that was a generational thing. Bruce was going to support anyone who was running against Richard Nixon."

And in the midst of the antihippie hostility in central New Jersey's small towns, Bruce says, supporting any candidate felt like taking a risk. "I voted," Bruce says. "For the first time, so I must have been thinking about [presidential politics]." And having some strong feelings about the issues, given what Bruce felt he'd risk by revealing himself to the authorities in Monmouth County. "To get involved in any sort of thing where you had to go in and identify yourself? That was going way beyond anything any of us cared to do. You must have needed some proof of identification, which people rarely carried. And an address, I'd imagine. I was floating probably in most of those days. I mean, in '72, where was I living?"

The politics that actually did affect Bruce's life stemmed from the growing conflict between the mentors who saw him as the lone singer-songwriter he had embodied since his first audition with Appel, and the ones drawn to the rock 'n' roll guitarist and front man he'd been for the vast majority of his career. John Hammond insisted that Bruce perform in the style he had brought to his audition, and Appel obviously shared his vision. But as the recording sessions set for early July edged closer,

Bruce couldn't stop hearing the new songs being played by a band. Certainly, a number of the acoustic songs slated for the album—"The Angel," "Mary Queen of Arkansas," and "Visitation at Fort Horn," to name a few—would find greater resonance in a more intimate solo setting. But "It's Hard to Be a Saint in the City" needed Manhattan's electric pulse, just as "Lost in the Flood" required boom and snarl to animate its post-moral wasteland. Cretecos felt the same way, and when the the issue got to Clive Davis's desk, he sided with Bruce and Cretecos.

To some observers at Columbia Records, Davis's overruling of Hammond seemed as rooted in the two execs' low-boiling professional rivalry as in the sound of Bruce's music. Hammond had certainly given Appel and Bruce the impression that his personal imprimatur guaranteed that Bruce would get a recording contract. That Davis had fallen just as hard for Bruce and signed him immediately implied that Hammond hadn't overstated his power. But forty years later, Davis takes care to dispel the notion. "John was an A&R man who came up with a lot of ideas," he says. "Some of [his artists] were signed, some weren't. But I do know that after John saw Bruce, he had to play his songs to me. John didn't have the power to sign artists." Nor to maneuver his new signing to the label's younger, arguably hipper subsidiary, Epic Records, which Appel recalls as Hammond's plans for his latest discovery. Appel wasn't crazy about the idea, and Davis, who stood to lose a promising talent from his own label's ranks, shot it down instantly. Bruce stayed on Columbia.

Davis's support of the full band sound allowed Bruce to pick up the telephone and call in the other members of the Bruce Springsteen Band. To Garry Tallent, the message sounded like anything but a herald of future glories. "He just asked if I could come up and help him record." Beyond the few days of recording he had on the schedule, Bruce offered no promises, no commitments, and no sense that his latest, rather dramatic revelation—he had been signed to a recording contract by one of the biggest and most highly regarded major labels—might require some clarity or even an explanation to the four musicians who had been playing at his side. Instead the band members realized that Bruce's new team of managers and label executives saw them as something less than vital to the next stage of his career. "We were like a band of hobos from New Jersey," Tallent says. "Just Bruce bringing in his pals."

If bringing along his buddies had truly been Bruce's highest purpose, it would have been safe to assume that Steven Van Zandt would be there. They'd spent so much of the last seven years working toward this very moment. "I was his best friend, and sort of a consigliere since birth," Van Zandt says. They'd shared so much music, and worked together so closely for the previous two years, Van Zandt had no doubt the collaboration would continue through Bruce's debut record and beyond. "I knew what he wanted to hear," he says. "But I was too close. They couldn't go straight to him and manipulate him without me being the rock. Or at least that's what they thought, so Mike Appel decided I was unnecessary."

The other musicians saw the conflict building from the opening take on the first recording date. "Steve was there for the first session," Tallent says. "But he had an opinion [about how things should sound], and Mike didn't want another opinion." Appel, on the other hand, says he had no role in Van Zandt's quick ouster. "Bruce decided he wasn't necessary," he says. "I think he just decided that having another guitarist at that time was not the right musical mix. And you must remember that Bruce can play guitar pretty damn well too."

No matter whose decision, Van Zandt didn't get a chance to take his guitar out of its case. His sole contribution to the album came when he punched the reverb tank on the back of his amp to create the blast of thunder that kicks off "Lost in the Flood." He got the news just after that session. "I can't remember if Mike told me or if it was Bruce. I think it had to be Bruce. And yeah, it was a downer. Very depressing."

For Bruce it came down to professional survival. "Don't forget, here was a guy making his first record. And they didn't want no band!" he says. "John Hammond wanted what he'd kind of seen from across his desk." And while he had only just managed to convince Appel and Hammond (but mostly Clive Davis) to let him use a rhythm section on some of the songs, their appetite for layered guitars—or even one halfway noisy electric guitar—had already reached its limit. "I felt like I came in undercover," Bruce says. "I always knew that some point when I got rolling, for me rolling was full-out [electric band music]. But there was no interest in that at the moment."

And what of the talk of static between Van Zandt and coproducers Appel and Cretecos? "They didn't *know* Steve. Really, there just wasn't interest in moving in an electric guitar. They were like, 'We'll go *here,* but we're not moving *there.*' I accepted it as a compromise between John Hammond and the record company and the record that I was trying to get Mike to make as producer. And I think I was also very caught up in the one-man, one-guitar, your-song thing. I was in the middle of that reinvention of myself. And that's what we ended up with."

Van Zandt went back to New Jersey, laid his guitar aside, and didn't pick it up again, he says, for almost two years. Hearing this, Bruce furrows his brow. "Is that true? I don't know, he may be being dramatic, but maybe not." Van Zandt: "I was working construction, running a jackhammer, and played football on the weekends." Bruce, recalling the incident now, laughs: "Oh, he *did!* He got a real job! What got into him?" When a football-related incident snapped one of Van Zandt's digits, he started playing a lot of piano to strengthen the finger. Feeling the itch to play in public again, he formed a bar band that included a drummer whose cousin had scored a job playing in the stage band for the early-sixties singing group the Dovells, famous for "Bristol Stomp" among others. They recruited Van Zandt to be the bandleader for the group's tours, and the musician put down his jackhammer for good. "We were on one of those oldies package extravaganzas. And it was fun for me. I got to meet all my heroes."

The recording of *Greetings from Asbury Park, N.J.* began in early July with full-band sessions held at 914 Sound Studios, located in the out-of-the-way (and thus inexpensive) town of Blauvelt, New York, located about forty-five minutes northwest of Manhattan. Appel and Cretecos ran the control room, with deference to their artist, who directed the band from the studio floor. The sessions were crisp and businesslike; closer to a gathering of music professionals than the kind of all-for-one, one-for-all vibe that had knit together Steel Mill and the Bruce Springsteen Band. With so many padded walls and glassed-in booths separating Bruce, Appel, and the Asbury Park crew, it was easier for everyone to focus on his own licks than on what this new twist in their leader's career meant to their own futures. Instead Bruce led the musicians, minus Van Zandt, through "For You," "It's Hard to Be a Saint in the City," "Lost in the Flood," and "Does This Bus Stop at 82nd Street?" Recording the basic tracks took two days, Tallent recalls. When they were done, the farewells in the 914 parking lot were as casual as they were indistinct. As far as anyone knew, it could well be the last time they would ever play together. Tallent and Sancious headed back to their lives in Richmond. Lopez went back to his boatyard. "And as far as any of us knew," Tallent says, "that was it."

Bruce, Appel, and Cretecos spent another week or so perfecting the full-band tracks and then turned their attention to the acoustic songs Bruce would perform on his own. Working with a sense that the album should be divided evenly between acoustic and electric songs, they recorded five songs with Bruce accompanying himself on guitar and, in one case, piano: a nearly eight-minute morality tale about war called "Visitation at Fort Horn," the impressionistic biker ballad "The Angel," a late-night noir tale called "Jazz Musician," the non–Middle Eastern ballad "Arabian Nights," and a dreamy circus performer lament called "Mary Queen of Arkansas." The relatively speedy sessions ended in early August, with the tapes handed over to Columbia within a few days. When Clive Davis turned his ear to the tapes, he liked what he heard. The songs were just as well constructed and beautifully observed as they had been on Bruce's studio demo. The band arrangements added zest without obscuring the all-important lyrics. They were, in short, great album tracks. But would any of these deeply felt, wildly imagined songs find their way onto the nation's radio airwaves? After a day or two, Davis picked up the phone and dialed Bruce directly.

"I asked him if he'd consider writing some additional material," Davis says. Specifically, he added, at least one or two tracks that he could imagine being played on the radio. "That's always a touchy subject with artists. But part of what made Bruce so special was that he didn't take offense."

Not even close, in fact. "I said, 'Well, that's probably true,'" Bruce said. "So I went down to the beach and wrote 'Blinded by the Light' and 'Spirit in the Night.' So that was a good call. They became the two best songs on the record."

Adding the new songs meant calling for another day or two of band sessions. But with three-fifths of his musicians down in Virginia and the clock running down, Bruce came up with another plan: Lopez would play the drums, but they'd hire well-known session pianist Harold Wheeler to handle the keyboards, and Bruce would, through the miracle of overdubbing, handle both the guitar and the bass. And he had one more card to play too: another Asbury Park musician he'd gotten to know a bit over the previous year. Bruce could already hear the recorded songs in his head and knew that the key musical element could be played only by Asbury-based saxophone player Clarence Clemons. The sax player, then the front man for Norman Seldin and the Joyful Noyze, was happy to come up and record, and as Bruce suspected, his Junior Walker–inspired riffs gave the songs just the right rhythm and blues feel. Clemons and Lopez hung around to overdub backing vocals and hand claps, and once the new songs replaced "Arabian Nights" and "Jazz Musician" on the master tape, the final lineup for Bruce's debut album was complete.

Job done and final test pressings stamped, Bruce returned to Bradley Beach while Appel and Bob Spitz took an acetate of the new album to Los Angeles to build excitement and new connections in the West Coast's entertainment capital. They took a room at the notorious Hyatt House hotel/rock 'n' roll star hangout on Sunset Boulevard[1] and made the rounds of music executives, Appel's well-placed friends, and record company *machers*. Everyone got a preview of the new album, along with the usual dose of Appel-style bonhomie and braggadocio. He'd picked himself a winner, he wanted LA's musical core to understand. No one had wanted to believe him, but now the whole world would know that Bruce Springsteen, and the man who had discovered him, were the real thing.

All that got thrown aside when Bruce called their hotel room at ten o'clock one night and told Appel that he had decided that the abstruse, seven-minute "Visitation at Fort Horn," had to be stripped off of the second side of *Greetings*. It was too long, Bruce insisted. It dominated

---

[1] Also known as the Riot House, which gives you an idea as to the general vibe of the place, which was loud, rowdy, and, for many guests of the era, fogged over in Tequila Sunrises, appealingly slinky women, and narcotics.

the end of the album and stole focus from "Spirit in the Night" and "It's Hard to Be a Saint in the City." It simply had to go, Bruce said.

Appel took the news badly. Didn't Bruce know that Columbia had already accepted the finished record, had mastered the entire thing, and pressed dozens of test copies? Changing anything now would force the label to junk everything, remaster the entire album, print new tests, and more and more. "Mike was going nuts," Spitz says. "We were sure Columbia would pull the plug; he'd already pushed them to the limit." Appel steeled himself for outrage when he phoned the news to Hammond the next morning. Instead the A&R man took up Bruce's cause immediately. "Whatever Bruce wants," he said, "is how it's going to be."

Indeed, when Bruce appeared one day carrying an old-fashioned "Greetings from Asbury Park, N.J." postcard (with illustrated beach and boardwalk scenes incorporated into the letters), he told Appel that this picture was as perfect for the album cover as its message was for the album's title. As far as he was concerned, that was the end of the discussion. Except for that Columbia had a rock-solid policy for new artists: every debut album cover *had* to feature a large photograph of the artist(s), the better to create an indelible image for the record-buying public to latch onto. When he left the room, Appel turned to Spitz. "This'll be a disaster," he said. "No one's gonna know who he is!" But then, Columbia already knew that, which was why it had its hard-and-fast rule.

Then Appel, Spitz, and Bruce met with Columbia's chief art designer John Berg. Entirely confident that the taciturn, no-nonsense Berg would shoot down the postcard instantly, Appel let his client present his idea, figuring they'd all move on to more realistic options after that. Instead Berg gave the "Greetings" postcard a long look and nodded thoughtfully. Reaching into his drawer, he pulled out a thick stack of similarly vintage postcards. "I gotta tell ya, I'm a huge postcard fan," Berg said, handing his collection over to Bruce, who dove in excitedly while Berg went back to examining the Asbury Park card. "This is absolutely what we're going to do," the designer said. "This is brilliant. It's perfect." Appel was speechless. "We thought it would kill us," Bob Spitz says. "But we were so wrong."

Borne up by the enthusiasm of both Davis and Hammond, Bruce and his gang were as protected in the Columbia empire as any unknown,

unproven act could be—at least for the moment, as power and loyalties
in record companies shift all the time, usually without warning. The sales
reports that would come in after the album's January 1973 release would
be crucial. And although they didn't know it at the time, the acetate
copies of the record were already winning Bruce friends around the company's sales, publicity, and A&R offices. Al Teller, then working in the
company's sales department, made a habit of listening to all the advance
acetates that came his way. Mostly he played them as background music,
but if something made him look up from his work, he says, he'd give it
a closer examination. So while Teller had never heard of Bruce Springsteen when he lowered the needle on *Greetings*' opening side, it only took
about eight bars for Teller to drop his pen. "I listened to the whole thing
straight through," he says. "Then I called in some product managers and
said, 'You gotta hear this!'"

Acetate discs were too fragile to withstand more than fifteen or
twenty plays; generally a week's worth of repeated listening. But it took
only a day of listening parties for Teller to wear the disc's grooves down
to nothing. Heading home that evening, he focused on the task at hand:
selling the product. But who the hell is Bruce Springsteen? How could
Teller drum up interest in an artist whose street rat poet's sensibility
ran so counter to every popular radio format? Fortunately, his daylong
in-house sales campaign—and the other execs who got the same charge
from their own acetates—seemed to be sparking an intra-office movement. "Everyone liked it," Teller says. "But some of us *really* loved it."
Particularly a young promotions man named Paul Rappaport, a sharp-
eared A&R executive named Steve Popovich, and, in the label's Texas
outpost, a promotions man named Michael Pillot.

All of them in the thrall of a thirty-five-minute album of songs
written and performed by an obscure twenty-three-year-old from the
Jersey Shore. Most of them could barely describe what they had fallen
for, let alone why they had all been so enraptured so quickly. But in
the midst of the river of music running through Columbia's offices and
hallways—at the very home of Bob Dylan, Paul Simon, Miles Davis, and
the Byrds—this unknown new artist had swept them up in his own current. And just that quickly, they were converts on their way to becoming

evangelists. And it wouldn't be long before others spoke of them—sometimes derisively, sometimes as the highest possible compliment—as Bruce Springsteen's apostles. "We all got affected by his aura," Popovich said a few months before his death in 2011. "Some things have that draw. You believe so deeply, you have such a focus on it. That's what happened for Bruce. To us he was an underdog, from nowhere, and people picked up on that."

NINE

I AM FINALLY, FINALLY, WHERE I'M SUPPOSED TO BE

CLARENCE CLEMONS INSISTED THE STORY was true.

The thunder, the lightning, the gale-force winds blowing across the Jersey Shore. Just another late-summer Nor'easter. Except that this storm became part of a rock 'n' roll legend in which the karmic explosion triggered by the meeting of two musicians nearly reduced Asbury Park's Student Prince club to rubble right there on Kingsley Street. Or something. Whatever, the incident took place in September 1971, months before Appel, Hammond, Columbia, and all the rest. But it set the tone for what was about to happen, so . . .

"I swear on a stack of Bibles that that door blew off its hinges," Clemons told me a few weeks before his death in June 2011. "I swear on *two* stacks of Bibles. And it was a sturdy door. The front door. The wood one with the lock, so when you close that door the place is closed, okay? A big, heavy fucking door. And when I opened it, it blew down Kingsley. Tumbling north, toward the Wonder Bar. That really happened."

Garry Tallent is less sure. And he was there with everyone else, taking a break from his bass duties partway through the Bruce Springsteen Band's nightlong show at the club. When it comes to the dramatic entrance of Clemons, and the dramatic departure of the front door, he shrugs. "I don't remember the stormy night," he says. "And people came in to jam all the time, so I don't recall. Look, it could well be. But you think it would be memorable, though."

Asked directly, and only a few months after Clemons's death, about the Student Prince door question, Bruce turns solemn. "It did. That's for certain." And what of the people—the *band members*—who insist it didn't? "They would be wrong."

Bruce and Clemons were thinking back to late September 1971, a few days after Bruce had caught part of the Joyful Noyze's set at the Wonder Bar. The band was led by keyboardist Norman Seldin, but Bruce's ex-girlfriend Karen Cassidy sang lead vocals for the group, and she had been telling Bruce about this charismatic sax player who shared the front of the stage with her. When the set ended, Cassidy went over to greet Bruce. "I asked him what was going on, and he had this gleam in his eyes," she says. "He asked about Clarence, and I just laughed. 'I knew it! You're gonna steal him!'" No matter. Cassidy walked over to the sax player and pointed out Bruce, nursing a Pepsi at the bar. "I told him I had a friend who I knew was gonna be a really big star, and he needed to come meet him," she says. When the Bruce Springsteen Band settled into the Student Prince, just a flew blocks down Kingsley Street, she took Clemons to check out Bruce's band. It meant walking through a rainstorm, but Clemons didn't care. He packed his saxophone into its case, and off they went.

When Clemons stepped into the Student Prince, the ripped-off door tumbling away behind him, his eyes fixed on the skinny white boy he'd met a few nights earlier. Bruce and the band were taking a break, but Bruce saw him coming and, he said many years later, felt transfixed. "Here comes my brother, here comes my sax man, my inspiration, my partner, my lifelong friend."

Some kind of vibe hung in the air, to be sure. And when Cassidy pulled Clarence over to say hi, the horn player pointed to the saxophone he had carried through the rain. Would it be okay to sit in during the next set? Well, of course it was okay. A few minutes later Clemons stepped onstage with the rest of the band and listened for the count-off. They began, he recalled, an unnamed instrumental.

"I will never, ever forget the feeling I got when we hit that first note," he said. "It was so urgent, so real, so exciting to me. It was like I'd been searching for so long, and now, thank God, I am finally, finally, where I'm supposed to be."

Bruce felt it too. Even in the midst of an impromptu jam session, held in a dingy bar with half of a half-capacity crowd paying half of its attention to the music, the onstage chemistry crackled. "Standing next to Clarence was like standing next to the baddest ass on the planet," Bruce wrote later. "You were proud, you were strong, you were excited and laughing with what might happen, with what together you might be able to do."

"And that," Cassidy says, "was it."

Actually, it would take nine months for Bruce to track down Clemons at another gig. But when he showed up at the Shipbottom Lounge in Point Pleasant that night in June 1972, Clemons insisted that Bruce come up to jam with his band. Bruce had to borrow a guitar, but they all knew the same rock and soul oldies, and the groove they found at the Student Prince came right back. The two musicians traded telephone numbers when the set was over—Bruce misspelling his new friend's last name as "Clemens"—and pledged to stay in touch. This time it took only a couple of weeks for Bruce to track down the Joyful Noyze and jam alongside Clemons one more time. The feeling between the two musicians grew even more that night, and when the sets ended, they went off together to get a drink (Bruce, at twenty-two, had started having a sip every now and again) and talk for a while. The early-morning drink stretched into a dayslong spiritual adventure. "We went down South and went to bars, talking and listening to music nonstop for two or three days," Clemons told me. "It's all a blur now, but I get tingles when I think about it."

Given the gleam in his eyes, it was difficult to figure if Clemons intended the story to be a journalistic account of actual events or an allegorical tall tale about his spiritual bond to Bruce. But once again, Bruce confirms the entire story, right down to the strange green glow of the liqueur that nearly capsized both musicians and the buddy sitting with them. "I had only just started drinking, so I was rolling with whatever came my way at the time," Bruce says. "My take on it at the time was like, 'I don't like none of it, so I'll drink any of it.' But then we had a run-in with this green Chartreuse.[1] Clarence could probably slug the bottle,[2] but me and a pal of mine [remembered only as "Jimmy"] got caught in the middle of it. We started to bang some of it back, and my pal made a beeline for the door, heading straight for the curb. I think I broke out in a sweat. It was pretty funny."

As Clemons unspooled the facts of his past—growing up in Norfolk County, Virginia, of the 1940s and 1950s with his longshoreman dad and proper, no-back-talk teacher mom—he described his early life as a holy quest: an unconscious, years-long pilgrimage to the one musician power-ful enough to accompany him through the gates of transcendence. "I was always searching for something," Clemons said, describing the gospel choirs he heard on Sunday mornings and the shimmer of the saxophone he unwrapped on his ninth Christmas. Afternoons of gridiron heroics in high school and at the University of Maryland Eastern Shore stadium were meaningful but still, he knew, not a part of his destiny. The outlines of that revealed themselves only during the thousands of hours he spent with his bedroom record player, honking along with sax heroes King Curtis and Boots Randolph. The radiance in the young man's eyes pushed him even further. Nearly from his first gig with his first neighborhood band, Clem-ons was the visual focus of every performance. Built larger than life, with a rich voice and magnetism to match, Clemons's steps shook the stage while his glittering tenor sax connected the histories of rock, R&B, jazz, and gospel music to the promise of next Saturday night.

Graduating with a sociology degree in 1964, Clemons had a shot at a football career with the Cleveland Browns, but it ended when a freak car

---

[1] A bright green liqueur distilled by Carthusian monks in France, who use 132 plants to flavor the stuff, which gets its color from the plants' chlorophyll.

[2] Not according to Clarence: "It was so powerful, we were like—Holy *shit!* That guy shoulda stopped us from drinking this! So then we stopped drinking for a little while."

accident shattered his knees. Clemons moved to New Jersey and took a job as a counselor for emotionally disturbed kids at the Jamesburg Training School for Boys, where he and his first wife, Jackie, doubled as caretakers, a job that came with an on-campus apartment. Clemons played in bands at night, first in a soul-jazz cover band called the Entertainers, and then in Norman Seldin's Joyful Noyze, a tight, crowd-pleasing cover band popular enough to be booked months, and sometimes a year, in advance. Hired on the strength of a single sit-in session, Clemons quickly became a frontman for the group. He was also a lightning rod for club owners who couldn't abide seeing a black face in their establishments. Seldin, to his infinite credit, didn't care what they thought. "One guy called me a fuckin' nigger lover," he recalls. "I said, 'We're not playing the gig, then. Go to hell.'" Business picked up soon enough—Clemons's magnetic presence didn't hurt—but Clemons kept his horn with him on his off days too. If he drove past a lively looking bar and heard music coming out, he'd stop immediately and head inside, just in case he could get a shot at sitting in with the band. "I call that my searching time," he said. "The time I spent trying to find Bruce."

In the fall of 1972, the object of his search realized that the thrill he'd felt that first night Clemons had stood next to him on the Student Prince stage had not been an illusion. Whatever doubts Bruce might have nursed were vanquished by Clemons's sax work on "Blinded by the Light" and "Spirit in the Night." When Bruce and Appel figured that the time had come to book some full-band shows, Bruce made a round of calls to re-form the five-piece Bruce Springsteen Band as his backing group. Lopez and Tallent came aboard happily, and when Sancious begged off to finish his own debut album (and sulk about Bruce having snatched his bass player), Bruce tapped Danny Federici to rejoin as his keyboard player. Then he called Clemons and asked him to join. Clemons didn't hesitate, although he knew that meant walking out on Norman Seldin, who complained bitterly about being left in the lurch. "I was enraged," says Seldin. "I said, 'Clarence, it's a one-in-ten-million shot!' And I couldn't see him fitting; I saw him as part of a Herbie Mann jazz quartet thing. But like it or not, that's where he was gonna go."

Clemons fit so easily into Bruce's tight-knit crowd that it felt like he'd always been there, maybe because he'd been just beyond the fringe of their scene for so long. Clemons already knew Tallent from the bassist's days as the lone white face in central New Jersey's crack rhythm and blues outfit Little Melvin and the Invaders. "Melvin told me, 'You should meet this white boy! This funky white boy!'" Clemons said, recalling the nights he subbed for the group's regular sax player.

"He already knew all the guys at the Danelectro factory," Tallent says. "And he was Clarence, so we hit it off right away." Federici, already delighted to be back onstage with his Steel Mill cohorts, soon came to recognize Clemons as a reliable partner in his offstage capers. And whatever crankiness Lopez displayed toward his new bandmate had more to do with having another alpha male moving into his pack. A loyalist to the core, Lopez bit back on his anxiety and accepted Clemons into the musical fraternity he still knew he'd started.

Bruce greeted the band in a hail of backslaps and promises of a steady $35 weekly salary that he assured them would grow once they started playing more and bigger shows. They were all in it together, just like they'd always been, he said. Still, this would not be a band in the way that Steel Mill, or even the five-piece Bruce Springsteen Band, had been. "I wasn't interested in being *in* a band," Bruce says. "I might be interested in *having* a band. I loved playing with them . . . but I learned through Steel Mill that the small-unit democracy was dead."

The musicians heard the same thing from Appel, who made it as clear as glass that his only real concern was caring for his one and only client, Bruce Springsteen. "It wasn't Steel Mill anymore, nothing like the band of brothers we used to be," says Lopez. "We were hired hands. And you always knew, in the back of your mind, that you were expendable." Bruce didn't see it in such stark terms. "They were the guys I knew," he says. "And I wasn't looking for great players. I was looking for people who understood how to play in an ensemble together, people who were individual enough, that had character and their own kind of color." These guys had all that, plus years of common history. "I'd had a lot of life experiences with these musicians before we went in the studio; the people who were willing to assist me in grabbing the sound that was in my head."

Given something as significant as a new major-label album to stand with, the as-yet-nameless group was excited to convene for three days of rehearsals at a hotel lounge in Point Pleasant. They then drove to West Chester State College in West Chester, Pennsylvania, to fill a brief bottom-of-the-bill slot for comedians Cheech & Chong on October 28. From there they turned back north to headline a Halloween concert that Tinker West produced at the Long Branch Armory. Afforded enough time to play a full set, Bruce performed the first part of the show by himself and then brought out the rest of the group for a more rambunctious slate of tunes. His shows would retain that acoustic-electric structure for most of the next year.

The next few weeks brought more performances, mostly opening slots at the Kenny's Castaways club on Manhattan's Upper East Side. But the most memorable show on the late-autumn–early-winter schedule turned out to be the afternoon show Appel had booked them to play on December 7, a special concert for the convicts of Sing Sing prison. For Bruce, the show would be a landmark, since he would be the first member of his family to see the inside of Sing Sing since Anthony Zerilli's penal journey in the late 1930s and early 1940s. Bruce kept that to himself, although Appel, already pitching the prison show as a hook to music feature writers, would have loved the extra angle. And he could use the help: Appel had blizzarded his pitches to the journalists whose attention would be crucial to *Greetings*' success in January. But the only reply came from Peter Knobler and Greg Mitchell, two Bob Dylan–fixated *Crawdaddy* magazine editors and staffers. The writers got to Appel's office on the morning of the seventh, chatted a bit about Bruce and his new record, and then piled into Appel's car to connect with the band's van and caravan their way to Ossining. "Bruce was scruffy and easy to talk to; just another guy in his sweatshirt, jeans, and boots," Mitchell says. "They were all so approachable and grateful for our attention."

Set up in a prison chapel jammed with hard-eyed offenders, they tuned their instruments with their backs to the crowd and then nodded uneasily as Lopez counted in the first song. They launched into the tune, but somehow the sound seemed to make the convicts more aggrieved than they'd been a few minutes earlier. They concluded the first number to a few pissed-off shouts from the back and then kicked into a second song. "That didn't go down with the inmates either," Mitchell says. Minds seizing up with images of the recent riots at the Attica prison across the state, the group's confusion spun toward low-grade panic. Then Jim Fainer, the soundman who had come up from Tinker West's shop for the day, stuck an ear out beyond the range of the stage monitors and realized that the group's PA system wasn't working. "I'd plugged it in backward," he admits. The system crackled to life just as Bruce called for Buddy Miles's acid R&B hit "Them Changes." Finally able to hear, the prisoners roared happily and pounded their hands to the backbeat. They bellowed their delight when the song ended, and as Bruce and the gang prepared to count in the next tune, "a short, squat, bald black guy with bunched muscles came rumbling down the aisle like the law was still after him. He got past the guard, hit the stage at a gallop, reached into his shirt, and pulled out . . . an alto sax!" (From Mitchell's and Knobler's *Crawdaddy* story.)

Bruce called for a twelve-bar blues in the key of C. The band members leaped to it, and they all stood back while the mystery sax man blazed away. And it might have been awkward and painful, except, as Mitchell and Knobler recounted, ". . . he was great!" Miracles never cease. And when he jumped back into the arms of the guards, Bruce led the applause and then crowed into the mike, "When this is over, you can *all* go home!"

The *Crawdaddy* writers stuck with the band for its show at Kenny's Castaways that night. "I didn't get any sense of what kind of writer he was or if he was good," Mitchell says. "But I liked him and the band, and we were impressed enough, just based on their vibe, to drop everything and go see the gig." They joined an audience of about thirty restive clubgoers, most of them too engaged with their drinks and friends to glance at the source of the music coming from the small stage across the room.

The group played another three nights at the club, then took off almost three weeks before heading west to Ohio to play bottom-of-the-bill support for the retro-1950s comedy/nostalgia band Sha Na Na's shows in Dayton (where the promoters believed they had booked someone named

Rick Springsteen)[3] and Columbus. Then they motored back to the Jersey Shore to wait the five days before the official release of Bruce Springsteen's debut album, *Greetings from Asbury Park, N.J.* on January 5, 1973.

"Madman drummer bummers, and Indians in the summer, with a teen-aged diplomat / In the dumps with the mumps as the adolescent pumps his way into his hat."

That's Clive Davis talking. Sitting at his desk. Gazing squarely into the dark eye of the video camera recording his performance for eventual replay in the offices of radio programmers, regional distributors, and record store owners all across the United States of America. "I wanted to make very sure that people got the uniqueness of his lyrics," says Davis. Indeed, they sounded remarkably distinctive coming from the mouth of a forty-year-old record company president dressed in shirtsleeves and a tie. "I wouldn't say it was Broadway caliber," says then marketing chief Al Teller. But the fact that Davis had taken that much time and effort to let the music industry know exactly how much belief he had in this particular artist was a significant card to throw down. "Clive's presence had massive gravitas," Teller says. "And every office got handwritten notes [about Bruce] from him. He was deeply involved in every aspect" of the record's release and promotion.

But in a company built on personal taste and individual loyalties, the label president's say-so went only so far. Particularly when it came to a scruffy, unknown quantity whose songs bore no audible relationship to anything else on the hit parade. "I wouldn't say there was overwhelming enthusiasm for *Greetings*," says Ron McCarrell, then the twenty-two-year-old manager of Columbia's college publicity program. McCarrell didn't need to hear a Springsteen pep talk, since he had already seen one of the shows at Kenny's Castaways. That performance, with its acoustic and electric set list, struck McCarrell as disjointed; the work of an artist "still trying to figure out what worked and what didn't." So why did it grab him by the lapels and pin him to the back of his chair? McCarrell shakes

---

[3] Apparently confusing Bruce with Australian musician factor Rick Springfield, whose first hit song "Speak to the Sky" had just been released.

his head. "Something special . . . he hadn't found it yet, and neither had we. But it was there." And like John Hammond, Clive Davis, and the small but growing cult of believers inside Columbia's offices in CBS's Black Rock building on Sixth Avenue, he was determined to do whatever it took to make Bruce Springsteen a star. Paul Rappaport says, "I remember jumping up and down on a sofa begging for money for live broadcasts, yelling, 'We're on the verge of rock 'n' roll history!' It was definitely like a brotherhood. Everyone was on the same mission."

As per Davis's orders, the regional sales reps made the rounds of radio stations and record stores, playing Davis's video reel on their suitcase-sized Fairchild video machines, papering the place with promotional displays and sales posters. Radio ads started playing on major-market FM radio stations just after the new year: "Bruce Springsteen packs more images into one song than most artists do on their entire albums!" When the albums finally emerged from their boxes on the morning of January 5, the public anticipation had built to—well, not very much. But excitement grew markedly in the Springsteen homelands of Richmond, Asbury Park, and especially Freehold, where Victor Wasylczenko transformed his record shop's windows, display shelves, and nearly all of its wall space into a gallery of *Greetings* album covers, posters, and promotional photos. "It looked like all I was selling was Bruce," he says. "My mission was to get everyone who came into the store to buy the record." It wasn't nearly as effective as the record store owner had hoped. "I sold more Partridge Family albums than I did of Bruce that first day. I had *record-breaking* numbers on the Partridges, in Bruce's hometown, the day his first record came out."

And maybe it wasn't surprising. *The Partridge Family Notebook* came with the throw weight of a still-popular weekly network series—whereas *Greetings* sounded as squirrelly as the bearded character framed by the postage stamp borders on the back cover looked. Casual observers could feel safe assuming that they had stumbled upon another sad-eyed troubadour chasing after Dylan's pixie-dusted boot heels.

Those who dropped the needle on *Greetings* found themselves confronting something else: a collection of twisty, wordy tunes whose individual styles, sounds, and production values were linked by a voice that sounded as weathered by life as it was eager to dance circles around it.

Kicking off with a double-quick journey down the guitar neck, "Blinded by the Light" careens into a whirlwind of tinkling guitars, bass zooms, and light-handed drum fills, all colliding with a braying sax before falling in line for the first verse, in which Bruce uncorks the hurricane of memories, observations, and fantasies that form the first of what he later called a series of "twisted autobiographies." And it's all here. The unruly drummers, Little League games, horny teenage boys, speeding hot rods, crumbling amusement parks, ill-intentioned local authorities, and the corn dogs sweating grease on the weather-beaten boardwalks. Only in this vision, the action plays out in an otherworldly glow: they're all racing to get somewhere else, all on the hunt for something bigger, if only a glimpse into the heart of the infinite whatever.

The discursive storytelling picks up again in the high school outcast memoir "Growin' Up," then pivots to the present in the urban fantasia of "Does This Bus Stop at 82nd Street?" Here the New Jersey rube marvels at the Technicolor swirl of advertisements, strip club signs, and the many-hued throngs churning on the sidewalk until he glimpses something as fleeting as it is beautiful: a woman tosses a flower, a man snatches it from the air, and their connection sweeps the music and everything else aside.

The pair of acoustic songs, "Mary Queen of Arkansas" and "The Angel," have their striking images, and, in "The Angel"'s case, a shimmering piano and acoustic bass (played by session pro Richard Davis) to set the mood. But viewed in retrospect, both songs are most interesting for the clues they offer about Bruce's budding authorial vision. In "The Angel," it's the allure of the open road and the danger that lurks in its shadows; while "Mary" traces the vision at the core of the still-undreamed "Born to Run": the perpetual yearning for somewhere else. "But I know a place where we can go, Mary," the song concludes, "where I can get a good job and start all over again clean."

Darkness looms. It's all over the spiritually apocalyptic war ballad "Lost in the Flood" and rumbling like the D train beneath every line of "It's Hard to Be a Saint in the City." And its sweet, ruined aroma perfumes "For You," the stunned lover's ambivalent farewell to a luminous but emotionally damaged girlfriend who may have just fulfilled her own suicidal ambitions.

"For You" is a killer—perhaps *the* killer—track on the album. Or it would be if it wasn't followed by "Spirit in the Night," the storybook retelling of that road trip to Greasy Lake. Here the midnight love story plays out à la *A Midsummer Night's Dream,* where the action is sanctified by the magical spirits spinning through the branches. Bruce had felt the magic in the air that night. Perhaps it's not a coincidence that "Spirit"'s musical presence is defined by Clemons's saxophone. You can glimpse his own magically realistic form in the scene too and hear the echoes of the heavens-wracking storm that, in his telling, heralded his arrival into his musical brother's arms. Which makes it all the more frustrating to consider how absent the band feels on *Greetings*, even when the musicians are a central part of the songs' arrangements.

With one ear trained on Hammond's front-porch tastes and the other on Cat Stevens's hugely successful records, Appel and Cretecos use the guitars and keyboards as a less-heard-than-felt musical foundation. Lopez's playing (on the studio's standard kit rather than his own instrument) is mixed with an emphasis on the low end (all toms, bass drum, and no snare), while even Bruce's guitar, capable of soaring and screaming onstage, has all the punch of a rumor about a guitar. Maybe this had as much to do with Bruce's musical preferences as anything else. "The music I'd been writing on my own was more individual than the material I'd been working up with my bands," he wrote in the *Greetings* essay in his 2001 lyrics compendium, *Songs*. "The independence of being a solo performer was important to me."

Now in a romantic relationship that felt more substantial, and necessary, than any of his previous attachments, Bruce decided to cross two emotional barriers at once: he put his name on an apartment lease and asked Diane Lozito to move in with him. She accepted his offer instantly. But Bruce insisted chivalrously that he get the opportunity to face both of her parents and ask for their permission first. Thinking strategically, they started with Diane's mother, Rita.

"He came to dinner, and Mom loved him. She thought he was

charming," Lozito says. Charmed, yes. But Rita Lozito still wasn't quite convinced that Bruce represented the future she hoped for Diane. "She still told me to stay with [previous boyfriend] Kale because he was in law school and would have a real job."

Stung but not entirely defeated, Bruce called Diane's father, Mike Lozito, in New York and impressed him too. Although not enough for the old man to forget his own wanton ways, which he traced back to the part of his upbringing that took place among other jazz musicians in New York's nightclubs. "They were so similar," Lozito says of her father and her boyfriend. "But he still said, 'Nope. Musicians will always fool around.'"

If Bruce and Lozito were disappointed by her parents' disapproval, neither of them was going to let it stop them from living their lives. Bruce bought a pair of cheap wedding rings to fool the property owners (most of whom rejected unmarried couples), and eventually found a one-bedroom apartment in the seaside neighborhood of Bradley Beach, about five minutes south of Asbury Park. Asked for a recent pay slip or some other proof that he would be able to manage the monthly rent, Bruce came back to the landlord toting a recent copy of *Newsweek* that noted his being signed to Columbia Records. "Then they figured he was legit, even if he was such a shabby guy," Lozito says.

In the confines of his own home, Bruce's public facade eased, revealing the tender, and sometimes explosive, heart of an emotionally vulnerable young man. "There was a lot of physical closeness, a lot of hugging and holding each other," Lozito says. "It was perfect, because I'm five five and he was five nine, and so we fit like a glove. He had a hard time sleeping at night, so I'd sit up watching TV with him while he wolfed down all this junk food: sodas, cakes, all this horrible stuff. We were so similar—both moody, both with tempers. But he was also controlling, and paranoid about people from outside our immediate circle. I could never tell my friends where we lived, and if I was going to see them, I had to meet them somewhere else."

And yet Lozito could not be taken lightly, as Bruce would relearn whenever one of their discussions got heated. "Diane was an aggressive Italian girl, and they'd have these big arguments," Albee Tellone says. "I heard rumblings about physical stuff. Like, she'd come after him, and he'd have to fight her off." Clarence Clemons, soon to become a regular visitor, shared the same memories. "Diane was such a ball of fire! She didn't take *any* shit from him, but she loved him and stayed with him. They were like two kids, so in love with each other. And they were exciting to be around. Always." Bruce, for his part, smiles and shakes his head. "Oh, yeah," he says. "She was a real scrapper."

And yet Diane still couldn't bluster her way past his guitar and writer's notebook. Feeling drawn back to the piano, he bought a battered spinet and moved it onto the apartment's enclosed sunporch, where he spent hours musing on the characters passing by on their way to the beach. Whatever he couldn't see from his sunporch Bruce would discover during his own boardwalk strolls, absorbing the maneuvers of the bikers, the drunken shouts of teenage partiers, and the boardwalk waitresses—the same hot rods-and-pinball scene he'd lived in for five years, only now he could see it in new shades of romance and poignance, sensing the chill in the shadow of the neon and the sadness haunting the waitress's exhausted smile. In his imagination, the scene had all the romance of the cowboys, outlaws, angels, and devils filling the books, movies, and songs that reflected the nation's real and imagined history. And once it all wove into his fantasies, the songs that emerged were so richly detailed and so full of feeling that they had the power to cause domestic unrest. "When he wrote 'Sandy,' Diane got pissed," Tellone says. "She thought he was cheating on her: 'He's writing about some damn waitress on the boardwalk!' But he was writing about *her*, and she just didn't get it."

Sam McKeith got it the moment he first heard Bruce playing with his band.

An ambitious young booking agent at the vast William Morris Agency, McKeith had already carved himself a niche booking soul acts all over New England. But as his company mentor had cautioned him, McKeith's success with black acts made it too easy for the company's (entirely white) elders to pigeonhole him as a token black guy who would never see beyond the beer-and-chitlins circuit. But that would be too limiting to build a major career, so McKeith came into the fall of 1972 determined to extend his reach into the rock 'n' roll mainstream. He had already peeked into one of Bruce's solo shows at New York's Max's Kansas City that summer and came away liking the stark visions in his songs. So when Bob Spitz (whom McKeith had worked with when Spitz produced student shows at Pennsylvania's Albright College during his undergrad days) called a few weeks later, all it took was a listen to a live tape featuring the same songs being performed live by Bruce and his band. Now McKeith felt electrified. "I was determined to put everything I had into making this guy happen," he says. McKeith got things rolling in the last days of 1972 with opening slots at a pair of Sha Na Na shows in Ohio. Back home by December 31, Bruce celebrated the New Year with Diane and then greeted 1973 with bags packed and his determination in overdrive.

With *Greetings* set to come out on the fifth, they hit the new year running, starting with a four-night stand opening for the comedy-rock team Travis, Shook, and the Club Wow at Bryn Mawr's Main Point club in Bryn Mawr, Pennsylvania. After that, they had a day to rest, then hit the road for Boston and an eight-night gig opening for the folk-blues guitarist David Bromberg at Paul's Mall. From there it was on to weeks and then months on the rock 'n' roll circuit in the upper-right corner of the United States. At times this new life as a major label artist, complete with publicity and financial support from Columbia, felt thrilling.

Ushered into the studios of Boston's influential progressive rock station WBCN-FM for an interview with popular host Maxanne Sartori, Bruce was tickled to the point of silliness. Opening with the band's Salvation Army arrangement of "Satin Doll" (sax, accordion, tuba, and guitar), he quickly noted that this right here was his very first radio interview, and so he needed to say hi to his mom, which he did to much in-studio laughter. From there Bruce alternated stumbly, good-humored interview segments with acoustic performances of *Greetings* songs, including a spirited take on "Blinded by the Light" featuring Jimmy Cretecos, chief roadie Albee Tellone, and a Columbia publicist named Ed Hynes on backing vocals. "This is my new single, kids!" Bruce told the audience. "If you come down to the store to buy it, I'll autograph the 45 label!" Interviewed by the *Asbury Park Press*'s Barbara Schoeneweis a few days later, Bruce showed up in a beat-up green leather jacket, a wrinkled shirt, jeans, and weathered boots. Worn down and freaked out by the prospect of sounding like he'd cashed in his roots for glam-rock stardom, Bruce mumbled in "a characteristically sullen manner" about his life as a major-label recording artist. "It's weird working for a big company," he told Schoeneweis, adding that "it was like pulling teeth to get me to sign" Columbia's recording contract.[4] Looking back to his Asbury Park era, he spun more myths, claiming that he'd had a habit of breaking up bands in midset if he didn't like what he heard. "The world does not need another four-piece rock 'n' roll band, and the market needs less to be flooded with more junk," he said. Bruce refused to answer any questions about his new music, his family background, or his professional future, telling Schoeneweis that everything she needed to know could be heard on his album. But when she asked what had made his new songs so irresistible to John Hammond, Columbia, and the nation's critics, Bruce couldn't help betraying a glimmer of pride.

"Well, it's me."

Bruce's live shows were dominated increasingly by his work with the band. He'd start with one of his solo acoustic songs or he'd come out with Tallent and his tuba and a sax-bearing Clemons to make the warped calliope sound for "Circus Song" (soon to evolve into "Wild Billy's Circus Story"). Then Bruce called for the rest of the band, traded his acoustic guitar for his just-purchased Fender[5] and counted off the new instrumental opening to "Does This Bus Stop at 82nd Street?" And this was where the hushed, sepia-toned poet-musician heard on *Greetings* burst into full, electric color. Reimagined as a kind of Van Morrison R&B workout

---

[4] An exaggeration, to put it mildly.

[5] In search of a new look and sound to launch his career as a recording musician in late 1972/early 1973, Bruce paid a visit to Petillo's music store in Ocean Township, New Jersey, in search of a new instrument. He came away with a rebuilt 1953 Fender Telecaster, its original neck replaced with one from a '50s-era Fender Esquire. He'd seen, and heard, the guitar played by other Asbury Park musicians before. "It just made its way round the local music scene 'til it ended up at Petillo's," he says. "That's where I found it, for a hundred and eighty five bucks." The very legible "Esquire" on the tuning peg head has long led fans to believe the guitar is a full-blooded Esquire. "I say it's a Telecaster, though that's a little incorrect," he continues. "It's a mutt, if you will."

(think "Domino"), only faster and grittier, the new "82nd" opened at full blast and then rose higher. By the end, the concluding image of the matador catching the falling rose, now set to blazing sax runs and a band on overdrive, sounded joyous. An invitation to a party already in full swing.

Swing they did, into the swampy funk of "Spirit in the Night," and then an express-line version of "It's Hard to Be a Saint in the City," now all raunchy guitar, pulsing bass runs, and drums shaking the floor. Bruce rarely played the album's all-important single, "Blinded by the Light" ("It's got too many words," he explained in a radio interview), preferring to either reach back a couple of years for "You Mean So Much to Me" or to the growing list of new songs that he'd written with both ears tuned to how they would sound in the hands of his guys on the stage. "Thundercrack," about the Bronx-raised Diane and her beguiling way on the dance floor, grew into a showstopper, thanks to the instrumental dramatics created by its reeling stop-start structure. That song became an early add to the playlist, and a standard show closer from January onward. And that tune arrived in the company of "Rosalita (Come Out Tonight)," another Diane tribute that wove a south-of-the-border lilt into its triumphant tale of love, rock 'n' roll, and liberation. Particularly when the singer grabs his girl, hits the highway, and pledges to never look back: "'Cause the record company, Rosie, just gave me a big advance!"

"All people have to do is see the band," Bruce said in another interview. "It doesn't matter if the place is empty or full . . . the guys in the band play right from the heart every time. They're a great bunch of guys, and they put out every night, all the time." Even at the beginning of the year, when most of the shows were booked in the Northeast, the pace and rhythm of a traveling band required immense amounts of stamina. The group's original asking price of $750 per gig rarely covered the weekly bills for the gas, oil, food, and salaries that kept it on the road—to say nothing of what it cost Appel and Cretecos to keep the lights and phones on at the management office. "We actually had to borrow a van to move the gear in," says Albee Tellone, the folk musician from the Upstage who joined up as a roadie (and soon became road manager). Tellone joined another Upstage regular, the golem-sized, Celtic bluesman Big Danny Gallagher, in a bare-bones crew often rounded out by Cretecos, who pulled triple duty as tour manager, soundman, and lights operator. Most often they traveled in two cars: the borrowed Dodge Maxivan, the rear seats of which had been taken out to make room for guitars, keyboards, and amps, and a station wagon for the band and staff. Sleeping space was nearly nonexistent, although you could squeeze in between the amps and guitars to catch a few hours in the van. When the band's gear expanded enough to require a U-Haul trailer, it became another haven for the band's exhausted and/or infirm.

Perpetually broke and forced to cadge sleeping space in dorms, locker rooms, or with friends and shirttail family members, Bruce, the band, and the two-man crew knuckled down and rarely complained. The $35 weekly salaries weren't always on time and sometimes never showed up at all. Tellone charged thousands of dollars' worth of gas on his own credit card and rarely found himself at the top of Appel's reimbursement list. No matter, there was always another gig to play, another load-in, another crowd to convert. Then everybody hauled the gear back into the van, grabbed a burger (if they could find one), and piled back into the cars for the three-hundred-mile drive to the next club, where they'd do it all over again. On and on they went, squirming for room in the smoky car, with Bruce entranced by the radio and Clemons right there with him, declaiming on the great songs and arguing bitterly when Bruce's tastes conflicted with his.

Everyone came with his quirks, although none could compete with crewman Big Danny Gallagher, who often became enraged when anyone tried to tell him what to do, as when Lopez asked the roadie to help set up his drums onstage. "Big Danny literally told Vini, 'Who the fuck do you think I am, your slave?'" Tellone says. "And I said, 'Technically, you are. A roadie's *supposed* to be an indentured servant.'" Gallagher didn't care. He shook his head, snorted, and stomped off to grab a smoke and a beer.

"If I didn't know [the music] was good, I never would have stuck with it," Garry Tallent reflects. But his wife had a job, and so they had some money coming in. And after so many years of rehearsing, playing, and dreaming, finally something seemed to be happening. He could see it most clearly during the multinight gigs they played in Boston, Bryn

Mawr, or in any town where Bruce had either never played or never made much of an impact. But now things seemed to be swinging, slowly but surely, in their direction. Starting in midweek, they usually played the first show to sparse crowds. "Then we'd play, maybe do a little radio," and as the word spread, the crowds thickened, and the response became more electric. "By the weekend, the place was packed and rockin'."

When the audience included a critic from a major metropolitan newspaper, such as Neal Vitale from the *Boston Globe*, the buzz became even buzzier. "The show was a delight," he wrote after seeing the band at Oliver's nightclub. "It became obvious, as Wednesday night faded into Thursday morning, that this had been the sort of gig to be long remembered: the feeling was that of having seen a totally brilliant, unique, soon-to-be-giant artist in his early days before he becomes a star."

TEN

LISTEN TO YOUR JUNK MAN—
HE'S SINGING

ALL PUBLICITY, UPBEAT-TO-RAVE REVIEWS, AND executive belief
aside, those freshly pressed copies of *Greetings from Asbury Park, N.J.*
stayed on the shelves. An internal Columbia sales sheet from March 19,
1973, showed that seventy-four thousand copies had shipped to record
stores, but with weekly sales at a trickle, most of those albums would be
coming back as returns—liabilities on CBS's quarterly docket. Meanwhile, Loudon Wainwright III, another singer-songwriter declared an
inheritor to Dylan,[1] sold three times as many records with his *Album
III*, thanks largely to his novelty hit "Dead Skunk." Six days earlier, in
a memo dated March 13, CBS publicity executive Sal Ingeme urged his
staff to double down on promoting Bruce's neglected single, "Blinded by

[1] Who, it bears mentioning, was only thirty-one at the time, quite productive, and nowhere near needing an inheritor.

the Light": "I'm sure that you all know how important it is for us to exert a *major effort* in busting both the single and the album by this artist."

When the group's first West Coast tour, supporting blues singer-harpist Paul Butterfield's new band, Better Days, got cancelled at the last moment (just after Bruce and band had made the marathon drive west), Columbia and Sam McKeith worked quickly to book enough replacement gigs to make the trip worthwhile. A Columbia-sponsored showcase at the Troubadour club on LA's Santa Monica Boulevard had been planned to feature the newly signed rock-folk-harmony band Pan, which played the evening's opening set. But even as the late-night undercard with only thirty minutes to play, and hobbled by a blown guitar amp that compelled him to switch to piano for most of the set, Bruce and the band turned a room full of chattering industry regulars into a rapt audience. To Peter Philbin, a young rock critic for the *Los Angeles Free Press*, the half hour with the New Jersey folk rocker felt like a revelation. When the set ended, Philbin trailed the band to the alley behind the club and introduced himself to the still-sweating Bruce. They talked for a few minutes, and when Philbin got home he pounded out an ecstatic review. "Never have I been more impressed with a debuting singer," he wrote. And while noting the new artist's similarities to Dylan, Philbin went on to declare Bruce "a total original" with "the remarkable ability to take his audience anywhere he wanted to go."

Bruce and the band made a quick jaunt to Berkeley, then returned to LA to open for Blood, Sweat and Tears at the Santa Monica Civic Auditorium. When Philbin went backstage, Bruce and Appel both recognized him and beelined over to shake his hand and thank him for his review. Noticeably more relaxed than he'd been in the alley behind the Troubadour, Bruce got Philbin going on his favorite records and bands, and when it emerged that the writer was a Van Morrison aficionado with a serious passion for the ethereal *Astral Weeks,* Bruce's eyes lit up: that was one of his favorite albums too! "Call me when you get to New York," he rasped.

Swept up in the music and the prospect of becoming a part of such a talented musician's blossoming scene, Philbin quit his job at the *Free Press*, packed up his stuff, and moved to New York. "I wanted to see more

of what this guy was about," he says. "And once he lets you in, you're in."
Philbin found a job with CBS Records' international publicity offices,
where he soon became one of Bruce's most impassioned advocates in
the company. A lucky break for Bruce, since he would soon need all the
friends he could get.

Back on their home turf in mid-March, Bruce and company got back to
the nightclub and college circuit, bouncing from the seven-night headline
gig at Oliver's in Boston to a variety of opening slots with the touring
bands of the day. Sha Na Na here, Lou Reed there, then Stevie Wonder,
then the Beach Boys. Rhode Island, Pennsylvania, Ohio, Connecticut,
and then the occasional headline show at the Main Point and so on. The
grind was relentless, the road ahead endless, so you had to be a believer.
Not just in Bruce's abilities, although that was obviously the point of
entry. But more importantly, in the core beliefs that propelled him forward: that no matter how corrupt the world may seem, certain things remained pure; that these things deserved to be respected; and that rock 'n'
roll was the most important of these things. "There was no separation,"
Tallent says. "We traveled together, we lived together; it was still kind of
like all for one and one for all."

The road, and the sacrifices that life required, drew them close
enough to recognize, and see into, one another's flaws and foibles. And
make no mistake, the band didn't just *look* like long-haired, largely unshaven eccentrics. They acted like it too. Consider the seraphim-cheeked
Federici, with his endless schemes and Danny-centric perspective on
personal responsibility. Tallent kept his thoughts to himself until something tripped his scarily detailed memory for virtually all historical facts
regarding pop, rock, soul, and country music of the past seventy-five
years. Meanwhile, Lopez's volcanic approach to problem resolution only
intensified with the pressure, exhaustion, and poverty of touring. The
drummer never shied away from meting out two-fisted justice, and his
reputation as a rough-and-ready brawler only got worse, Lopez says,
when Bruce started calling him "Mad Dog" on stage. As he says, Lopez
wouldn't back down for anyone. Including Clemons, who figured that he
had become Bruce's go-to protector and foil, and bitterly resented anyone

who threatened his sense of being the first among equals in this musical enterprise. If they managed to keep it relatively cool for the time being, the air between the big men crackled.

Bruce's own conflicts generally played out in the confines of his own thoughts. Already torn between his loyalty to his bandmates and his own creative independence, he also had to consider his commitment to the machine that had sprouted around him. If he could keep all that out of his mind, then came the visions, memories, and haunted spirits that played across his mind's eye; the internal disturbance that had compelled him to cling to his guitar in the first place. So everyone else in the band knew to give the guy some breathing room. Until he went out to buy himself something for dinner. Because that absolutely, positively, required a physical intervention.

"Bruce was still eating like a teenager, buying all his food at the convenience store," Albee Tellone says. "His idea of a meal was Ring Dings, Devil Dogs, and a Pepsi. We'd finally have to say, 'Man, put that shit down. You need to have real food: A steak! Some fish! A salad!'" If Bruce put up an argument, they'd simply hijack him, with Clemons grabbing one elbow, Big Danny Gallagher gripping the other, and Tellone leading the way to a restaurant with real, human sustenance on the menu.

Appel, in his guise as stern but loving authority figure, wielded his power with such whip-cracking exuberance that he seemed determined to aggravate everyone he encountered. So while the manager spent most of his time in New York, agitating for publicity, gigs, and the greater good of Bruce Springsteen, his jaunts with the band were always memorable. Something about that drill sergeant's hat put an extra edge in his rounds of the facility, barking orders and raining intimidation on everyone who stumbled into his path. "He just went into character with that hat," Tallent says. "Marching around like a little Hitler. I may have called him that, even." But Appel was also a charming, charismatic guy with a consuming devotion to his client. "It's all true," Tallent says. "And it was classic music biz stuff because he really believed in Bruce. He took out a second mortgage to keep the band on the road, all those things. So I don't care what anyone says about Mike. He made it work."

• • •

When Bruce felt uncomfortable playing at a certain venue or for a particular audience, he couldn't resist the urge to follow his most subversive impulses. At one executive-packed show in New York City, he spent his entire set playing slide guitar with his microphone stand riding the strings. The squeal ricocheting around the room sounded more like a wounded cat than the eloquent solos he could play with two hands. "I brought about ten executives with me that night, and it was so awful he cleared the room," Peter Philbin says. Flown to Los Angeles to play one of the A Week to Remember shows that Clive Davis produced to celebrate Columbia Records' most important artists, Bruce started strong with a tight, bluesy "Spirit in the Night." But given a muted reaction from the industry-heavy crowd, the famously electric performer became so subdued onstage that Davis cornered him later to give him the most basic of pointers: "You might want to consider using the vastness of the stage," he said. "Because . . . you're just *standing* there."

Bruce never liked playing for people whose enthusiasms could be traced to the bottom line of their paychecks. That his own thirst for success had steered him to the point of performing at CBS's annual sales convention in San Francisco curdled the artist's blood. Hustled onstage in the smoky wake of the fireworks-and-lasers spectacle put on by the Edgar Winter Group, Bruce came out seething. Given a fifteen-minute limit for his set, he played more than a half hour, ending with the mini-epic "Thundercrack," made even longer by a comic rap in the middle and a series of meandering solos that would have tried the patience of his most dedicated fans. Such as John Hammond, who glowed with frustration when he confronted his wayward artist backstage. "What are you doing, Bruce?" he cried. "You can't follow bombast with something like *that!*" Bruce shrugged and left it at that.

It had less to do with Hammond than with the mix of ambition, appetite, and self-control roiling in Bruce's stomach. What part of himself would he have to give up to be successful? And how would he feel later if the virtues he grasped so stubbornly turned out to be nothing more than animations of his own fears? "When you're young and vulnerable, you listen to people whose ideas and direction may not be what you want," Bruce told writer Robert Hilburn of the *Los Angeles Times* a few years later. "If anyone ever told me I was going to make [my first] record [almost entirely] without guitars, I would have flipped out. I would not have believed him. But I did make an album like that." And now the only thing worse than failing his new patrons was realizing he had surrendered so much of himself to become what they wanted him to be.

In the spring of 1973, Appel called Bruce with big news: Columbia's smash pop/jazz group Chicago (for whom the Bruce Springsteen Band had opened in 1971 when they were still known as the Chicago Transit Authority) had offered them a slot as the featured opener on their summer tour of basketball arenas. Riding its first number one album and a three-year string of hit singles, Chicago stood solidly at the height of its career. And once the group's manager-producer Jim Guercio saw Bruce play Max's Kansas City during the summer of 1972, he had been eager to help however he could. "I thought he was fucking great," Guercio says. When the time came to plan his group's next national tour, Guercio made sure that Bruce got a shot at the opening slot. "I thought they'd all get along," Guercio says.

Even if the pay ($1,000 a night) took them a step down from the $1,500 they'd been averaging since mid-February—and they were rarely invited to ride on the headliners' private jet—Bruce and the band did share the higher grade of hotels, food, and drink accorded to chart-topping bands in the early seventies. "And the best part was the guys in the other band," Bruce said in 1974. "They were great guys, just really, really real." Hanging out together at night, the bands' parties took place to the sound of Chicago bassist-singer Peter Cetera playing Polish music on Federici's accordion. On one particularly rowdy night in Hartford, Connecticut, a group of Chicago guys took Lopez and one or two other band members on a trek to find some friendly women that the Chicago guys knew from a previous visit to the city. The whole mob, plus Bruce and the rest of his guys, spent the rest of the night having a giggly, wee-hours party in the hotel pool.

The shows themselves weren't always as convivial. Given the constraints of union rules and the crowd's patience, Bruce had to boil his usual ninety-minute set down to a tight forty, with no time for encores. Bruce started the tour with full access to Chicago's sound and video systems, but after a night or two, Chicago's crew reined in the volume. They switched off the video screens a night or two after that, reducing the impact of Bruce's performance to a dull ripple off in the distance. "I did that tour because I'd never played big places before," he told writer Paul Williams in 1974. But the nightly displays of audience lassitude rattled Bruce's confidence. "I went insane during that tour," he said. "The worst state of mind I've ever been in, I think, and just because of the playing conditions for our band."

Demoralized and angry, Bruce cornered Appel and told him he would never again play an extra in some other band's superstar tour. "From now on, we're a club act, and we'll work our way up from there." As Peter Philbin says, Bruce's stand was both gutsy and foolish. "Chicago was as big as they came," he says. "When a new act that isn't in favor with anyone just walks off their tour—well, that doesn't go down well with the label. And Bruce had a number of those incidents."

Worse, he had just lost his most important supporter at the company. Despite the golden reputation that Clive Davis enjoyed in the rest of the music industry, the years of internecine struggle with former president Goddard Lieberson, among others on the Columbia/CBS executive floors, caught up with him in the final days of May 1973, when Davis got fired amid allegations that he had misused company money to pay for his son's bar mitzvah. A lot of accusations, most involving crimes much more sinister than the cost of a boy's bar mitzvah reception, had torn through CBS offices that spring. But for Bruce, the threat was more simple. Without Davis backing him up in the top office, his position at Columbia had started to crumble.

When they had a long drive to the next gig, Bruce liked to ride with Albee Tellone in the equipment van. Perched on the passenger seat, he had the space to open his notebook and let his imagination wander through the world that flashed past the windshield.

Everywhere, fragments of stories jumped out from the storefronts, the street signs, and the faces walking the sidewalk, chatting on the corner, and carrying a wading pool out of a small town Woolworth's. When they passed a roadside strip club announcing the return of a popular dancer, Bruce wrote "Kitty's Back" on the page, building a door to an urban noir of dealers, schemers, and faithless, irresistible women.

Eyes open wide mile after mile, Bruce traced a vision of modern American life as viewed by the perpetual passerby. All of it reminded him of his own life. "We spent hours talking about everything," Tellone says. "My ex-wife, his ex-girlfriends, music, and songwriting." When he focused on the words he'd scratched onto the page, Bruce often collided with the disengaged student he had been in high school. "He needed the basics," Tellone recalls. "He was catching up, he had his thesaurus and rhyming dictionary with him, and he'd find words and ask if they worked in this or that context."

Bruce didn't read a lot of books, so he used movies as tutorials on narrative writing, dramatic pacing, and the significance of the characters' voices and relationships. He looked to the directors' visual imagery to see how one well-shot scene could reveal ideas and themes that the dialogue could never carry. Bruce found a rich conceptual vein in a 1959 Audie Murphy Western about a pair of frontier teenagers whose first journey to the big city nearly corrupts them both. Glimpsing himself in their story, Bruce wrote the film's title into his book: *The Wild and the Innocent*. Which became all the more vibrant when he saw the same story reflected in the faces of the musicians who accompanied him from town to town. "There were just a lot of characters around; everybody had nicknames. A lot of street life, and the boardwalk," Bruce says. "I was drawing a lot from where I came from. I'm going to make this gumbo, and what's my life?" Bruce already knew the answer to that question. "Well, New Jersey. New Jersey is interesting. I thought that my little town was interesting, the people in it were interesting people. And everyone was involved in the E Street shuffle: the dance you do every day just to stay alive. That's a pretty interesting dance, I think. So how do I write about that? I found it very compelling, and I also wanted to tell my story, not somebody else's story."

Recording sessions for Bruce's second album began at the 914 Sound Studios in mid-May. Given how crucial touring was to the group's week-to-week income, the sessions were squeezed into dayslong increments through late September. The postmidnight recording (so aggravating to Hammond, who figured Appel was trying to keep him away) was actually part of a scheme hatched with chief engineer Louis Lahav to record for free while studio owner Brooks Arthur was home in bed. The arrangement worked perfectly until Arthur arrived unexpectedly one night and realized what was going on. "He wasn't happy," Tallent says. "Let's put it that way."

Working on the cheap had become second nature. While Bruce and the rest of the band made the daily two-hour drives to and from Blauvelt for the sessions, Lopez and Federici set up a tent in the studio's parking lot and camped out. When David Sancious got tired of Richmond and moved back into his mother's house in Belmar, New Jersey, Bruce invited him to rejoin the band on piano, thus relegating Federici to the organ, accordion, and other incidental keyboards. None of which pleased the Phantom, particularly when his younger colleague came on like a section leader. "He'd get up and come over to me and say, 'You shouldn't play that, you should play this,'" Federici told writer Robert Santelli in 1990. "That really disturbed me. So we didn't have a good rapport." What they both shared, however, was a dedication to the band and its leader.

Bruce walked into the studio with a thick stack of songs, many of them well polished from months of live performances. But as the album found its voice, it resisted some of Bruce's most reliable showstoppers. Crowd favorite "Thundercrack" fell out of consideration early, along with "Zero and Blind Terry," "Seaside Bar Song," "Santa Ana," and the one song everyone agreed sounded like a killer single: Bruce's smoldering R&B ballad, "The Fever." All sacrificed for the same all-important yet perfectly ambiguous reason: they didn't fit into the movie Bruce imagined himself writing and directing. Set partly on the Jersey Shore and partly in the New York City he'd discovered—and then reimagined as the setting for his own variations on *West Side Story*—the album became a series of stories about liberation: through music, through friends, through lovers, through the realization that even a junkman like Fred Springsteen can walk with his head held high and a song on his lips.

Given Bruce's renewed passion for full-band rock 'n' roll, it's fitting that the first moments of the album's opening song, the not-quite-title track "The E Street Shuffle," feature a horn section tuning up to play. Quickly organized, they play a brief intro to a high-spirited R&B guitar riff (lifted from 1963's "The Monkey Time," by Chicago soul singer Major Lance) establishing the groove for the horn-fortified band to leap into. From there, Bruce describes a typical night in the lives of the street kids and hustlers populating this mythical E Street[2] on party night. Nothing all that significant happens. But everyone finds his or her way to the party, and when the band kicks into gear, the revelers whoop, converge on themselves, and dance. Horns blaring, rhythm section gliding at top speed while the clavinet bops and that guitar riff slinks and slides, the building lifts off its foundations, and the entire enterprise floats skyward.

By the end, the tune's main characters, Power Thirteen and Little Angel, slip away from the dance floor, "and they move on out down to the scene." Perhaps to the quieter end of the boardwalk, where the acoustic guitar-wielding narrator of "4th of July, Asbury Park (Sandy)" looks past the carnival lights and corn dog haze for something more substantial. He's already tasted the forbidden love of his boss's daughter, but whether escape is a real option or just another illusion remains a mystery.

From there the adventure abandons the shore for downtown New York City for "Kitty's Back," which strings its Tom Waits–meets–*The Aristocats* lyrics across sprawling instrumental jams highlighted by the first and last epic guitar solo Bruce captured in the recording studio.

Flip to the album's second side, and the opening piano chimes of "Incident on 57th Street," in which Spanish Johnny and Puerto Rican Jane[3] find a lovers' respite in the midst of gang warfare, police incursions, and a noirish heat wave. Here liberation comes in the vague promise of another part of town "where paradise ain't so crowded." But as in Shakespeare's original, paradise doesn't last: Johnny vanishes in search of easy money, leaving Jane with the shakiest of promises: "We may walk until the daylight, maybe."

The album's closing song, the nearly ten-minute ballad "New York City Serenade," brings the album back to the big city, where even the street hustlers teeter between grandeur and nonexistence. David Sancious's Tchaikovsky-meets-Mingus piano intro sets the dramatic tone

[2] Named for the quiet, residential Belmar street where Sancious lived with his mother.
[3] Whose literary antecedents are made clear in the second verse, as Johnny acts the "cool Romeo" while Jane follows her heart like "a late Juliet."

of the piece before dissolving into a pattern of simple chords joined by Bruce's acoustic guitar and the slap and swoon of congas, played by Bruce's boyhood neighbor, Richard Blackwell. Singing in a near whisper, Bruce describes his own version of *West Side Story*, where the rumble is for dignity and the small pleasures that come with being alive. So while a vibes player in a jazz club might indulge his own glorious melancholy onstage, he can't rival the grace of the trash collector patrolling the street with satin on his back and a song on his lips. "Listen to your junk man, listen to your junk man," Bruce whispers. "He's singing, he's singing, he's singing . . ."

All the romance and heartbreak, the veil of spotlights, and the windblown highway. A nomadic existence held together by music, camaraderie, and duct tape. And also an image evolved to fit the dreamy-urban-poet persona that inhabited so many of the songs on the album. The photograph on the album's back cover revealed Bruce as a street corner poet, wonderfully bedraggled in black Converse sneakers, a wrinkled green tank top, bracelet on his wrist, and leather belt tight around his whippet waist, surrounded by other scroungy but intriguing characters. The height and breadth of Clemons, barefoot in shorts, shirt open, floppy cap on his head, and kerchief knotted on his neck; Lopez, looming above everyone with Hawaiian shirt agape and stone-and-gristle midsection in clear view. Sancious, also barefoot, sports a black daishiki, while Tallent, all long hair and thick beard, stands next to the angelically tressed Federici, whose smile has the sparkle of a man who really, really wants you to buy his duck.

In the thrall of *The Wild, the Innocent & the E Street Shuffle*, Bruce's entire personality seemed to have shifted. Asbury guitar hero Sonny Kenn, still the senior man on the Jersey Shore circuit, recalls checking out a show in East Brunswick, after which he was surprised to discover that the fresh-faced rocker he remembered had become something else entirely. "He was doing his cool thing, crouched up in the corner of the dressing room going [*in a breathy hipster voice*] 'Heeeeey, maaan'—this whole Tom Waits thing. Which was weird to me, because that wasn't the guy I knew." Kenn shrugs. "But I still think *The Wild and the Innocent* is one of his greatest records. It's so experimental, it's damn everything. If he'd stopped there, that would be enough for anyone's career."

Still, *The Wild, the Innocent & the E Street Shuffle* faced a less than ecstatic reception at Columbia, due both to *Greetings'* commercial failure and the unclassifiable nature of the new album's sound and structure. Even Hammond bristled when he realized that the lead single, "The E Street Shuffle," clocked in at a Top 40–busting four minutes and twenty-six seconds—at least a minute longer than nearly every other song on pop radio. With Clive Davis gone from the corner office, Bruce's star had been eclipsed by the just-signed Billy Joel, whose piano-based melodicism leaned much more mainstream than the New Jersey street poet could ever be. What's more, Joel had come to the company through the just-elevated A&R chief Charles Koppelman, who had sworn to make him a success. And if the time and investment that required came at the expense of another young artist, well, welcome to the record industry.

Released on November 11, *The Wild, the Innocent & the E Street Shuffle* sold a bit better than *Greetings* had done the previous winter, moving about two thousand copies a week during its run through the Christmas season. The initial critical reception reached the same heights as *Greetings*: *Rolling Stone's* Ken Emerson called it one of the year's best albums, while *Creem's* Ed Ward pronounced it "great." Other critics largely followed suit. As for radio, some FM stations on the East Coast and in the Midwest started spinning "Rosalita," due largely to the evangelical ministrations of DJs such as Ed Sciaky in Philadelphia and Kid Leo in Cleveland, both of whom fought hard to convince their bosses to both play Bruce's records and simulcast his shows when he came to town.

But like the characters in "New York City Serenade," Bruce still splayed between triumph and collapse. On the one hand, each show created a new batch of converts, many of whom hauled a carful of buddies to the next show, and when those guys filled their cars, and then the clubs, with their increasingly enthusiastic friends, club owners took notice. As did Bruce's fellow artists, whose managers sent letters to Appel declaring that they would rather *not* be on bills that featured an opening set by Springsteen, whose gentle backstage behavior secreted the heart of a far too loud, way too spellbinding, crowd-destroying lion. As Tallent recalls, even solid compatriots Jackson Browne and Bonnie Raitt (or their booking agents) went through periods of avoiding having Bruce as an opener. "We were still friends and all," says Tallent. "But I think there were a couple of times they felt they weren't received as well as they were used to being."

But even the slightly swifter pace of sales for *Wild* didn't meet Columbia's expectations for a truly up-and-coming artist's second album. By the first weeks of 1974, the more dispassionate members of the company's power structure—for example, the accountants tracking the numbers on the quarterly profits-and-loss statements—began to murmur. Where is this Springsteen guy headed, exactly? Wasn't he the sulky freak who played such a bummer set at the convention in San Francisco?

"We had a lot of meetings about the artist roster," A&R executive Michael Pillot says of that winter. "And there was a lot of talk about dropping Bruce." Not everyone from the company remembers the moment as being that dire. "His sales certainly weren't up to expectations," says Clive Davis's successor, Bruce Lundvall, who goes on to say that the first show he watched Bruce play that winter convinced him that the kid would become a star. "And I reported that back, too."

Bruce's most devoted supporters at Columbia remained on high alert. When whispers about the campaign to drop Bruce got to chief publicist Ron Oberman, he pounded out a fierce letter, cosigned by a half dozen other staff converts, pleading with Koppelman to give Bruce one more chance. The declaration of belief bought a little more time, but that still didn't make Bruce a popular face in the Columbia offices. When newly appointed CBS president Walter Yetnikoff noticed how much time Bruce spent slouching in the office of his buddy Peter Philbin, the top exec instructed his employee to cut it out immediately.

"That kid's not selling any records for us!" Yetnikoff railed. "He's not going anywhere. Now he's distracting you, and I want it to stop."

As Philbin recalls it, he shot right back.

"Fuck you!" he said. "Don't you know who that kid's gonna *be*?"

Yetnikoff gaped for a second and then stormed off without another word. But he didn't fire Philbin for his impudence, and he didn't drop Bruce from the label, either. Instead Yetnikoff approved a compromise strategy in which Columbia/CBS would advance Bruce and Appel just enough money to produce a single. "We gave him the assignment of making a good record," Lundvall says. "If it turned out to be good, the company would fork over the money to produce the rest of the album. But if it didn't, well, they'd all have to try again."

Bruce accepted the challenge (he had no choice), but not without some resentment. "They want to stick their fingers in my pie," he told J. Garrett Andrews of Brown University's *Daily Herald* in the spring of 1974. "I don't need it. Just let me make my music and leave me alone. They're bugging me for a single. I don't know, maybe they mean well, but I doubt it."

What he thought of their motivations didn't matter. As Bruce entered 1974, his future—professional, personal, emotional—came down to one final play. A make-or-break single that would either keep them moving forward or herald the end of the line.

ELEVEN

HYPERACTIVITY WAS
OUR BUSINESS

STEPPING ONSTAGE BENEATH THE CRUMBLING, water-stained acoustic tiles of the Nassau Community College's student union on December 15, 1973, Bruce nodded to the scattered applause and sat on a stool. Danny Federici, sitting just behind and to the right, waited silently while Bruce, teasing the strings of his acoustic guitar, made a short introduction. "Goin' back to that fateful summer of '73. Girls all walkin' up and down the boardwalk, kids playin' on the pinball machine." Whispering now: "It's just around the fourth of July . . ." After a hushed duet of "Sandy," the band members came up, strapping on their instruments and then turning their attention to Davy Sancious, stirring up the piano keys for his largely improvised intro to "New York City Serenade."

Maybe fifty or sixty students sat in front of them. Bruce, wispy-bearded but close-cropped in his tight shirt and jeans, directed the band with typical precision, moving from the unhinged "Spirit in the Night" to a lockstep version of Rufus Thomas's "Walking the Dog" built around abrupt stops, silent moments ended by a whistle blast or Clemons's muttered "What it is!" signaling the band to flip the switch back to full blast. The game went back and forth, gaining momentum until a stop came with no whistle or sound, just Bruce gazing blankly into the crowd. He held the pose for ten, fifteen . . . *twenty* seconds, then swiveled his head owlishly, upping the tension as he regarded the crowd. Then a small shrug of his shoulders, capped by a light *Huh!* that snapped the band instantly into the song's next verse, to the cheers of the crowd. The last song, the whipsawing "Thundercrack," gave all the players spotlight turns, leading up to Bruce's climactic guitar solo, most notable for his Chaplin-esque mugging during the slow, near-silent part, his face twisting to mime the effort of the bending of a string and the growl of a low note. When Clemons honked a sour note on his instrument, Bruce stopped everything, his face rent by comic exasperation. "Why do I pay these guys fifty dollars a week? For that?"

The inside joke was that Clemons, Lopez, Sancious, Federici, and Tallent, now dubbed the E Street Band, had become a central part of Bruce's performances and reputation. Everyone got multiple solos during the shows, and a perpetual invitation to play whatever he felt, no matter how long it took. "I don't believe in having a band where they're just scraping away behind me," Bruce told an interviewer in 1974. "I want 'em to be happening . . . I got a bunch of guys who play great, let 'em out there. Let 'em play. It's just, *take* it, and when you're done, let me know, and we'll *all* do something."

Like on the new speed-jazz arrangement of "Blinded by the Light," in which Bruce's guitar commented on virtually every line of lyrics, answered by Federici's organ swoops, Clemons's best King Curtis honk-and-scream, Sancious's spider-finger blues, and Lopez's speed-freak fills. Goaded onward by the velocity of the band and the flashiness of his brethren, the drummer would somersault so far beyond the tempo that bassist Tallent began to doubt his own ability to count to four. "Vini would go into a fill, and when it came time for us to come down on the one, he wouldn't be there. He'd give me a nasty look, and I'd think, 'Uh-oh, I'm in trouble here.'" But danger and speed go hand in hand, and the only thing more exciting than racing toward destruction came when everything snapped back into place, only to career off in another direction. "Hyperactivity," Bruce said many years later, "was our business."

Mike Appel pursued his end of the business with the same manic energy. Hearing that the CBS sales team would be convening in Nashville in February, Appel booked a show just down the street from the executives' hotel as a guerilla attempt to woo the force back into Bruce's corner. So, okay, the scheme turned out to be a bust: even after Appel papered the place with fliers, nobody on the CBS team showed up. The repudiation only made Appel that much more determined to make the company, the music industry, the *entire world*, fall under Bruce's spell. And so he became even more outlandish.

Appel celebrated the holidays by hand packaging and then sending lumps of coal (charcoal briquettes, actually) to the radio programmers who refused to give Bruce a chance on their airwaves. He also infamously dialed a big-desk honcho at the NBC television network to talk him into prefacing the Super Bowl—*the Super Bowl!*—with Bruce standing alone on the 50-yard stripe, performing an antiwar song called "Balboa vs. the Earth Slayer." All that, and the written, telephoned, telegrammed, buttonholed-on-the-sidewalk hard-sell pitches to all and sundry. Often followed up by letters, calls, and so forth that could turn hostile if he sensed resistance. "Was I too aggressive or outlandish?" Appel asks. "That's what some people say. But that crazy, reaching-for-the-stars attitude permeated the early years. And look where it led."

And wasn't it a reflection of what Bruce and his hurricane-grade band were doing onstage? "Sure, Mike's abrasive. He's got that New York thing," says born-and-bred Angeleno Peter Philbin. "But I never saw a manager who believed more than Mike. He had total belief." So much, in fact, that Appel could no longer express his quest in the terms of mere rock 'n' roll or show business. "Bruce Springsteen isn't a rock 'n' roll act," he swore to friends, colleagues, and especially producers, bookers, program directors, and anyone else who would listen, "He's a *religion*."

Like any true apostle, Appel would sacrifice whatever it took to push Bruce another step up the mountain. If saving money meant halving original employee Bob Spitz's salary and then eliminating his position because little brother Stephen Appel had graduated high school and would work for free, then bye-bye Bob Spitz. Then coproducer-comanager Jimmy Cretecos vaporized, either because he could no longer identify a glimmer of hope in Bruce's financial future or as a result of some far more shadowy internecine tussle that no one will talk about in detail. Particularly the soft-spoken Cretecos, who sounds pained as he explains that he's suffered enough for his short role in Bruce's career and won't say a word about any of it, no matter how much there is to tell.

Still, Appel endured his own crisis of faith that winter. Worn down by two years of struggle, unpaid debt, and frustration, he found himself considering the benefits of tearing up Bruce's contract, steering him toward another manager, and letting that guy do whatever Appel couldn't to catapult Bruce to where he deserved to be. But then he'd listen to one of the albums or catch a show, and hope swelled, faith ran fresh, and the crusade went on. Something, Appel knew, had to change. They just had to keep pushing. And in early 1974, that meant precisely one thing: isolating the true essence of Bruce Springsteen, his music, his band, his voice, his vision, and distilling it into no more than four minutes of uncompromising yet radio-friendly rock 'n' roll music.

Recently broken up with Diane Lozito, Bruce reclined on the bed in the small house he'd rented in the West End region of Long Branch, New Jersey. Notebook folded open, guitar in hand, he strummed idly, his line cast into the depths of consciousness, waiting for an idea to present itself. A chord progression, a snatch of melody, some kind of visual image, whatever. Then three words fell onto his tongue: *born to run.*

The title of a half-remembered b-movie? Airbrushed words blazing across the flank of a '64 Chevy he spied on the Ocean-Kingsley circuit in Asbury? Bruce had no idea. It didn't really matter anyway. "I liked it because it suggested a cinematic drama I thought would work with the music I was hearing in my head," he wrote in the late nineties. He came up with chords, the verse reminiscent of the Beach Boys' Brian Wilson–composed love/lust/car drama "Don't Worry Baby," and tried to imagine where the song would go from there. Like Wilson (working with lyricist Roger Christian), Bruce's highways led to bigger ideas and more urgent feelings: "The cars only interested me as vehicles for writing my songs."

In Bruce's consciousness, the street racing scene defied the social and economic strictures that kept the underprivileged, the young, and the outsiders from becoming who they were meant to be. "Jersey's a dumpy joint," he told writer Jerry Gilbert of the British music paper *Sounds* that same winter. "I mean, it's okay, it's home. But every place is a dump." This realization, despite (or arguably, because of) its adolescent simplicity, had become entwined with his passion for rock 'n' roll. "Escape was the idea," he said to Eve Zibart in 1978. It connected everything, from Chuck Berry's "School Days" to Dylan's "Stuck Inside of Mobile with the Memphis Blues Again." "The song is a release. It's an expression of the humdrum, the daily existence that you break out of."

Drawn to a brighter, more urgent version of the drama that had fueled his music for more than a decade, Bruce dismissed his alter egos and stood alone at the center of the screen, climbing into the car and feeling the wheel vibrating in his own palms.

In the day we sweat it out on the streets of a runaway American dream / At night we stop and tremble in heat / With murder in our dreams . . ."

From there it all came pouring out: the surfers shivering in the breakers; the cars rumbling down Highway 9 to identical towns farther down the Shore, the metal-flake hot rods turning slow circles on the Asbury Park circuit. "Like animals pacing in a black, dark cage, senses on overload," he wrote. "They're gonna end this night in a senseless fight / and then watch the world explode."

Everyone, everywhere, all souped up with no place to go.

It's a death trap! A suicide rap! We gotta get out while we're young / 'Cause tramps like us, baby . . .

Then it all comes back to the three words, and the governing realization that spurred the composition of the song and everything that would follow.

. . . we were born to run.

It would take him months to get the words just so and even longer to capture the gleaming sound already playing in his ears. But he'd found the heart of the song, the chords and melody ringing so true that he could already sense that he'd tapped into something powerful. A song with the energy of "Thundercrack" and "Rosalita," only condensed to its most vital essence. "This was the turning point," he wrote later. "It proved to be the key to my songwriting for the rest of the record."

Bruce, the band, and Appel got back to work at the 914 Sound Studios on January 8, 1974, spending a couple of days fiddling with rudimentary versions of both "Born to Run" and "Jungleland." The latter song, also new, had a setting, characters, and an omniscient perspective that flowed from previous urban epics "Incident on 57th Street" and "New York City Serenade." They went back to the road for a week or so, made another brief stop at 914, then off again, then back to the studio for thirty-six or forty-eight hours, then back to Boston, Ohio, or Virginia—wherever a crowd waited for another go-round of the E Street shuffle. For the moment, the here-and-gone schedule worked in Bruce's favor. The songs weren't there yet, and he still hadn't quite figured out how to evoke the glossy yet serious as death sound he knew the album had to have. So no hurry, particularly with the shows picking up so much steam. Every return visit to a club or a city brought in bigger audiences than the previous one, and as the crowds got larger, so did the money. The band's nightly quote from agent Sam McKeith had tripled from the previous year's bargain-basement rate of $750. And every so often, promoters in an established hot spot would put together a bigger show, and they'd score a small jackpot: for example, netting a sky-high $4,200 for one night in Richmond, in late January.

Given a year's worth of experience among a slightly higher orbit of performers, Bruce put more emphasis on his wardrobe, trading wrinkled T-shirts and hoodies for gleaming white T-shirts, usually set off by a vest or sweater. Even Bruce's facial hair got itself together, graduating from the Spanish moss stage to something closer to a dark, filled-in beard. The crew tightened up its act too,[1] with a new generation of crew guys experienced enough to anticipate and fix "the fuck-up factor," as they called it, before a club manager's mistake or stray communication could screw up the night's show. And if they needed someone to have a frank and useful discussion with an underperforming or annoying presence, that's where Lopez came in. Only sometimes he didn't think things through before he launched the missiles. And other times he aimed them at his own friends and compadres.

Everyone knew Lopez had started the original band. That he brought in Federici, who helped take stock of Bruce's skills before they both asked him to join in with them in the winter of 1969. Lopez and Bruce had played together ever since, and while the drummer knew which one of them wrote, sang, and played lead guitar on their songs, he also knew which one was, on at least one level, the senior man in the organization. Look at the picture on the back of *The Wild, the Innocent & the E Street Shuffle,* and you can see it yourself: Bruce leaning against the windowsill with Clemons, everyone else seated or slouched, while Lopez stands tall behind them, shirt open and muscles rippling like a conquering hero. "[Fans] called me Bruce for the longest time because of that picture," Lopez says.

The drummer took some heat from critics for his offbeat sound, but not from his boss. "He had this wildly eccentric sound," Bruce recalled thirty years later. "A fabulous style that totally fit those [first] two records." And yet Bruce knew his third album would have to sound more focused. They would have to act that way too, which was where Lopez's fists got in the way. Particularly when the decreasingly subtle feud between the drummer and Clemons got out of control. One ridiculous argument[2] in the house they shared with Federici didn't end until furniture was splintered, walls punched through, and Clemons wielded a heavy stereo speaker as a deadly weapon. "I figured I'd scare him," Clemons

---

[1] Both Albee Tellone and Big Danny Gallagher had moved on by the end of 1973.

[2] Stemming either from Clemons's unwillingness to clean up the kitchen after a marathon session of marijuana smoking or because, in the sax player's words, "Vini finally just pissed me off."

said. Message received. "He grabbed me by the throat, and then I was the bouncing ball," Lopez says. "He was big, you know. After that, I moved out of the house."

Lopez's five-year tenure with Bruce hit its death spiral during an early-February recording session in Blauvelt. At one point in the evening, Stephen Appel showed up bearing the band's weekly salaries. But when Lopez counted and realized the take was several hundred dollars lighter than usual, his fiery instincts took over. Storming out of the studio, Lopez found Stephen chatting with Louis Lahav in the lounge. Already roaring about the money, Lopez either shoved the cash into Stephen's chest with enough gusto to accidentally knock him down (Lopez's version), or else he punched him in the face hard enough to send him through an open door and into the next room (Stephen's recollection). Either way, Bruce saw the whole thing.

"Bruce leaped up like a crazy man," Stephen Appel says. "He screamed, *'What are you doing!?'* and Vini just ran out into the woods."

Stephen peeled himself off the floor and stalked out to his car, but Bruce caught him before he could climb in. "He said, 'What the hell just happened?' and I said, 'You were there!'" The teenager screeched away a moment later, leaving Bruce to decide if he should chase his renegade drummer through the wild or return to the studio, where the rest of the band waited.

Two days later Bruce knocked on Lopez's door in Bradley Beach, where the drummer stored the guitarist's stage equipment. When he came inside, he delivered the news in a chilly monotone.

"Hey man, you're fired."

Lopez shook his head. What did Bruce mean?

"You're not in the band anymore."

The drummer tried to bargain: he'd fucked up, he knew it. And if his drumming was a problem, he could practice more. Whatever, he deserved a second chance. Everyone gets a second chance, right?

"Nope," Bruce said. "No second chances. It's a dog-eat-dog world."

Lopez: "I could tell he felt bad about it. But he was Bruce about it too. Just a little bit detached." Lopez wouldn't accept it. He cajoled. He argued. He nearly begged. Then he remembers it getting uglier. That Bruce called him a shitty drummer. That critics and friends had long urged him to find someone else for the job, and now he had no choice. Finally, Lopez pointed to the door and told him to get the fuck out, right now. "Ordinarily, I'd help him carry his stuff out to the car," Lopez says. "But at this point, he could do it by himself."

The first audition went to Johnny Arnzt, a hard-hitting Asbury Park regular whom Tallent and Federici had played with as teenagers. But when Sancious brought in Ernest "Boom" Carter, the versatile Richmond drummer that he and Tallent had played with in the first iteration of Sancious's jazz-fusion trio, he fit in immediately. "This guy *plays* the damn drums," Bruce told a reporter during Carter's first tour with the band. "He knows the subtle. He don't beat the drums, he don't smash the drums. He's understated. A very subtle cat."

Carter was also fast enough on his feet to play a show less than a week after they started rehearsing together. Mike Appel had already cancelled a handful of dates in order to give the drummer a chance to get the hang of the band's songs and style. But the owner of the Satellite Lounge in Cookstown, New Jersey, refused to accept the cancellation. Everything was set up, the tickets were sold, this was going to be a huge moneymaker for him. And they were going to let an unrehearsed drummer upend the whole thing? No fucking way. So Appel cited a litany of other reasons: the recording sessions, exhaustion, and what about the gas crisis? The nation's supply had dried up. Drivers had to wait for hours to fill their tanks. They could end up stuck in south Jersey with no gas and no way to get home.

"I'll take care of that," the guy said. And if they didn't show up, by the way, he'd take care of *them*. "The word we got was that he had people who were going to shoot us if we didn't play the gig," Tallent remembers. "The big quote was something like, '*I know where you live.*'" So as it turned out, they *could* work a gig into their break. And when the show ended and the time came to drive back to New Jersey, the gas came to them, delivered to the club's parking lot by a pair of state troopers.

So even if they couldn't find their own albums in record stores within walking distance of the clubs they played,[3] the months of touring—and a scattering of enthusiastic disc jockeys—began to pay off, and not always where they expected it. Swinging through Texas and Arizona in the spring, they played to a nearly empty room in Dallas but found an enthusiastic mob in Houston, a riotous club crowd in Austin, and, astonishingly, a sold-out concert hall in Phoenix. "I have no idea why we became so popular in this particular spot," Bruce told a reporter after the show. "We don't sell out a place that size, ever. So what happened here don't happen. I don't know what's goin' on down here."

A few weeks later, in April, Bruce and the band drove to Boston to play a string of shows at Charlies Place, a small bar off of Harvard Square in Cambridge. Standing in the mist before the evening's late show, reading the Boston *Real Paper* review of *Wild* posted on the wall, Bruce heard the voice of the clean-cut young man now standing next to him.

"Whaddaya think?" the guy asked, pointing to the review.

"It's pretty good," Bruce said.

Eyes gleaming behind his wire-rim glasses, the guy held out his hand and introduced himself. His name was Jon Landau, and yes, that was his name on the story. Bruce laughed, shook his hand, and stuck around to chat for a moment. Then he went backstage to pull things together for the show. Landau went inside to find the guy who had brought him to the show—a music writer named Dave Marsh—and find a place to sit.

When the show began, Landau could only gape. Transfixed by Sancious's improvised opening to "New York City Serenade," the critic was knocked backward by the full-tilt attack of "Spirit in the Night," "Kitty's Back," and "Rosalita." During the encores, Landau was on his feet, howling like a creature whose only contact with serious rock criticism would come when someone rolled up a newspaper and used it to swat its furry ass.

After the show, Landau introduced himself to Appel and hung

---

[3] Intracompany rumor and anecdotal accounts from shop owners indicated that someone high in Columbia/CBS's power structure had ordered the sales reps to compel retailers to trade their copies of *Greetings* and *Wild* for Billy Joel's first Columbia album, *Piano Man*, released the same week as Springsteen's second LP.

around to chat about Bruce and the intricacies of record production. "The next day I got a call from Bruce, and we talked for several hours," Landau says. An eagle-eyed reader of reviews, Bruce had already fixed on the part of Landau's review that criticized the production of Bruce's first two records, and after having read that same beef in a variety of reviews, he needed to know exactly what Landau meant. "One thing led to another, and we just talked, just drifted all over the place, and we agreed to talk some more. That was the beginning."

When Bruce and the band came back through Boston a month later to open for Bonnie Raitt at the Harvard Square Theatre, Landau showed up again. This time his step had lost the bounce that carried him through that night at Charlies. In a crumbling marriage, doubting his own commitment to his craft and to the rock and soul music that had inflamed his imagination since he was a boy, Landau was also scant hours from his twenty-seventh birthday. Feeling crushed and faded, the writer sat by himself, his face as empty as the life he thought he'd built for himself. Right until the lights faded and the music began. Because that's when Landau felt it all again, even more strongly than before.

> Springsteen does it all. He is a rock 'n roll punk, a Latin street poet, a ballet dancer, an actor, a joker, a bar band leader, a hot-shit rhythm guitar player, an extraordinary singer, and a truly great rock 'n' roll composer.

And something else, too. A tonic for the soul. A flash of hope across the murkiest skies he'd ever encountered.

> When his two-hour set ended, I could only think, can anyone really be this good; can anyone say this much to me, can rock 'n' roll still speak with this kind of power and glory? And then I felt the sores on my thighs where I had been pounding my hands in time for the entire concert and knew that the answer was yes.

Four decades later it's still a breathtaking piece of writing. A cry for help, a declaration of purpose, a call to arms. A piece so hotly emotional that

Landau spent years feeling sheepish about it. "I was writing to myself, writing to the reader, and I was writing to him."

> On a night when I needed to feel young [Springsteen] made me feel like I was listening to music for the first time. I saw my rock and roll past flash before my eyes. And I saw something else. I saw rock and roll's future and its name is Bruce Springsteen.

Even if it came from an alternative-to-the-alternative newspaper in Boston, the May 22 column hit the music industry, and especially the offices of Columbia/CBS Records, with the force of a thunderbolt.

"That got people's attention," CBS marketing executive and Bruce booster Ron McCarrell says. "We'd been hanging by our thumbs, hoping we were right. That bolstered our feelings." And single-handedly revived the company's interest in an artist it had all but abandoned. Suddenly the reps snapped back into gear, pushing Bruce's records back into shops nationwide, accompanied by a promotional campaign pegged almost entirely to Landau's column. "I remember turning the quote into a poster for record shops," McCarrell says. "And that was kind of the beginning of what led into the massive campaign for *Born to Run*."

You'd think Bruce would be thrilled. And he was. Except for the part of him that hated it. "I [was] just getting over the Dylan thing," Bruce said to the UK *New Musical Express*'s Tony Tyler in 1975. "And I'm sitting home thinking thank God people seem to be letting *that* lie go, and phwoooeeee! '*I have seen.*' No! It can't be!"

So okay, Landau's column had meant a lot to Bruce. But seeing it dragooned into yet another massive hype campaign? "It was like they took it all out of context and blew it up, and who's gonna swallow that? It's going to piss people off, man. It pisses *me* off. When I read it [in the ad], I wanted to strangle the guy who put that thing in there."

Though, of course, the advertising guys had taken the critic's proclamation in the *exact* context he had intended. But to Bruce, the distinction between a critic's well-considered praise and the screamy hype of record company posters couldn't be larger. "It's like I'm always ten points down, 'cause not only have you got to play, you've got to blow this bullshit out of peoples' minds first." Only the music mattered, which explained why Bruce forbade Appel to produce T-shirts and other merchandise bearing his name and image, a purist move that also served to choke off a revenue stream that could help sustain the still-sputtering organization.[4] And although only a small number of promoters had reason to ask about booking shows in arenas, Bruce made it clear that he had no intention of playing in halls that would dilute the connection he could establish in clubs and smaller theaters.

Appel, for one, thought his client had the right priorities. "We were the wonder boys," he says. "If we were going to invest time and money into anything, it had to add up to something cool for the performance. That was the driving force. The payoff was the artistry."

As the spring warmed into summer, momentum for the live shows grew. The promotions staff at Columbia/CBS turned the three-night, six-show mid-July stand at New York's Bottom Line club into a showcase for all the industry figures, journalists, radio programmers, and DJs who might be tempted to see the show for themselves. This time, virtually all of them clamored to be included. And Bruce came through like he'd never done in the industrial spotlight, turning in tight, fiery shows that linked rocked-up versions of his own songs with performances of the Crystals' "Then He Kissed Me"[5] and Chuck Berry's "No Money Down" that invested the oldies with the depth and passion of rock 'n' roll liturgy. And early drafts of "Born to Run" and "Jungleland" upped the ante that much more. Back in Phoenix at the end of the month, tickets for a return to the 2,650-capacity Celebrity Theatre sold out so quickly the promoter added a late show, which also sold out. The band's take for the night added up to $11,500, nearly three times what it had ever made for a single night's work.

The heat growing behind Bruce began to overwhelm even the

---

[4] And also created a big opportunity for local entrepreneurs to retail their own Springsteen/E Street Band T-shirts, stickers, and so on to the fans, often at a nice profit.
[5] Revised to "Then She Kissed Me."

commercially successful acts that had booked him to open their shows. When a last-minute call from the producers of the Schaefer Music Festival in Central Park at the Wollman Rink resulted in Bruce's being booked to open for Anne Murray, Appel implored the Canadian pop singer's manager to let his client come on after the headliner, as an undercard closer. The manager took up Appel's invitation to see one of Bruce's shows but still came away unconvinced. How could any regional band, no matter how energetic, disrupt the charge that Murray would create with middle-of-the-road hits such as "Snowbird"? But his reasoning failed to calculate the number of hard-boiled fans from New York and New Jersey that Bruce would draw. Let alone how they would react when their local hero had to clear off the stage to make room for Murray. But the show went on as Murray's manager wanted. "They regretted it later," Appel says.

They were unstoppable, until David Sancious came to Bruce with the dismaying news that he had been offered a solo deal with Columbia's sister label, Epic. So he was leaving the band and, worse yet, taking Boom Carter with him. As these things go, it was a friendly split. Both musicians agreed to stick around for the next month to give Bruce time to find their replacements. Instead Bruce (almost certainly in league with Appel), didn't say anything to anyone for a few weeks, hoping that the pianist and the drummer might change their minds and stick around. They didn't. So in early August Appel placed a notice in the Musicians Needed section of the *Village Voice*'s classified ads, seeking a drummer ("No Jr. Ginger Baker's" [*sic*]), a pianist ("Classical to Jerry Lee Lewis"), along with a trumpet player ("Jazz, R&B, & Latin"), and a violinist. "*All must sing. Male or Female. Bruce Springsteen and the E. Street Band. Columbia Records.*"

More than a hundred musicians responded, leading to two months of auditions to sort through something like sixty drummers and nearly as many pianists. And none of them made the grade until a pair of young but already seasoned New York professionals showed up. Max Weinberg and Roy Bittan, drummer and pianist, respectively, came in separately but with similarly long and diverse musical histories. North New Jersey-ite Weinberg had made his professional debut as a six-year-old phenom performing with Herb Zane's wedding band, which made pianist Bittan, from the Rockaways district of Queens, a relative newcomer, given his more traditional high school band start. Intriguingly, both had spent significant periods playing in Broadway shows, so the two musicians were well schooled in the accompanist's trade of combining creativity with consistency, while always keeping their eyes and ears open to what was happening around them.

Bittan had seen Bruce and the band at a club earlier that year and came away swooning. "I could tell where they were going," Bittan says. "I could sense they needed to be more of a rock 'n' roll band." Called in to audition, Bittan sat quietly while Bruce played the chords to "She's the One," and when invited to play whatever he felt, the pianist responded immediately. "I heard the Bo Diddley beat and reacted to it, just came up with a part, thinking, 'I don't know if this is gonna go over.'" But Bruce nodded, the rest of the band fell in, and off they went. "New York City Serenade" came next, minus the introduction, and then Fats Domino's "Let the Four Winds Blow." It seemed to go well, Bittan thought.

Weinberg, by contrast, had never seen or heard Bruce play. But he'd heard good things about him, and then the "No Jr. Ginger Baker's" line caught his eye. He can't say why, exactly, since he already had a full-time gig in the musical *Godspell* and took classes at Seton Hall University during the day. "And I already knew that bands always break your heart," Weinberg says. And yet he called for an audition. Curious enough to go but ambivalent enough to not make a fuss about it, Weinberg showed up at SIR, the gear rental and rehearsal space in midtown Manhattan, with nothing more than a snare drum, a hi-hat, and a kick drum. Given that the drummer right before him had come equipped with a miniature skyline of shimmering cymbals and sparkly tom-toms, Weinberg's three-piece set made, as he puts it, "quite the minimalist statement." They played for three hours, working through rock rhythms, shuffles from Chicago and New Orleans, and more.

But the real litmus test came when Bruce abruptly turned around and waved his arms. No warning, no explanation, but Weinberg still did exactly the right thing and stopped on a dime. Bruce smiled and relaunched the tune. Then waiting another half hour, in midsong and without even a backward glance, throwing his right hand into the air. This proved pivotal. "You were the only guy who hit the rim shot," Bruce told Max many years later. "That's when I knew I'd found my drummer."

With Bittan on board too, the new conglomeration rehearsed for ten days, and then warmed up with a pair of unannounced (and yet quickly sold out) sets at the Main Point club in Bryn Mawr. And then the E Street Band got back on the road.

Bittan and Weinberg blended well into the ensemble, both contributing new musical possibilities and easygoing personalities that softened a lot of the tension that had built among the others over the years, shows, and miles. "There was a lot of adjustment, because we were family, and suddenly they were a part of it," Clemons told me. "But we got used to them pretty quick because they were so good. And then it was like the band grew up overnight."

But when the road led back home, the twenty-four-year-old Bruce felt anything but grown up. By early 1974, his relationship with Diane Lozito had fractured into a montage of arguments, fights, breakups, and fraught reunions and would inevitably lead back to the same conflicts that had broken them up before. Lozito was impetuous and pugnacious, Bruce was controlling and stubborn. Lozito liked her share of public attention, but Bruce required all of it for himself. What they shared was a fierce passion that drove them mad in the worst possible ways, especially when the relationship began to shatter. When Lozito tried to leave, Bruce chased her down and brought her home, even when she begged him to leave her alone. When she moved secretly to Nantucket, thereby avoiding his informal network of spies (fans on the Jersey Shore can be so helpful), he stewed alone until he spied Lozito's friend Debbie Schwartz one day in Central Park. The fact that she was standing on the side of a stage upon which he was currently performing for several thousand concertgoers (at the Schaefer Festival show back in July), did nothing to contain his bitter curiosity.

"He walked right up to me and said, 'Where's Diane?'" Schwartz (now Debbie Colligan) says. "You're in the middle of a show!" she shouted back. Bruce didn't care. In fact, he needed to know *right now.* Feeling pressed, Colligan admitted that Lozito had been with her in

Nantucket but had just moved to Boston. "I could only live with her for two weeks!" Colligan shouted. "She's crazy!" Edging back to center stage, Bruce nodded and shouted back, *"I know!"*

"What was really ironic," she says, "is that they were playing 'Spirit in the Night,' which he had written about her."

Now the love songs he wrote were more haunted than spirited. A no-longer-quite-so-young lover's tales of romance, obsession, and promises broken by time, circumstance, and worse. The early, longer version of "She's the One"—much of its lyrics later repurposed for "Backstreets"—begins in erotic fixation (the woman with the killer graces and secret places), and then spins through memories of broken myths, lost challenges, abandonments, and a love "just like the sun." The lyrics are scattershot, overstuffed with clashing images, situations, and narrative threads. But "She's the One" was a work in progress. And just like the barely started album for which it was intended, it would be done, Bruce insisted, when it was done.

TWELVE

THEN AGAIN,
LET'S JUST LET IT RIDE

WHEN THEY HAD A FINISHED mix of the "Born to Run" single in the early summer of 1974, Mike Appel invited Columbia president Bruce Lundvall to the studio. Lundvall sat quietly as the tape rolled. When the final notes faded, he looked over at Bruce. "You just made a hit record," he said. To Lundvall's surprise, Bruce shrugged it off. "He didn't believe me," the executive says. "But I told him it was a smash and sent him back to make the rest of the album."

You might think that sweeping praise from the top executive in his record company would have eased the make-or-break burden that Bruce lugged with him. You would be wrong. Because whenever he listened to the first two albums, all Bruce could hear were the things he wished he'd done differently. The overstuffed lyrics, the stilted sound, the distance between what he needed to say and what came out of the speakers. "He wanted to write as directly as the great songwriters did," Appel says. "We kept talking about it: balance, balance, balance."

Which sounded a lot easier than it turned out to be for Bruce, who spent hours laboring over every syllable in his notebook, along with every note that came from every instrument and every nuance of every sonic texture. Everything, he decreed, had to serve a distinct purpose. "He kept coming back with different sets of lyrics," Appel says. "Something like five versions of 'Born to Run' alone. 'How's this one, Mike? What do you think of these ones now?' Finally, I told him to go and pick out his favorites himself—I was done."

Bruce was just getting started. Still convinced that this might be his last shot at making a record, he couldn't allow for any compromises. This record had to say it all. Nothing could ever be more important. Partly because the songs he wrote were drawn from his deepest, most primal experiences. But also because Bruce's travels and his deepening grasp of the political and cultural flailing of the era[1] had convinced him that his sense of spiritual abandonment resonated on levels far beyond his own experience.

"People were contemplating a country that was finite," Bruce recalled of the post-Nixon America of 1975. In a culture awash in irony and disbelief, he needed to create a work that reestablished rock 'n' roll as a cultural force with the power to inspire and even create change in your life, in your town, in the world around you. Which meant making an album that both carried the spirit of rock 'n' roll tradition and stood as a vital testament to its own times. Would it be the greatest rock 'n' roll album ever made? Possibly not. But that didn't mean he shouldn't put everything he had into giving it a shot.

Appel, nothing if not a cheerful megalomaniac, was right there with him, no matter how excruciating the process. And Bruce seemed determined to make every step a pitched struggle against the limits of philosophical debate and physical endurance. "You think there's a right way, which is a fallacy," Bruce said to *Rolling Stone*'s Joe Levy three decades later. But, he continued, if you're young and screwed up enough, losing

---

[1] The criminality of the Nixon administration, the inglorious end of the Vietnam War, the gnawing economic and environmental crises, the Watergate scandal, and Nixon's humiliating resignation in 1974.

yourself in work can be far more appealing than being aware of, and directly confronting, your own dysfunction. "It was the only way I knew how to work," Bruce said. "It was fun, but it was exhausting. I think intentionally exhausting."

When Barry Rebo, the videographer who had been tracking Bruce's career since the Steel Mill days, drove up to Blauvelt to shoot some recording sessions in January 1975, he found Bruce, Appel, and the band looking as sad and translucent as ghosts. A year since they started work on the "Born to Run" single and first attempted a skeletal version of "Jungleland," they had a total of one song finished. Bruce had composed a handful of new songs, including "She's the One" and "Wings for Wheels," [2] both of which they had added to the band's live set. [3] With trained professionals Roy Bittan and Max Weinberg on board, Rebo expected the recording to flow more smoothly than before. Instead the overnight session became an endless series of false starts, faltering equipment, off-kilter takes, and increasingly dispirited attempts to rally for another try.

Even the ten o'clock dinner in the control room, full of stories, jokes, and bouncing balloons, crackled with tension. Anyone glancing up to the studio window could spy a piano tuner working frantically to adjust the studio's perpetually out-of-key piano. When the tuner warned Appel that the instrument had structural problems and would never hold a tuning for more than thirty minutes or so, Appel nodded but shook off the man's $10-an-hour offer to be present and ready to work all night. They simply did not have the cash to pay for it.

Back in the studio at eleven, Bruce, the band, and their production team knuckled down for another run at "Jungleland." With Bruce clad in a T-shirt and bomber jacket in the vocal booth, he counted off the song and then closed his eyes to sing the first verse. They got only halfway into the second verse before Appel called a halt through the control room intercom, explaining that the instruments had fallen out of sync in one

[2] An early title for "Thunder Road," with sloppier lyrics and a "Rosalita"-like dance party ending.
[3] Both of which featured verses and digressions that would eventually be repurposed into entirely different songs, such as the middle section of the early "She's the One," which led to "Backstreets."

verse. A moment later they began again, tripped, and then started again. When they got through an entire take, Appel punched the button on his microphone. "All right, that was a great take as far as we're concerned!" he crowed. "What do you wanna do, Bruce?" Springsteen shrugged. "Do another one," he said. "Do it this time with—"

Appel, back on his microphone, didn't seem to hear. "What a great take. Isn't it great to have one under the belt?"

Another try. Bruce in his booth, eyes shut, dancing and swinging his arms as he sang, swept up in the music. Then the *skronk* of the control room intercom button. "Bad take!" engineer Louis Lahav barked. "Why?" Appel asked. "Rushed." Bruce sighed, and they started again, getting all the way through to the end. Everyone agreed that one came out near perfectly—except for Bruce, whose forehead puckered as he contemplated a four-beat piano transition from the first section into the sax solo in the middle. "You think them chords are making it in the middle?" he asked. As Appel contemplated the need to revise the design of the song yet again, Bruce led the band in a sloppy but cheerful attempt at Cole Porter's "Anything Goes."

More tries at "Jungleland," more breakdowns. Between takes, Bittan sat at the piano looking confused, searching for new chord inversions that might sound better in the song. But why did these ones suddenly sound so wrong? In the control room, a gloomy Appel muttered the obvious: "It's out of tune again. Should we tell Bruce?" Still in the isolation of his vocal booth, Bruce opened his eyes and saw Rebo's camera just on the other side of the glass. "Barry, uh," he said in a friendly but firm voice, "you can't be doing this when I'm doing this." Then he called for another take.

"That was murder," says Jon Landau, whom Bruce had invited to come in and see what they were up to. "I was there for some of that, it was just murder. Terrible." Already familiar with the ways and means of modern recording studios, Landau felt scandalized. Every professional facility he'd worked in or visited had its own piano tuners, electricians, and audio experts poised for action whenever sessions were going on. If something broke midsession, the trained techs could either fix it in moments or get one of the replacements the management had stockpiled in storage.

"What I saw in these sessions is that he could not get any momentum going because of these interruptions," Landau says. Speaking to Roy Bittan, also no stranger to recording sessions, he discovered they shared the same frustrations. "I remember [Bittan] saying, 'What the fuck are we *doing* in this place?'"

The scene played like a joke about a perfectionist being driven mad. Only none of it seemed remotely funny. Except, at some distance, to Bruce's pal, ex-bandmate, and then manager-producer of Southside Johnny and the Asbury Jukes. "Anytime it takes six months to make a single, something's obviously going wrong," Steve Van Zandt said thirty years later. "Who can tolerate that? How anyone had the patience for it is beyond me. You should be able to knock that out in about three hours."

Something needed to change. And so Bruce picked up the telephone and made another call to the man whose words had already changed his career for the better. Bruce had seen his new album's future, and its name was Jon Landau.

A month after his *cri de coeur* ran in the *Real Paper*, Landau had surgery to help remedy his Crohn's disease, a degenerative intestinal condition. After a long recovery that included an extended stay in the hospital and months of bed rest, Landau emerged at the end of the summer feeling better than he had in years, even though his marriage to the film critic Janet Maslin had recently ended. He relocated to New York City in late autumn and received an invitation from Bruce to spend an evening in Long Branch. But when a blizzard choked off the highways that morning, Landau called to suggest they try again another day. "But I sensed as we were talking that he really wanted to get together that day," Landau says. Bundling up, he took a train from Pennsylvania Station, weathering delays and snail-like progress to arrive in Long Branch five hours later. At Bruce's place that evening, the host spread his album collection across the floor, and the two music obsessives started spinning their favorites, digging into the songs on every conceivable level: the architecture of the music, the narrative structure of the lyrics, the singer's tone and feeling, the interplay of drummer and bassist, and on and on. When they got hungry after midnight, they drove down to the open-all-night Inkwell in Long Branch for dinner. Back at Bruce's an hour later they kept going until dawn and then went back to the Inkwell for breakfast. At nine in the morning, Landau caught a bus back to the city.

"He was just an interesting person, and I was curious," Bruce says. "I'd missed out on the world of ideas that comes with a real college education, but I was really drawn to people who knew how to use words or knew how to express their ideas. I thought, 'There's a connection there with what I'm doing.' The life of the mind is just as important as the life of the body." For Landau, the experience had just as much personal significance. "That stays in my mind as a bonding moment that took things to another level for me. I think for him too," Landau says. "I think making that choice to go down there in the snowstorm was a significant statement to myself and to him. And this was at the time when things began to coalesce with *Born to Run*."

On the surface, they could not have been more different. Landau, raised in an intellectual family that moved from Queens to Lexington, Massachusetts, when he was a junior high student, usually glided a step or two beneath his school's top students but still acquitted himself well enough to land in Brandeis University, where he majored in history while also pursuing avid interests in philosophy and American cultural history. But Landau's real passion kept him focused on music. Turned on to Pete Seeger and the Weavers as a five-year-old (one of the benefits of being raised by leftist intellectuals), Landau started guitar lessons in second grade, working through his Mel Bay instruction books right up until the dawn of rock 'n' roll in the mid-1950s. "It was that bang, bang, bang of 'That'll Be the Day,' 'Johnny B. Goode,' 'Good Golly, Miss Molly,' the whole series of records," he says. "'Rock and Roll Shoes,' 'Sweet Little Sixteen.' God, did I love *that* record. I just dove into the whole thing. I loved them all." At eleven, Landau took solo subway trips from Queens to Brooklyn in order to see Alan Freed's rock spectacular at the Paramount Theater on Saturday afternoons. He listened to the Top 40 on New York's WMGM-AM every night, tracking the list's fluctuations with a yellow pad and a pencil. "'Sweet Little Sixteen,' I remember, got up to number two, and some song like 'The Purple People Eater' kept it out of number one," he says, shaking his head at the injustice of it all.

Landau fell hard for the rhythm and blues artists of the mid-1960s (Aretha Franklin, Otis Redding, Sam and Dave, among many others), and pored over their records too. He played guitar in a high school band, and when he got to Brandeis, Landau joined his friend Tom O'Connell, a student at Tufts University, in a Simon and Garfunkel–esque duo they called Jelly Roll. The two worked up their own songs, which they performed to some measure of local acclaim. Offered a small recording contract and an opportunity to travel to Nashville to make demos with professional musicians, Landau chose instead to abandon his career as a performer. "I was afraid," he says. "I'm not sure if I fully realized it or not, but I did not want to be out front. I wasn't built for that."

At the same time, Landau started writing record reviews for Paul Williams's *Crawdaddy* magazine, then in its earliest iteration as a photocopied journal featuring serious critical writing about rock, rhythm and blues, and other forms of pop music.[4] *Crawdaddy* developed a small national following, and a year or so later another aspiring young publisher from California named Jann Wenner sent Landau a dummy copy of the music-and-youth-culture magazine he planned to launch in the fall of 1967. Impressed by the prototype for *Rolling Stone*, Landau signed on as a critic and columnist, and his reputation and influence rose along with the magazine's. When Jerry Wexler, the great A&R man and producer at Atlantic Records, called to pay his respects, Landau took the opportunity to meet the man and learn as much as he could about the inner workings of the music industry and the intricacies of record production. Asked by another industry friend, Elektra Records publicist Danny Fields, to write a critical analysis of the MC5, a politically radical protopunk band the label had just signed, Landau produced a detailed twenty-page report. When the label dropped the MC5 six months later,[5] Landau recommended the

---

[4] Williams, also a student, was almost certainly the first American writer-editor-publisher to even attempt such a thing.

[5] Not for lack of sales of the band's debut album, *Kick Out the Jams,* but because its title song, and the album version of its cleaned-up lead single, included the prominent use of the word *motherfucker*, which at the time made them too hot to handle.

band to Wexler, who said he'd bring the group to Atlantic but only if Landau promised to produce its next album.

Landau took the job, and the partnership worked surprisingly well. "He'd done his homework and knew everything about records, which earned him a lot of points with me," says MC5 guitarist Wayne Kramer. Landau helped the chaotic band clarify its musical vision, advised Kramer on how to organize its business structure (which until that point had been run through manager John Sinclair's commune), and improve intraband communications. "Jon got us talking honestly, like in a therapy situation," Kramer says. "We'd have these meetings where he'd be saying, like, 'Well, Wayne, how do you feel about this?' 'And Fred [Smith, the quintet's other guitarist], how do you feel about what Wayne just said?' It raised us to a new level of consciousness."

The resulting album, 1970's *Back in the USA*, got ripped by critics and fans for sounding way more restrained than any band of fire-breathing revolutionaries ever should, but the months Landau spent working with them struck Kramer, at least, as one of the MC5's most happy and productive periods. "I pressed him hard to be our manager," the guitarist says. "But he was adamant that he didn't want to be a manager, he just wanted to produce records." Landau did go on to produce albums for Livingston Taylor, James's younger brother, and a talented songwriter on his own account, and to attempt one with the J. Geils Band, a Boston blues-rock band he brought to Wexler and Atlantic Records. But the J. Geils album didn't get off the ground,[6] and when Landau's digestive system grew increasingly knotted with Chrone's disease, he rededicated himself to the quieter life of writing criticism. Widely acknowledged as one of the nation's best practitioners of the still-young practice of serious rock criticism, Landau told friends that he'd like to be known as the King of the Rock Critics. He was kind of joking. But also kind of not.

Landau's first contribution to *Born to Run* had been on his mind for more than a year: get the hell out of 914 Sound Studios. "*Do* something about this!" Landau beseeched his friend. "You're a world-class artist,

---

[6] Though they would soon become an acclaimed and then top-selling band.

you deserve a world-class studio!" Finally convinced, Bruce went to Appel and told him to find a new studio. When the recording sessions picked up again in March, the operation moved to the Record Plant in midtown Manhattan. And although Appel still wasn't convinced they needed another expert in the studio, Bruce's word still reigned, and Appel slid over to make room for the album's third coproducer: Jon Landau.

"Jon loved Bruce," Appel says. "He wanted any part he could play. There would have to be room for both of us." Landau agreed. "Mike was pretty practical, and he saw what Bruce wanted, and he did his best to adjust," he says. The resulting tension appealed to Bruce, who had learned the benefit of being the pivot point between two opposing forces as a boy living with two sets of parents at his grandparents' house. So while Landau and Appel struggled for his ear, Bruce could take rich advantage of his partners' strengths, turning to Landau for structural and narrative advice, while relying on Appel's mastery of detail to make certain every note sounded exactly right. "We got along," Landau says of Appel. "I was in the lead on a great amount of the stuff, but Mike's endurance is tremendous. When you got into the real fine detail that I might lose patience with, Mike was a slogger." It also helped that they were all too focused on the album to fuss over personality and turf conflicts. "There was nothing duplicitous about Jon," Appel says. "We just never really got to know each other."

As Appel told biographer Marc Eliot in 1989, "the most important thing [Landau] did was to kick-start the album and get Bruce off his butt." Indeed, Landau's fresh ears helped Bruce locate some obvious cuts and fixes. "Jungleland," for instance, lost a melodramatic Spanish-style intro with drums, maracas, and passionate violin runs, in favor of an elegant prelude that featured violinist Suki Lahav's[7] skills to much better effect. Landau also helped streamline the arrangement of "Thunder Road." But for all the clarity he brought, Landau also encouraged Bruce's tendency to overthink every note, strum, and organ stop. As Landau

[7] Louis Lahav's wife, who had been playing shows with the band since the fall of 1974, most strikingly on a lovely piano-violin-voice arrangement of "Incident on 57th Street."

admitted later, it often took Appel's late-night wails—"Guys! We're makin' a *rekkid* heah!"—to get them back into gear.

Appel also recalls fighting to convince Bruce and Landau to back down in their struggle to include "Linda Let Me Be the One" and "Lonely Night in the Park" on the finished album. "I said, 'You really think those shitty songs can stand next to 'Backstreets' and 'Thunder Road'? That's what you think? Fuck that!'" Appel proved just as stubborn, and correct, when he fought to keep "The Heist," subsequently renamed "Meeting Across the River," on the finished album. Musically, the song's piano, standup bass, and muted trumpet seem closer to the romantic street poetry on "New York City Serenade" and "Incident on 57th Street" than to the chrome-detailed rock 'n' roll they were crafting for the new record. But this time the music and lyrics had been honed to the barest essentials, all crafted to underscore one man's last, desperate shot at redemption.

They had so many other details to tangle with, so many hours, days, weeks, and months to adjust the precise tone of this guitar solo, or the fingertip glissando in that piano intro, or the best way to mix the multitrack recordings down into the shimmering but emotionally powerful sound Bruce needed to hear. He began to think of the album as a musical novel, the individual songs fitting into a larger, unified story. And like a novel, the chapters—or songs, in this case—had to dovetail, contrast, and ultimately enhance one another. So while "Thunder Road" might sound perfect in its full-band arrangement, it might better suit the album in a completely different context, with a completely different sound and message. At one point, Bruce tore the fully-wrought song down to its foundation, rebuilding it as a brooding acoustic guitar piece with a completely new melody, stripped-down chord changes, some different words, and the climactic "I'm pullin' out of here to win" exhaled like a sigh of defeat.

The process felt slow, grim, and tortuous. When Tallent's wife visited a session one evening, she wound up spending eight hours watching Bruce try to coach the band through an eight-bar instrumental passage in one song. "When she left, she said, 'Don't *ever* take me to a recording session again!'" Tallent remembers. The guys in the band, of course, had no options. "All we could do was hold on. Smoke a lot of pot and try to stay calm," said Clemons, who spent sixteen hours playing and replaying every note of his "Jungleland" solo in order to satisfy Bruce's bat-eared attention to sonic detail.

When the sessions finally ended, Bruce described the era as an endless loop of unplayable parts, unfixable mistakes, and unmixable recordings. The experience, he told the *New York Times'* John Rockwell in late 1975, was "like a total wipeout. It was a devastating thing, the hardest thing I ever did." The fact that Bruce actively resisted help from more experienced hands, particularly when it came to mixing final versions of the songs, only made it more difficult. For all that he required absolute control over every aspect of the album, holding that much authority also multiplied his psychic burden. The closer he clutched the thing to his chest, the less of it he could see, or comprehend.

Steve Van Zandt dropped in one day to see how things were going, and found Bruce, Landau, and Appel trying to coach a handful of high-dollar session horn players[8] through their parts on "Tenth Avenue Freeze-Out," an old-school R&B romp that celebrated Bruce's spiritual connection to the band. As always, the process dragged on for hours. Increasingly frustrated and burned out, Bruce approached his old friend, then lying on his back on the control room floor. "Whaddaya think?" he asked. Van Zandt looked up from the carpet. "Me? I think it sucks." Bruce recoiled and then issued a sharp snort. "Well, then *fix it!*" he snapped and plopped down hard into a chair.

"It sounds like a myth, but that's one story that's actually true," Van Zandt says now. So as his dispirited friend watched from the control room, Van Zandt climbed to his feet, pushed through the studio door, and walked to the center of the studio floor. "Okay, boys!" he called. "You can toss those charts away now." Working on his feet, Van Zandt pointed to each horn player in turn and sang him his new part. After a quick horns-only run-through, Van Zandt gestured to the engineer to roll tape. And when the track played again, it knit perfectly with the bouncy

---

[8] Including brothers Michael and Randy Brecker (trumpet and saxophone, respectively), sax player Dave Sanborn, and trombonist Wayne Andre.

Stax-style groove they'd been chasing all evening. At which point Bruce turned to Appel. "Let's get this boy on the payroll," he said. Van Zandt accepted his old friend's offer, but, he says, mostly because he didn't think he was making that much of a commitment.

"As far as I knew, Bruce's thing was over," he says. "They had seven gigs booked, and that was it. So the offer I got was really, 'Hey, come out and play these last seven shows with us.'" Which felt exactly right, since Van Zandt's central project—managing, producing, and writing for the Asbury Jukes—was starting to pay dividends now that they had become the most popular bar band on the East Coast. Even so, and no matter what had happened between them in the last few years, Van Zandt still considered himself to be Bruce's true consigliere. When his buddy beckoned, Steve would be there, no questions asked. "And then I ended up staying seven years."

Mixing the tracks—the process of filtering, enhancing, and then blending together the many individual performances that make up a multitrack recording—quickly bogged down into another tortuous process that dragged until the dawn of July 20, just hours before Bruce and company were due to launch their summer-fall tour in Providence, Rhode Island. Finally escaping the Record Plant struck the entire band as an enormous relief, but the emotional respite didn't last long.

Five days later Appel showed up at the band's hotel in Kutztown, Pennsylvania, with an acetate pressing of the master recording of *Born to Run*. With Bruce, his new girlfriend, Karen Darvin, and the entire band gathered to listen, Appel placed the disc on the inexpensive portable record player Bruce took on the road and let it spin. When the last notes of "Jungleland" faded out, the band whooped, applauded, and reached out to slap hands. Stephen Appel, still serving as road manager, noticed that his big brother's eyes glistened with tears. Relief seemed to blow in through the open window, except for Bruce, who sat with his face clenched, staring into the carpet. "I dunno," he said darkly. "I'd do things differently." Beard abristle, he jumped to his feet, snatched the acetate from the turntable, and stalked out to the hotel courtyard, where he flung it into the swimming pool.

What was wrong? How about *everything*. The sax parts sounded like a bad Bruce Springsteen imitation. (That's when Clemons stalked out of the room.) The piano drowned out the guitars. The mix had the clarity of a shit storm. All this time, all that work, and *this* was the best they could do? And in conclusion: *"Fuck!"* No longer quite so happy, the rest of the band drifted out of the room, bound either for their rooms or (more likely) the bar. Alone with the brothers Appel, Bruce swan dived into the gloom. Did he understand that an acetate never sounds as good as the finished album? Did he take a moment to consider that the portable stereo he'd just been listening to, with its plastic speakers, tin tonearm, and Easy-Bake Oven design, might not even be capable of reproducing the dense, intricate recordings they had made? Apparently not.

Bruce was too busy declaring the entire project a waste of time. A cruel satire of rock 'n' roll. Overheated dogshit. Appel dialed Landau, who had gone to California to check in with his colleagues at *Rolling Stone*, told him what had happened, and handed the phone to Bruce. Thus began, as Landau recalls, a "combative" conversation. "My point was . . . part of the job is finishing," Landau says. "I was saying, look, you can't and will not be able to put every thought, every idea, and every creative impulse onto one record." From this point forward, Landau insisted, Bruce should take all of his new ideas and put them in his notebook for the *next* record. "There *is* going to be a next record, believe me," he swore.

Bruce remained unconvinced. He hung up the phone and looked over at Appel, now reclining in a chair and shaking his head. "Fuck it," Appel said. "Let's scrap the whole thing. I mean, obviously. Just *fuck* it." He kept going, talking about how he'd break the news to Columbia's Bruce Lundvall the next morning. Sure, he'd be pissed. But that's showbiz, right? And maybe, Appel continued, they could let the label release the "Born to Run" single as a stopgap, and then rerecord the songs live in the studio without any overdubs or Phil Spectorian witchcraft? That'd work. Or better yet, they could record some shows and use the live performances of the new songs as album tracks. Anything was possible, right?

"I was being crazier than him, see?" Appel says. "Now *he* had to be the voice of reason." Bruce, Karen Darvin, and the two Appels all piled into Mike's car and headed for the turnpike back to the city. They were maybe halfway home when Bruce started to laugh. Quietly at first, then uproariously. "He thought it was hilarious that Mike was so crazy," Stephen Appel says. "Suddenly he was in a great place. Both Mike and Jon had said exactly the right things to him. I never saw Bruce happier than on that car ride." By the time they got back to New York, Bruce shrugged off the last six torturous hours with a wave of the hand. "Then again," he said, "let's just let it ride."

Born to Run would be released in exactly a month.

The band swung through a few of its more reliable cities in early August, girding for a five-night, ten-show stand at the Bottom Line in the West Village. The shows sold out instantly—not a major feat given the club's four-hundred-seat capacity—but once again, the crucial factor had less to do with the paying fans than with the CBS-comped tastemakers, critics, and industry *machers* who would decide exactly how the much-anticipated album by the so-called future of rock 'n' roll would be received. "The whole world came to those shows," Van Zandt says. "And not in a supportive way, either. It was more like, 'Okay, *show* me something!'"

So Bruce did, with eight compact but intense ninety-minute performances that mixed selections from his first two albums with songs from the new record and sixties covers (the Beach Boys' arrangement of "Then I Kissed Her," the Searchers' "When You Walk in the Room," and Ike and Tina Turner's "It's Gonna Work Out Fine") that shed light on Bruce's connection to rock's foundations. And while the band played with its usual fire and discipline, Bruce performed like a man possessed. He waved his arms, broke into a strange herky-jerky dance (imagine a marionette with fifty thousand watts of AC running through its strings), and then leapt off the stage to dash across the lines of tables as enthralled clubgoers tried to slap his hand and grab their drinks at the same time. Back onstage he flirted with the girls in the front, shouted out to his relatives sitting in the back, and told elaborate shaggy-dog stories about his childhood and his days with the Castiles and Steel Mill.

Celebrities came in flocks, including actor Robert De Niro, who took special note of Bruce's pre-encore "Are you talkin' to *me?*" routine (which the actor later transmuted into a creepy highlight of his performance as a psychotic in 1976's *Taxi Driver*), along with director Martin Scorsese, who came away eager to cast the rocker in one of his movies. When Clive Davis showed up with Lou Reed in tow, the former Columbia president[9] could barely believe how far the shy folkie he'd met in 1972 had come. "I was stunned, actually," he says. "He was the best live performer I'd ever seen in my life." When Davis came backstage to say hello afterward, Bruce wrapped him in a hug and whispered slyly into his ear, "Am I moving around enough for ya now?"

The publicists at Columbia/CBS were making plenty of moves of their own. Directed by label president Bruce Lundvall to spend $250,000 to get the word out as far, wide, and as inescapably as possible, Glen Brunman designed the *Born to Run* sales campaign like a D-day invasion, with multiple forces poised to attack in calibrated waves. Starting with posters and stand-up displays for retail stores, they rode the reviews and features stirred up by the star-packed run of shows at the Bottom Line, all setting the stage for the scores of ads placed in newspapers to herald the album's release at the end of August. An endless barrage of Bruce this and Bruce that, all of it illustrated by striking portraits of the bearded, curly-haired artist looking like a poet biker in his black leather and jeans, an Elvis Presley button on his chest (or sleeve, depending on the shot), clutching his now weathered Fender and a pair of Converse sneakers hanging from the guitar's tuning pegs. And right there you could see the whole album in front of you: the essence of fifties rock 'n' roll and the beatnik poetry of sixties folk-rock, projected onto the battered spirit of mid-seventies America.

And if that didn't seem iconic enough, take a long look at the album itself: the black-and-white shot of Bruce—cloaked in black leather, guitar in hand, Elvis button on his strap—leaning hard on the mighty shoulder of Clemons, whose white shirt is set off by a broad-brimmed black hat and, of course, his radiant black skin. For in this picture, Bruce knew, resided the heart of the band: unity, brotherhood, a small fulfillment of

[9] Already installed as president of Arista Records.

the American ideals of strength, equality, and community. The essence of e pluribus unum, as filtered through the unity of rock 'n' roll and rhythm and blues. "A friendship and a narrative steeped in the complicated history of America begin to form, and there is music already in the air," Bruce wrote thirty-five years later, describing the picture in the foreword to Clemons's whimsical memoir, *Big Man*. "The album begins to work its magic."

As image creation goes, it worked on every level. The visual union of Elvis, Dylan, and Marlon Brando, with a touch of Stagger Lee looming over his shoulder for bad-ass measure. And if that bit off a big chunk of cultural iconography, the songs themselves dug even deeper with their visions of young love, small towns, rumbling highways, and the wicked fast streets of the city. And thrumming beneath the entire tableau, the spark of hope, and the promise—shaky, but still—that an American road can take you anywhere you had the imagination, courage, and luck to find. But in the midst of the Gerald Ford administration, after a dozen-plus years defined by assassinations, war, political corruption, and the collapse of the flower child/hippie/Woodstock culture, the sound of such belief—particularly from a veteran of the same cultural conflicts—was stunning.

But there it is, right from the rusty music-box opening of "Thunder Road," as Bruce's voice, sounding younger and clearer than on his earlier records, greets a girl as she steps into a twilight breeze. He's a social reject, and she's an outsider, both left to pray for chances that never come. So the singer holds out the only thing he has left to offer: the engine in his car and the highway leading out of town. "Hey, the night's bustin' open / These two lanes will take us anywhere!" The band detonates, but Bruce, singing in a strikingly rich and powerful croon, crowns everything. "That must have come straight out of [the Orbison] records," Bruce says of his new vocal technique. "That big, round operatic tone. I just loved the sound of [Orbison's] voice, and I gave it a shot. Just said, 'Well, here I go.' And I didn't get there. But I got someplace." Indeed, the stereo speakers boil over with romantic urgency. Even when the lyrics glow purple (the killer in the sun, the talking guitar, the screaming ghosts), the belief in Bruce's voice keeps it riveting. Bruised, burned, and somehow unbowed, he's taking the American ideal at its word, betting it all on the open road and his own stubborn will. "It's a town full of losers, I'm pulling outta here to win!" On a hero's journey that flows as much from *The Iliad* as it does from *The Wild One*.

Every song plays for the heart; every piano intro, organ line, drum fill, and bent guitar note is meant to revive a memory, trace a scar, point to the future. The light-footed "Tenth Avenue Freeze-Out" serves as the E Street Band's creation myth and a meditation on the transformative power of friendship. The squealing guitars in "Night" paints the Ocean Avenue–Kingsley Street circuit as a last-ditch arena for working-class glory, while the alternately brooding and explosive "Backstreets" casts its broken teen romance against a dying, spiritless city. Flip the album, and a blast of drums erupts into the bombast of the album's title track. Faster, harder, and more deliriously phrased than the companion piece at the start of the first side, "Born to Run" plays like a meld of Dylan's "Like a Rolling Stone" and the Beach Boys' "Good Vibrations." As in the former, the imagist lyrics of "Born to Run" (the cages, the suicide machines, the velvet rims, the hemipowered drones) define a strikingly new vocabulary. And like the latter, the layered music is powerful enough to make lyrics all but unnecessary. Woven together, it all comes at hurricane force, blowing houses apart, ripping trees from the earth, hurling cows into the next county.

"She's the One" cuts back to musical basics, stringing its tale of obsessive love to a Bo Diddley beat played with the subtlety of an approaching tank. But such is the pain of lust; such are the pleasures of a powerfully fucked-up romance. The corner-bar jazz of "Meeting Across the River" casts its doomed hero in a 1950s *cinema noir*, only to send him into shadowy streets already buzzing with the action described in the album's climactic piece, the 9:23 epic "Jungleland."

Here a violin prelude gives way to piano and Bruce's elegiac tale of the renegade Magic Rat, who joins forces with a barefoot girl only to be chased off by the "maximum lawmen," antagonists to the city's street gangs, rock bands, empty-hearted lovers, and every other character tramping the streets. And on this night, they're dressing like visionaries, waving guitars "just like switchblades" and then wielding their knives with balletic grace. The Magic Rat and the barefoot girl slip off together, and their connection stops the city in its tracks. A lone saxophone blares across the night, and when the ineffably sad melody concludes, everything has changed. Singing in a somber monotone, Bruce recounts the death of the Magic Rat, gunned down not by the cops or a rival but by his own tender heart. Just that quickly, the streets burn, battles rage, dreams vaporize. When the smoke clears, the devastation is so complete that even the poets have been struck dumb. "*They just stand back and let it all be.*"

As the critics would say, *Born to Run* lived up to every promise ever made about Bruce Springsteen. From the breezy opening moments of "Thunder Road" through the blood-borne passion of "She's the One" and "Night," the restless ambition fueling the title track, and the tragedies in "Backstreets" and "Jungleland," the album stood as a summary of the previous twenty years of rock 'n' roll, a portrait of the moment, and the cornerstone of a career that would reflect and shape the culture for the next twenty years, and the twenty to follow. Like the Beatles' American debut, *Meet the Beatles*, Bob Dylan's *Blonde on Blonde*, Elvis Presley's first album, and Nirvana's *Nevermind*, *Born to Run* established a sound and identity powerful enough to permanently alter the perceptions of those who heard it, whether they liked what they heard or not. "It was the album where I left behind my adolescent definitions of love and freedom," Bruce wrote. "*Born to Run* was the dividing line." Nearly four decades later, it still is.

THIRTEEN

A CLASSIC CASE OF BE CAREFUL WHAT YOU WISH FOR

THE CRITICAL APPRAISALS GREETING *BORN TO RUN* read like news accounts of the second coming. "The purest glimpse of the passion and power of rock 'n' roll in nearly a decade," sang the *Los Angeles Times*' Robert Hilburn. Which sounded pretty good until you read the thoughts of the *New York Times*' chief music critic, John Rockwell: "Mr. Springsteen's gifts are so powerful and so diverse that it's difficult even to try to describe them in a short space . . . you owe it to yourself to buy this record." Pick up *Rolling Stone*, and there came Greil Marcus, one rock critic who could score a few points against Landau in an intellectual knife fight, declaring *Born to Run* "a magnificent album that pays off on every bet ever placed on [Springsteen]." At *Creem* the review came from the nicotine-yellow fingers of Lester Bangs, the gonzo critic whose acidic pen could reduce overblown music and musicians into a foul-smelling puddle. But while Bangs acknowledged the whiff of Barnum in Columbia's publicity campaign ("one of the biggest hypes in recent memory"), his enthusiasm for the music itself overwhelmed everything else. "Bruce Springsteen is an American archetype, and *Born to Run* will probably be the finest record released this year," Bangs wrote. And there was more: "In a time of squalor and belittled desire, Springsteen's music is majestic and passionate with no apologies . . . [and] we can soar with him, enjoying the heady rush of another gifted urchin cruising at the peak of his powers and feeling his oats as he gets it right, that chord, and the last word ever on a hoodlum's nirvana."

As the momentum behind *Born to Run* strengthened, so did the tidal conclusion that the album, like Bruce himself, was nothing short of heroic: God's gift to the culturally blighted 1970s. Which put the New Dylan business to shame and added that much more momentum to the skepticism of writers and critics who didn't have an ear for Bruce's music but did have an eye for the magical blend of hype and herd mentality. And what could anyone make of the many connections between the über-critic circuit and Springsteen's already incestuous inner circle? Any observant reader of rock magazines and other youth culture journals would recognize Landau's name from his many reviews and columns, and from his record review editor title at *Rolling Stone*. And while the reader might not guess that Marcus and Landau were longtime friends—and that the former had in fact recommended the latter for his editorship— she could undoubtedly entertain herself wondering if Marcus's personal and professional bonds to Landau (his titular editor at *Rolling Stone*) might have influenced his enthusiasm for *Born to Run*.

And, of course, Landau was also a close friend of the writer Dave Marsh, who had escorted Landau to his first Bruce show in the spring of 1974, introduced the two men, and then encouraged Landau to publish the "I Saw Rock and Roll Future" column at Boston's *Real Paper*. It would be more of a leap to suggest that Marsh, who came up through the Detroit-based offices of *Creem*, had somehow bedazzled Bangs into writing his rave review. But Marsh had also written a glowing profile of Bruce that *Creem* published the month before Bangs's review ran, which reintroduced the thought of insider groupthink. Either that, or the canniness on the part of a lightly educated New Jersey guitarist who had intuited that any artist who could fuse Bob Dylan's subterranean braininess with Elvis

Presley's sexual outrageousness would be the very image of the brainy rock critic's fondest imaginings. So maybe it wasn't difficult to understand what the *New York Times*' Henry Edwards meant when he proposed, just after the first wave of *Born to Run* reviews flooded the media, that "if Bruce Springsteen didn't already exist, the critics would have had to invent him."[1]

And there was more to come.

Months after issuing the edict that Bruce would give no print interviews that weren't guaranteed to be a part of a cover story (a bluff move that grew into a necessity when the wave of attention swelled to tidal proportions), Appel got a call from an editor at *Newsweek* saying that the magazine was ready to commit to putting Bruce on its cover. Both of the nation's leading newsweeklies had already devoted column inches to Bruce, starting with *Time* magazine's generous coverage of both *Greetings* and *The Wild, the Innocent*, while *Newsweek* ran a midsized, interview-free but largely upbeat[2] feature pegged to *Born to Run*'s release in late August. This time, however, *Newsweek* wanted to publish a deeply reported piece. "In those days having an entertainer on the cover was a hallowed bit of ground," says Maureen Orth, the *Newsweek* writer assigned to write and lead the reporting for the piece. "But [the editors] loved him, and when I saw him perform in Asbury Park I thought, 'Oh my God, he's a great, great performer.'"

Still, the buzz coming from sources who had spoken either with Orth or the staff reporters also working the story indicated that *Newsweek* planned to focus on Bruce less as a dynamic new artist but as the latest in a series of industrially created pop idols.

When *Time* magazine culture writer Jay Cocks got wind of the

[1] Arguably unfair and yet interesting aside: Edwards's next major project was writing the screenplay for the Bee Gees/Peter Frampton movie adaptation of *Sgt. Pepper's Lonely Hearts Club Band*, the most reviled rock 'n' roll–based movie ever. Completely unexpected punchline: Edwards was a friend of, and continues to be spoken of generously by, Dave Marsh. Go figure.

[2] Save for the suggestion that *Born to Run* would benefit from the sort of ironic detachment Bette Midler put into her act. Which is akin to criticizing Midler for not having Neil Young's jagged way with a guitar solo.

Newsweek story-in-progress, what he heard made him think that his competitors were out to trash their subject. A fan of Bruce's first two albums who heard *Born to Run* as a significant addition to the American rock 'n' roll catalog, Cocks took *Newsweek*'s plans with two kinds of umbrage: he hated letting the crosstown rivals run away with the Springsteen story, and he especially hated the snide package they were, by all indications, wrapping him in. "I thought it would have been a killing representation of an important American artist," Cocks says. "I thought *Time* magazine should make a countermove. And I'd always wanted to write about him. Plain and simple." Marching into the office of his editor, Martha Duffy, Cocks explained what *Newsweek* was up to and pitched his idea of taking them on head-to-head. Duffy got it all immediately and convinced the magazine's top editors to let them go after their own Springsteen cover story.

When Orth learned that her crosstown competitors were also on the case she went back to Appel and Bruce to argue that they were making a big mistake. "Bruce wasn't big enough to sustain both covers, given what they meant," she says. "I said, 'You're going to live to regret this.'"

For the editors of the magazines, the dueling stories became a game of chicken. While both recognized the absurdity of putting the same somewhat obscure pop star on their covers in the same week, neither could imagine backing down, particularly when gossip about the dueling stories swept across the media filled canyons of midtown Manhattan. "Pretty outlandish, eh?" Appel says, blue eyes sparkling with glee. But even as Bruce seemed on track to appear on both of America's leading newsweeklies, the never-ending avalanche of publicity, reviews, and coverage made him feel increasingly queasy. "I used to feel I was always in control," he grumbled to the UK *New Musical Express*'s Andrew Tyler. "Now I'm not so sure." Talking to Cocks, Bruce said he had no idea what the "commotion" could be about. "I feel like I'm on the outside of all this, even though I know I'm on the inside." When *Newsweek*'s Orth got her interview, Bruce called his new notoriety a nuisance. "*What* phenomenon?" he asked. "We're driving around, and we ain't no phenomenon. The hype just gets in the way." And if Bruce thought the *Born to Run* publicity had already grown to absurd proportions, he was kidding himself.

Dated October 27, but available a week earlier, the *Time* and *Newsweek* covers hit the country on the same day. Unsurprisingly, the double-barreled magazine coverage created its own moment in the media culture. Cocks's story in *Time*, titled "Rock's New Sensation," celebrated his subject's achievements while also sketching his past (in the terms that Bruce chose to reveal it) and the outlines of his daily life. Orth's piece (reported in part by Janet Huck and Peter S. Greenberg), led with a "Making of a Pop Star" headline on the magazine's cover, while the story itself veered between favorable accounts of Bruce's shows and music, and at times caustic analyses provided by *New York Times* critic Henry Edwards (whose anti-Springsteen essay served as the first critical take in the piece) and by Joe Smith, the president of Columbia's main competitor, Warner Bros. Records. Smith compared Bruce to Elton John and Warners's own James Taylor and found him wanting.

Speaking now, Orth says her only intent was to write an accurate portrayal. "I felt like I needed to report the story out," she says. "It's balanced, just not worshipful." If she was blowing the lid off of anything, Orth continues, it was the star-making machinery—from Columbia's publicity offices to Mike Appel—that she saw as manipulating and twisting a young musician whose work she really did believe in. "I was finding out stuff that made me think that this kid was getting batted around. An innocent kid who was shy and maybe not so sophisticated at that point. Who was thinking of Bruce?" Still, the *Newsweek* story ended by comparing Bruce to Coca-Cola as another heavily advertised product his customers called the Real Thing—Coke's central advertising slogan at the time. Cocks and *Time* focused on "Thunder Road"'s notion that there really was magic in the night, and for a lot of fans, no matter their reasons, Bruce was it.

If other people worried about what the stories said, Bruce was too busy fretting that their existence would mark the precise point where his music, reputation, and soul would be consumed by the spotlight. At first he kicked himself, furious that he'd let himself become just another celebrity. "He was worried fame was evil," Stephen Appel says. "He saw it ruin peoples' lives. People lost themselves in their own caricatures." So while Mike Appel savored his promotional triumph, and the E Street Band guys reveled in what all the attention could mean for their group's future, Bruce simmered in his hotel room in Los Angeles. "That was beyond anything anyone could have wished for," Steve Van Zandt says. "And he was *pissed!* But I was laughing. I thought it was fun." So did Garry Tallent, who first glimpsed the magazines while dashing through the Dallas airport to make a flight to the band's next show. But the bassist had another thought too: "It was a classic case of *be careful what you wish for*."

Bruce passed the magazines' publication day playing pinball with Columbia promotions man Ron Oberman in an American Legion bowling alley and then shooting pool at the home of former CBS executive Frank Shargo. Back in New York, some members of the publicity team at his record company were beginning to think their new star might not be wrong about the caustic risks of overexposure. "When we first had the record in our hands, I remember saying, "It's time to step up! We gotta break down walls!'" says label publicist Ron McCarrell. "So we got a little carried away." That realization came a few weeks after some of Bruce's most fervent supporters sensed the possibility of a backlash. A&R man Michael Pillot had tried to slow things down somewhere between the Bottom Line shows and the record's release, only to learn that publicity campaigns work like rocket ships. Once they launch there's no going back. "The answer was, 'Nope,'" Pillot recalls. "They said, 'You wanted it to move, right? Now it's moving.'"

So while Bruce stalked Los Angeles like Hamlet-in-reverse, fretting endlessly over the wisdom of actions he had already taken, another, less public part of himself confronted the fact that he had not surrendered to all the publicity as much as he'd actively fueled it. "I could not have been on those covers if I didn't want to," Bruce told the writer Bill Flanagan in 1992. "I didn't have to do those interviews. I remember sitting in a room saying, 'Gee, do I want to do this? It seems scary.' But I [didn't] want to be sitting on my porch when I'm sixty saying, '*Oh, I shoulda, I coulda, I woulda!*' Hey! You got one ride. So I said, 'Let's go!'"

The first thing the *Time* and *Newsweek* covers achieved was to force Bruce out of the bungalow he'd been renting in Long Branch since the spring of 1974. A tiny, foundationless structure tucked between the large family homes on the block, the once easily overlooked house was now a magnet for the new crowd of fans whose determination to find their quarry overwhelmed whatever respect they might have for an ordinary person's privacy. Flushed out of that house—so quickly, in fact, that he abandoned the spinet piano upon which he'd composed so much of *Born to Run*[3]—Bruce rented a more remote house on a wooded hill in Atlantic Highlands. Quite a bit less glamourous than what you'd imagine a rock star's house might be, but it did offer a nice view of Sandy Hook Bay, and an extra bedroom for newly hired road manager Rick Seguso to stay in when the band took a few nights or weeks off.

The record itself sold remarkably well, even accounting for the hype, eventually reaching number 3 on the *Billboard* album chart, en route to selling more than seven hundred thousand copies by the end of a year (a significant achievement in 1975), and far more than that as the months and years passed. And though the "Born to Run" single stalled at #29 on the singles chart, the song served as a hugely effective calling card to record store owners and radio programmers, and became a guaranteed crowd killer in concert.

Beyond that, the success of *Born to Run* did little to alter the day-to-day existences of anyone in or working for Bruce and the E Street Band. Yes, the touring vehicles evolved from cramped Ford club vans, to a surplus Red Bank city bus retrofitted with rickety metal-framed bunks, to an actual touring bus. But the entourage still slept in cheap hotels (when they didn't sleep on the moving bus), subsisted largely on truck stop food, and received no happy surprises in their weekly paychecks. "It's nice to have a hit record," Tallent says. "But we were thinking, 'It doesn't *feel* like we have a hit record. It still feels like we're destitute.'"

It also didn't feel like the entire nation had been swept up in Springsteen mania. For while CBS's publicity department had grown quite generous with its financial support for tour advertising, radio outreach,

[3] The interior lid of which had been signed by Bruce and every member of the E Street Band to mark the completion of *Born to Run*, according to house owner Marilyn Rocky. The piano stayed there for years until one departing tenant took it out to the street with the trash. It may or may not survive somewhere on the Jersey Shore.

and so on, Bruce remained a stranger in most of the American South, Midwest, and the West coast. In some corners of the nation, the promoters could pay little more than the $2,500 the band had commanded for shows in early 1974. But no matter where he played, or to how many people, his shows had grown even more explosive than before, due both to the excitement generated by the new album and Bruce's overwhelming fear that he'd wind up being a one-hit wonder.

Most nights he absorbed all of his fears and anxieties and transformed them into the rocket fuel he needed to catapult himself over the footlights and into the empty air above the crowd. Sometimes the pressure curdled his blood and left Bruce seething. Occasional defects in the sound system, particularly high-decibel blasts of feedback, inspired amp-kicking fits of outrage. Food could also become a serious point of contention, as in the New Orleans visit where road manager Rick Seguso shook up the menu at the postshow family-style dinners they all shared by replacing the usual order for fried chicken with chicken cordon bleu, one of the local caterer's specialties. Most of the gang cheered having something new on the menu. But when a feedback-frazzled Bruce sat down for his meal, he gazed dubiously at the sauce-drizzled, ham-and-cheese stuffed chicken breast on his plate, took a tiny bite, and then dropped his plastic utensils on his paper plate. "What's *this* shit?" he hissed. Seguso explained about the caterer, the culinary joys of New Orleans, and so on, but the musician glared back. "Well, *I* hate it!" At this, the road manager gestured around the table. "Nobody else is complaining." Bruce reached down, picked up his chicken, and hurled it at Seguso. "Then *you* eat it!" he roared, storming out of the room, down the hall, and, presumably, to the nearest Kentucky Fried Chicken outlet.

"I just said, 'Holy shit!'" Seguso remembers. "And everybody else was looking at me and going. '*Oooooohhhh!*'"

"I think Bruce was under a lot of pressure," Tallent says. "But he sure does have a hell of a right hand for a chicken cordon bleu."

The pressure became even more pronounced in mid-November when Bruce and the band—all making their first journeys outside North America—jetted to England for a weeklong microtour to prime the pump for the full European tour set tentatively for the first half of 1976. The first stop, at London's Hammersmith Odeon theater, would obviously be the most important show of the week. As Bruce's official London premiere, it would be his chance to break through to the city's cultural establishment: a prickly circle of critics and tastemakers who reserved their greatest scorn for Americans who buzzed into town thinking they had something to offer that the city of the Beatles, the Rolling Stones, and David Bowie somehow lacked. That Bruce and the E Street Band had such a distinctly American look and sound only added to the challenge. And when Bruce arrived at the venue, only to find the marquee aglow with a sign reading, "Finally, London Is Ready for Bruce Springsteen and the E Street Band," the publicity-singed musician flipped. The thick papering of "I Have Seen Rock and Roll Future . . ." signs and stickers on London walls upped his frustration all the more, and when he got to the theater and found the lobby and seats festooned with miniature "Finally, London Is Ready for . . ." signs, he erupted. Bruce ran from sign to sign, ripping them down, reducing them to shreds, and scattering the evidence like so much confetti.

The memory of the show traveled across the next three decades as a story about a disaster; the collision of a rattled artist with an aggressively unimpressed audience. It certainly didn't help that Bruce spent much of the show with a thick wool cap pulled down tight over his forehead and sometimes over his eyes. But as a much-subsequently released video and live album made clear, the first Hammersmith show wasn't anything close to a disaster. When the lights dimmed, Bruce stepped out to an excited ovation that became a rapt hush when he performed the voice, piano, and glockenspiel arrangement of "Thunder Road." From there, "Tenth Avenue Freeze-Out" electrified the room with its playful funk, while the unadorned piano intro for the less-known *Greetings* album track "Lost in the Flood" earned an excited burst of applause.

So maybe the crowd didn't have the electric charge of the ones Bruce had been facing in the United States. And yes, the quiet moments just before "The E Street Shuffle" invited one angry Cockney to cry out "*Oi! Turn the guitar up!*" Obviously, some observers enjoyed it more than others. Vivien Goldman, writing for the British paper *Sounds*, clocked the show as somewhere between "very, very good" and "so-so," concluding:

"the burden of being ordered to take London by storm proved too much for his slender shoulders." Somewhere else in the crowd, Monty Python's Flying Circus member Michael Palin agreed with a friend that "We came expecting the Messiah but got Billy Graham instead." Still, the shows in Stockholm and Amsterdam came off well, and the week-concluding return to the Hammersmith Odeon rocked harder and to greater acclaim than the opener a few days earlier. Still, Bruce and the band came home feeling beaten up.

"We had four shows, got sandblasted, and scooted home," Bruce says. But maybe he and everyone else had been too unsettled by their surroundings to see straight. "You're dealing with men who had never been anywhere," he says. "We couldn't find any cheeseburgers! Europe in 1975 was very European. So we ran back and didn't go back for six years. That wasn't by mistake."

Back in the USA, Bruce and the band celebrated the end of the Born to Run tour, and everything else they had achieved in 1975, with five nights of shows at the 3,119-capacity Tower Theater just outside Philadelphia. All of the performances sold out quickly, with the heaviest demand tilting toward the final show on New Year's Eve. With more than 90,000 requests flooding in for the 15,000 available tickets, an obvious question loomed: Why not admit that the band had grown too big for the city's theaters and start booking Bruce in to Philadelphia's Spectrum arena? The building could hold more than 18,000 for a rock concert, and given the size of the demand, Bruce could fill the basketball arena four, probably five times. And with cash flow still a perpetual problem, when they went begging for crowds in at least half the country (the Born to Run tour had actually lost money), why resist the opportunity for a big score when it came up?

Because Bruce wouldn't even consider it. Especially not at the end of 1975.

He'd compromised something with the packaging and selling of *Born to Run*. That had been a survival move—recall the desperation of the post *Wild, the Innocent* era. But here's the thing: *it hadn't required him to alter a note of his music.* He'd even held firm when Columbia tried to insist on having a pop radio–friendly short edit of the "Born to Run" single. And when it came to his actual connection to the world—the precious moments when he could look into the eyes of the people, expose his deepest feelings, and feel their energy flowing back into him—there could be no compromise. No echo-chamber sound, no fans stuck out on the upper decks miles away from the heart of the moment. That, Bruce assured anyone who asked, was not going to happen. Ever.

A brave stand. And yet it also put Bruce at odds with himself. Having worked so hard to project his art and vision to as wide an audience as possible, refusing to play bigger halls meant that he was also putting himself beyond the reach of a significant percentage of his fans. And if he really wanted to put on the most powerful shows in rock 'n' roll, that meant having the best band, sound, lights, and crew in the industry. All of whom deserved to be paid for their work, just as Bruce would be paid for his when the royalties from *Born to Run* rolled in. None of that could happen unless they opened the tent wide enough to welcome the crowds Bruce had invited in by making his breakthrough album.

"It's a problem," Appel admitted to the writer John Rockwell that fall. So maybe they could find a way to play Madison Square Garden without surrendering completely to its concrete-and-steel ambiance. They could, perhaps, hang a curtain to both eliminate the echo and block off the most far-flung sections. That was an option, anyway; something they'd work out in 1976, once they figured out what to do with the live recordings Appel had commissioned on the fall tour, thinking that the best way to leverage *Born to Run*'s success would be to release a multidisc live album showcasing Bruce's exalted performances while also exposing his new fans to the wonders they'd missed on the first two albums. Bruce still hadn't decided whether he was up for that, but he wanted to listen to the tapes before he made up his mind. Landau, while not an official member of the organization, wasn't shy about telling Bruce that he thought it was a terrible idea. But the competing opinions on the live album mattered far less than who had them, and why, and what they would do to assert their authority over what happened next.

In the end, it always comes down to the contracts. Appel's three agreements with Bruce, all five-year commitments, were headed into their fifth year. The manager-producer had long ago promised to reduce his percentages once Bruce broke through to the mainstream, and obviously that time had arrived. But Landau had arrived first. And once Bruce told him that neither he nor a lawyer in his employ had ever taken a serious look at Appel's contracts, Landau urged him to get it done as soon as possible. Bruce did, and emerged from the process rent by surprise, confusion, and anger. Appel, he now realized, had taken control of everything that mattered: his money, his songs, his recording career, everything.

And despite the promises his manager had made about fixing their contracts when Bruce became successful, that hadn't happened yet and wouldn't, it seemed, until Bruce agreed to extend Appel's contracts into the future. When a still-unhappy Bruce said that he was no longer entirely certain that he'd be renewing any of their contracts, Appel came forth with another surprise: he had, in his role as publisher, negotiated with Columbia/CBS to receive a $500,000 advance on the coming *Born to Run* royalties.

The company had approved the loan instantly, and now all the money was secured in one of Laurel Canyon Ltd.'s corporate accounts. Appel assured Bruce that he would get his contractually guaranteed fifty percent of the money even if he didn't extend his contracts. But if he agreed to sign the new contracts, he'd get 75 percent of the money. If he didn't, Appel, and Bruce, would be forced to live by the far more tight-fisted terms of the contract they both signed back in 1972.

Call it pop music business as usual. But that made it a sharp kick in the ribs for Bruce, because it had *never* been business as usual between Bruce and Appel. From the moment they had shaken hands in the winter of 1972, they had been crusaders, soldiers on a march to glory. Contracts say whatever contracts say, but as far as Bruce knew, or cared, handshakes and the promises they symbolized meant more. Or so he had believed. But as the spotlight followed him onto the stage of the Tower Theater on the night of December 31, Bruce didn't know what to believe in anymore. Except for the one thing that had always worked for him: plugging in his guitar, turning it up loud, and hurling himself into the music.

Coming out in his usual jeans and leather jacket, with a long, multicolored scarf draped around his neck, Bruce gaped for a moment at his band, who had surprised him by dressing in matching white tuxedos, and then launched into a searing, full-tilt "Night." After a quick nod to the band's fancy dress—"These guys look so sharp"—he counted off a starry-eyed, slow-dance arrangement of "Tenth Avenue Freeze-Out" before diving back into the charmed swamps of "Spirit in the Night." Next, Bruce indulged in a quick between-song nod to recent glories ("Seasons come, seasons go, ya get your picture on the cover of *Time* and *Newsweek*, but the bus never stops") and then led into an even more juiced than usual "Does This Bus Stop at 82nd Street?," ending with an exultant capper to the image of the girl throwing a rose to the lucky young matador: "and that's *me!*"

Then came something unfamiliar: an extended piano intro, a series of dark chords accompanied by ghostly wails from the sax and guitar, emphasized on occasion with a slithering cymbal roll. Bruce stepped to the microphone and spoke, his voice flat and grim.

> I used to live in this, uh, two-family house on the main street in town. And at night my father, he'd lock up the front door so the kids had to come through the back door, y'know. And he'd be sittin', he'd sit all the time in the kitchen. He'd turn out all the lights in the house, and he'd just sit there. He did that for as long as I can remember, y'know, until they moved away . . .

From there he described the late-night talks with his father. Finding Doug sitting alone at the kitchen table, the room lit only by the glow of his cigarette and the alcohol-and-burnt-tobacco haze in his breath, his asking Bruce to sit down and talk, and then his awkward attempt to gird his stymied paternal love with something useful: a peek into the cruelty of his own adult life, the need for mature men to put away their fantasies and brace for the worst life had to offer.

> Then he'd start screamin' at me, and I'd start . . . I'd start screaming back at him, and he'd be tellin' me all the time what a bad world it was. And I'd be tellin' him that it was my life.

Then he started to sing the opening lines of the Animals' "It's My Life," slowed down to draw out the tension in the verses before bursting into explosive full-band choruses. "I'm gonna make it for certain," he sang through gritted teeth. "I'm breakin' loose!"

The story of his father, his family, and his childhood, all the old terrors now tangled in his devolving relationship with Appel, in the consuming fear that everything he'd worked for, everything he'd achieved despite Doug's insistence that it could never come true, all of it was now vanishing before his eyes. Except for that he wouldn't let that happen, and so now he screamed it at the top of his lungs, with the entire theater riveted to his every word.

It's my life, and I'll do what I want!

He slashed at his guitar, his muscles coiled and tense, the veins in his neck taut and unyielding as he bellowed one last thing.

Don't . . . push me!

FOURTEEN

IT WAS ME AND YOU, BABY, I REMEMBER THE NIGHT YOU PROMISED

WITH A COUPLE OF MONTHS off and an album climbing to the one million sales mark, Bruce granted himself a few indulgences. He relished driving his eye-popping '57 Chevrolet and had orange flames painted on its bright yellow chassis—Elvis's pink Cadillac, only stripped down, bulked up, and trembling with symbolic horsepower. He got the car earlier in 1975, when "Born to Run" was still aborning and he felt drawn to the physical manifestation of the songs he'd written. "Rock 'n' roll is a fetishist's dream," Bruce said on Steve Van Zandt's satellite radio show in 2011. "The physical totems, the jackets or the shoes, they hold such unusual power in your imagination. There's a spirit power to it."

But once Bruce's face and his automotive iconography became so well known across the country his Chevy functioned like a bullhorn: *Bruce is here.* Fans on the street screamed and waved as he drove past. Others ran into traffic to knock on his windows when he waited at a red light. He'd pass cars going the opposite direction, only to see their drivers pull abrupt

U-turns in order to follow him. "He couldn't drive it anywhere because suddenly he was a target," Peter Philbin says. Bruce hid the car in his garage, and when he learned that Philbin was moving back to Los Angeles to take an A&R post at CBS's West Coast offices,[1] he offered to sell his pal the flaming Chevy for $1,000. A fraction of what it cost him, but that was still too rich for Philbin's blood, so the car stayed in Bruce's garage, where it remained until he sold it years later.[2]

Bruce also assigned Rick Seguso, the first of a chain of road managers who would serve as his off-road housemate, life assistant, and companion, to find the next place for them to live. This time Bruce wanted to rent a bigger house in a more remote area—a family-sized home where he could live comfortably, with enough room for the band to rehearse, possibly all night long if Bruce felt like it. A week or two later Seguso took Bruce to Telegraph Hill Road in Holmdel, New Jersey, to see a large house on a horse farm that had once been a cavalry outpost. The sprawling, slatted-wood structure had plenty of space for the band, its various instruments, amplifiers, and other gear. The deck out back looked out over a steel-bottomed, baking soda–cleaned pool—a refashioned horse wash—and to the rolling, grassy hills beyond. Bruce took one look and signed the lease so they could move in, although he still wasn't making enough money to cover the rent without Seguso's contribution. So even if the real money hadn't started rolling in, Bruce could glimpse the fruit of his hard work every time he walked through the door of his rented house, or caught sight of the hills rolling away from his living room windows. It was, at least, a momentary distraction from the gloom that had slipped behind his guitar and lodged in his chest.

Bruce's moodiness started early on the Born to Run tour, in the hours before the October 4 date at Detroit's four-thousand seat Michigan Palace theater. "I didn't want to go onstage," Bruce told Robert Hilburn a few

---

[1] An appointment made by CBS president Walter Yetnikoff as a reward for Philbin's prescience and fierce dedication to Columbia's new smash artist. "You were right, and I was wrong," Yetnikoff said. "I want you signing bands for this label."

[2] The Chevy is now owned by a private collector, and tours as part of the Rock and Roll Hall of Fame's 2009 (and now traveling) exhibit, "From Asbury Park to the Promised Land: The Life and Music of Bruce Springsteen."

years later. No matter how many good reviews *Born to Run* had received, no matter the ecstatic energy he felt flowing through the concert halls, the avalanche of publicity made him feel he'd become a cartoon. "I was being perceived as an invention, like a ship passing by." Sitting backstage, trying to focus on the performance to come, Bruce felt only detachment. He had nothing left to say, nothing more to reveal. It was already out there, being picked apart by ink-stained carrion who assumed that every note he played had been concocted by someone else. "But I knew where I came from," he told Hilburn. "Every inch of the way. I knew what I believed and what I wanted." That thought was enough to propel him back onto the stage with a need as deep as vengeance. And it worked. He went back at it again, the starry-eyed rocker making his stand in the same jeans, black T-shirt, and leather bomber that animated so much about where he came from and where he was going.

So no one would imagine the doubt in his heart, not even when the comic creation myth rap at the start of "The E Street Shuffle" came out like a rock 'n' roller's interpretation of *Waiting for Godot*: "Somewhere, there's someplace, somehow . . ." he began. "Even though it gets harder to come by. And, uh, somewhere, somehow, someplace. Maybe it ain't here now. But somewhere, somewhere tonight, Clarence, hit me! Sparks fly on E Street . . ."

With the $500,000 advance Appel took from Columbia/CBS on the line and tension rising, Bruce demanded new copies of all his contracts and sought counsel with the one person he was beginning to trust above all others. Bruce flew to Los Angeles, where Jon Landau had relocated temporarily in order to produce Jackson Browne's *The Pretender* album. Landau retrieved Bruce at the airport, and they ended up in a restaurant. The rift with Appel, Bruce said, was getting worse. He needed a lawyer to help him but had no idea how to find a good one. Landau made an appointment for him with his own attorney, Mike Mayer, whose quick read of the contracts made him cringe. Virtually every clause and subclause, he said, was a nightmare version of the current industry standards; they were so tilted against Bruce, in fact, that when entertainment lawyer David Benjamin, who worked with the team of Peter Parcher and Mike Tannen, who would soon take over Bruce's legal work, read them a few months later, he gasped. "[The contracts] had every trick in the book." So tricky, Benjamin says, it was hard to imagine that Appel would have, or could have, imagined them for himself. "Appel hadn't ever managed anyone before. He didn't *know* what every trick was." More likely, Benjamin says, the real author of the contracts had been Appel's lawyer Jules Kurz, "an old-time guy from the year *gimmel*," Benjamin says. The three-layer management-production-publishing contracts; the full ownership of Bruce's songs; the disparity in publishing income; the contractual distance between Bruce and Columbia Records. "He was full of those old-time tricks."

Back in New York and edging toward panic, Bruce paid a surprise visit to the apartment of Bob Spitz, Appel's former assistant, then working with Elton John's American management. When the doorman called up to announce the guest, the man seemed taken aback. Mr. Bruce, as the doorman called him, was "not in good shape." Assuming that his guest had boozed himself into a stupor, Spitz realized quickly that Bruce was sober but extremely freaked out. They hadn't seen each other since Spitz left his job at Laurel Canyon in 1974, but Bruce launched almost immediately into his anguished tirade about Appel. "That's when he told me the whole story," Spitz says. "That he thought Mike had fucked him and it was all over, so now he was working with Jon." But, of course, nothing could be quite that simple.

Landau, back in New York during a break in Browne's sessions, lived just a few blocks from Spitz, and Bruce invited him over. "We sat at my dining room table, and Bruce said, 'Please, anything you can remember; anything you can tell me to help me.'" When Spitz asked if he wanted to separate himself completely from Mike, Bruce shook his head. "I want Mike to produce me, but I don't want Mike to manage me." Landau seemed to agree, but Spitz was puzzled. "What's the problem?" he asked. "He already produces you." Bruce shook his head adamantly. "No. He gets too much money. He's robbing me blind."

If they needed firsthand testimony about Appel playing fast and loose with Bruce's money, they had come to the right place. "When a [royalty] check for Bruce came in, we used to take it to the Apple Bank on Fifty-fourth and Sixth and cash it," Spitz says. "[Mike would] put the money in the pocket of his Levi's jean jacket and pay for everything with it." When Spitz voiced reservations about his boss's idiosyncratic way of handling his client's money, Appel shrugged it off. "He'd say, 'We're gonna get it all back!'" Spitz recalls. In the bad old days, the point was difficult to argue because, as Spitz knew, Appel used his own money in precisely the same way, taking as little salary as possible when the Laurel Canyon accounts ran low. That was the only way to feed the cars, hotels, and salaries that kept Bruce and the band moving and working their way to the acclaim Bruce deserved. Who had time to keep neat books when they had a world to conquer? Bruce certainly didn't care about such niceties, and as long as the music stayed pure and their vision clear, everything else would take care of itself. And he knew Appel agreed with him. "I think Mike is the greatest, number one," Bruce told John Rockwell just before *Born to Run*'s release. "I don't go out there and do half. Mike understands this. He ended up takin' the heat for a lot of decisions I made."

And yet Appel was no longer the only man he'd met with the commitment, musical passion, and business expertise to complement his own strengths and shore up his weaknesses. And maybe Landau's intellectual and emotional sophistication would make him a much better partner for the next part of Bruce's journey. Nearly two years after Landau had pronounced him the incarnation of rock 'n' roll's future, Bruce remained convinced that the critic-turned-producer was the right man to get him there. Bruce took Landau's word so seriously it often seemed like the writer had already set up shop in Appel's management office. Once enthusiastic about the live album that Appel had already told CBS they would deliver as a follow-up to *Born to Run*, Bruce reversed himself abruptly when Landau argued that it was far too early in his career to produce such a summary document. Appel's ambitious plan to mount a summer university tour with their own six-thousand-capacity circus tent as a portable venue also died a quick death once Bruce heard Landau raise a few potential logistical problems. "And he [Bruce] got vitriolic, and he said it [was] the dumbest thing that he ever heard of," Landau said in a pretrial deposition. "He said, 'I can't believe that I ever thought of it for ten minutes!'" Landau sounded surprised at how quickly and radically Bruce's mind could change.

Other offers flowed in, some big enough to resolve Bruce's financial problems in the course of one performance. NBC offered $500,000 for an hour of prime-time television that Bruce could fill however he pleased. No way, Bruce said. A Philadelphia promoter dreamed up a massive July 4, 1976, concert at JFK Stadium, making it a kind of dream opportunity by offering to let Bruce handpick a dozen unsigned New Jersey bands to fill the undercard. And depending on ticket sales, he stood to earn at least $500,000 and as much as $1 million for his work. Once again Bruce shook it off. A stadium concert, he insisted, was the last thing he'd ever do.

Bruce's lawyers did work out a temporary truce allowing Appel to continue booking a two-month tour that would generate some income by hitting smaller markets they had never taken the time to play, such as Appalachian State University in Boone, North Carolina, and the Freedom Hall Civic Center in Johnson City, Tennessee. The project gained the not-so-elegant title of the Chicken Scratch tour, which would have seemed insulting to the towns themselves were Bruce and the band not so desperate for whatever dollars they could pull together in order to keep their houses heated and stomachs filled.

Still hoping that there might be a way to construct a situation where Appel and Landau could both work with him, Bruce went to his manager with an offer that could define their futures and resolve their contractual problems in one blow. Appel would have to agree to tear up the old contracts and work by the more equitable terms they had already ironed out. Plus, Bruce wanted complete control over his songs. And if Appel agreed to that, then they could keep rolling just as they had been. With only one more condition: from here on out, every aspect of their business relationship would be guaranteed by a handshake. Nothing more, and nothing less. "I was about contracted out," Bruce says. "Just very, very gun shy of whatever was going to happen next. But Mike and I had gotten to a place where I thought we had it all sorted out. It was between the two of us. But we did have an arrangement that we had settled on." Bruce went away feeling relieved. But then Appel talked it over with his dad. And when Appel Sr. told his son that he'd be a fool to tear up his very favorable contracts, Appel changed his mind. "The next day it was off," Bruce says with a small shrug. "I knew it had something to do with the influence of his pop, and that was the end of that."

Now it's easy for Bruce to shrug it off. But in the heat of 1976, Appel's abrupt change of heart was an affront. "He can't accept my word!" Bruce seethed to Landau. "Mike knows my word is worth a thousand percent, and he knows if I say I am going to stand by this stuff, I intend to stand by it. And *still* he's walking away from it!"

From there the conflict spiraled toward the civil courts. Bruce hired Mayer to carry his standard while Appel worked with Leonard Marks. The attorneys came with small armies of partners, associates, investigators, and paralegals, all poised to attack the variety of contracts and agreements that tied Bruce to Appel, and the both of them to CBS Records, the William Morris Agency, and so on. The two principals kept their distance from each other during the spring and early summer, playing close to the vest while their respective brigades girded for battle. Nothing much happened until mid-June, when Bruce's representatives informed CBS that the artist planned to start recording his fourth album in August, with Landau joining him in the production booth. Two weeks later Appel's troops shot back with a letter informing all and sundry that no such recording sessions would take place: given that Bruce's relationship with his label was as a subcontractor to Laurel Canyon Ltd., the actual signatory on the CBS contract, the agreement obligated the musician to work in accordance with Appel's directions and then deliver his recordings to the production company. And in early July Appel's lawyers made it clear that their client would not allow Landau to participate in any recording sessions with Bruce Springsteen.

Now that Appel had, in effect, taken his career out of his hands, Bruce had no option but to fight back as hard as he could. His lawyers filed the lawsuit on July 27, accusing Appel of multiple counts of fraud, breach of trust, and more. Appel countersued two days later, alleging a variety of sins committed by Bruce against his manager and the legally binding agreements by which they had agreed to live.

The most significant recording Bruce made that summer turned out to be the depositions he gave to Appel's lawyer, Leonard Marks, in the company of his own attorneys, the legal representatives for CBS Records, even more attorneys representing Jon Landau (who had also been named in Appel's suit), and Bernard Jacobs, a notary public of the state of New York. Thoroughly unschooled in every aspect of civil litigation (a fact that the lawyer Mayer and company should have anticipated), Bruce had no idea what to expect or how to function in what would be an antagonistic procedure.

Appel's attorney certainly brought the antagonism. Pushed repeatedly to answer questions that were either flummoxing (for instance, the endless series of questions about the precise job titles, duties, and salaries of his road crew) or designed to reveal Bruce's bratty rock star ways ("Did you stay in good hotels on your tours in 1975?"; "Is it a fact that you generally had a suite of rooms yourself?"), Bruce flipped. He shouted. He swore, referring scornfully to Mr. Marks, Esq., as "Lenny." At one point, Bruce climbed onto the conference table and jumped up and down in outrage. Then he leaped down, kicked open the door, and burst down the hall and into the women's bathroom.

A disastrous performance by any measure, and it eventually fell to the judge to take Bruce aside and explain exactly how his own testimony might be used to destroy his case. But when Bruce replaced Mayer with a team of attorneys led by Peter Parcher, his legal strategy shifted to take advantage of the raw anger behind Bruce's outbursts. According to Springsteen, attorney Mike Tannen, Landau, and others, the team realized that Appel would never settle until he came to understand that his relationship with Bruce was beyond fixing. When the deposition picked up again Bruce still spoke heatedly, but with a distinct strategy behind what he was saying and how wrathful he seemed when he said it. "I never looked at Mike Appel, and I found out that I don't own a fucking thing that I wrote . . . He told me I had half my publishing, and he lied to me . . . I have been cheated . . . every line of ["Born to Run"] is me, and no line of that [expletive deleted] song is his. I don't own it. I can't print it on a piece of paper if I wanted to. I have been cheated." Bruce repeated the phrases like a chorus. "He lied to me!" "He was dishonest with me!" "He betrayed my trust!"

If that didn't make Bruce's feelings about Appel clear, he had also written a mournful new ballad called "The Promise." Set on the highways of the Jersey Shore, the lyrics told Bruce's story in the words of a street racer whose hand-built speedster, the Challenger, shared the name of the surfboards that Tinker West made in the factory where Bruce had lived and worked with Steel Mill. Throughout, the song weaves the icons of Bruce's own life—the familiar roads and factories, the hardworking rock band "lookin' for that million-dollar sound," Highway 9, and even Thunder Road, the glittering highway that leads to everything that happens on *Born to Run*. But in "The Promise," all of those youthful visions have been stolen, battered, and left for dead on the side of the road. In the end the racer sees himself as a ghost, drifting across a desert as empty as his spirit has become. "When the promise is broken you go on living, though it steals something from down in your soul," he sang. "Like when the truth is spoken, and it don't make no difference / Something in your heart grows cold."

Bruce performed an early version of "The Promise" at the Monmouth Arts Center in Red Bank on August 3, and then played it consistently as he tweaked the song through the nine-month streak of shows they dubbed "the lawsuit tour." An instant fan favorite, "The Promise" joined "Something in the Night"—another dark ballad featuring dreamers who realize, too late, that making it all come true can be the worst thing that can happen—as a clear harbinger of where he was headed. Still, the emotional core of the evening came most often in "Backstreets" and the heated spoken-word passages that dominated the transition from the song's final verse to its howling close. As heard in a particularly fiery performance at the Palladium theater in New York City on November 4, the band faded to Bittan's piano and the light chiming of Federici's glockenspiel. Bruce stood alone in the spotlight, speak-singing softly at first.

> It was me and you, baby. It was me and you, baby. I remember the night when you promised. I remember, I remember, the night. The night you promised . . . You swore that it was me and you, you promised it was me and you. You promised it was me and you.

He stopped for a moment, his voice becoming a harsh, descending wail in the microphone. Federici's chimes became the sound of church bells.

Mesmerized by the music on Fred and Alice's living room radio, circa 1952. *Courtesy of Cashion Family Archive*

Douglas Springsteen at work in Freehold's M&Q factory, spring 1964. © *George J. Evans Photography*

Anthony and Adelina Zerilli, Bruce's grandparents on his mother's side, on their wedding day. *Courtesy of Springsteen Family Archive*

Bruce and Ginny Springsteen dancing in the Randolph Street house, circa 1953 . . . *Courtesy of Cashion Family Archive*

. . . and dancing some more at a family gathering in the late '00s.
Courtesy of Cashion Family Archive

Bruce and Ginny on the Jersey Shore, circa 1955. *Courtesy of Springsteen Family Archive*

The extended Springsteen clan gathers in 1961 to celebrate the christening of Bruce's cousin Grant. Bruce stretches out to the left; Alice and Fred Springsteen sit on the far left; Dave "Dim" Cashion is to Fred's right; and Doug and Adele Springsteen are in the back row, second and third from the right. *Courtesy of Cashion Family Archive*

Bruce at thirteen, showing off for the camera. *Courtesy of Springsteen Family Archive*

The Castiles in 1966—high school kids already more than a year into their careers. Left to right: George Theiss, Bruce, Frank Marziotti, Paul Popkin, Vinnie Maniello. *Courtesy of Billy Smith Collection*

Standing proud during their first stand at Greenwich Village's famous Cafe Wha. Left to right: Bruce, George Theiss, Curt Fluhr, Paul Popkin, Vinnie Maniello. *Courtesy of Billy Smith Collection*

Child in the early months of 1969, just after their union at the Upstage club and a few months before they had to change their name to Steel Mill *(left to right):* Danny Federici, Vinnie Roslin, Bruce, Vini Lopez. *Courtesy of Billy Smith Collection*

Bruce and new bassist Steve Van Zandt celebrated as local heroes in the pages of the *Asbury Park Press,* 1970. *Courtesy of Billy Smith Collection*

BRUCE SPRINGSTEEN   STEVE VAN ZANDT

In his element with Steel Mill in the early fall of 1970. *Courtesy of Billy Smith Collection*

Onstage at the Main Point in Bryn Mawr, 1973—Bruce, Vini Lopez, Clarence Clemons, and Garry Tallent, with Danny Federici just out of camera range on Bruce's left.
© *Peter Cunningham /petercunninghamphotography.com*

Bruce with girlfriend Diane Lozito, the inspiration for "Rosalita," "Thundercrack," and others, at the Main Point in Bryn Mawr, circa 1973. *Courtesy of Diane Lozito Collection*

Bruce, Mike Appel, and Clive Davis. © *Peter Cunningham /petercunninghamphotography.com*

(Below) Taking a moment away from the lawsuit woes of 1976 with girlfriend Joy Hannah *(far left)* and friends. *Courtesy of Joy Hannah Collection*

(Above) Bruce, at the crucial Bottom Line shows in August 1975, uses Clemons for shelter from Kitty and the oncoming storm of *Born to Run* acclaim. © *Bob Leafe*

Jon Landau, the self-proclaimed king of the rock critics, at the *Rolling Stone* offices in 1970. © *Jann Werner Collection*

Shooting for the moon and stars with Clemons, and just behind the saxophone, Federici. ©*Bob Leafe*

Taking a break from the *Darkness* sessions with Van Zandt and photographer Eric Meola in the Utah desert in August 1977. © *Eric Meola*

Bruce watches a dark cloud rising from the desert floor in Utah, August 1977. When he got back to the studio, he had a finished lyric for "The Promised Land." © *Eric Meola*

Bruce playing softball with the E Street Kings, a team made up of the band and friends. They played against local radio stations and club staff for fun for a few summers in the mid-1970s. © *Cliff Breining*

Making the bells ring and the lights flash somewhere on the Darkness on the Edge of Town tour, 1978, with Clemons, Roy Bittan, and Steve Van Zandt. © *Frank Stefanko*

Bruce and the E Street Band in its *Born to Run* to *Born in the U.S.A.* lineup. Left to right: Bruce, Garry Tallent, Danny Federici, Steve Van Zandt, Roy Bittan, Max Weinberg, and Clarence Clemons. © *Frank Stefanko*

Bruce in mid-meltdown at the September 22, 1979, Musicians United for Safe Energy concert, leading ex-girlfriend and professional photographer Lynn Goldsmith onto the stage before having her ejected from Madison Square Garden. Number one fan Obie Dziedzic (just to the left of the Jethro Tull T-shirt, in glasses) looks horrified. © *Bob Leafe*

With actress girlfriend Joyce Hyser on Christmas morning, 1981, New Jersey. *Courtesy of Joyce Hyser Collection*

In his bedroom of the house Bruce rented on the shores of a reservoir in Colts Neck, New Jersey, 1982, just after recording *Nebraska*. The painting behind him is the result of a paint-by-numbers project and may have come with the furnished home.
© Frank Stefanko

Musclebound and blasting the biggest noise imaginable, Bruce launched the *Born in the U.S.A.* album, tour, and era in 1984.
© Lawrence Kirsch /musicfoto.com

Hired just days before the start of the U.S.A. tour, singer Patti Scialfa soon became an integral member of the E Street Band and in Bruce's life.
© *Bob Leafe*

Bruce and Julianne: The newlyweds walking outside the reception for their 1985 wedding in Lake Oswego, Oregon.
© *Brent Wojahn*/ The Oregonian

After the *Born in the U.S.A.* mania ebbed, and the complexities of married life grew around him, Bruce started work on the more intimate *Tunnel of Love*. © *Pam Springsteen*

Living in Los Angeles in the early '90s, and traveling widely through the rural southwest, Bruce found the voices and stories for *The Ghost of Tom Joad*, and another step forward in his writing. © *Pam Springsteen*

Still partners . . . *Courtesy of Jon Landau Collection*

Four years after the awkward "Blood Brothers" reunion, and despite Bruce's last-minute fears, the 1999 reunion with Clemons and the rest of the E Street Band proved enormously successful. *© Rocco Coviello / roccosphototavern.com*

With Steve Van Zandt sharing second guitar duties with Nils Lofgren, the twenty-first-century E Street Band sounded more powerful than ever. *© Rocco Coviello / roccosphototavern.com*

While the deaths of Danny Federici and Clarence Clemons gave the Wrecking Ball shows a poignant mood, Bruce's performances (here in Boston, 2012) seemed undimmed by time and age.

© Rocco Coviello / roccosphototavern.com

We swore. I remember, I remember . . . we promised, we promised. You said that when the kids rang the bells . . . you said that when it was midnight, that when it was midnight and it rang, when the kids rang the bells, when the kids rang the bells, we both promised. That when the kids rang the bells . . . we swore. We swore. We swore. We swore. We said we'd go!

Then the piano and the bells chimed together, gaining volume just as Bruce's voice climbed into a frenzy.

You said . . . you said we'd go! . . . When the bells were ringing! When the kids ring the bells! When the kids rang the bells, you said. You promised. You promised. And you lied. You lied! You lied! You lied! You lied!

Then a sweaty hand reached into the air, Weinberg hit a rim shot, and just like that, they all switched back into the climactic recitation: "Hidin' in the backstreets, hidin' in the backstreets . . ."

Every word, every incantatory phrase, every scream of outrage confirmed what the lawyers and record executives had already concluded about the battle between Bruce and Appel: that the money was the least of it; that the accusations of fraud and contractual violations were actually a veneer above a much more emotional struggle. "These were two people who were essentially married, who had broken down walls for each other and together," reflects David Benjamin.[3] "And it was a great partnership when it worked." But as in so many early marriages, one of the partners fell under the influence of someone else. "Look, I've been divorced; I've been there," Benjamin says. "So just as important as Mike was, he was the starter marriage. Jon took Bruce to places Mike probably couldn't. And when one of the partners falls in love with someone else, the hurt in the old marriage becomes magnified."

[3] Bruce shook up the legal team soon after his disastrous deposition, taking up with a more litigation-savvy team that included Benjamin, seasoned litigator Peter Parcher, and Mike Tannen, the latter of whom worked closely with Paul Simon during the 1970s.

• • •

Given a stretch of free time between tours and legal procedures, Bruce spent time with his new girlfriend, a blessedly trouble-free college graduate from Little Silver, New Jersey, named Joy Hannan. They had met on the dance floor of the Stone Pony nightclub in Asbury Park. He invited her to see a movie with him a few nights later, and the couple spent the next year or two in what seemed like an extended summer romance.

"I was his best buddy," Hannan says. "We'd go the beach, we'd hang out at the Pony, I took him sailing. He and I basically had fun." Driving around central New Jersey in the rusty white pickup that Bruce called the Supertruck, they talked about everything but his career and legal battles. Still, Bruce's ear for music dominated the air around them. Hannan's memories of their time together all come with the sound of Tammy Wynette singing "Stand by Your Man." "If he liked a song, we'd hear it over and over and over again," she says. At one point, Bruce played the Wynette country classic for a solid month, straight. "He just loved country music, that twang. And he really appreciated a well-turned phrase." Bruce belted along to the radio whenever he liked the song it played. And when a local station happened to spin a Frank Sinatra ballad while they were driving through a blizzard in Hannan's Asbury Park neighborhood, Bruce pulled his truck to the curb, took his girlfriend by the hand, and pulled her gently onto the street, where he waltzed her around the street singing into her ear as the snow fell through the streetlights.

Bruce also liked to hang out with his boys, going to movies, hitting the clubs to grab a few beers, check out the bands, and, when invited, jump up and jam for a few numbers. He felt particularly comfortable at the Stone Pony, a relatively new club on Asbury Park's Ocean Avenue. He'd become a favorite of Pony owner Jack Roig ever since the latter had glimpsed the star, fresh from his appearances on the covers of *Time* and *Newsweek*, digging deep into his pockets in search of the $3 cover charge while standing at the end of a block-long line for admission. "I said, 'Bruce! What the hell are you doing out here?'" Roig recalls. "And he *didn't* have the money. No wallet, no ID, nothing."

Bruce didn't protest when Roig took his arm and led him through the door. From there Roig bought him a beer and sat down to talk, and soon

Bruce began to think of the Pony as an extension of his own living room. He came regularly, put away his share of cocktails, and when the bar was really jumping, he'd cross over to the bartenders' side and do a little pro bono bartending. Something less than a seasoned mixologist, Bruce had no idea how to make proper drinks and even less interest in computing tabs and giving correct change. Instead he accepted the customers' money without looking, then handed back fistfuls of change that might add up to significantly more than what the drinks had cost. "I'm sure he cost me a fortune those nights," Roig said. "But he made it so much fun I couldn't worry about it."

Drunk or sober in the middle of the night, Bruce drove in an unorthodox style. No wonder Rick Seguso didn't flinch when Bruce called in the middle of one night with a sheepish but urgent request. He'd been pulled over in the Supertruck and couldn't produce his driver's license or his vehicle's registration. When he tried to tell the cops that he was Bruce Springsteen, they rolled their eyes, got out the cuffs, and hauled him off to the lockup. "They don't believe who I am," he whispered to Seguso. "Do we have any of those copies of *Born to Run* lying around?" The road manager grabbed a handful, along with Bruce's ID and car registration, and went to retrieve his boss. A few signed albums later, they let Bruce go home with a slap on the back and a friendly suggestion that he drive more carefully next time.

By the end of 1976, Bruce's rented house in Holmdel had become the center of his operations. So while the band rehearsed in the living room, an ad hoc managerial staff, spearheaded by road manager Rick Seguso, tended to business in offices set up in two unused bedrooms. Mike Tannen took care of the high-level negotiations and contracts up in New York, but the day-to-day strategy and planning came out of Holmdel, which had become particularly tricky, thanks to the cash that Appel still controlled, and his lawyer's campaign to attach all of Bruce's concert proceeds until the legal scrum could be resolved. As a result, Bruce, the band, and their crew found themselves in a terrible pinch. They no longer had enough money to propel the operation on the road, which was the only place they could earn the cash to pay the salaries that would keep the band, crew, roadies, and other employees working.

"Oh yeah, we were broke before, but now we were even broker," says Garry Tallent. "We'd made this big record, and we had nothing to show for it. Nothing. We were basically destitute." Out on the road, the inescapable metaphor for their situation was the bargain basement tour bus they'd started using: a rumbling beast with an engine that couldn't quite muster forty-five miles an hour in the flats, and then gave out completely when attempting to scale a hill with the weight of a full load. Passengers had to hoof it uphill until they caught up to where the bus idled at the summit, waiting to take them down the far side of the hill. Bruce made a few concessions to his and the band's financial straits, even allowing Seguso to talk him into playing basketball arena shows in Phoenix and Philadelphia albeit with a custom-made black curtain intended to improve the acoustics while also blocking off the sections with the worst sight lines in order to maintain a semblance of intimacy. "He was dead against it," Seguso says. "But otherwise we couldn't afford to pay people what they were worth, or keep the show on the road."

Back home, the band members faced even more complicated challenges. No longer guaranteed a steady paycheck—with so much money getting sucked into the legal black hole, they had to take IOUs many weeks—domestic life grew harsh. Particularly given the ghosts of the bonuses and base-pay raises they had expected in the wake of *Born to Run*. When Tallent checked out a Springsteen/E Street tribute band playing in a bar near his apartment in Sea Bright, he learned that the tribute bassist made three times more for playing Tallent's parts than Tallent earned for creating, recording, and then playing them around the country.

The winter grew frigid. Heating oil cost more than ever, and worldwide acclaim did nothing to keep the icy Atlantic breeze from slipping through the cracks in their window frames. In the past, the band members could earn some extra cash during breaks by taking side gigs or playing sessions for other artists' records. But now that Bruce could sense the entertainment media itching to write his professional obituary—the kid-hits-it-big-only-to-tumble-back-to-earth narrative having such obvious commercial possibilities—a strict, if unstated, policy took effect: no breaking ranks. No gabbing to reporters about how dismal things had become. More than ever, loyalty ruled. Take it for the team, suck up the suffering, and everything else will come together in its own time.

But they'd been hearing that same speech for more than four years. At least half of the E Street Band stumbled into the first days of 1977 thinking they could glimpse the end of the line with Bruce. Nearly eighteen months since *Born to Run*, and still unable to start recording a follow-up, it seemed safe to assume that they had already lost all of the momentum the hit record brought them. And it wasn't like the making of *Born to Run*, or even the months of acclaim they earned for it, had been carefree. "Playing in a band is fun, by definition," says Roy Bittan. "But in the background, it was always like the Grim Reaper was just around the corner waiting to end Bruce's career."

Did they all have to go down with him? Bruce wasn't the only one who had dedicated his life to music. They'd all been playing just as long as he had, often in the same swim clubs, Hullabaloos, boardwalk bars, and all-night clubs. They'd all contributed to his success, and even if Bruce was the sole author and spirit behind *Born to Run*, the band's work hadn't gone ignored. They'd all fielded calls to work on other artists' sessions; some even had invitations to join other successful bands. Both Bittan and Weinberg, for instance, had been offered work playing on the sessions for Meat Loaf's *Bat Out of Hell* project.[4] Bruce didn't like the idea, but he liked it even less when a couple of band members applied for unemployment benefits to help tide them over. But as the money dwindled further and no legal resolution seemed in sight, the intraband situation festered. When Bruce left a rehearsal early one day, the other musicians began to talk about packing their things and going their own ways.[5] As Van Zandt remembers it, the situation seemed close to a breaking point.

[4] Which eventually rode its *Born to Run*–esque sound to septuple-platinum status.
[5] Whether all of this talk was limited to this informal conversation or if it led to another, more organized band meeting, is unclear—memories differ. Van Zandt, who has the most precise version of events, says that there was a real meeting, with Bruce not in attendance, and then a straw poll kind of vote that resulted in an even 3–3 split, with Clemons, Bittan, and Federici thinking it was time to go, and Weinberg, Tallent, and Van Zandt voting to hold things together. But Tallent and Weinberg have zero recollection of being at any kind of meeting and dismiss the entire notion that there would even be anything for anyone to vote about, since they were individual players working for Bruce.

"That was a real crisis," he says. "So I left the rehearsal and thought, 'Oh no, this is the end! I gotta do something to keep the band together!'" Working in consigliere mode, Van Zandt kept the discouraging words away from Bruce and went straight to Steve Popovich, the former Columbia executive and perpetual Bruce fan who had recently jumped to CBS's other label, Epic, where he'd signed Southside Johnny and the Asbury Jukes. Popovich and Van Zandt kept in such constant contact that the guitarist didn't try to be cagey about how close the E Street Band had come to imploding. "We gotta find some money!" Van Zandt reported. Either that, or the band wouldn't last another week. Popovich responded immediately: "Don't panic. Sit tight. Let me figure something out."

From that moment, keeping the band together became Popovich's crusade too. "I *lived* in Freehold, man," he told me a few months before his death in 2011. "My family was there. When I fought with my wife, I'd figure out where Bruce and the band were playing and go there. That was my healing thing." Unwilling to sit back and watch his favorite band fall apart, Popovich dialed Van Zandt with just the right offer: he'd signed ex-Ronettes singer Ronnie Spector to Epic. Billy Joel had written a Ronettes-style song called "Say Goodbye to Hollywood" to be the lead single for her comeback album. Now they needed a great rock 'n' roll band to help her cut the song. Who would be more perfect than the E Street Band? And given the reputation they'd built with Bruce, he had no problem paying everyone double the union scale for their services. "He was talking like five hundred, six hundred dollars; about three weeks' salary for everyone," Van Zandt says. Bruce, who was both a Ronnie Spector fan and acutely aware of his band's financial straits, not only okayed the side gig but also showed up to play guitar. Everyone took home his check, and the storm ended. "We never discussed breaking up again," Van Zandt says.

When Bruce hears a boiled-down recounting of all of the above, he shakes his head. "I don't know, everybody has a different version of it. The band might have had those discussions amongst themselves, but I don't think anybody discussed it with me. The only thing I remember was that times were tough. There was a Ronnie Spector session that Steve produced. I went in and played guitar on it or something, but I don't remember a connection between any of those things."

Still needing cash to fuel the next tour, Bruce's booking agent, Sam Mc-Keith, asked his William Morris Agency bosses to grant his client a loan secured by future receipts. When they counteroffered a much smaller loan, secured in part by Bruce's signing a new contract with the agency, Bruce found himself in a bind. From 1973 to 1975, McKeith's strategic bookings had proved so instrumental in building Bruce's popularity in the East, and those odd little pockets in the Southwest (Austin, Phoenix, Houston) that the agent was one of just three people thanked by name on *Born to Run*'s inside cover. As he'd acknowledged, Bruce owed a piece of his success to McKeith's labors and thus owed him some loyalty. "I liked Sam a lot," Bruce says. "If there had been anything to keep me there, it would have been him."

But then Frank Barsalona, president of the Premier Talent booking agency, came down to New Jersey and offered a no-strings loan for $100,000, big enough to finance the last leg of the lawsuit tour in early 1977, and also the kind of good-faith-and-a-handshake deal that could win Bruce's heart forever. "He came down and said, 'Hey, you need some help? I'm your man,'" Bruce recalls. "And that was the beginning of a beautiful relationship, you know?" Barsalona didn't even suggest that Bruce sign a deal with him, although Bruce did eventually sign with Premier. His touring career is still managed by agent Barry Bell.[6]

---

[6] Bell first met Bruce, and got to know Appel and the rest of the organization, while working with Sam McKeith at William Morris, and so the story of his jump to Premier and into what had been McKeith's chief agent status is a bit complex. Bell had first agreed to join forces with Appel to form an independent booking agency with a roster headlined by, but not limited to, Bruce. Those plans crumbled when Appel refused Bruce's offer of a handshake contract. Meanwhile, Bell socialized with Bruce (their respective girlfriends were neighbors), quit his job at William Morris, and accepted a better job at Premier. McKeith's defenestration, according to Bell, was a result of Bruce's disenchantment with the Morris agency and for his being too close to Appel. McKeith, on the other hand, believes that Bell, like many junior agents before and since, simply built his own personal bond with Bruce and used it to leverage him away from McKeith and William Morris, and into Premier, where he would serve as Bruce's chief agent. That said, other factors

At the same time, Mike Tannen worked out an agreement with Yetnikoff to sign Bruce directly to CBS once the Appel situation got resolved—and this time with superstar-caliber royalties of $1 per album sold. In the wake of some damaging information that had come to light in the last few months (including a deposition from Bob Spitz that recalled Appel admitting that any sensible judge would find his contracts "unconscionable"), Bruce's and Appel's lawyers negotiated through the spring, and in May 1977 they reached an agreement: Appel would receive $800,000 in cash and keep 50 percent of the publishing rights to the twenty-seven songs Bruce had published through Laurel Canyon. Everything else, including the rights to all his future songs, belonged to Bruce.

With Appel no longer a threat, the demonic image he had taken on in Bruce's eyes faded to reveal the man he had always been: the two-fisted, tough-talking warrior with the golden heart; well intended but tragically flawed. Another in the line of men who had helped raise Bruce, who had carried his amps, played their hearts out on his stage, sometimes got caught double billing him for their telephone calls, and peered back at him from the other side of the bathroom mirror. So when his lawyers informed Bruce that Appel's current standing in the courts had become sketchy enough to strip him of far more—perhaps everything—Bruce shook his head. "I don't want to hurt this guy," he told Tannen. "I want to get away from him, but he was there when I needed him. Whatever he gets, he deserves."

The day the money changed hands—when Appel gave over Bruce's royalties for *Born to Run* and everything else, and when CBS issued the $800,000 advance for Bruce to give Appel—Bruce walked out of the CBS building onto Avenue of the Americas, looked at the checks in his hands, all payable to Mr. Bruce Springsteen, and laughed. "Look!" he said to Joy Hannan. "I'm a millionaire!" They both knew it was temporary: he'd be handing the $800k to Appel within a few hours, and a significant

---

were also in play, and McKeith still seems peeved by how it all went down. And given the personal/professional travails he was on the verge of encountering, the whole episode is one of the less cheerful in Bruce's long career. But, as Mike Tannen says, such is life in the entertainment industry.

percentage of the royalties would go straight to paying debts, back salaries, and such. But they still beelined to the nearest phone booth, crowding in together as he dialed his parents' number in San Mateo. When Adele picked up, he shouted, "Hey, Ma!" and told her the news. "It was cute," Hannan says. "His parents were so excited for him, and he was so happy the lawsuit was over." They'd all come quite a distance since that snowy day in 1964 when he pointed out the Kent guitar on the other side of Caiazzo's music store window and asked, "Please, ma," for Santa to bring him that one.

FIFTEEN

THERE'S ALWAYS ROOM TO THROW SOMETHING OUT

WHEN THEY TOOK A DINNER break, you could see it in the way they arranged themselves at the long table in Bruce's dining room. In the middle, you'd find most of the musicians—Max Weinberg, Roy Bittan, Garry Tallent, Danny Federici, Clarence Clemons—bunched together with Bruce's road manager–chief assistant (Rick Seguso at first, and then Bob Chirmside) and whoever else happened to be around. Bruce reserved the head of the table for himself, with oldest pal, coguitarist, coarranger, strategist, and all-around co-conspirator Steve Van Zandt seated at his shoulder. "It was like this rolling conversation between Bruce and Steve," Weinberg says. "And the way it worked went exactly like stories I've heard from Charlie Watts about how Keith [Richards] and Mick [Jagger] work together. They had this incredible partnership. Bruce was the visionary. He had the songs, though they weren't always fleshed out. Steve was like this great mechanic—he was the guy who could turn the wrenches."

And that's how it ran for the year and a half after *Born to Run*. The band members gathered at Bruce's Holmdel house each day at two o'clock, went to his wood-paneled rec room, took up instruments, and got to work. Smoothing down the rough patches in the live arrangements, putting their stamp on cover songs, shaking up their own old songs, and learning the new compositions Bruce had in his notebook. Kicked into higher gear by the pressure of the lawsuit, impending financial disasters, and more, Bruce's songwriting grew even more prolific than before. Put a guitar in his hand, sit him at the piano, or give him a quiet moment, and just wait: tunes came bubbling out, often in twos, threes, sixes, or more. He brought them all in, sometimes completely written, others little more than a verse, a riff, and a scrap of lyric. Or maybe just a word, as with one four-chord rocker first aired in the rehearsal room when its entire lyric was the word *badlands*, sung over the chorus. And always, more to consider. Bar band stompers about pretty girls and fast cars; smoldering love ballads; goofy, R&B-based plaints about mean girlfriends; pensive sketches of renegades, racers, helpless lovers, haunted highways strung between failure and hope.

To Steve's ears, Bruce's new songs rang like church bells. The pop tunes—"Ain't Good Enough for You," "Fire," "Rendezvous," and so on— had the verve of the late-fifties and early-sixties rockers that had electrified their transistor radios when they were teenagers, while "Talk to Me," "It's a Shame," and "The Brokenhearted" had the majestic swing of classic soul music. Other songs evoked different but similarly crucial strains of rock, soul, and country, and as heard along with the emotionally intricate songs addressing Bruce's legal, musical, and existential struggles ("The Promise," "Something in the Night," "Breakaway," and "Racing in the Street," to name a few), it amounted to the most vital, important music Bruce had ever made. "It's this stuff that he completely ignores about himself that is, to me, his highest evolution," Van Zandt says. "It's *easy* to be personal. It's *easy* to be original, believe it or not. Pink Floyd is easy. 'Louie Louie' is hard. *Sgt. Pepper*'s—yeah, great. But 'Gloria'? Harder. Give me those three chords and make 'em work? *That* is the ultimate rock 'n' roll craft/ art/inspiration/motivation. That's the whole thing!" Hearing this, Bruce shakes his head and laughs. "That's my buddy, you know," he says. "He's very particular about the things he likes."

Landau presented Bruce with a different set of influences. Musically as steeped in the roots of rock, soul, and country music as Van Zandt was, he was also, as Bruce describes him, a formalist who believed that the best way to capture the riotous energy of rock 'n' roll was to perform it professionally, record it clearly, and then mix it cleanly enough to reveal the nuances in each instrument's tone.[1] As Bruce knew, Van Zandt and Landau were going to disagree about a lot of things—another iteration of the Appel-Landau dichotomy he'd created for *Born to Run*. As he told filmmaker Thom Zimny in 2010, he had his reasons. As he admits, placing himself between two powerful influences has come naturally since he was a toddler. "It's the rule of three," Bruce says. "My grandmother, my mom, and me. Mike, Jon, and me. Jon, Steve, and me. And that still exists."

Drawn to the darkly comic family stories of southern writer Flannery O'Connor, Bruce also felt a connection to the emotionally fraught characters in *The Postman Always Rings Twice, Double Indemnity*, and the other noir novels of James M. Cain. "Those things were very in tune with my inner life, and something about my childhood," he says. "Those noir heroes, the sand was always shifting underneath them." The doomed atmosphere in noir fiction resonated with his Catholic spiritual identity. "That feeling of being rubbed up against and trashed, and you can't get out from underneath it." What could be more noir than living in a world patrolled by a tempestuous God whose consciousness is as unknowable as His all-seeing eye is judgmental?

Taking up Landau's attention to subtexts in films, Bruce now watched his favorite Westerns and B movies with an eye for cinematic history and technique. Bruce absorbed films on more levels than he'd ever known existed; even the drive-in screen seemed to widen, revealing symbols, messages, and insights he had never considered consciously. The new perspective also gave Bruce a new comprehension of his own work, particularly when it came to the virtues of stark images and simple,

[1] The best non-Springsteen example of Landau's signature sound can be found on Jackson Browne's *The Pretender,* produced by Landau in 1976. As compared to Browne's more rustic albums, *The Pretender* fleshed out his usual acoustic guitar, piano, fiddle, and lap-steel-guitar blend with enough strings, horns, gospel, and cross-cultural exotica to give the artist's self-revelatory lyrics a global sweep.

unadorned narrative points. Listening to Hank Williams and the other essential country music songwriters helped Bruce to whittle songs down to their barest essentials: a few chords, a straightforward melody, plain-spoken, conversational lyrics. Solo breaks were short and to the point, and mostly reiterations or slight variations on the melody.[2] "It's an austere record," Bruce says. "I was stripping everything down, making everything very straight-ahead."

Bruce stumbled on one of his most significant influences by accident while flipping through the TV channels late one night. Coming across an old movie about unsettled farmers trying to make their way in the Depression, the film starred Henry Fonda as an Okie named Tom Joad. Bruce missed the first half of the film and never did catch its name. But the tale of an impoverished family searching for work and dignity riveted him. At dinner the next night, he mentioned it to Landau, who knew instantly what he'd seen: John Ford's 1940 adaptation of John Steinbeck's *The Grapes of Wrath*. They talked about the film for a while, and soon Landau recognized a shift in Bruce's sense of his next album. "He seemed to take a turn toward a different way of looking." As Bruce told TV interviewer Bob Costas in 1995, Ford's movie[3] never left him. "There was something about the film that sort of crystallized the story for me," he said. "Something in that picture that always resonated throughout almost all of my other work."

As on *Born to Run*, this batch of songs focused on the working-class characters Bruce had always known. The neighbors, teammates, and classmates who, like Bruce, were at the point in life where you're mature enough to understand the need for steadiness but still young enough to yearn for something more. Only now, on the other side of his success, Bruce had come to understand what time and experience can do to the most closely held dreams. He was exploring the real start of adulthood, Bruce told his go-to documentarian Thom Zimny in 2010. The point in

---

[2] "Adam Raised a Cain" being the obvious exception to this rule, but even here, Bruce's screaming evocation of emotional chaos serves a distinct purpose in the song's narrative.
[3] Bruce didn't get around to reading John Steinbeck's original 1939 novel until he met the author's widow many years later.

your late twenties when you're grown up enough to realize that "life is no longer wide open. Adult life is a life of a lot of compromise. And that's necessary. There are a lot of things you do want to compromise on, and a lot you don't." None of which you'd assume would apply to a rock 'n' roll star whose most recent album had sold, by then, more than a million copies. "We'd had this one success," Bruce told Zimny. "But I . . . went back to Asbury Park millions of dollars in debt."

In the wake of his enforced two-year exile from the recording studio, another question loomed: would anyone beyond his cult of mostly East Coast fans remember who Bruce was or be interested in the long-delayed follow-up to his big hit? The music scene had changed radically since 1975, the leading edge of rock 'n' roll now defined by the raw, aggressive sound of the Clash, the Sex Pistols, and the Ramones. Once again Bruce could feel the Grim Reaper's chilly breath on the back of his neck. Once again he went into the studio half convinced that this would be the final hurrah. "[I] didn't know, this might be the last record I ever make," he told Zimny. "Everything I had, I had to get it out *now*, on this record. There may be no tomorrow—just this moment."

But on the other hand, if it turned out that fame and privilege continued to define his existence, that might be even worse. Even his brief journey through the mass-media tinsel machine had "separated me from things I'd been trying to make connections to all my life. And it frightened me because I understood that what I had of value was at my core. And that core was rooted in the place I'd grown up, the people I'd known, experiences I'd had."

To put it another way, he was already damned for having become famous. If this record failed, he'd be damned for being forgotten. He was, simply, *damned.* Maybe that suspicion comes easily to Catholics. But for Bruce, the acrid taste of hellfire had less to do with the righteous fury of God than with the dark spirits that fumed inside him, both tormenting and igniting his desperate needs, just as they had ignited the anguish that continued to blaze in his father's lightless kitchen in California. "A lot of the songs [from that era] deal with my obsession with the idea of sin," he told Zimny. "What is it? What is it in a good life? Because it plays an important place in a good life, also. So how do you deal with it? You don't get rid of it. How do you carry your sins?"

The path to his own redemption was as clear as it was vertiginous: "More than rich, more than famous, more than happy, I wanted to be *great*." It wouldn't be easy. In fact, it was the *opposite* of easy. "He needed to try as hard as he could, 'til he's bleary eyed, delirious, and collapses in some way, emotionally or physically," Roy Bittan observes. "That level of creativity you can't just consciously get. There's something underneath you tap into. And when you do that, you're coming from another place." Bruce knew it too. "It was both self-indulgent and the only way we knew how to do it," he told Zimny. "The obsessive-compulsive part of my personality was that I was driving [everyone] crazy because I could. I was a dangerous man to be around."

Road manager/home front factotum Rick Seguso figured that out the hard way. Having been handed some basic managerial chores during the lawsuit era, Seguso figured he'd run with the ball. Maybe they could put together an in-house management company, thereby allowing themselves to function without having to rely on unfamiliar and perhaps ill-intended outsiders. Bruce didn't say yes to the idea, but he also didn't say no, which put Seguso in the curious position of being in charge of nothing but responsible for a lot. Working in such an undefined role led to trouble when Seguso had to reconcile the band's tour dates with the obligations that Clarence Clemons had taken on by accepting a role in Martin Scorsese's 1977 film *New York, New York*. When a two-night stand in Philadelphia in October became a conflict for what Seguso describes as a last-minute call for the sax player to be on the set in Los Angeles, the film's star, Robert De Niro, called Bruce to complain. The actor and musician were friends, but movie fan Bruce admired De Niro's work so much that when the actor started seething in his ear, he became furious at Seguso too. Uninterested in his employee's recounting of the film producers' often late and occasionally incoherent messages, Bruce presented one command: "Fix it!" Thrown into a panic, Seguso pleaded with the Philadelphia concert promoter to knock back the date of the second show by twenty-four hours, thus allowing Clemons time to take one red-eye flight to California, where he'd do his scene, and then take another red-eye back to Philadelphia to do the second show. But Seguso still felt tainted by the mix-up, and it wasn't long before Bruce let him go.[4]

With Seguso gone, Bruce called on Bobby Chirmside, another veteran crew member, to fill the road manager's job. Which, of course, didn't end when they got off the road. "The thing is, you gotta move in," Bruce said. Chirmside, who lived with his parents at the time, had no problem with that. Oh, but Bruce had one more question: "Do [your parents] have any extra furniture? 'Cause all I've got is a Buckaroo pinball machine, a desk, two beds, a nineteen-inch portable TV, and a pool table. And that's it." Chirmside moved in a few days later, living room sofa in tow, and Bruce's existence in the ten-bedroom house on Telegraph Hill Road moved into a new era.

Ordinary days at home began around eleven o'clock or noon, when Bruce shuffled out of his bedroom and fixed himself a bowl of Cheerios for breakfast. Fueled up for his day, he usually climbed into his dusty white pickup truck, cranked up a Hank Williams tape, and rumbled off to search the public library stacks for new books, troll the antique stores in Long Branch, or take a walk on one of the beaches or boardwalks. "This was really his loner period," says Chirmside, who stayed home to scrub the dishes, push a few loads of Bruce's jeans, T-shirts, and sweatshirts through the wash, and then hit the supermarket to stock the kitchen for the next few days. When Bruce returned home in the midafternoon, he had a sandwich and then either fiddled at the piano or took an acoustic guitar into his bedroom. He spent hours each day working on new songs, concocting a chord progression and then singing or humming a melody over the top. A snatch of lyrics appeared next, sometimes from the pages of his ever-present notebook. He'd work like that for hours at a time but never said a word about what he had worked on or how it was going.

"When you're writing well, you're not exactly sure how you've done

---

[4] Seguso admits that he was also drinking more than usual that winter, and thus landing in some regrettable situations, none of which helped his case around Holmdel.

it," Bruce says. "Or if you'll ever do it again. You're looking for the element you can't explain. The element that breathes life and character into the people or situation you're writing about. So to do that, you've gotta tap something more than . . . well, it can't just be math. There's got to be some mystical aspect to it. And when that third element arrives, it's sort of one and one makes three." The perpetual romancing of the muse, and the constant (if self-generated) pressure to make his work more and more powerful kept Bruce's focus locked on his work. Not that he didn't have time for friends, girlfriends, and nights out at bars. But all that fit in around the edges of a life dominated by its own internal visions, machinations, and riddles.

As Bruce had warned Chirmside, the decor in the Telegraph Hill house redefined *sparse*, with its emphasis on stacked books, crates of albums, and scatterings of magazines. Imagine the bachelor digs of an English major with a music fixation and a Monmouth County library card, and that'd be about right. A pool table and bumper pool table filled one back room. Gold records and other industry awards ended up in the closet, but Bruce saved his most prominent display spaces for the paintings and dioramas that fans sent to express something about their feelings for their favorite songs and albums. "Someone sent in a box with a gravel road and a hot rod on the road, and a sign reading 'Thunder Road,' and he put it on his mantel," says Lance Larson, a veteran Asbury Park musician and friend of both Bruce and Chirmside. "We were not allowed to fuck with that stuff. He'd get pissed—*'Don't touch that!'* He cherished that stuff."

The intensity of Bruce's feelings for his fans came to be symbolized in the form of Obie Dziedzic, whom he'd first met as a teenage fixture in the front row of Child/Steel Mill concerts in 1969. Dark haired, owl eyed, and shy, Dziedzic kept a respectful distance from her hero for the first year, even as she left homemade meals for Tinker West and the other crew members at the band's soundboard. West pointed out Dziedzic to Bruce, and he began to look for her near the stage, and was rarely disappointed, since hardly anything could keep her away from his shows. When Steel Mill played its final gig at the Upstage in 1971, Bruce called out to Dziedzic from the stage and made a place for her at the band's table at the postgig party they held in the Green Mermaid coffee bar. Dziedzic stayed just as committed during the Bruce Springsteen Band era, so Bruce began to call on her to drive him to the Student Prince shows. Ever since, Bruce made a habit of putting her name on his guest list at every show he played. When he got popular enough to play theaters and then arenas, he inserted a clause into his standard performance contract calling for a pair of tickets—front row center—to be left at the box office with Dziedzic's name on them. Every night. No matter what city or country. "She's like patient zero," Bruce says. "The genesis point. It was like, 'Look! We have a fan! She came more than once! She does the things a fan does!' She carried that for us, and still does."

When Van Zandt got serious about managing and producing Southside Johnny, he hired Dziedzic to be his assistant. She remained with him until 1977, when Bruce insisted that she come work for him instead. ("What about Steve?" she asked. "Don't worry about him," Bruce said, with a wave of his hand.) From there she became an integral part of Bruce's staff, buying his groceries, running his household errands, cleaning his house, tending to his wardrobe, and cooking the dinners he chose from the menus she'd crafted to broaden and add real nutrition to his stubbornly adolescent palate. Amazingly, it worked. Bruce let Dziedzic maneuver him into eating vegetables and sauces beyond the tomato-based kind you ladle onto spaghetti. When Lance Larson came over for supper, he was always surprised by Bruce's staunch demand that no food ever go wasted from his table. "If I left a little salad on my plate, he'd look at me: 'You gonna eat that?' And if I was already into the chicken parmesan or whatever, he'd eat it off of my plate, like 'Whaddaya doing? Gimme that salad! It's *healthy* for you!'"

If Bruce felt like going out, the three of them piled into the truck or one of his other cars and made for the Stone Pony. Bruce usually tossed back a beer or two, maybe with a shot of Jack Daniel's. But while Chirmside and Larson got swept up onto the dance floor, Bruce stuck close to the bar, chatting with friends or just watching the band, feeling the buzz of another party at full, booze-fueled throttle. "He's very into himself, is the thing," Larson says. "We'd say, 'Oh great, he's comin' to watch us have experiences, and then he's gonna write about 'em!' So it was like, 'Hey, Bruce, you need some more songs? Come on!'"

Women edged up to say hi, old friends were always on hand, and when the music got going, Bruce pulled a woman into the crowd and worked up a glow. If midnight stretched to two or three and he'd been dancing with the same girl for a few hours, he would slip out quietly, helping his friend up into the cab of his truck and drift away down the block. And just when Chirmside and Larson started to think he wouldn't be back, Bruce reappeared. "He treated them like they were his sisters," Larson says. "He dropped 'em off, then came back to pick us up." As his buddies knew, Bruce's love life now revolved around Lynn Goldsmith, a well-known music photographer who also happened to be a striking, long-haired brunette possessed of the same operatic passions that had drawn Bruce to Diane Lozito just a few years earlier.

Recording sessions for the do-or-die fourth album began at the Atlantic Studios in midtown Manhattan a week after the legal settlement separated him, once and for all, from Appel. With Bruce and Landau coproducing, and Van Zandt assisting with arrangements, the gang settled in for the long haul.

The problems began with Max Weinberg's drums, and the seemingly impossible pursuit of a miking setup that would make his instrument sound like a drum rather than a drumstick hitting a drum. Only later would they realize that the flaw they could never quite fix was a result of faulty rigging in the studios. But for Bittan, the unrelenting quest for God's own drum sound also registered as foot-dragging: an anxious artist's subconscious attempt to avoid the soul-abrading struggle he required to draw out his best work.

The sessions crawled through the summer. Then in September everyone moved to the Record Plant, where work continued through January 1978. Unlike the *Born to Run* sessions, this nine-month process moved quickly from song to song, with Bruce leading the band through the enormous catalog of songs they had started working on at his Holmdel house over the last year, along with the new songs that continued to come to him. By the end of the recording sessions, they committed something like seventy new songs to tape, knowing that at least 80 percent of them would end up on the reject shelf or be given away to another artist.

Southside Johnny and the Asbury Jukes ended up with "Talk to Me" and "Hearts of Stone," which suited Van Zandt's purposes. But when Bruce showed up with the Elvis-inspired fifties rocker "Fire"[5] and the torrid love song "Because the Night" only to reject them both, Van Zandt could only walk away grumbling. "Bruce was constantly giving away his best stuff or not releasing it. It's all part of his thing." Landau, even with one eye on industrial matters—publicity, radio, retail outlets, and sales—still understood Bruce's creative purpose. "I think he may have suspected that if 'Fire' had been on the album, that would've been the hit, and that would've defined [the entire album]," Landau explains. "He couldn't put 'Fire' on there and tell the record company that it *can't* be the single. He would have lost control of that." So, Bruce figured, better to be proactive and keep the song out of sight.

With so much top-shelf material written and recorded, Bruce entered a new frontier in his lost-in-the-wastelands style of production. Rather than spending months obsessing over the intricate dynamics of each song, he'd deliver a landslide of raw material and then spend months sifting through the heap, choosing, sorting, polishing, and dumping. Then he'd start all over again until some larger narrative revealed itself. So for all that Bruce thrived on the simple joy of rock 'n' roll, he was even more determined to give his music an intellectual and emotional gravitas. He wanted the music to be powerful enough to reflect his life and times while also redefining the possibilities of American rock 'n' roll.

In a lot of ways, it all went back to Elvis Presley, whose naive brilliance had fused white culture with black music. The accidental big bang that had blasted popular culture into Technicolor ignited a revolution and, as quickly, became the basis of a rapacious cottage industry that sapped Presley of his magic until he was too sad and weak to dance. For years the King of Rock 'n' Roll's steady devolution served as the leading example of American capitalism's most sharklike impulses. All of which became clear in the insider tell-all *Elvis: What Happened*, which Bruce (along with Van Zandt and several other guys in the band) had been

---

[5] Which Bruce had written thinking he might pitch the song to his boyhood hero as a possible new single.

reading. Still, Bruce felt Elvis's charge strongly enough to turn the story of his 1975 attempt to visit the King by jumping his Graceland manse's gates into a fine piece of self-deprecating, hero-worshiping stage banter. More recently, Bruce had bought tickets for the concert Presley had scheduled at Madison Square Garden in September 1977. When news of Presley's death radiated across the TV networks on August 16, Bruce took the news hard. "He was really upset; just incredibly pissed off," says Chirmside.

Two days later Bruce, Van Zandt, and photographer Eric Meola flew together to Salt Lake City, threw their bags into the back of a red, 1965 Ford Galaxie 500XL convertible, and drove into the heat warp of the desert, making for the sandy, one-lane roads that skirt the mesas, connecting the ranches and Indian reservations to the towns, to the cactus raising its arms toward the distance. With Meola scoping the terrain for photogenic remnants of the twentieth-century frontier, Bruce and Van Zandt charted Presley's decline, and how his cocoon of oldest, closest friends had coddled their magisterial pal all the way into his grave. Elvis had considered the Memphis Mafia guys to be his best friends in the world. But when his head began to slip beneath the surface, they didn't say a word. "All those guys, all his friends, abandoned him," Van Zandt said. They collected their salaries and left the King to drown in pills, silence, and a book about Jesus he would never finish.

They drove straight through for the first thirty hours, chasing Bruce's curiosity down every dirt road, following the ruts until they forked into another road or simply vanished into the rocky desert floor. When they came across a little general store, they parked by the gas pump, bought some Cokes, and gave Meola enough time to take out his camera and squeeze off a few shots. Bruce and the car, Bruce and the frontier, Bruce and the cannonball clouds that ribboned the sunlight. Set loose in the fly speck desert towns, Meola hoped to evoke the same melancholy that Robert Frank achieved in *The Americans*, a seminal collection of portraits that revealed the underclass of the 1950s and 1960s in their desolate towns and broken neighborhoods. Bruce connected with Frank's work at first sight; like John Ford's *The Grapes of Wrath, The Americans* depicted the world he saw when he shut his eyes. Meola, who had introduced

Bruce to Frank's photography, edged into his terrain by shooting in black-and-white, which also helped draw out the texture of the desert and the magnitude of the mesas jutting from the desert floor. An enormous thundercloud grumbled over the peaks one hot afternoon, packing thunder, lightning, and winds that swept the dust until it merged with the clouds. "It was like a Biblical storm, like something I'd never seen before," Meola says.

They watched the storm come and go, and then went back to driving, moving until well after midnight, when they found a dusty street that had once been a central road in a small town. Only a few houses remained, along with a pack of dogs that chased around in the blackness, howling after the creatures in the brush. Pausing for a few hours' sleep, Bruce stretched out on the front seat, while Van Zandt took the back, leaving Meola with the big, flat hood of the car. "It was hot as hell, with those dogs howling down the street," the photographer says. When dawn came, they woke up, shook the cobwebs from between their ears, fired up the engine, and took off again, heading back to Salt Lake City for the flight home.

Meola came home with with his desert portraits and the series of shots showing Bruce with the car as the storm rises above the peaks behind him. Bruce had his own way of internalizing the trip across the arid Southwest, spinning the harsh beauty of the desert together with the ghost of Elvis, the heat-bedazzled dogs, and the lightning storm into another testament to the spirit he recognized in the untamed land. "Gonna be a twister to blow everything down / That ain't got the strength to stand its ground," he wrote in the final verse, going on to describe a storm devastating enough to strip away the tender dreams and follies that make a person too vulnerable to stand a chance in the raw frontier: "Mister, I ain't a boy, no, I'm a man," he declares. "And I believe in the promised land."

When the sessions moved to the Record Plant, Bruce and Landau made straight for the studio floor, where they went over the songs still left to record, talking it all over in the stuttering shorthand of like minds. Bruce took up his Fender and played an early version of "Come On (Let's

Go Tonight)," while Landau snapped his fingers, bobbed his head, and pitched in a little harmony. When Bruce looked up, Landau nodded excitedly. "That's great. Really great. What else you got cookin'?" Bruce put down his guitar and led the way to the piano, where he opened his notebook and went back to playing the "Come On" verse, focusing on the passing references to Elvis Presley's death. "The power of the images," he said, "was that they weren't the central part of the song, but sorta, you know—"

LANDAU: —tangential. It's good. It's very good. It's sophisticated.

BRUCE: It kinda states it [Presley's death] as a fact, but . . . I don't know, it's sort of strange.

LANDAU: [quoting from lyrics] "Some came to witness, some came to weep." That's a great line. A very important distinction there, like, the curious and the . . . it's great. Really great.

Bruce flipped a few pages, put his hands back on the keys, and laid out the first chords of what would become "Candy's Room." In this iteration of the song, the central image is a mysterious house; a walled-in mansion that draws the narrator to its gates, where he peers across rolling lawns to see a woman's face gazing back through the glass.

LANDAU: That's great. That's really great. It's got such detail, so sharp . . .

BRUCE: I'm trying to work simpler, clearer images, really.

LANDAU: You got it, you really got it. This is just as vivid as in the past, only . . .

Bruce nodded happily and went back to singing.

LANDAU: This is great, the way she comes in here—

BRUCE: Yeah, it kind of gives it a sexual thing, like—

LANDAU: —the inside of the house is the female thing, and the outside of the house is the male thing.

BRUCE: Exactly.

LANDAU: The formal construction is unbelievable.

BRUCE: It's a real cinematic thing. But the words aren't really together; I can't figure it out . . .

LANDAU: It's very together.

When Bruce stopped playing, Landau smiled and nodded his head.

LANDAU: That's great. It's scary. It's blowing my mind to hear all this stuff after so much time. And to hear it sound so together . . . The combination of the first set you show me for "Come On," and the first set you show me for this . . .

BRUCE: "I think this is real. This is real. We got good stuff."

Landau went back to the control room, and when Van Zandt wandered in, Bruce seemed practically giddy when he told his aide-de-camp that more new songs were on the way.

BRUCE: We're gonna be rehearsin' this week.

VAN ZANDT: Are you crazy?

BRUCE: Nope, I'm serious.

VAN ZANDT: What are you gonna throw out?

BRUCE: I can't think of somethin'. But I'll think of somethin'.

He spun on his heel and hunched to play, pounding out chords while Van Zandt grimaced and shook his head.

Bruce, from over his shoulder: "Remember, there's always room to throw something out!"

Musically austere, lyrics stripped down to sepia portraiture, *Darkness on the Edge of Town* sets out to describe the underbelly of America's everything-all-the-time culture. The backdrops shift from song to song, moving from Asbury Park to the Dakotas to the Freehold of the 1950s to the Southwest to the industrial flats to the highway and beyond. But the real setting is that same forgotten America that Frank had captured in the backwaters of the nation's cities, towns, and wilderness. "Lights out tonight, trouble in the heartland," runs the first line of "Badlands," the martial rocker that opens the album. "Adam Raised a Cain," the next song, turns the focus in the opposite direction, confronting his own demons in the form of his sad, angry father.[6] A tense, heavy-footed blues, "Adam" rides Federici's church-gone-wrong organ, call-and-response vocals, and Bruce's own slashing guitar into the sinful heart of the father, the son, and the world around them: "Daddy worked his whole life for nothing but the pain," he howls at the song's conclusion. "You inherit the sins, you inherit the flames."

Again, the personal twists into the political and the sociocultural springs from the tangled roots of individual lives. The deafening industrial floor in the bleak country ballad "Factory" (new lyrics for the musical body of "Come On [Let's Go Tonight]") opens the door for "Streets of Fire" and its gospel-of-the-damned portrait of an outcast in a society redolent with sulfur. "Something in the Night" describes the same vision from the post–"Born to Run" perspective, where even a successful escape can end in disaster. "You're born with nothin', and better off that way," he sings. "Soon as you got something, they send someone to try and take it away."

Speaking to the *Washington Post*'s Eve Zibart just after the album's release, Bruce acknowledged that his vision had darkened. "There's a little more isolation in the characters, less people on the record," he said. Describing "Darkness on the Edge of Town," which would become the album's title track and closing song, to Dave Marsh in 1981, Bruce cast the album as a journey to the core of individual existence. "The guy at the end of 'Darkness' has reached a point where you just have to strip yourself of everything to get yourself together."

As he'd done with the songs on *Born to Run*, Bruce built the finished songs from key lines, phrases, and images that bubbled up from his notebook, surfaced as lines in other songs, or started merely as telling phrases scribbled into his book (such as "driving force," "night shift," "with death

---

[6] Coaching mixer Chuck Plotkin on how the song should sound, Bruce described a movie scene showing two young lovers sharing a picnic in a sunlit park. The sun would be shining, the grass would be emerald, the ducks paddled across the pond before them. Then the camera would zoom out to reveal, just behind them, a human corpse lying in the bushes behind them. *Aiieee!* "This song," Bruce told Plotkin, "is the dead body."

in their eyes," "the outsiders," "hot rod angels in a promised land," and so on) only to emerge as part of another, completed song. What they all had in common was their place in the vocabulary Bruce had concocted to describe his own interpretation of where he had been and what he had seen during the two or three years he had lived since *Born to Run*.

Bruce's experience plays out repeatedly across the album, finding its most vivid forms in "Racing in the Street" and "Darkness," both of which conclude with their narrators on the far side of their respective ambitions, wondering if their achievement could possibly be worth the sacrifice the fight required. In the plangent "Racing," the triumph turns out to be the struggle itself, and the questing spirit that can fill the most mundane life with a kind of sanctification: "For all you shut-down strangers and hot-rod angels rumblin' through this promised land," he sings, "tonight my baby and me are gonna ride to the sea / And wash these sins from our hands." The narrator in "Darkness" reaches a similar, if less affirming, conclusion, since his vow to keep going also requires an acceptance of the emotional isolation that comes with "wanting things that can only be found / In the darkness on the edge of town." Singing wordlessly over the song's (and the album's) final moments, Bruce evokes the opening bars of "Something in the Night," and the chill cloaking the entire album: the creeping suspicion that the things that make you feel the most alive will turn out to be some combination of unobtainable, worthless, and self-destructive.

All of which dovetails perfectly with the last lines of "The Promise," and the spiritually destroyed racer who finally admits he had always known his road led to nowhere: "Remember, Billy, what we'd always say / We were gonna take it all and we were gonna throw it away."

SIXTEEN

BIG MAN! ARE THEY STILL STANDING?

FINISHED WITH THE RECORD IN the spring of 1978,[1] Bruce set out to design the prerelease publicity campaign with as much authority as he had brought to the recording process. He visited the cover-printing plant to make sure the cardboard reproductions of Frank Stefanko's cover portrait didn't nudge his face too far into the pallid or tangerine registers. Still feeling singed from the aggressive ballyhoo of earlier years, Bruce met with CBS publicist Dick Wingate in Los Angeles to warn him off a

[1] Following a monthslong mixing session that again cycled through confidence, frustration, gloom, anguish, and then surrender, before a nearly panicked Landau called Los Angeles–based producer Chuck Plotkin and told him "The album won't mix!" Sitting at the panel a day or two later, Plotkin queued up "Prove It All Night," listened to Bruce chatter about how screwed up the song was, and how maybe only a new guitar solo could fix it, and then waved him aside. "Look, we'll push some buttons and move some levers, and it's not gonna be hard." Two hours later Bruce and Landau were so happy with what they heard that Plotkin became a pillar of a Springsteen-Landau-Plotkin-Toby Scott (Bruce's chief engineer) team that remained more or less in place until 2001.

massive Bruce Is Back campaign. "If it were up to me," he told Wingate, "no one would know the album was coming out 'til it was in the stores." As a result, there would be no magazine story pitches, no interviews, no advance tracks granted to strategically chosen radio stations. All the world needed to know, Bruce decreed, was that Bruce Springsteen had a new album out, and this is what it looks like.

Released on June 2, *Darkness on the Edge of Town*[2] came into the world facing plenty of competition: the Rolling Stones' acclaimed *Some Girls* album, plus new releases by album-rock stars Bob Seger and Foreigner. "I remember us looking at the release schedule, trying to figure out how we might do," Wingate says. CBS's management clearly wanted the album to be huge, even given the artist's resistance to splashy promotion. Magazine and newspaper ads ran the week before and then the week of the album's release. Television ads (a rarity in those days) aired coast to coast on Memorial Day weekend. When disc jockeys at New York's WNEW-FM and WPLJ-FM jumped the gun by playing lead-off single, "Prove It All Night," during the embargo period, CBS quickly filed cease-and-desist orders, unwilling to let even the most staunch supporters disrupt its promotional plans.

Released to another chorus of euphoric reviews ("Springsteen aims for moon and stars; hits moon and stars" read the thumbnail review in *Rolling Stone* that summer) and a quick hop into the Top 10 of *Billboard*'s album chart, the album still didn't stick. Lead single "Prove It All Night" peaked at number 33, while the next try, "Badlands," sputtered at 42. "*Darkness* was kind of floundering," Landau recalls. "It didn't have legs.

---

[2] The album went through a variety of alternate titles, including (jokingly) *Viva Las Vegas*, an idea that got started when Bruce led the band on a jammed version of the old Elvis tune and Landau imagined a cover illustration showing Bruce's name on the old International Hotel's marquee, with the rest of the Vegas strip reduced to a ghost town. A more serious option, *Badlands*, bit the dust when former Asbury musician Billy Chinnock (by then relocated in Maine) turned up with an album and single called *Badlands* too. Knowing that Chinnock was close to Garry Tallent, Bruce blamed his bass player for tipping the name to the other musician. Tallent swears he did no such thing. "I said, 'Maybe he saw the same Martin Sheen movie *you* did!'" Tallent says. Bruce didn't, and apparently still doesn't, buy it. Tallent: "He says, 'Say what you will, but I know that you did it.' And I say, 'Believe what you want, but I still didn't do it.'"

And it certainly wasn't having the impact of *Born to Run*." Worried that the album would be seen as a commercial failure, Bruce reexamined his resistance to publicity. "I realized that I worked a year—a year of my life—on somethin', and I wasn't aggressively tryin' to get it out there to people," he told Dave Marsh. "I was superaggressive in my approach toward the record and toward makin' it happen . . . And then when it came out, I went, 'Oh, I don't wanna push it' . . . It was ridiculous to cut off your nose to spite your face . . ."

Realizing that many of the postrelease problems he and *Darkness* were having resulted from lacking a full-time manager to help plan and execute such complex campaigns, Bruce turned to Landau for help. They'd already spoken in theoretical terms about his coproducer signing on for an ongoing role in Bruce's organization. But, as Landau admits, he was an unlikely choice to become anyone's manager. For while he had picked up some expertise in the ways and means of the record industry, Landau lacked the formal business and accounting training that a top-shelf artist would require from his or her most highly placed associate. But when Landau pointed out his obvious weakness, Bruce just shrugged. "You're a smart guy. This stuff is not rocket science. We trust each other, and that's all that matters." They worked out a basic agreement in a matter of minutes, Landau says, and agreed to give each other a six-month tryout before making everything official. "And," Landau concludes, "there was no looking back."

With one close friend in the manager's chair, Bruce helped shift the *Darkness* campaign into higher gear by opening up to Dave Marsh, then an associate editor at *Rolling Stone*, to fuel a cover story about the new album and tour. Published in mid-August, Marsh's story ("Bruce Springsteen Raises Cain") played out across Bruce's dayslong tour stop in Los Angeles, where a series of shows, parties, and Fourth of July celebrations allowed Marsh to gaze deep into the artist's past, abiding philosophies, and passion for rock 'n' roll. The most vivid portrait of Springsteen to date, the article was also striking for its unabashed advocacy of its subject. "I always saw myself as an advocate journalist," Marsh writes in an e-mail. "I have never, ever, adopted the pretense of 'objectivity,' which I think is silly and does more harm than good."

So while neither Marsh nor *Rolling Stone* mentioned the author's friendship with Bruce, or his longtime relationship with Landau, or his integral role in introducing the musician to his coproducer-manager,[3] his account of Bruce's trip through Los Angeles bristled with thoughts, adventures, and acts of rock 'n' roll so pure and beautiful they read like mythology even though they're so obviously true. So here's Bruce arm in arm with his fans in the front of LA's Forum arena, ordering security guards to back off from his communion with the audience during "Spirit in the Night": "You guys work here or something?" he shouted into the microphone. "Get outta here—these guys are my friends." Over here we find Bruce in the same venue shrugging off the rave reviews his concerts had received: "Big deal, huh? I gotta tell you, I only levitate to the upper deck on Wednesdays and Fridays. And I don't do no windows." When news breaks that Bruce's next appearance will be a surprise show at the four-hundred-seat Roxy on Sunset Boulevard, here are a thousand fans jostling for position outside the box office. When it turns out that a significant percentage of the seats for the show have been set aside for industry figures, here's Bruce starting his performance with an abject apology. "I'd like to say I'm sorry, it's my fault," he declares. "I wasn't trying to turn this into a private party, 'cause I don't play no private parties anymore, except my own." Huge cheers, and then he snaps the band into a supercharged cover of Buddy Holly's "Rave On," the start of a three-and-a-half-hour rock 'n' roll extravaganza that leaves *LA Times* critic Robert Hilburn in a panic, wondering how he can tell readers that this night's show was even better than the previous night's show at the Forum, which he'd just called one of the best musical events in the history of Los Angeles.[4]

[3] "It was perfectly obvious that I was granted a great deal of access," Marsh writes. "It was, or should be, perfectly obvious that any writer given that access is a 'friend' of the person being written about, or perceived as one." Still, in later books and articles, Marsh was careful to acknowledge his connections to Bruce and company.

[4] According to CBS promotions man Paul Rappaport, Landau set up the club show to stir up buzz that the Forum shows had failed to ignite. "We need to do something to blow this town apart," he told Rappaport. "We didn't *dent* anything." Once Landau booked the Roxy for the July 7 show, Rappaport helped set up a live broadcast on then dominant KMET-FM, and performed a variety of other tasks that did indeed give

And even cooler, as if anything could be cooler, here's Bruce in the wee hours of the fifth of July, leading an assault on the embarrassingly large *Darkness on the Edge of Town* billboard on Sunset Boulevard, which he, Clemons, and Tallent, along with an eager platoon of crew members, deface with a hand-scrawled "PROVE IT ALL NIGHT" sprayed across the bottom, the work signed with a slightly smaller "E STREET." "I wanted to get to my face, and paint on a mustache," he told Marsh a few hours later. "But it was too damn high." All of which reads as screen ready as Bruce's own cinematic lyrics. Until Marsh poses a question about the billboard caper that, purposefully or not, compels Bruce to reveal the canniness behind his rowdiness:

> MARSH: "Were you worried you'd get caught?"
> BRUCE: "Naw, I figured if they caught us, that was great. And if we got away with it, that was even better."

In other words, if he had to get arrested in order to reestablish himself as rock 'n' roll's truest anticelebrity and regular guy, that would not be a problem.

The raves for the Darkness tour had started with the opening show in Buffalo, on May 23, 1978, and didn't ease up from the first swing through the usual East Coast hotspots (Boston, Philadelphia, the New York–New Jersey corridor), the Midwest swing, and the first West Coast haul down to Los Angeles in early July. Still, ticket sales didn't always follow suit. So while most of the theaters they visited were smaller than the ten-thousand-seat Kiel Auditorium in Saint Louis, where more than a third of the house went unsold, large sections of the country had either

---

Bruce's Los Angeles visit the electricity a single Forum show didn't. Sitting in a bar chair just before dawn the morning after the show, Rappaport was approached by Bruce, who said he'd heard how much work the publicist had done to make the show happen. "You have no idea how hard I'm trying to make this go," he said, talking about his career. "I can't thank you enough for helping us do this." At which point, Rappaport recalls, the musician took his left hand, brought it to his lips, and kissed it.

forgotten about Bruce since *Born to Run* or had never experienced the E Street show before. "We got nothing in the South, really," Van Zandt says. "Austin was good, some other places in Texas were okay. Philly was good, Boston, Cleveland, some places in Texas. The rest of the country was soft. I remember playing to a lot of empty houses. A *lot* of empty houses."

But as Premier Talent's Frank Barsalona made clear, the point of this tour was to make the entire country a hot spot for Bruce. Not by publicity or the grace of album reviews and national coverage but by showing up everywhere that would have them and playing as hard as they could, night after night, until every significant city or crossroads had a chance to experience their power. As if Bruce, or anyone in the band, needed to be told the virtues of working the road. But given the chance to wreak rock 'n' roll havoc everywhere and take prisoners nowhere, Bruce's natural intensity became all the more overpowering. "It all ties in with the records and the values, the morality of the records," he told Marsh. "There's a certain morality to the show, and it's very strict. Everything counts. Every person, every individual in the crowd counts. To me."

Increasingly obsessed with the technical quality at the shows (particularly in the larger halls), Bruce extended the afternoon sound checks into three-hour marathons of jamming, correcting mistakes heard at the previous night's show, rehearsing whatever new song(s) he wanted to add for the evening, and staging new theatrical bits to add dimension to his more grandiose comic stories. Then came Bruce's painstaking ritual of patrolling literally every section and corner of the theater or arena, microphone in hand, listening for gaps in the amplification, drum tone, and, worst of all, echo. And if it turned out that things weren't just exactly right, for whatever reason, Bruce stopped everything until they, and he, had gained control over that subsection of the hall. Such were the dimensions of Bruce's expectations, and his overwhelming need to fix every problem and right every wrong that might stand between himself and his audience. He owed them his best, just as he owed it to Barsalona, Landau, every member of the band, the crew, and especially the fans who came out every night in search of something more perfect than they could find in their daily lives. In Bruce's mind, the burden was as tormenting as it was inspiring.

"Everybody had pressure on them, but mostly it was Bruce, because it was his name out there," says Garry Tallent. "He [became] very dark, sometimes difficult to be around. Just in a bad mood a lot of time, always ready to hit somebody." True enough, steely-eyed perfectionism had always been a central pillar in Bruce's musical career. But what became increasingly clear as the tour rolled into the summer was that Bruce's performances had gone from being displays of poetic craft and visceral release to something more like a crucible, a ritualistic ordeal of baring his own soul, reaching out for the communion and creating an energy powerful enough to carry the audience, and himself, to a kind of rock 'n' roll salvation.

When Bruce and the band hit the stage, they all came dressed in variations of the trim-cut, monochromatic blazers, trousers, and button-up shirts Bruce now favored. Often he set off his look with a thin tie, usually knotted loosely around an unbuttoned collar. Together with his clean-shaven face and shorter (if perpetually mussed) hair, the look he exuded was somewhere between urban poet and hassled salary man, although the sharp-toed boots emerging from his cuffs added rock 'n' roll spark, particularly when he was up on his toes, guitar at the ready, leaping to "Badlands"'s opening chords. The first hour of the show focused on the new songs, with "Spirit in the Night," and its traditional leap into the arms of the crowd, holding a key spot during the opening sequence.

Digging deep into the fabric of the *Darkness* songs, Bruce worked with Bittan to craft original piano-and-organ intros for the tunes he liked to introduce with the new, often haunting stories he'd composed. He added new or revised lyrics to "Streets of Fire" and "Darkness on the Edge of Town," and rearranged "Factory"'s opening verse into an atonal drum-and-organ-drone funeral march. The rockers also gained intensity, none more spectacularly than "Prove It All Night," which rode a Bruce–Van Zandt guitar duel into becoming a twelve-plus-minute showstopper. Van Zandt's arrangement of the unreleased "Because the Night" doubled down on the guitar fusillade, while renditions of new or largely unknown[5] songs such as "Point Blank," "The Ties That Bind," "Independence Day," and the vintage but rarely heard "The Fever" churned with the same friction between dread and hope. As a visual performer, Bruce prowled the stage like a warrior, hoisting his Fender like a sword in one moment, wielding it machine gun–style in the next. In the climactic sprint through "Rosalita," "Tenth Avenue Freeze-Out," and then into the oldies-dominated encores, Bruce's face ignited, and his dancing grew frantic. When the crowd surged to the stage, his boot heels seemed to leave the ground altogether. *Zoom*, he leaped onto the piano, standing up to boogie in the spotlight. *Whoosh*, he sprang down to the stage, only to clamber to the top of the tall speaker stack, where he struck a hero's pose and then danced to the chorus before hopping back down to his microphone to hit the final verse of the last song. By the end, he was bathed in sweat and bent over, hanging onto the mike stand as he bellowed, raw voice and all, his final confession: "*I'm just a prisonerrr!* . . . [long pause for breath] . . . *of rock 'n' roll!*"

In the heat of the moment, washed in the light and noise of another triumphant performance, it rang like a promise. Then the stage lights dimmed, the audience streamed for the exits, and the crew dismantled the lights, drums, amplifiers, and keyboards, lugging them all back to the trucks. From there it was back on the bus, back to the highway that led to the next hall in the next city where the next crowd of fans and potential converts were waiting to see him do it all again.

The tour stretched through the summer, barnstorming back through the South, turning north at the East Coast, where Bruce and company played back-to-back sellouts at Philadelphia's Spectrum arena. Following a night off, they played three straight sellouts at New York's Madison Square Garden before taking another run around the eastern hot zone and then heading back to the Midwest.

The traveling and backstage setups both reflected and amplified the

---

[5] Unreleased by Bruce, "Because the Night" was familiar to audiences due to the Patti Smith Group's hit (#13) version, released that same spring.

pressures of the tour. Bruce, the band, production crew, management team, and their various assistants rode to gigs on a pair of buses defined by their top-ranking passengers. The Bruce-led bus, also known as the Quiet Bus, had a few rows of seats, a dozen small bunk beds, and a separate chamber at the back where the front man could sleep or relax in privacy.[6] The other bus, captained by Clemons, was the Party Bus, populated most heavily by crew members, hangers-on, and anyone else in the touring party (such as Federici) eager for a night of beer, booze, music, laughter, and many not-quite-legal substances.

You didn't want to do any of this in Bruce's sight, however, or screw up something bad enough to make him suspect that your personal indulgences were affecting your commitment to the show. So when Bruce made an unexpected visit to the band's dressing room just before a show at Boston's Music Hall, things turned explosive once he walked through the door.

"I was with him," road manager Bobby Chirmside remembers. "And when we walked in, one member of the band was holding a cocaine spoon up to the nose of another member of the band. And they got caught. And it was like time froze." Watching from a few feet away, Clemons could only stare: "I just thought, *'Oh, shit!'* And then all the first guy could say was, 'Oh, hi. Do you want some?' And Bruce said, 'Uh, no.'" As Chirmside recalls, the color flooded into the bandleader's cheeks, and his muscles tensed with fury.

"If. I. Ever. Fucking. See. This. Again." Chirmside heard him snarl. "I don't care who it is. They're *gone*. On the *spot*. I'll fire them." He spun on his boot heel and clomped back to where he'd come from. When Chirmside got to Bruce's dressing room, he gave the still-furious bandleader a few moments to calm down. "Then I said, 'Boss, are you serious? You'd fire them on the spot?'"

---

[6] Which seems pretty luxe until you realize that the vehicle's large and not particularly quiet engine rumbled and roared scant inches beneath the bedroom's floor. The place vibrated when the driver switched on the engine, and when he shifted into high gear, the noise was overwhelming. How Bruce managed to sleep in there is anyone's guess. And attempting anything like thoughtful contemplation, let alone relaxation, seems even more far fetched. But after playing high volume rock 'n' roll for three-plus hours night after night, maybe he didn't even notice the sound.

Bruce didn't hesitate. "Absolutely," he shot back. "I could replace *any* of those guys in twenty-four hours." Then he thought for a moment. "Except for Clarence. Replacing Clarence would take some time."

Indeed, the Scooter and Big Man legend was a crucial part of the band's onstage chemistry. So even as Bruce's new music tilted away from sax-laced rhythm and blues, Clemons's hulking profile, so often cloaked in silk suits and carried with an elegant blend of sweetness, artistry, and urban menace, remained Bruce's key foil. He was the shoulder to lean on in midsolo, the glowering vision of Stagger Lee, the golden sax gleaming as heroically as Bruce's own six-stringed Excalibur. So even if Bruce was also likely to call to Van Zandt for onstage musical and theatrical support, his bond with Clemons—and the enactment of racial harmony, mutual admiration, and the power of fraternal love—gave the concerts their mystical glow. "The spontaneity between us was so amazing," Clemons told me a few weeks before his death. "I'd start each show wondering, 'Where is he gonna take me today? Where's the music going to take us? What can we do today to really fuck 'em up?'"

When they got deep into the encores, well past the point where an ordinary band would be back on the bus, and it would have been perfectly okay to give one last wave and call it a night, Bruce turned to Clemons to read the crowd for him. "He'd say, 'Big Man! Are they still standing?'" the saxophonist remembered. And if Clemons peeked out from behind the curtain and saw the crowd crushed against the stage and screaming for more, he'd give the nod, and Bruce would holler to the rest of the band, "Boys! Let's go back out there!"[7]

If only because Bruce had nothing else to do that night. Nor anything the next day besides waiting for the next show to start. And according to Clemons, the rest of the band felt exactly the same way. "Man, the other bands back then, they always wanted to get back to the party," he says. "But for us, the party *was* onstage. That was our joy. Not what might

[7] Clemons also swore that at a stop in Atlanta that year Bruce responded to the sight of fans streaming down the aisles by bolting outside and sprinting to the theater's front door to order them back to their seats. "We ain't done yet!" Which sounded apocryphal even as he said it, but Clemons insisted it was true.

happen afterward. We left it all onstage, all the time." Except for whatever he brought onto his own personal party bus, of course—but given the Big Man's shamanic sense of music and life, that was all part of romancing the spirits and letting them shoot right through you.

As a tour-credentialed photographer and Bruce's girlfriend, Lynn Goldsmith saw it all unfold from the inside. Her black-and-white photographs from the Darkness tour[8] reveal the rock 'n' roll road as a daily grind of jarring contrasts, from the dust-wreathed buses to the truck stop breakfasts, to the cramped and often tumbledown dressing rooms. Suitcases erupt in tangles of unfolded shirts and loose socks. Meals come from steam trays and are served up on plates stamped from Styrofoam, with plastic utensils on the side. The scene pivots 180 degrees when the house lights go down and Bruce and the band step onto the stage. Elevated by the lights, noise, and his music, Bruce strides like a rock 'n' roll superhero. He strikes poses with his battered Fender, towers over his followers, sweeps his fingers over their heads, stands among them in the aisle, cuddles into a lap here, rests his head on a shoulder there. Then comes Clemons, a vision in white and gold, blowing his horn like a much larger and cooler Gabriel.

Then they're backstage again, Bruce collapsed but elated on a folding metal chair, and then glaring into Goldsmith's lens as she finds him scrubbing off the sweat in a locker room shower. She's careful to keep the perspective above the waist, but the hardness in his eyes describes the tension in their personal/professional relationship. Goldsmith is welcome into his most private space, but her camera, and the power it affords her, is not.

The feeling was mutual. Already a well-respected photographer in the rock 'n' roll world, Goldsmith spent much of her time with Bruce worrying about what the relationship would do to her professional reputation. "I didn't want to be known as anything but Lynn Goldsmith," she says. "I didn't like the idea of working like I did while being Bruce's girlfriend.

[8] Many of which are collected in her book, *Springsteen Access All Areas*, Universe/St. Martin's, 2000.

It was not a positive thing to me." Other pictures show the tenderness between them: Bruce dancing goofily to the music in his dressing room; slouched in front of his living room television, the week's *TV Guide* flopped open next to him on the sofa. But it was always an on-again, off-again relationship, Goldsmith says, for which she takes as much blame as her ex might place on himself. "At that period, I always did a kind of come here/go away [with boyfriends]," she says. "I wasn't capable of loving someone in the way I would have liked to have been loved at that time. As his girlfriend, I really wasn't there for him."

So onward. During the same Los Angeles visit that included the Roxy show, Bruce met Joyce Hyser, an effervescent young actress. Raised in Philadelphia, Hyser graduated high school at sixteen and moved west to try to work as an actress. When the tour settled at the Sunset Marquis hotel on Sunset Boulevard, Hyser came to say hello to a friend who was married to a crew member. When Bruce saw the sparkle-eyed brunette by the pool, he was smitten enough to ask the actor Gary Busey[9] to introduce him. They talked for hours, Hyser recalls, and she liked him instantly. But she hadn't come to Los Angeles to become another star's girlfriend. "I wanted to make it on my own and be an artist in my own right," she says. "But he was so incredibly sweet." Bonnie Raitt, who also happened to be at the hotel that afternoon, felt the sizzle between them too, and wrote "*This is where Joyce and Bruce met*" on the wall just above where they had been sitting.

When Bruce invited her to come with him to San Diego for the next night's show, Hyser agreed, on the condition that she stay with a friend rather than in his hotel room. He thought that was a fine idea. "He was getting out of his relationship with Lynn, and he said to me that he had never in his life had a one-night stand, and I thought, 'How is that even possible?'" she says. "He was a huge star. But he had also never smoked a cigarette and never smoked a joint, and I'm like, '*Shut up!* Is this the beginning of the bullshit?'"

Well, yes and no. "I meant in the context of musicians, not actual

[9] Then winning enormous praise for his breakthrough performance as the titular character in *The Buddy Holly Story*, and thus years away from his latter-day career as a cheerful, if occasionally dangerous, Hollywood weirdo.

people," Bruce says. "Particularly in the early days you were always dependent on the kindness of strangers. I think I had a general sense that it was bad karma to fuck with the citizens. But rules were always made to be broken, and if someone rang my bell, or if a circumstance presented itself . . ." You can imagine why he didn't bother completing the sentence.

Whatever, the couple bonded, and by the fall they were constant companions. When Bruce moved from Holmdel to a rented ranch house on the edge of a reservoir in Colts Neck, an exurban area ten minutes east of Freehold, Hyser helped him to furnish the place by cruising the neighborhoods around Monmouth County on garbage day in search of cast-off chairs and tables others had left by the curb.

Whatever they couldn't get for free they bought at the warehouse-sized ABC Carpet & Home in Lower Manhattan or dug out of one of the tiny antique shops Bruce favored in Long Branch. Bruce also rented a small apartment in Los Angeles's middle-class Miracle Mile neighborhood to use when Hyser worked in Hollywood. And when they drove north to visit his parents in San Mateo, the couple either slept in the tiny guest room or, if other relatives were around, on the living room floor. "We barely ever saw other celebrities, and we didn't hang out with other rock 'n' rollers," Hyser says. "We'd go to movies or go out for dinner. Our life was small, and mostly revolved around family."

He preferred to keep his personal life as uncomplicated as possible, but something about his relationship with Lynn Goldsmith made it impossible to negotiate a clean breakup. Having traveled to New York to see his Madison Square Garden shows in late August, Hyser had only just arrived at Bruce's room in the Navarro Hotel when Goldsmith rapped at the door. Infuriated to find Hyser and her suitcases in the room, Goldsmith spoke some angry words before Bruce steered her into the hallway to talk it over. When he came back inside, Hyser says, he looked mortified by his own inability to control his personal life. "She was angry, I was upset, and he felt horrible for so many reasons." Three-plus hours spent wringing himself out in front of twenty thousand fans in Madison Square Garden restored Bruce's spirits for the evening. But when his mood descended between tours, Bruce often sought refuge in a desert hotel in

Arizona, where he'd spend days or weeks by himself strumming his guitar, scribbling in his ever-present notebooks, and contemplating the emptiness on the horizon.

"I think Bruce was afraid of being happy, because it would screw up his creative force," Hyser says. "At least at that time, he created from a place of anger, not from a place of happiness. I think he was extremely analytical, but pain scared him, too. And at that point, he had never been to therapy."

SEVENTEEN

THAT'S YOUR TIME CLOCK,
MY FRIEND

BRUCE AND THE BAND ENDED the 115-stop Darkness tour with a pair of New Year's shows at the Richfield Coliseum, just outside Cleveland. From there he had three months to catch his breath and write songs for his next album, which they planned to start recording in New York City. Absent the lights, noise, and cheers, Bruce's thoughts turned back to the faces he'd known in his childhood and the daily routines that kept them marching from one day to the next, even as it cut the lines around their eyes. That world didn't seem to exist anywhere on the road he had been traveling for half of his life, but he could see it all around him. In the eyes of his sister Ginny and her husband, Mickey, already celebrating their tenth wedding anniversary with their kids running at her feet. Bruce could blame his job, the road, and the extreme focus he brought to work. But most of the other members of the band and their crew still managed to have real lives at home. Bruce saw it all, from a distance.

"When you're thirty years old or twenty-nine, those are things that start to drift across your landscape," he says. "Those were just things I became interested in writing about. Because I hadn't written about them previously, although it was certainly the roots of the place that I grew up in and the people that I knew."

But no matter how much time he spent with Joyce Hyser, no matter how simply he tried to live, Bruce couldn't resist clinging to his isolated ways. By happenstance or design, he'd constructed a life built for one. And so he took up his pen and sketched what he imagined he was missing. "*The River* was me moving into an area where I just thought about those things or I started to try them on," Bruce says. "So you're trying on that identity for a few minutes and what it feels like to sing this out. It moves you closer to where you're moving in your personal life sometimes."

Picking up where *Darkness* left off, the new songs sprouted from the fundamental sounds and voices heard in early rock 'n' roll and country records. Three, maybe four chords, simple verse-chorus-verse construction, and stories described in the language of regular people. No omniscient commentary, no poetic revelations, no anthemic declarations of purpose. Just snapshots of the real world as viewed through the hopes, labors, fears, joys, and struggles of the unheralded many. The people, Bruce said, who might not shake up the world but kept it spinning from day to day.

The sessions started in March 1979 at the Power Station, a New York recording facility that included a gym-sized, hardwood-lined (and uncarpeted) room designed to capture the clamor of a rock band playing on the stage. Neither Bruce nor Landau had thought of recording there until Weinberg, Tallent, and Bittan came back from recording Ian Hunter's *You're Never Alone with a Schizophrenic* album. Their raves about the space's live atmosphere spurred a change of recording plans. "We figured we'd throw up the room mikes, get the snare crashing, make a lot of rock 'n' roll noise, and cut some music that felt very explosive," Bruce says. "I wanted a record that combined the fun aspect of what the band did along with the story I was telling."

The words of the moment became *live* and *immediate*. Which would have signaled a more relaxed style of business if they had any effect on Bruce's single-minded pursuit of rock 'n' roll perfection. It didn't, so what had once been endless overdubs and replaying of individual parts morphed into endless full-band takes, all of them grinding through the same song for hours and hours, waiting until Bruce and/or Landau finally decided that the second run-through from a day and a half ago had been the best of them all. Other times Bruce trashed the first twenty or thirty takes because he'd thought of a better melody, different words for the chorus, or an entirely new song built from the first's broken-up parts. Then he had to put all that together, sing it with heart, *and* play exactly the right guitar solo while every member of the band played their parts flawlessly. By the end of the first day, Van Zandt had already had enough. He called Bruce aside and told him he was done. "I said, 'Listen, I'm sorry, but I can't do this again,'" Van Zandt recalls. "'You carry on, but I quit. I'm splitting.' And he said, 'No, no, it's going to be different this time!'"

Van Zandt was having none of it. The real problem, he told Bruce, was that his production team—Landau, engineer Jimmy Iovine, and Chuck Plotkin—"didn't have a fucking idea about what they're doing." Speaking thirty-one years later, he reins in his critique of everyone except Bruce and his pathological work habits. "They all had their talents, I knew that. But contemplating the whole fucking *years* it was gonna take to make a record, I couldn't do it. Didn't have the patience. And that's when he said, 'No, no, I want you to produce it with me.' And that's a direct quote."

As ever, Van Zandt pursued truth and beauty through the rough edges of garage rock and the bejeweled chime of sixties pop. Leading off with "Roulette," a hurtling rocker inspired by the recent near-catastrophic failure of safety systems at Pennsylvania's Three Mile Island nuclear power plant, Van Zandt pushed the band to attack its parts with the savage intensity of punk rockers. Weinberg, encouraged to play like the Who's explosive too-wild-to-live drummer Keith Moon, slammed his tom-toms with seismic force. The song came out sounding so overpowering that Van Zandt told the drummer to play the same way for the rest of the sessions. "The songs Bruce was writing then were pretty thrashing and wild," Weinberg says. "He and especially Steve kept referencing Keith Moon. But I think that was one of the instances when Steve was at odds with Jon, because Jon really preferred the Stax style, which was far more economical."

Weinberg nearly lost his job during the *River* sessions, due in part to the stylistic drift that started during the early weeks of recording. Combined with a sense of time set askew by speeding up and slowing down with the emotional peaks and valleys of Bruce's live shows, the drummer found himself out of favor with Landau, who made a strong enough case about Weinberg's unreliable playing to convince Bruce to take his drummer aside and tell him to get help, and fast. Hearing that Landau had already mentioned subbing Los Angeles's ace session man Russ Kunkel (Jackson Browne, James Taylor, and so on), Weinberg hired a teacher, stripped away everything he thought he knew about timekeeping, and rebuilt his precision in short order.

Settling in for what they thought would be five weeks of recording (it eventually stretched to eighteen months), the group worked according to Bruce's favored schedule, laboring from seven in the evening straight through until nine in the morning. After a few sessions with star engineer Bob Clearmountain,[1] they settled in with Neil Dorfsman, a junior engineer who was so excited to work with Bruce that he told his Power Station bosses he'd do Bruce's sessions for free.[2] As the days turned to weeks, crawled into months, and then stretched to a year and then even longer than that, Dorfsman took note of the intricate balance Bruce maintained between his mismatched coproducers. "Steve was the vibe-meister," Dorfsman says. "He was almost like a liaison: the guy who would round up the band, get everyone in the room, get them psyched to play." Landau, on the other hand, struck the engineer as "extremely smart and perceptive. And like most artists, Bruce needed a sounding board; someone to reflect back what was happening in a semi-objective way. Jon didn't say much, but his presence was calming. Many months later Bruce said, 'You must wonder what Jon does,' but I already figured it out. He could get things moving with just a couple of words."

Night after night, the band members set up in their stage positions,

[1] Who had to leave in order to fulfill previously made obligations, although he would later return to help mix some songs.
[2] Kicking off a career that would include engineering and production work with Bob Dylan, Paul McCartney, Sting, Dire Straits, and many others.

girding for the next deluge of new songs Bruce would surely bring in. Some were more fragmentary than others, but when one felt close to acceptable he'd add it to his list. When they finished one song, Bruce flipped through the notebook he kept on a music stand until he found a song that fit the moment. "Ah, here's somethin'," he'd say, fingering the chords on his guitar as the other guys listened. If the tune was relatively complex—more than three or four changes, with a chorus and a bridge—he taught it to the band in sections, running through the chords and melody and sometimes calling for a particular feel or riff he wanted to hear from individual players. Bruce tracked the sections alphabetically in the order of their unveiling. But this was a trick. The actual structure of the song, which he would reveal just before they started playing, had nothing to do with the alphabetical order. The "C" piece might well be the opening figure, while the "E" section aligned with the first verse, the "B" was the bridge that led to the concluding vamp ("D"), and so on. Kind of a weird way of doing business, but as Garry Tallent recalls, Bruce wanted to keep his players on their toes. "He didn't want us too confident with it," Tallent says. "He was trying to keep Roy and myself and maybe some others from overplaying."

If a new song came with a basic, three-chord rock 'n' roll foundation, Bruce kept the spontaneity alive by counting off the first take without telling anyone how it went or even what key they should play in. "He'd just say, 'Follow me!' and we'd go," Tallent says. "We'd hear the song for the first time while we were recording it."

Bruce was far more careful about recording "The River," a terse acoustic ballad that told the story of a young couple bound—by an accident of teenage conception, social expectations, and the absence of opportunity—to the same working-class grind that had consumed the lives of their parents, and their parents' parents. Another sacrifice on the twin altars of organized religion and America's class system. "The River" also happened to be a word-for-word description of the life that Bruce's sister Ginny had lived since her accidental pregnancy, at eighteen, and early marriage to Mickey Shave. Written in the first person, "The River" is shot through with empathy and no small amount of anger. By the final verse, the narrator thinks back to those youthful moments of love and promise as a setup for the life that has claimed them. In the end, he's left with the most dispiriting of riddles: "Is a dream a lie if it don't come true / Or is it something worse?"

For Ginny, who hadn't known that her brother had written a song about her, hearing its live premiere at Madison Square Garden was unnerving, to say the least. "It was wonderful that he wrote it and all, but every bit of it was true," she says. "And here I am [in the audience], completely exposed. I didn't like it at first—though now it's my favorite song."

"The River"'s premiere took place on September 21, 1979, in the midst of the shortened set that Bruce and the band played during the Musicians United for Safe Energy "No Nukes" fund-raisers, a series of five concerts organized by an all-star consortium of politically active pop artists. Hoping to build a global protest against nuclear energy—and the specter of deadly accidents that could sicken or kill hundreds of thousands, as the Three Mile Island incident nearly did—chief organizers Jackson Browne, Bonnie Raitt, Graham Nash, and John Hall appealed to dozens of the era's top performers.[3]

Bruce, as a critically acclaimed up-and-comer with a notoriously fanatic local following, seemed an obvious choice for the lineup, but even given his longtime friendships with Browne, Raitt, and Hall (the latter of whom he'd met at the Cafe Wha? in 1967), the Jersey icon seemed a long shot for the bill. After all, Bruce had avoided lending his name to political events since the George McGovern fund-raiser in 1972. "I felt my music carried its own power," he says. "When something works [on its own artistic terms], there's a sense of the world." Trying to mix in a specific political agenda, on the other hand, too often reduced what should have been art into dogma. But by the summer of 1979, Bruce had started to think again about using his music to fuel the causes that rang his conscience's chimes. "I was searching around for some way to connect

[3] The board members themselves, plus Nash's partners David Crosby and Stephen Stills, the Doobie Brothers, Carly Simon, Tom Petty and the Heartbreakers, Chaka Khan, Raydio, Gil Scott-Heron, Jesse Colin Young, Sweet Honey in the Rock, and others.

what I was doing musically with some tangible action," he says. Climbing aboard a movement started by friends he respected seemed like a good way to start, so while Bruce stopped short of contributing a statement to the shows' concert program, as all the other artists had done, he felt entirely committed. "I felt I would make whatever statement I needed to make from the stage," he says. "And also by just being there—[because] what I wouldn't have done is offer the power of my band casually. Because that was something I believed in and was very serious about."

As Jackson Browne recalls, Bruce's commitment to appear had the desired effect. "He was kind of an icon, with a sense of rebellion and honesty," he says. "Having someone like Bruce on the show gave us a validity and legitimacy among people in the street." Booked to headline the final two shows at Madison Square Garden (the MUSE organization also put on a massive free concert in Lower Manhattan's Battery Park on September 23, which Bruce skipped), Bruce came to his shows with more than the usual performance anxiety clinging to his back. Six months into recording, the new album had yet to take shape in his mind. And if a pair of gigs could be a momentary distraction, he also had to confront the pressure of such high-profile shows, along with the fact that he hadn't been onstage with the band since the end of the Darkness tour nine months earlier. He would also have to edit his usual three-hour set to ninety minutes, tops, to make room for all the other artists on the bill. Worst of all, Bruce would turn thirty on September 23, meaning that he would almost inevitably have to acknowledge his landmark birthday during his set on the night of the twenty-second.

That last one freaked him out the most. When Danny Goldberg, the producer of the concert movie documenting the shows, asked Bruce how it felt to hit his thirties, the musician made it clear that he wasn't the least bit happy about it. "He said, 'Oh man, it feels really different,'" says Goldberg, speaking in the robotic voice of someone only just holding himself together. "It probably doesn't seem like that big a deal to him now."

Still, Bruce was one of the younger artists on the stage, and given his enormous following in and around New York, he was the hottest draw: sales for the last two shows had lagged until Bruce signed on, at which point they sold out instantly. Thus he was afforded a level of deference the other artists either couldn't, or didn't want to, claim for themselves. So while the other performers shared team-sized dressing rooms, Bruce and the E Streeters camped out in a private area accessible only to holders of official Springsteen credentials. Later, Goldberg had no problem finding footage of the other stars chatting and cavorting together backstage; the only glimpse of Bruce, he discovered, was a ten-second snippet of him greeting Jackson Browne's little son.

Certainly, the twelve-song set Bruce and band played on the twenty-first became precisely the slam-bang finish everyone in the hall had hoped to witness. A combination of Springsteen anthems ("Born to Run," "Thunder Road," "Rosalita"), unreleased new songs ("Sherry Darling" and "The River," much to Ginny Springsteen's surprise), and high-intensity performances of oldies ("Detroit Medley," "Rave On"), the performance left Bruce drenched, wrung out, and predictably ecstatic.

Things took a less appealing turn the next night when the birthday greetings started coming over the footlights. When one fan handed up a cake, Bruce hurled it back onto the heads of the crowd packed tight around the stage. He finally acknowledged the roll of his internal odometer in his usually jokey introduction to the as-yet-unreleased frat-rock song "Sherry Darling." "Okay, this is my big birthday party tonight," he said. "I'm officially over the fucking hill. Can't trust myself anymore.[4] So let me hear some party noises!" Which he did, delivered with enough gusto to propel him through the second half of the set and right into the encores, which ended with a particularly crazed performance of Gary "U.S." Bonds's "Quarter to Three," extended to nearly ten minutes of throat-tearing screams, razor-wire guitar solos, dancing, guitar swinging, amp jumping, and more. And they were still blasting away at full, joyous power when Bruce glimpsed a too-familiar face in the crowd and felt something snap.

According to Lynn Goldsmith, he shouldn't have been surprised, let alone aggravated. She had been a key MUSE volunteer for months, serving as the event's head of photography. Charged with shooting her own

---

[4] Referring to the 1960s mantra that no young person should trust anyone over thirty.

pictures and coordinating the other photographers working for the event, Goldsmith had responsibilities backstage and on the camera riser eleven rows back from the front of the stage. Though generally cordial in their postromance relationship, things remained awkward enough for Bruce to request that Goldsmith make herself scarce from his part of the backstage area when he was preparing to go on.

"He came over to my house, and we made a plan, just he and I," the photographer says. In her telling, Goldsmith described where she had to be during the evening, and said she'd get another photographer, Joel Bernstein, to shoot Bruce's backstage area once he arrived. "He'd come at a certain time, I'd go to the front [of the stage]. And I wouldn't go backstage after that. I thought the whole thing was fine after that."

It wasn't. So while Goldsmith shot the first of Bruce's two shows without incident, the second show, with its unhappily received birthday celebrations, turned sour before Bruce saw his ex-girlfriend with other photographers clustered on a platform above the eleventh row. "She was real close right in front, and that's in Bruce's field of vision," road manager Bobby Chirmside says. First Bruce started to pace the stage; then he glared up at Goldsmith until they made eye contact. "He gets down on one knee, and kind of bent his finger at me like, '*C'mere,*'" Goldsmith says. "I knew that look in his eye, and I wasn't going there." When Bruce saw Goldsmith packing up her gear, he leaned over to Clemons and shouted "*Watch this!*" Then he leapt off the stage and into the aisle. Goldsmith tried to vanish into the crowd, but it took only a moment for him to grab her arm. "I was saying, 'Please stop, you're hurting me,'" Goldsmith recalls. But Bruce could not stop. He twisted her arm so hard she thought it would snap. Surrounded by rows of stunned and unhappy faces, he pulled Goldsmith down the aisle and then up the stairs to his microphone at center stage.

"Ladies and gentlemen!" he shouted. "This is my ex-girlfriend!" Goldsmith tried to laugh it off in front of the crowd, but then he marched her to the edge of the stage and pushed her into the arms of Chirmside, ordering him to throw her out of the building. Chirmside put his arm around Goldsmith and held her more gently than Bruce had done. But he still escorted her down to the arena's inner tunnels, where she realized he was following his boss's orders. "She said, 'Bobby, you're not really going to throw me out, are you?'" Chirmside says. "I said, 'I'm not. But I've got to hand you over to security, and then *they're* going to have to throw you out.'"

Humiliated and furious, Goldsmith marched out into the night. The other MUSE stars had no idea what had happened, or why. "I just kind of stood there with my mouth hanging open," Browne says. The understanding backstage was that Goldsmith—despite her leadership role among the MUSE photographers—had violated an agreement to stay away from Bruce's performance. And yet this didn't make Bruce's behavior any less ugly or shocking. "It was kind of Bruce's personal thing hanging out there." Browne says. "And I know Lynn; she's a great gal. It sounds like a misunderstanding that played out in a very dramatic way."

The drama only got more intense when Joyce Hyser, who had been seated in the arena, burst through the dressing area's door, cheeks burning with outrage. Bruce hadn't told her about the brewing conflict with Goldsmith, so when she saw her boyfriend plucking his ex out of the crowd and announcing her as his girlfriend, Hyser—who obviously had missed the "ex" part of his rant—could assume only that she had been had. Storming in Bruce's direction, Hyser was intercepted by Browne, who guided her into a dressing room and put his arms around her shoulders to calm her down.[5] They were still standing like that when an elated Bruce came skipping down the stage stairs, followed by his band, singing the chorus to the Village People's "Macho Man" in his wake. "He's all pumped up, then he finds Jackson with his arms around me, and I'm a sniveling *mess*," Hyser says. Seeing his current girlfriend in the California singer's arm refired his temper. "*What the hell is going on here?*" he snarled, prompting frantic explanations from both Browne and Hyser. Bruce ended the evening begging Hyser's forgiveness, but even when he and Goldsmith bumped into each other at the Sunset Marquis hotel in Los Angeles a year later, he refused to apologize for anything. Instead,

[5] Browne says he remembers consoling Hyser, but not the part about having his arms around her. "But she was *fine*. Anyone would want to put their arms around her. She was *ridiculously* fine."

Goldsmith recalls, Bruce blamed her for his public tantrum. "He said, 'Why did you do that?' and I just laughed. 'Why did *I* do that? Why did *you* do that?' Then we both started laughing."

Bruce felt much more in control when the time came to oversee his part of the *No Nukes* movie set to premiere in theaters during the summer of 1980. Although Goldberg recalls Bruce as being uniquely warm and charming throughout, the musician still put the production through his own kind of wringer, starting with the songs the filmmakers wanted to use in the film and on the album. The original cut that Goldberg and codirector Anthony Potenza made included four songs from Bruce's sets: "The River," "Thunder Road," "Stay,"[6] and "Quarter to Three." But when Bruce came in to look at his segments and weigh in on their look, feel, and sound, he had a problem. Given the gravity of the concerts, and his own desire to be taken seriously, he didn't want his party music to dominate his appearance in the film. So "The River" and "Thunder Road" could stay, but "Stay" and "Quarter to Three" had to go.

He was never rude or peremptory, Goldberg says. Mostly, Bruce responded to the producer-director's entreaties by not saying anything. And when Goldberg came up with the right explanation about how the narrative of the film, which already included more segments about energy technology than the majority of concert movie attendees would tolerate, required the climactic rush of a Bruce Springsteen encore, Bruce nodded. "He gave me a hug and said, 'Okay, I get it. You can use these songs,'" Goldberg says. "It was one of the great moments of my life."

From there Bruce took residence in the editing bay, watching his scenes with the precise eyes of an auteur, calling for different shots or angles.[7] And when Bruce got into the sound editing studio, he fussed with the mix at such microlevels and macro length that Goldberg had to beseech Toby Scott (Bruce's trusty engineer, called in to oversee the

[6] Performed with Browne, who had a hit with his 1977 cover of Maurice and the Zodiacs' 1960 chart topper.
[7] The Lynn Goldsmith incident had been edited out of "Quarter to Three" long before Bruce saw a frame of the film, for obvious length, discretion, and nobody-wants-to-see-*that*-again issues.

music mixing in Bruce's segments) sometime between midnight and dawn that union rules governing payment for film industry engineers had just put them in an overtime pay bracket ("It was like double-double-golden-overtime-overtime, I think," Scott says) that could bring the production to its knees. "We wrapped it up a couple of hours later," says Scott.

Work on Bruce's new album continued through the end of 1979 and into the winter of 1980. Attempts to edit the new material into a single album came to nothing. They kept recording, and when the boxes of session tapes hit three hundred and kept growing, they sent a crew member to buy a gigantic 10 foot x 10 foot x 10 foot road case to use as an in-studio storage locker. When they ended a session and loaded the new tapes into their storage container, they secured it with several chains and locks. Soon the box—called the Bruce Springsteen Memorial Couch or the Houdini Box—became a visual metaphor for the seemingly endless project.

As with his previous two albums, Bruce couldn't stop thinking, and worrying, about the record. And the more he stewed, the more energy he had for writing even more songs. As Hyser remembers, his mind churned constantly, forever absorbing and analyzing the things he saw, heard, lived, and felt, channeling them through his guitar and then into scraps of verse he wrote into his notebook—or, if his binder wasn't available, onto notepaper that piled up on the coffee tables, counters, and end tables where he sat when inspiration hit. "He always had his guitar," Hyser says. "Bruce was very romantic but very single-minded about nothing getting in the way of his work, including relationships and friendships. That's what sustained him at that time . . . and it was just constant."

When the bill for recording time hit $1 million and kept climbing, CBS president Walter Yetnikoff visited the studio to make sure Bruce understood that it only *looked* like the company was footing the bill for all their work. All those charges would end up being paid for through Bruce's own royalties. "His response was, 'How better can I spend my money than on my art?'" Yetnikoff says. "What was I supposed to tell him?' *'No! You should spend all your money on drugs!'*?" Bruce was just as convincing when he insisted that *The River* could only work as a double album. Record company chiefs tend to hate that sort of thing (double albums cost more in the shops, thus selling in lower numbers), but when Bruce told him that a single album didn't give him enough space to say what he needed to say, Yetnikoff says he was powerless to respond. "You can't argue with that. You can't respond except to say, 'All right! You win!'" Still, Yetnikoff had little sympathy for Bruce's fixation on achieving the most perfect of all perfect mixes. "I said, 'You know what? Nobody gives a fuck about the snare drum sound,'" says Yetnikoff. "I said, 'Let me mix your record. Just show me the voice button, and I'll mix the fucking record. And don't worry about the snare drum—nobody hears it. Another musician might, but everyone else is listening to your voice!'" Bruce passed on the offer.

At the start of the sessions in 1979, Bruce had brought in "Hungry Heart," a cheery pop tune built around a piano riff he borrowed from the Four Seasons' 1964 hit "Dawn (Go Away)." He ran the band through a handful of takes and then lost interest when he decided it sounded too airy for the hard-bitten album he'd envisioned. True enough, earlier drafts of "Hungry Heart" sketch a dark story, admitting "Sometimes I can't explain the things I do / I guess I did it 'cause I wanted to." The title phrase also appears in an earlier, even bleaker version of "Stolen Car," in the narrator's admission that the end of his marriage came because "I fell victim to a hungry heart." Even "Hungry Heart"'s recorded lyrics—which begin with the narrator deserting his family and then describe the start and end of another relationship in a single sentence ("We fell in love, I knew it had to end")—seems out of step with its breezy music. Nevertheless, Bruce abandoned the song, deciding to give it to the Ramones for their next album. Landau, on the other hand, refused to let it go. In this he had an enthusiastic partner in Van Zandt. "It just had this groove," Van Zandt says. "Something about this song. So I said, 'Let's get some extra high harmony on it.'" They called in Mark Volman and Howard Kaylan, cofounders of the harmony-centric sixties band the Turtles ("Happy Together," etc.) to add a touch of Beach Boys to the backing vocals. Thinking that Bruce's Big Voice croon made the song sound a bit too *mature* for Top 40 radio, Plotkin sped up the tape to give the vocal a more boyish lilt. "We got up to Mickey Mouse speed 'til we backed it down," Landau says. Finished tinkering, Van Zandt handed the mixing duties over to Bob Clearmountain, already known for his ability to give potential hits just the right coat of gloss. Excitement all around.

Until they played the completed track to Bruce, who shook his head. He still didn't like it. Too pop, too lightweight. So just hand it off, just like they'd done with "The Fever," "Because the Night," and "Fire," the latter of which had climbed to number 2 on the *Billboard* Hot 100 for the Pointer Sisters in February 1979. So, conversation over. Except that it wasn't. As both Van Zandt and Landau knew, the time had come for Bruce to have a real hit song on Top 40 radio. "It's a complicated moment," Van Zandt says. "You really need it to be the right hit single at the right time, or else your rock credibility goes away. But this is our fifth album. We've paid our dues. And this felt right."

Eventually convinced that "Hungry Heart" did fit on the new album and would serve nicely as the project's lead-off single, Bruce gave up worrying about the corrosive effect of the Top 10. Then he began to look forward to seeing what a hot single might do for his career—particularly when CBS publicist Paul Rappaport pulled him aside in October to tell him how strong the response from radio programmers and other industry factota had become. "I told Bruce, 'Hey, *ka-ching!* That song's gonna be a hit!'" Bruce beamed. "Great!" he said, "I've been wanting to get some new tires for my 'Vette!" Rappaport laughed. "I said, 'You can probably buy a whole Corvette *factory* when this is over.' He just looked at me like I was crazy and walked away."

Bruce had no idea. Released on October 17, 1980, *The River* bolted for the top of the *Billboard* album chart, selling more than 1.5 million copies in the run-up to Christmas. "Hungry Heart," released four days after the album, was ubiquitous on Top 40 radio throughout the fall, climbing to number 5 of the singles chart. None of Bruce's previous singles had even come close to the Top 10. By the time the band got to the Rosemont Horizon arena in northern Illinois on November 20, the chiming sound of the hit song's intro so excited the crowd that Bruce couldn't get the first line of the first verse out of his mouth before the fans drowned him out, shouting every word in perfect unison. "Bruce's eyes were popping out, like '*Holy shit!*'" Rappaport remembers. "He's always let the crowd do the first verse ever since, but that was the moment. The shock on his face, the pure delight. That was priceless."

Set adrift on opposing currents of ecstasy and dread, *The River* reveals as much about Bruce's internal life as he'd ever displayed in public. The mostly live performances (the basic band tracks were often enhanced with overdubbed vocals and/or guitar and saxophone solos) emphasize the big studio's ambient blend, giving the songs a barroom feel that trades the precision of "Born to Run" and "Darkness on the Edge of Town" with the power of the full band's instrumental wallop. "I wanted to cut some music that felt very explosive," Bruce says. "I wanted to combine the fun aspect of what the band did along with the story I was telling. Find a way to combine those things and create a bigger picture of what we did out in front of the people."

Thus the legion of new fans who would push *The River* to quintuple-platinum status were introduced to a performer and band whose approach was defined by what Bruce describes as "desperate fun": a joyful noise meant to keep the encroaching gloom at bay, if only for the moment. Singing with the raw voice of an embattled ordinary guy, Bruce narrated his stories as directly and unromantically as possible. "I was interested in what adulthood meant," he says. "That was a life that I was not living, but seeing from the outside looking in, I admired it in a lot of ways. I thought it was certainly the roots of the place that I grew up in and the people that I knew." People who lived and worked hard, and who celebrated their glories and assuaged their wounds to the sound of barroom rock 'n' roll.

From a distance, the simple joys of rock 'n' roll are all over the album, from the Delta House rock of "Sherry Darling" (with cheers and chorus singing concocted in the studio), to the taut drums and guitars on "The Ties That Bind," "Two Hearts," and "Out in the Street." But just as "Hungry Heart"'s joyous music belies its uneasy core, "Cadillac Ranch"'s celebration of America's most luxurious gas-guzzler, complete with its shout-outs to famous hot-rodders Junior Johnson, James Dean, and Burt Reynolds, lead to the long black Cadillac that takes all its passengers on a one-way trip.[8] The narrator of "Ramrod" also has death on his mind, even as he pushes his automotive slang into the red zone of sexual metaphor. "This guy . . . he's there, but he's really not there anymore," Bruce told Dave Marsh in 1981. The song's last line, "Give me the word now, sugar, we'll go ramroddin' forevermore," made the shadow of death inescapable, at least to its author. "I don't know," he told Marsh. "That's a real sad line to me sometimes." Thirty years later it's easier for Bruce to put his finger on why: "When you make your big choices in life—who you're going to be with, where you're going to live, what you're going to work at—there's a very natural clock that starts ticking. And that's your time clock, my friend."

And so even as *The River* traces the human toll of economic and social inequity (particularly in the title track, "Jackson Cage," and "The Price You Pay"), the real-life verities of adult romance ("I Wanna Marry You"), and the chill of emotional isolation ("Stolen Car"), the entire journey is geared to end, with the richest possible symbolism, with the bloodied wreckage and shattered body we find in "Wreck on the Highway." "So at the end of the record, that's what gets introduced," Bruce says. "The highway's closed at a certain point. You have a certain amount of miles that you can make. It's a recognition of mortality."

[8] See also the lyric sheet photo that traces the song's inspiration to the real Cadillac Ranch, a long line of half-buried Cadillacs made by the conceptual art group known as Ant Farm (Chip Lord, Hudson Marquez, and Doug Michels) installed just outside Amarillo, Texas, in 1974.

EIGHTEEN

DELIVER ME FROM NOWHERE

THE 140-STOP RIVER TOUR KICKED off in Ann Arbor, Michigan, on October 3, 1980, hauling through virtually every major city in the United States before playing a final stateside show in Indianapolis on March 5, 1981. A first-ever full-length European tour was scheduled to start in Brighton, England, on March 17. But when the cold he'd been fending off at the end of the stateside tour floored him for more than a week, Bruce came to understand how much the US tour had drained from his tank. Leery of venturing back to the United Kingdom with something less than all cylinders wide open and roaring—particularly to London, from which he still felt he'd been spanked and sent home in 1975, Bruce and Landau rescheduled the twelve British shows to be the last stops on the European itinerary.

Heading into the opening concert in Hamburg, Germany, on April 7,

Bruce's pretour nerves frazzled a bit more when the local promoter warned that Hamburg audiences were notoriously undemonstrative. Just because they're sitting there silently with blank looks on their faces, Bruce heard, didn't mean they weren't having fun per se. Just don't expect an American-style eruption of energy. "So the audience sat through the first set, just *nothing*, until we came back and opened the second set with 'Badlands,'" Bruce recalls. "Then they rushed the stage, and that was it for the rest of the tour. Just mayhem every place we went."

The wild reception chased them across Europe and into Britain, running particularly hot at London's 12,500-seat Wembley Arena, which Bruce and band filled completely each night of their six-night stand in late May and early June. "It was startling," Bruce says. "If I were to list some of the high points of being out there working, that tour was one of them."

Van Zandt was just as stunned. "We break Europe, and we've made it. We are a success. And it's like, wow! We really did it! Fifteen years in the making, y'know." As Premier Talent's Frank Barsalona had promised, Europe was, and remains, a lucrative market for Bruce.

Even more important, the tour allowed Bruce and everyone else in the E Street touring party to look at the world from somewhere beyond American soil. Starting out as provincial Americans protected by the insularity of the rock 'n' roll tour bubble, the journey through other lands, cities, and communities presented an entirely new perspective. So many of the people they met, particularly the young adults they found in the coffee shops and pubs, had come to see America as a forbidding imperial presence. "This kid accused me of putting missiles in his country, and I was like, 'What are ya talking about? There's a guitar in that case, not a missile,'" Van Zandt says. "But it wouldn't leave my head until I realized that when you leave this country, you're an American. It's not Democrat or Republican, taxi driver or rocker. It's just *American*. And we're supposedly a democracy, so you are responsible for what your country does."

Bruce had already voiced his fears of the incoming Ronald Reagan administration onstage the night after the deeply conservative politician's

election on November 4, 1980.[1] His anxieties, particularly when it came
to the new president's bellicose stance against the Soviet Union and the
Eastern bloc of nations, had already been realized in western Europe,
where an influx of American missiles and personnel evoked forty-year-old
memories of marching soldiers and rampaging tanks, along with fears of
the modern chemical warfare that could reduce their lives into so many
clouds of poisonous dust. Soon the narrative of the shows confronted
the idea of America itself, in all its beauty and failings. Bruce had already
introduced a striking cover of Woody Guthrie's "This Land Is Your Land"
in late December, noting sharply that the folk tune so many people considered a fireside sing-along was intended as a rebuttal to the starry-eyed
triumphalism in Irving Berlin's "God Bless America." Adding John Fogerty's Vietnam-era "Who'll Stop the Rain" and "Run Through the Jungle"
drew out the social commentary already girding "Thunder Road," "The
Promised Land," and especially "Badlands."

At the same time, Bruce focused his reading on American history, in
search of stories and analyses that gave new perspective to the accepted
saga of pilgrims, patriots, great men, and Manifest Destiny. Joe Klein's
Woody Guthrie: A Life sketched a real-life portrait of the roads, work
sites, and campsites visited by the Joad family in Steinbeck's *The Grapes of
Wrath*, while Henry Steele Commager and Allan Nevins's *The Pocket History of the United States* described the nation's development from a populist perspective that reflected his own experience as a child of the lower
working class. "I never heard anyone talk about politics in my neighborhood," Bruce says. "It might have come up once in school, because I came
home one day and asked my mother if we were Republican or Democrats.
She said we were Democrats, because they're for the working people. And
that was the extent of the political conversation in my entire childhood."

Raised to view the American story through the eyes of the downtrod-
den, Bruce could connect his parents' struggles with the larger dynamics

---

[1] "I don't know what you thought about what happened last night," he told the audience at Arizona State University's arena the next night. "But I thought it was pretty
frightening."

of a country prone to forget its most vulnerable citizens. To be a Springsteen in Freehold meant knowing all about vulnerability and the taste of the ashes scattered upon the people who couldn't summon the power to fight for themselves. It was the same story he'd written about his father in "Adam Raised a Cain," the flame-lit portrait of a man forced to work a lifetime "for nothin' but the pain." Only now he could recognize Doug Springsteen's struggle in a larger context: as another glimpse of the underside of the American Dream. The story of the man whose perspective on American-style progress came from beneath its razor wheels.

So much of Bruce's ambition, and the unrelenting energy he had focused on building his career, had been fueled by his determination to avoid his father's fate. In the midst of his biggest success[2] the time had come to turn his attention, and more important, his audience's attention, to the Americans whose nation had left them behind. After all, a significant percentage of his friends and fans were the people who suffered at the hands of a top-down socioeconomic structure. "We were at that very moment out and engaged with the people who were on the other end of the stick," Bruce says. "So that became a regular part of the show. I still reserve a small part of the evening for a public service announcement. I do believe that there's a section of my audience that's involved with what I'm doing, so I address them, and it feels like a natural thing to do."

Back in the United States in mid-June, Bruce took his first step into a cause that had been playing on his conscience since his late-seventies encounter with Ron Kovic, the maimed Vietnam vet, antiwar activist, and bestselling author of the politically charged memoir *Born on the Fourth of July*.[3] Bruce found a paperback edition of the book while on a road trip through the Southwest and read it in a desert motel somewhere between Phoenix and Los Angeles. Hanging out by the pool at the Sunset Marquis a few days later, he saw a wheelchair-bound man rolling over to say hi. Bruce spoke to the guy for a few minutes before he realized that

[2] Bruce would end the River tour with all the profits he hadn't seen after Born to Run and the mammoth Darkness tours.
[3] Later adapted into a hit movie starring Tom Cruise.

the man in front of him was the author of the book he had just finished. "It was really strange," Bruce said to Will Percy for *Double Take* in 1998. "I said, 'You wouldn't believe this, but I bought your book in a drugstore in Arizona, and I just read it. It's incredible.'" Kovic took him to a veterans' center in the Venice neighborhood and later put him in touch with Bobby Muller, a wounded vet who had started a national organization for his and Kovic's contemporaries, the Vietnam Veterans of America (VVA).

Hearing in 1981 that Muller's organization had run out of money and would be forced to close its doors, Bruce invited him to a show at New Jersey's newly opened Meadowlands Arena in July, and then asked him to stay late so they could talk. In the midst of that conversation, Bruce, Muller, and Landau hatched a plan: when the tour came back to Los Angeles in late August, they would make the opening concert at the Los Angeles Sports Arena into a benefit for the VVA.

With a legion of veterans, many severely wounded, watching from a specially built deck on the side of the stage, Bruce started the show with a brief but emotional speech. Describing America's Vietnam era as a long walk through a dark alley where thugs attack some people while others walk past without looking up, he urged the audience to throw a lifeline to the war's victims. "Unless we're able to walk down those dark alleys and look into the eyes of the men and the women that are down there and the things that happened, we're never gonna be able to get home," he said. Muller spoke next, concluding his speech by observing that rock 'n' roll had always been the one thing that bonded his generation of Americans. "So let's not talk about it, let's get down to it, *let's rock 'n' roll it!*" Bruce kicked the band into Creedence Clearwater Revival's "Who'll Stop the Rain" and let it rip for nearly four hours, straight through the long-lost Bob Dylan–Roger McGuinn anthem "Ballad of Easy Rider," an extended "Detroit Medley," and then back to the start of his own rock 'n' roll life with a wild run at "Twist and Shout."

A transformative event for the VVA and a significant step for the Vietnam vets movement in general (Muller later said, "Without Bruce Springsteen, there would be no Vietnam veterans movement"), the show also allowed Bruce to address the memory of Bart Haynes, the "swingin' little drummer" the Castiles lost to the war in 1967, and Joe Curcio, a

Freehold Regional classmate who had gone into the service with all the fire and energy of an eighteen-year-old kid and then returned two years later as a shattered spirit, his shoulders stooped beneath the weight of what he'd seen and done. As Curcio recalls, Bruce had always gone out of his way to be kind to him during his dark years, even when he found him in a barroom or on a sidewalk collapsed beneath his burden and whatever he had consumed to numb his distress. "I was kinda screwed up, but he was always nice," Curcio says. "Bruce is special like that."

Special enough to realize that his own onstage tales of avoiding the war (throughout the seventies, Bruce spun wild tales about his attempts to convince the US Army he was crazy) might strike some veterans, or their survivors, as less than funny. All of those tactics were common in the late-1960s,[4] but that still didn't seem to justify Bruce's celebrating a scheme that resulted in other Americans serving in his stead. Particularly given the crowning irony that Bruce needed only to submit his medical file—and its notes about the concussion and knee injury he'd suffered in his 1968 motorcycle accident—to be shooed out with 4-F stamped on his forehead. By the time he told the same story to introduce "The River" in the early eighties, all traces of slapstick were gone. When the audience cheered his failing the army's physical exam, he cut them short: "It ain't nothin' to applaud about."

On a night off from the River tour in Denver, Bruce went out to see Woody Allen's film *Stardust Memories*. As he described it later to Dave Marsh, his solitary evening took a turn at the popcorn counter when a teenage fan came up to shake his hand. Noticing that Bruce had come alone, the guy invited the musician to watch the movie with him and his sister. Bruce said sure, and the three watched Allen's acidic take on fame together. When the lights came up afterward, the teenager looked stricken. "Jesus, I don't know what to say to ya," he said. "Is this the way it is? Is this how you feel?'" Bruce reassured him he never felt besieged

---

[4] A lot of the Asbury Park musicians took their draft-beating instructions from Billy Chinnock, who turned his own successful strategy into an easy-to-follow formula for friends facing the same ordeal.

by fans, which relieved the guy enough to invite the musician to come back to the family's house and meet their parents. Bruce didn't hesitate to say yes, and after a brief you've-gotta-be-kidding-us scene at the door (resolved when the guy ran into his room and returned with his copy of *The River*, holding the cover portrait next to the real Bruce's face), they welcomed Bruce like long-lost family, cooking up a late dinner for them all to share, and then sitting at the table for hours telling him all about their lives, ambitions, and all the rest. Talking to Marsh, Bruce was nearly breathless as he described the scene. "You get somebody's whole life in three hours," he said. "You get their parents, you get their sister, you get their family life, in three hours. And I went back to that hotel, and I felt really good because I thought, 'Wow.'" As he'd already said, it was one of fame's most rarified privileges. "That is something that can happen to me that can't happen to most people."

And it wasn't an isolated experience. As Bruce told Fred Schruers in his *Rolling Stone* cover story published in January 1981, another fan had recently come up to tell him he had just spent ten hours on a bus in order to celebrate his twenty-first birthday at that night's concert. What's more, being able to tell that to Bruce face-to-face was the most important thing that had ever happened to him. "In ten minutes I'll know more about him than his mother and father do, and maybe his best friend," Bruce told Schruers. "It's just a real raw, emotional thing; it's like the cleanest thing you ever felt. You gotta love the guy. If you don't, there's something the matter with you."

But there's also something the matter with a thirty-one-year-old man who feels most comfortable engaging in such brief, fan-to-star encounters. And while Bruce invested the largest part of his energy in giving his audiences a night of music thrilling and genuine enough to be personally transformative,[5] he came away each night feeling less like a man reveling in the company of his twenty thousand new friends

---

[5] As Jon Landau recalls, the River shows grew even longer than the Darkness shows had been. Eventually Bruce realized he was losing control of himself. "I remember there was one night in LA when it was 1:20 a.m. when he came off the stage," Landau says. "I remember him reflecting, 'I'm going too far.' We didn't break one o'clock much after that."

than like a seduction artist creeping out of a lover's bedroom with his shoes in his hand. "I'd rather go on the bus to another city than stay [after a show]," he told the *Los Angeles Times*' Robert Hilburn. "I don't like staying. It's funny. It makes me feel uncomfortable." As did the thought of having a permanent home of his own rather than the crash pads and the lightly decorated rental houses he had cycled through for more than a decade. Even when he bought a three-bedroom house in Los Angeles where girlfriend Joyce Hyser stayed when she was working in town—often with Bruce's sister Pam as a housemate—when Bruce came to town, he usually avoided his own house in favor of the ease and anonymity of the Sunset Marquis hotel. "Bruce really loved the hotel life," says Hyser. "He loved being on the road."

Then in the midst of her four-year romance with Bruce, Hyser had plenty of opportunities to feel the tension between her boyfriend's sensitivity and his reflexive need to hide behind the barrier he'd erected to keep his inner self from other people. So while Bruce was happy to include his girlfriend in Springsteen family events, and went on to bond with her father, he never seemed all that upset when she shrugged off his occasional musings about getting married. "One reason why we stayed together as long as we did was that we both always had one foot out the door," she says. "Everyone had an escape route." Bruce traced the limits of his own commitment to Hyser by comparing his life to a totem pole, upon which one force would always rule above all others. "Honestly, there was nothing more important than his career," Hyser reflects. "That's what it came down to at the end of the day." That, and the understanding that their relationship had to bow to his need for privacy. "His whole thing in those days was, 'When I want to see you, you need to be here, and when I don't, you need to be gone.'"

The River tour ended with two shows in Cincinnati in mid-September 1981, after which the entire band, plus wives, girlfriends, management, and key E Street staffers traveled to Hawaii to celebrate Clarence Clemons's wedding to Christina Sandgren, whom he'd met in Scandinavia during the group's European swing that spring. Bruce served as the sax player's best man and led the entire band in a long set of oldies and originals during the reception. Returning to his latest rental house in New Jersey, he contemplated the posttour silence with mixed feelings. Finally flush with the long-delayed rewards of rock stardom, he had the financial freedom to do virtually anything he could imagine. Except for that he couldn't imagine anything he wanted to do other than to write and record a new album, or be on the road, or jam at the Stone Pony or in Clemons's new club, Big Man's West, a few klicks up the Jersey Shore in Red Bank.

"It was definitely a closing to a certain earlier section of my life, the initial section of the traveling and touring and those early records," Bruce says. "There was more contemplation. I was thirty or thirty-one, and something turned me back around toward my early childhood. That moved me into *Nebraska*, so that was pretty telling. I'm not sure what brought that music around, really."

Probably the same thing that compelled him, night after night, to climb into his car and drive the streets of Freehold, visiting the empty space on Randolph Street, where he had once lived with his grandparents; the duplex on Institute Street where he had been a schoolboy; and then the duplex on South Street where he'd lived as a teenager. He had no idea what he was looking for, Bruce admitted later. But that didn't stop him from going back. No matter where he was, memories of the Randolph Street house, and the shattered remnants of the life his grandparents had lost when their daughter died, fell over him. When he saw *Badlands*, the 1973 Terrence Malick film based on the exploits of teenage mass murderer Charlie Starkweather and his fourteen-year-old lover, Caril Ann Fugate,[6] the disconnection in the characters' eyes, the sense of living so far beyond meaningful social engagement that the rest of the world spins into a blur, brought him back into the house's chilly living room. "I was trying to capture the mood of what the house was like when I was a child," he says. "Austere, haunted . . . just this incredible inner turmoil."

The song Bruce first called "Starkweather" took shape quickly, the transposition of his childhood memories into the Midwestern murder

---

[6] In 1957 Starkweather, with Fugate in tow, went on a bloody rampage from Nebraska to Wyoming, killing eleven people he happened to come across.

saga made easier by his reading of Ninette Beaver's book-length description of the killings and a vintage state map of Nebraska he'd turned up somewhere. Pairing it with another freshly written song, "Mansion on the Hill," set the emotional terrain firmly in his Freehold youth, so while the stories ranged from undisguised autobiography ("Used Cars," "My Father's House," "Mansion on the Hill"), to bleak accounts of criminals, cops, and gangster wars ("Johnny 99," "Highway Patrolman," "Atlantic City"), to "Born in the U.S.A.," a bitter account of the life of a small-town Vietnam veteran, the same mood of desolation wove the songs into a unified whole. From song to song, story to story, and character to character, the same images and thoughts repeat, often word for word: "I got debts no honest man can pay," declares the last-chance narrator in "Atlantic City." The same phrase appears in "Johnny 99," this time from the mouth of a just-convicted criminal begging the judge to send him to death row.

Where poverty doesn't loom, spiritual emptiness does. "Deliver me from nowhere" declares the incipient psychopath talking himself in and out of a murderous rage in "State Trooper." Less threatening, and yet similarly lost, the narrator of "Open All Night" pins his hopes on the radio dial: "Hey ho, rock 'n' roll, deliver me from nowhere." And if the explicitly autobiographical songs lose the criminal element, the air of anguish is just as thick. Recollections of a summertime party in "Mansion on the Hill" (the name clearly reminiscent of Anthony Zerilli's House on the Hill) filter through the stalks of corn where the uninvited young narrator hides with his sister to take in the music and lights. Memories of accompanying his father on trips to an auto dealership play as exercises in humiliation in "Used Cars," while "Reason to Believe," which in any other setting would be the title of a rousing anthem, unspools as existentialism. "Still, at the end of every hard-earned day, people find some reason to believe," he concludes. It's that *some* that makes all the difference. Put your faith in this, put your faith in that. For all the good it does, it might as well be nothing at all.

The already-performed "Bye Bye Johnny" turned up on the same list of songs, along with another crime spree drama, "Losin' Kind"; the lovers-on-the-run ballad "Child Bride"; a pent-up lust song, "Pink

Cadillac"; and another portrait of economic and personal impoverish-
ment called "Downbound Train." Throughout, the same spiritual void
yawned beneath the characters' feet. "It's the thin line between stability
and that moment when time stops and everything goes to black," Bruce
wrote of the album in his 1998 collection of lyrics, *Songs*. "When the
things that connect you to your world—your job, your family, friends,
your faith, the love and grace in your heart—fail you."

Accustomed to recording home demos of his songs on an off-the-shelf
boom box, Bruce decided to trade up to a professional-grade home tap-
ing setup. He sent his guitar tech, Mike Batlan, to get a Teac four-track
recorder, figuring the extra tracks would allow him to add an extra guitar
part, overdub a harmony vocal, add percussion, or whatever flavoring he
thought might help the band get a sense of how he wanted the finished
tracks to sound. Whatever mixing he needed to do could be performed
on a high-grade but still off-the-shelf Panasonic beat box, which was just
good enough to handle the at-home demo work he had in mind.

   A technically demanding songwriter would have sprung for a more
reliable mixing unit, especially since this particular beat box had been
through some rough months. Earlier that fall Bruce had brought it along
on a boat journey that he and Garry Tallent were taking on the Navesink
River. They were rocking and rolling their way up the river until the
water turned rough. "This wave came over the bow, hit the beat box, and
shut it down," Bruce says. He hauled the dead machine back to Colts
Neck, put it on his couch,[7] and forgot all about it until a week or so later,
when he was watching television in the middle of the night. "Suddenly,
pchhhk-chhhk-kapow! I hear this sound, and it scared me, man. *What the
hell is that!?!* Then a few more explosions, and bang! The thing came blasting back on." When it worked again the next morning, Bruce put the box
back into his pile of active electronic gear, and when he called in Batlan
to help him record his new batch of songs, they both assumed that the
resurrected Panasonic was ready to work.

[7] Why Bruce would choose to store a drenched tape player on his *living room sofa* is anyone's guess. He was a young guy living alone, and it's too absurd a detail to not be true.

Batlan reported for duty early on the afternoon of January 3, 1982, and followed Bruce up to his bedroom, where he'd set up the Teac and a couple of microphones on a desk. Neither of them knew exactly how the equipment worked. But with the factory instruction booklets at hand, Bruce took up his guitar, waited for Batlan to point the microphones in the right direction, and performed the vocal and guitar tracks for "Nebraska." When Batlan rewound the tape and played it back, they were both pleasantly surprised to hear the song sounding just as Bruce had played it moments before. "We were like, 'Hey! It works!'" Bruce says. "It was completely haphazard and spur of the moment. But it was a nice thing, you know."

Working deep into the night, Bruce and Batlan recorded fifteen songs, with most of the basic tracking finished within four or six takes each. Overdubs were minimal, and after two or three days of mixing ("The sunken beatbox mix," Bruce calls it), they dubbed it down onto a cassette tape Bruce had picked up at a drugstore. With the process complete, Bruce slipped the cassette into his jacket pocket and carried it off to deliver it, along with a pages-long memo describing the songs' content and inspirations, to Landau's New York office.

Impressed by the power of the songs' minimalist narratives—and also by the yelping desperation in the performances—the producer-manager became all the more eager to escort Bruce back into the recording studio. So even if the overwhelming gloom in the recordings made him worry a bit about his friend's emotional state, the manager was confident that his artist had discovered a new horizon in his creative path. When Landau drove to Colts Neck to talk over the songs, he proposed recording most of them with small, folklike arrangements: acoustic guitars, stand-up bass, drums played with brushes. Nothing, he said, should stand between the hushed intimacy in Bruce's voice and the listener's ear. And yet enough of the songs invited a bigger, full-band sound, so Landau reserved the Power Station's gym-sized studio A, and Bruce called everyone in to start recording a few days later.

The first day in the studio didn't produce anything worth keeping. But when they got together the next afternoon, Bruce played the demo of "Born in the U.S.A.," then listened while Roy Bittan fiddled around on his just-purchased Yamaha synthesizer. When the keyboardist came up with a repetitive, high-pitched chord pattern that struck his ears as sounding just enough like Southeast Asian music to evoke the exotic jungle feel of Vietnam and Max Weinberg joined in with his pounding drums line, Bruce grabbed his electric guitar and counted off a first take. Recast as a pile-driving rocker, "U.S.A." blossomed in new shades of fury. Captured live in the studio, it required only a handful of takes to be declared finished. And also, to chief engineer Toby Scott and producers Landau and Chuck Plotkin, like something they'd never quite heard before. Scott: "We played it back, Chuck and Jon and I, and I said, 'This doesn't sound like the Bruce Springsteen of *The River*, but it sounds really good.' Just that live feel, with the drums going boom-crash, boom-crash. So we went on, and everything worked real quickly."

From there Bruce and the band went on a tear, recording finished (or all but finished) tracks drawn from the pages of his latest notebook of ideas, lyrics, and songs. After three weeks they had more than a dozen songs in the can, including "Born in the U.S.A." "Glory Days," "Cover Me," "Darlington County," "Working on the Highway" (evolved from "Child Bride"), a sizzling, funny take of "Pink Cadillac," and an early version of "My Hometown." They took a break after that initial rush, and when they reconvened a few weeks later, Bruce took out his cassette tape and said he wanted to shift gears for a while. They spent a few days working out arrangements to the taped songs in the music room at Bittan's house, but when they got back into the studio and tried to cut full-band versions of "Johnny 99," "Mansion on the Hill," "My Father's House," "Open All Night," and a few others, the feel was wrong. The intimacy in the original demo tape, along with the creeping gloom and mystery, had vanished. Part of the problem, Plotkin says, came out of the recording studio's tendency to conventionalize sounds, capturing them with pristine clarity. "But you don't want the *Nebraska* songs to be sweet and clean sounding," he says. "That's not what those songs are trying to convey."

The magic in the demo cassette, they realized, came out of its sonic flaws. The ghostly sound, the whimper in Bruce's vocals, the imprecise rhythms, and the remnants of river muck that brought out the desolation in the characters' stories. Soon it became obvious that the record Bruce needed to make of those songs was already rattling in his jacket pocket. "He turned to me and said, 'Tobe, can we master a record off of this thing?' and pulled out the tape," Scott says. "Then he tossed it at me. Literally." Taking it away to transform the demos into a releasable product, Scott realized how deeply flawed Bruce's and Batlan's attempts at recording had been. Bruce had never bothered to clean the heads of the recording console—a routine habit for engineers working with professional electronics. Neither man knew what the variable-speed knob on the console did, so they didn't notice that it had been set accidentally to run faster than normal. When Bruce finally did clue in and turned the knob to its normal, slower setting, the recordings all sounded sluggish. "Problems ensued," Scott says. Months' worth of problems, as it turned out. "I remember thinking the record would never get onto the disc," Plotkin recalls. "I was sitting around in a hotel room crying, it was so frustrating."

When the monthslong mastering process ended, Bruce and Landau brought their proposed next record to Walter Yetnikoff and Al Teller, the presidents of the CBS record group and Columbia, respectively, and were relieved to get upbeat receptions from both. Certainly *Nebraska* wouldn't be the global smash *The River* had been. But, as Yetnikoff proclaimed, the stark beauty of the music, along with what it represented in Bruce's artistic development, required that it be released and promoted. His colleague agreed. "Being a huge Bruce fan, I loved the record," says Teller. "But it was a small record, and would never be big." Teller said to Landau that as long as they were willing to accept sales of less than a million copies—and an advertising campaign that didn't hype the record as if it were destined to be the next *The River*—he had no problem with it being Bruce's new album. As Teller acknowledges, he and Columbia/CBS no longer had the authority to reject Bruce's albums anyway. "All they had to do contractwise was to submit a technically workable collection of ten to thirteen songs. Quality, content, and everything else was no longer a factor."

Released for the Christmas market in the fall of 1982, *Nebraska* emerged to a series of understated ads, the usual raves from the critic sector, and confusion from casual and serious fans alike. What happened to the Bruce who stomped and strutted across the spotlit stage? Where was the spirited kid who abandoned the loser towns and set out for the promised land? Who refused to surrender until the badlands—and all the authority figures who kept it churning—understood that they couldn't grind him into the dirt? Those declarations had never come for free: the darkness in Bruce's soul had always underscored his dreams of glory. But *Nebraska* offered nothing *but* darkness, from the plaintive howls prefacing the title track to the recurring crime sprees, arrests, trials, and life-ending prison sentences. The album pointedly lacked even a gesture toward salvation. Glance across the lyrics printed on the record's dust cover and run your eyes across the text. The concluding lines of virtually every song described the same spirit-crushing vision of life: "There's just a meanness in this world." "Let 'em shave off my hair and put me on that execution line." "I met this guy, and I'm gonna do a little favor for him." "Hey ho, rock 'n' roll, deliver me from nowhere." "Shining 'cross the dark highway where our sins lie unatoned." The promotional video for "Atlantic City," Bruce's first contribution to the new but already crucial MTV, was every bit as bleak, a washed-out black-and-white exploration of a beach city sinking beneath the lights and glitter just beneath the gambling industry's promises of wealth and glamour.

Still, *Nebraska* found its audience, a significant percentage of whom had either ignored Bruce altogether or dismissed him as a hype-driven lightweight. "I didn't know there was music like that, that was as impactful and as heavy as *Nebraska* was," says Tom Morello, a hard-edged eighteen-year-old punk rocker already on his way to becoming the leader of the sonic-destructo-punk band Rage Against the Machine. "The alienation that I felt was for the first time expressed in music, and then I became a huge superfan."[8]

With *Nebraska* finished, Bruce tried to return his attention to the full-band album they had started—and seemingly made a lot of progress toward finishing—in the winter and spring of 1982. But there were

---

[8] It actually took a few years from *Nebraska*'s release for Morello to absorb the album. But his experience is still emblematic, particularly among fans who didn't connect with the more commercial work Bruce would take on in the mid-1980s.

always more songs to record, more ideas to toss into the mix, more reasons to keep throwing the sledge against the stone until the earth cracked
open and God's wisdom beamed out. And yet, Bruce's thoughts swirled,
pulling him back to the same scenes he'd tried to exorcise with the *Nebraska* songs. Unable to free himself of the past, he packed a bag, threw
it in the trunk of his car, and collected his longtime pal Matty Delia[9] for
a cross-country road trip to the new house he'd bought in Beverly Hills.
The journey went fine, but their arrival only reignited the panic that
had pushed Bruce away from New Jersey. "I wanted to get right back in
the car and keep on going," he told Dave Marsh in the mid-1980s. "I
couldn't even sit still."

The fact that he was behaving just like Doug Springsteen, who often
hit the road in attempts to restore his sense of order, did little to ease
Bruce's dismay. "He definitely had a major psychological crisis right about
that time," Marsh says. "I could've been clearer in the book,[10] but wasn't
because I wasn't comfortable with it at the time. But I felt comfortable
with his depths to say the guy in 'Nebraska' isn't Charlie Starkweather. It's
him."

Still, Bruce underplays the significance of the moment, insisting
that tales of him running right back to his car and flooring it back to
the East Coast are overblown. "I might have wanted to," he says. "I had
bought a little house in LA and stayed there working on some music for a
while. But I didn't drive right back." Instead he had Mike Batlan install a
professional-grade home studio in his new house, located right off Sunset
Boulevard, near the Beverly Hills Hotel. Working with his new gear, he
spent the next five months in Los Angeles, writing and recording alone.

Even now, Bruce has a difficult time talking about what inspired his
journey, or what caught up with him when he arrived in Los Angeles.
Friends use words like "suicidal," but he speaks more generally. "Things
can come from way down in the well. It's in your DNA, in the way your

[9] A man whose many careers include motorcycle shop owner, equipment parts rental
shop owner, something that seems to involve booking and/or producing rock shows
at nightclubs, and who knows what all else. Bruce and Delia have been fast friends for
decades.
[10] *Glory Days*, Pantheon, 1987.

body cycles. You're going along fine and then, boom, it hits you." A pause. "So I found a psychiatrist within days of getting to Los Angeles, then when I got back east I found another guy in New York City."

Moving through 1983 with an evolving, if not entirely unified, sense of his vision and work, Bruce continued to write and record more songs. Working in his home studio, Bruce played and sang every part himself, expanding on the solo recording he'd launched with the *Nebraska* demo sessions a year earlier. The songs shared the unadorned structure and gloomy themes Bruce had explored on the earlier solo album, but with flickers of light that at least gestured toward the possibility of redemption. When James Lucas, the ex-convict narrator in "Richfield Whistle," gets caught stealing from his boss, the man refuses to send him back to prison, letting him go with a shake of his head and a sad sigh. "If you needed some extra money, Jim, all you had to do was ask." Lucas walks into a liquor store intending to rob the register, but the clerk's warm greeting ("Can I help you find something, friend?") stops him on the spot and sends him back into his wife's arms. Other songs trend darker, but "County Fair" goes in precisely the opposite direction, describing an ordinary summer party as a kind of heavenly vision, with all the neighbors dancing beneath the stars to "James Young and the Immortal Ones / Two guitars, baby, bass and drums / And they're rockin' out at the country fair."

Working at home, alone save for the presence of Mike Battan, Bruce savored the independence the new technology gave him. He enjoyed playing all the parts for himself, and what he couldn't play—such as anything beyond the most basic drum pattern—could be handled by the state-of-the-art drum machine he now owned. And using that much technology no longer felt like a punt, since the machine's metronomic beats suited the feel he was after. As the songs became nearly finished recordings, close to releasable, Bruce considered staving off the band album again. Or perhaps scattering just a few band tracks across an album dominated by his solo, home-recorded songs. But still, he couldn't imagine breaking up the band. When the time came for him to rock out at the county fair, he knew he wanted his guys with him. If only because he still had one more mountain to climb, and that was not something he could do alone.

So as the new work took shape and the clouds thinned above Bruce's head, the approach of 1984—the target date for a new album—brought a realization that the time had come to take the step he'd contemplated ever since Elvis, the Beatles, and every other rocker he loved had sparked a light behind his eyes: "A lot of currents came together. And at the point I got there, I was that guy. That's where I found myself. You can kid yourself that you're not, but then what have you been doing?"

NINETEEN

THE BLUE-COLLAR
TROUBADOUR

ALREADY AWARE OF THE CONNECTION between his onstage athleticism and the exultation that coursed through him when he was at the height of his shows, Bruce started looking for new ways to achieve the same endorphin-rich glow. At first he bought a bicycle and took it on long rides, following his nose down roads he'd never explored, often ending up calling home from ten or twenty miles away to tell Obie Dziedzic where she could pick him up. When a friend introduced him to a trainer who specialized in full-body workouts, Bruce signed on and found his way to the gym where the guy worked. The moment he stepped into a weight room it was like coming home.

"I was a big fan of meaningless, repetitive behavior," Bruce says. "And what's more meaningless than lifting a heavy object and then putting it down in the same place that you found it? There are probably other psychological reasons behind it, but otherwise it was a perfect match for me. The Sisyphean aspect of it just completely suited my personality."

The swelling muscles in his shoulders, chest, arms, and abdomen suited Bruce's vanity just as well, and with a regular running habit building up his wind and legs, Bruce took on a new glow and stature.[1]

Away from the gym, Bruce made a habit of visiting Club Xanadu, a modern dance club thumping away in the same Kingsley Street address where the Student Prince had once stood. Run by former Asbury Jukes trumpet player Tony Pallagrosi, Xanadu featured live acts on some nights, and house DJs who entwined early hip-hop beats with electronica, rock riffs, and the season's pop hits on other nights. Entranced by the hypnotic feel of the music, Bruce camped out at the bar and watched the new generation of Asbury Park music fans gyrate to the 120-beats-per-minute rhythms.

The club's star bartenders, Paul Smith and Buddy Gac, had their own followers, due largely to their endless good cheer and extravagant displays of energy. Dressed to impress, from their tight athletic shorts to the cut-off sleeves of their army shirts and the matching bandannas wrapped around their foreheads, Gac and Smith turned heads by hurling their cocktail shakers back and forth to the music. When the action on the dance floor got especially hot, they climbed up onto the bar to dance. Nothing fancy, but Gac did have this side-to-side boogie unique enough to raise eyebrows when another guy in a headband appropriated it on MTV in mid-1984.

Back at the Power Station in midtown Manhattan in the later months of 1983, Bruce, the band, Landau, Plotkin, and Scott continued to struggle over what the next album could or should be. Nearly two years since the sessions started with that amazing run in January 1982 (a dozen songs finished in three weeks) they had recorded sixty more tracks. All had their charms, most were release-worthy, and some felt like classics waiting for their moment in the sun. Once again, the litany of styles and moods could stretch to several albums for several different bands. "Lion's Den" and "Pink Cadillac" sounded like rhythm and

---

[1] Bruce shakes off direct questions about his achievements in the weight room, but when a visitor volunteers his own maximum bench press from the same era, Bruce chuckles happily. "Ah, I had ya beat! Not by much, though."

blues, while "Stand on It" and "Delivery Man" sprang from rockabilly. "Murder Incorporated" and "My Love Will Not Let You Down" rocked hard as nails, and "This Hard Land," "County Fair," and "None but the Brave" spun all of that together with strains of country, folk, and Bruce's own boardwalk sound. But even given all that—and so much more—the album refused to take form. By late summer, coproducer Plotkin had no idea where the project was heading. Bruce's tentative track list, which dispensed with "Working on the Highway," "I'm on Fire," and "My Hometown," among others, from the January 1982 sessions in favor of newer cuts, including "My Love Will Not Let You Down" and "None but the Brave," struck Plotkin as a conceptual mess. "I said, 'The record I'm hearing starts with "Born in the U.S.A." and ends with "My Hometown."' I wanted 'Working on the Highway' back, 'I'm on Fire,' and some other stuff we cut."

Focusing again on the album's earliest sessions, the album that began to emerge filtered the dystopian gloom of the *Nebraska* songs into the living world of love, work, and the hobbled pursuit of happiness. The martial beat and roared chorus of "Born in the U.S.A." could be mistaken for an anthem, while the buddies' road trip in "Darlington County" runs through small highway adventures before the narrator skips town with the image of his handcuffed pal receding in his rearview mirror. The central character in "Working on the Highway" pays for his love affair with a (slightly too) young girl on the Charlotte County road gang, and even the riotous "Glory Days" draws its light through nostalgia rather than faith in the future.

Heading into the first weeks of 1984, it seemed that the album, now named *Born in the U.S.A.*, was finished—until Landau declared that they still didn't have the right song to serve as the all-important, project-defining lead single. A song, he explained, that would serve as a direct statement of who Bruce had become; a self-portrait his fans could understand and see enough of themselves in to feel a direct, human connection. Hearing his manager's request/demand was not the least bit happy-making for Bruce, who cited the six dozen songs he'd already written and proposed that Landau write his own fucking song if he thought he could do better. When Bruce's anger subsided, he said he'd give it a try and went to his hotel to get some sleep. Back in the studio the next night, he opened his notebook to a freshly scrawled page, took up his guitar, and played through "Dancing in the Dark," a taut, melodic tale of frustration and isolation. Set in his own day-for-night world of recording studios, hotel rooms, and dark streets, the song started in high gear and kept pushing. When the verse pivoted into the chorus, Bruce's voice climbed with the chords. "You can't start a fire without a spark," he sang. "This gun's for hire, even if we're just dancing in the dark."

Rooted deep in Bruce's musical and lyrical terrain, "Dancing" still came through the speakers with a distinct Top 40 sheen. Recorded with Bittan's synthesizers at the top of the mix and Weinberg nailing a straight-ahead 148-beats-per-minute beneath Bruce's clear, urgent vocal, "Dancing in the Dark" was the most deliberate play for the mainstream he'd ever made. At one time, he wouldn't even have considered doing such a thing. But being older, more experienced, and secure in his abilities and stature didn't hurt. Neither did the blistering message he knew listeners would confront in the album's title track, and in the class consciousness that connected so many of the album's other tracks. In the midst of the Reagan presidency, and the "Morning in America" he described—despite the economic darkness just beyond the walls of the country's gated communities—Bruce felt pulled to leverage his music and image into a strong dissenting argument.

"I had an idea, and it was an idea that I had been working on for several records," he says. "It shot through *Nebraska*, all through *The River*, all through *Darkness on the Edge of Town*, and, really, right there on *Born to Run*. I was a strange product of Elvis and Woody Guthrie, and I pursued the pink Cadillac in my own way, but I was fascinated by people who had become a voice for their moment. Elvis, Woody Guthrie, Curtis Mayfield, Bob Dylan, of course. I don't know if I felt I had a capacity for it or just willed my way in that direction, but it was just something I was interested in. Probably because it was all caught up in identity." Bruce's self-exploration merged with his social, political, and commercial ambitions. "You cannot figure out who you are if you don't understand where you came from, what were the forces that work on your life as a child, as a teenager, and as a young man. What part do you have to play? How do you empower yourself?"

Bruce figured out how to empower himself the first time he'd stepped onstage with a guitar in his hands. He'd worked his way from the social invisibility of his Freehold boyhood to local and then regional popularity, and then rock 'n' roll stardom. *Born to Run* and then *The River* made him a cultural figure, and with a new album that he was already confident would take him higher into the public consciousness, he sensed an opportunity to make an impact far beyond the *Billboard* charts, the pages of *Rolling Stone*, and the concert arenas. He could represent another kind of American face: the ones who went to war, sacrificed their health and sanity, and were ignored when they got home; the workers who gave themselves to jobs that were as essential as they were taken for granted.

That was the grandest part of his reasoning, anyway, and it certainly helped assuage his fears of what such a resounding bid for superstardom might imply about his creative integrity, or what that level of success would do to the quality of his life. But those questions didn't even begin to slow him down. They had already hired the era's best pop/rock/dance mixer, Bob Clearmountain, to work his radio-friendly magic on the new songs. Given Clearmountain's reputation and track record (the Rolling Stones' hit "Miss You" and *Tattoo You* album, which included the smash "Start Me Up"; Huey Lewis and the News' multiplatinum *Sports* album; Roxy Music's hit LP *Avalon*; and many others), the option of swerving left was no longer operative. And that in itself signaled a dramatic shift.

"On *The River*, Bob mixed an album's worth of songs, and that didn't end up being the record we used," Bruce explains. "He wasn't as dysfunctional as we were, so he worked quickly. We wanted to take a very long time thinking about it. Or I did, and everybody else wanted to follow along. We put those things together with glue and tape and, uh, plenty of talent. But moving to Bob was an acknowledgment of a place I'd gotten to in my recording work; an acknowledgment that I had those ambitions. I had to say I'm using this one and not that one because I think that this one is going to reach an audience that that one may or may not. So I had to acknowledge my ambitions, I had to acknowledge that we had moved into a level where we were now going to be interacting with professionals."

Still, the mixer of hit songs was flabbergasted to hear the master tracks for "Dancing in the Dark." "It's actually pretty different from the rest of the album. It's got a really commercial groove to it," Clearmountain says. "And it just took a few hours to mix—a very simple job, and still one of the easiest records I've ever mixed. But when I put that up, I just thought, 'Whoa, this sounds like a hit song! Where'd *that* come from?'" As Landau says, it came straight from the ambitions that he and Bruce had always shared, which had drawn them together in the midst of *Born to Run*, steered them to make *Darkness on the Edge of Town*—a solid seller after its initial fizzle—and governed Bruce's eagerness to have the similarly ambitious Landau sign on as his manager in the summer of 1978. "If you weren't interested in having an enormous impact and success, you wouldn't have picked me to work with. Because I am interested in those things," Landau says. "How Bruce saw himself, his role, his career, and all of those things was diverse, it wasn't just one thing. But he did want—*we* both wanted—to have tremendous success. And everything that we did together culminated in *Born in the U.S.A.*"

To make sure they were on the right track with the just-completed single, Bruce picked up an acetate copy of the song and took it with him down to Asbury Park's Club Xanadu. Taking his usual seat at the bar, he ordered a beer and a shot and waited for the place to fill up. When the dance floor overflowed, he handed the disc to the DJ and explained what it was. Bruce didn't want any fuss. "Don't tell anyone what it is," he insisted. "Just put it on, and we'll see what happens." The DJ got it spinning, and when he faded out the other song and turned up the volume on "Dancing in the Dark," the dancers flew into overdrive, and the whole club seemed to levitate above Kingsley Street. "The place went wild, then all of the sudden we were dancing on the bar," Paul Smith says.

Columbia/CBS chiefs Al Teller and Walter Yetnikoff started their dancing when Landau invited them to the recording studio to preview the follow-up to *The River*. They all got along famously—particularly in the wake of *Nebraska*, which the company helped push to gold-selling status before Christmas, and then to platinum a few months later. Pretty good for anyone's album, and close to spectacular for a set of spooky acoustic demos. Landau had already made it clear that the new album shared a lot more in common with *The River* than with *Nebraska*, so they came in expecting something that would sound like a hit. They weren't disappointed.

"They start playing it," Teller recalls, "and I'm listening with two distinct heads: my fan head and my professional head. And my fan head is loving it. But my professional head is going completely bonkers. I'm hearing one hit after another. There's like five, six hits on there, and I'm already sequencing the singles in my head." Turn up the album yourself, and you'll hear it too. From the first blast of drums and synthesizer on the title song to the searing guitar, interlocking keyboards, and danceable rhythm on "Cover Me"[2] to the ringing cowbell, snare blasts, and carnival organ–piano blend on "Darlington County," distinctively new and yet still rooted in the soil of the common-man America he'd always known. Tallent's bass is both economical and melodic. "Working on the Highway" evokes rockabilly and the English Beat at the same time, while "I'm on Fire" sounds like a Johnny Cash tune infused with neon. With one last song to play, Landau stopped the tape and told the story about how it had taken them until just weeks ago to realize that the album still lacked the perfect hit single, and how Bruce had gone off to give it one more try. "And I think we got it," he said, nodding for the engineer to restart the tape. That's when they heard "Dancing in the Dark."

"I think I hit the studio ceiling," Teller says. Yetnikoff soared right alongside. "I don't know if I wet my pants, but I may have. I've done that other times," Yetnikoff says. "I was as rabid a fan as the fourteen-year-old girl in New Jersey. Sometimes record executives actually *like* the stuff they're dealing with. And I was very turned on by what Bruce had become as an artist, and what he meant to the musical world, the rock 'n' roll world."

---

[2] Written originally for the R&B singer Donna Summer, who specialized in disco hits that sounded a lot like rock 'n' roll songs.

Teller turned back to Landau and told him to prepare for a ride like he and Bruce had never taken before. "I don't make predictions very often," Teller says. "But I told Jon, *guaranteed* him, that the album was a smash hit number one record. That we'd sell tens of millions of albums in the US, and get at least a two-and-a-half-year run out of it. I told him they'd do two touring cycles behind this, and that *this* ['Dancing'] is a smash hit number one single."

When Bruce came in—he'd been lurking, and perhaps listening in to the executives' reaction, in the room next door—Teller wrapped him in a victory hug. "Forget about it!" Teller raved. "This is going to be your most spectacular album. Easily." Barring one small hiccup ("Dancing" never quite got past Prince's "When Doves Cry" to number one) every one of Teller's predictions came true.

When Landau had asked Bruce to write a more personal song, the musician had produced "Dancing" and "Bobby Jean," the latter a yearning rocker that bid farewell to a longtime friend. Whether he's singing to a romantic partner or an old pal isn't clear. The name in the title is sexually ambiguous, and the lyrics don't tip one way or another. What is entirely clear, however, is the bone-deep connection between friends who have had each other's back since they were awkward teenagers. "Now there ain't nobody nowhere nohow / Gonna ever understand me the way you did," Bruce sings. And the love in his voice is just as vivid as the hurt in the chorus: "Now I wished you would have told me / I wished I could have talked to you / Just to say good-bye, Bobby Jean."

Generally not the sort of thing Bruce would, or could, say to someone's face. But "Bobby Jean" was directed to one distinct person to address one very specific fact: Steve Van Zandt had left the E Street Band. And maybe it shouldn't have been a surprise, given that the guitarist had been muttering about leaving ever since the start of the *River* sessions in 1979. Bruce's insistence that Van Zandt become a full-fledged member of the production team had kept his childhood pal on board for the time being, but Steve's frustration had mounted again during the 1982 sessions for *Born in the U.S.A.* Van Zandt formed his own band, the Disciples of Soul, to clear his palate during the break and quickly produced a debut album of biting, overtly political music called *Men Without Women* (1982), which he followed with a lengthy tour of Europe. A second album, 1984's *Voice of America*, followed, along with another tour. But while Bruce went out of his way to be supportive of his pal's solo work—contributing parts to the first album, although he's uncredited—the distance opening between them grew increasingly obvious, even if Bruce refused to acknowledge it.

Also unacknowledged, and far more upsetting to Van Zandt, was the deflation of his influence in the production team—and on Bruce's ear. For a long time, the balance between Landau and Van Zandt had been tense, but productively so. "Jon on his right and me on his left. Jon representing the career, the business, the narrative end," the guitarist says. "Me representing rock 'n' roll, the street, where it was coming from. A healthy balance, and it proved to be quite successful."[3] Van Zandt had been a central influence on the wildly fruitful January 1982 sessions that produced the majority of the songs that ended up on the finished *U.S.A.* album in 1984. Between that and the massive success of "Hungry Heart," which Van Zandt had helped rescue from Bruce's indifference, he felt like claiming what he considered his due.

"At a certain point, I needed my role to expand," he explains. "I knew exactly what he sounded like, exactly what the band sounded like, exactly what he heard in his head, and how he needed the next album to sound. That's what I thought, anyway." Instead the pendulum swung in the opposite direction. "All of a sudden I could tell he wasn't hearing me. I'm not getting through. That was new to me, and I wasn't comfortable with it." Hearing this in 2011, Bruce looks puzzled, then shrugs. "Steve's very particular about the things he likes," he says. "And sometimes my buddy feels a little underappreciated."

As Van Zandt recalls, his relationship with Bruce grew tense, then chilly, then edged toward the spiky. "I felt our relationship was in a little bit of jeopardy. And I thought the way to preserve the friendship was to leave. I knew if I stayed, the rather civilized disagreements were about to

[3] Although Landau's feeling for the music was also bone deep, just as Van Zandt could be a canny manager. If anything, their skills matched too closely.

take a turn for the less civilized." Van Zandt made fleeting appearances at the full-band sessions during the spring of 1983 and then didn't turn up at all for the fall 1983–February 1984 recording work. Still, neither Bruce nor Van Zandt spoke publicly about their split, both referring to the Disciples of Soul as a side project. And as far as Bruce was concerned, Van Zandt was still on board for the world tour he and the E Street Band had planned to start in the summer of 1984.

In February 1984 Bruce recoiled visibly when he saw a news report on MTV announcing that Van Zandt had split from the E Street Band. "That's a bunch of bull!" he sputtered to his weekend guest, fellow guitarist Nils Lofgren.

"I was shocked," Lofgren says. "I know Bruce is very private, and God knows the aggravation he's learned to live with, with rumors and all that." Bruce first met Lofgren in 1970 at the Avalon Ballroom audition on which Steel Mill had pinned its hopes during its brief San Francisco residency. Lofgren burst out of the gate earlier than Bruce, first as Neil Young's sideman and then as the leader of a trio called Grin, which gained a cult audience in the early seventies. They bumped into each other from time to time on the club circuit after Lofgren went solo in 1973 and when he got dropped by his record company in 1984, Bruce made a point of reaching out.

"I was down in the dumps. Then he said, 'Why don't ya come up for a weekend?'" They hung out for a few days, lighting up their evenings by checking out a couple of local clubs and stepping up to jam with whoever was playing. "That was his thing," Lofgren says. "The band would find a couple of guitars, Bruce would lead us, and everyone fell in line." The weekend was a tonic for Lofgren's spirits. "It always helps to go to a couple of bars and hold your own with Springsteen next to you. But mostly we listened to *Born in the U.S.A.*, and I thought it was a great, great record." So when they saw the MTV news break, Lofgren didn't resist the temptation to offer his assistance. "I said, 'Well, if you do need a guitar player, I'd love an audition.' He looked up and said, 'Really?'" Then they went back to watching videos.

When Bruce made a final pitch to keep Van Zandt on board, he made sure that his friend knew how wild the buzz surrounding *U.S.A.* had

become. "He had a sense the record was going to be successful," Van Zandt
says. "I think he legitimately wanted me to share in what he felt I deserved,
since I had coproduced the album and was a big part of it." They talked for
hours, briefly kicking around the prospect of the Disciples of Soul joining
the tour as the opening act, with Van Zandt playing both ends of the show.
But given that Bruce never had opening acts—and on this, of all tours,
he couldn't imagine limiting his own stage time—the idea didn't stick.
Van Zandt also wasn't crazy about Bruce's newly supersized commercial
ambitions. When you can sell a million or two million albums and fill
sports arenas while still having a generally normal offstage life, working
to become a global superstar seemed ridiculous. Nevertheless, Van Zandt
says the talk, and his decision to finalize his departure from Bruce's band,
marked a significant moment in their friendship. "It wasn't a fight, but
it was a very deeply emotional moment," he says. "A kind of emotional
reconciliation. An acceptance that we were going our separate ways. A
separation of brothers going their own ways, for their own reasons. It was
emotional, and disappointing. But not adversarial at all."[4]

In early May Bruce called Lofgren at his home in Maryland. "Hey, if ya
feel like it, you can come back up and do a little jamming with the band."
Lofgren answered just as casually ("I said, '*Sure!*'") but inside his head,
lights flashed and alarm bells chimed. "I'm thinking, 'What's *that* mean?
Jamming? Why?'" But, of course, he knew what it meant. Ever the A student, Lofgren went immediately to a bootleg-collecting friend, borrowed
a few of Bruce's shows, and wrote out the chord charts to every song he
heard. Lofgren's buddy also had a bootlegged tape of the still-unreleased
Born in the U.S.A., so he wrote down those charts too. Taking a commuter jet to a tiny airport in south New Jersey, Lofgren found Bruce
waiting for him in the parking lot. As Lofgren had assumed, he had been
summoned to audition for Van Zandt's position in the band. But the
guitarist still felt taken aback when they got to Bruce's house in Rumson,

[4] As of the summer of 2011, Van Zandt says that Bruce still hasn't said a word to him
about the inspiration for "Bobby Jean." "People say it's about me; I don't know that it is,"
the guitarist says. "If it is, it's nice, y'know. But we've never talked about it, to this day."

New Jersey,[5] and discovered the rest of the E Street Band sitting around the dining room table. Bruce slid into one empty chair and gestured toward the last chair, sitting alone at the foot of the table. "So I went, '*Damn!*' But look: who else if not me?"

The band rehearsed in Red Bank, in the empty building that had once housed Clemons's never quite profitable nightclub, Big Man's West. Lofgren played with the band for a couple of days and packed up his guitars at the end of the second day feeling good about what had happened. No matter how it turned out, he'd given it his best shot, he figured. Bruce vanished into a side room in the moments after they'd quit playing, and when he came out, Lofgren went over to give him a thank-you hug. Bruce just smiled.

"He said, 'Look, I talked to everybody. It feels good to us. So do you want to join the E Street Band?' I said, 'What? You mean now? Like a full member of the band? Not just a sideman?' And he said, 'Yeah. Join the band.' So I said, '*Absolutely!* Count me in!'" Lofgren flew back to Maryland that night, packed up everything he'd need for a tour, threw it into his car, and drove back up to New Jersey.

He had five weeks before the opening date of the tour, set for Saint Paul, Minnesota, at the end of June. Lofgren took over the guitar parts without much sweat, but he had a tougher time doing all that while also summoning the grit and power for Van Zandt's high vocal harmonies. Bruce, however, already had a solution on hand. He called Patti Scialfa, who had managed to do all the growing up that Bruce and Van Zandt had asked her to do when she tried out for Dr. Zoom and the Sonic Boom thirteen years earlier. Bruce had considered adding a female voice to the band even before Van Zandt left (Scialfa had auditioned months earlier, in fact), so when he offered her a backup singer job, she jumped at it and became the first woman to become a full-fledged member of the E Street Band. Scialfa, a willowy redhead with sparkling green eyes and a playfully sexy stage presence, had been a fixture on the Asbury Park scene for so long that her joining did little to disrupt the E Street boys' club.

[5] The first home Bruce managed to buy in his home state, purchased with some of his proceeds from the River tour.

She also came with serious academic credentials, including a music degree from New York University and training from the jazz conservatory at the University of Miami's Frost School of Music. Scialfa had spent years busking and playing club dates with her all-woman band Trickster (with Soozie Tyrell and Lisa Lowell), and toured and recorded as a vocalist for both David Johansen and Southside Johnny and the Asbury Jukes. "Patti saved my ass," Lofgren says. "She got thrown in even later than I did, but Patti can sing anything."

First came the video. In 1984, with the three-year-old MTV established as the hub of the nation's (and increasingly the world's) pop music culture, any bid for mainstream success had to include a video that showcased the artist's single, while also establishing his or her image and the mood of the new song and/or album. Bruce had resisted MTV's gravitational pull in the bleak "Atlantic City" video in 1982, but his heady ambitions for *Born in the U.S.A.* required a much more industry-friendly campaign. Still, Bruce, who fell in love with music the old-fashioned, AM-radio-driven way, was wary. "I kind of agreed with him," Teller says. "I knew that videos hampered people's ability to comprehend the music in their own way." But Columbia's president also knew how the music business worked in 1984, and Landau said he'd try to make something happen.

When the manager came back to show what they came up with while working with director Jeff Stein (best known then for *The Kids Are Alright*, his spectacular 1979 documentary about the Who) for a day in the Kaufman Astoria film studios in Queens, New York, Teller was baffled. Rather than featuring the band or any kind of onstage setting, the video featured Bruce alone. Appearing on an all-black set and dressed in black pants, a white, sleeveless T-shirt, thin black suspenders, and a thick black bandanna tied across his forehead, Bruce looked mostly like a mime with ants in his pants. Set loose on the empty soundstage, Bruce lip-synced the lyrics while doing his best back-and-forth boogie, with occasional 360-degree spins for odd measure. And that was the whole production, until a white-suited Clemons popped in to simulate his saxophone solo at the end of the song. "No background, no band, that was it," Teller says. "It really just showed you how uncomfortable he was with videos." When the executive caught Landau's eye at the end of the clip, he shook his head. "Jon and I just looked at each other, and I said, 'No way!'" [6] Landau, he says, nodded—almost as if he'd expected Teller to say that—and said he'd try to come up with something else.

Then a miracle occurred. Bruce agreed to not only shoot a real performance video but also cooperate with the Hollywood-style enhancements suggested by director Brian De Palma, who had helmed the bloody horror movie *Carrie* and the even bloodier gangster movie *Scarface*. Shot onstage on the first night of the Born in the U.S.A. tour in Saint Paul, DePalma's video began with a boots-up pan of Bruce, dressed in new blue jeans and a short-sleeved white button-up. Dancing to the opening bars of the single, he came into view as a popcorn movie version of himself, shiny to the point of seeming premoistened, with a silly grin on his face. With artificial smoke floating behind him, Bruce and his similarly shiny band members pantomimed their parts while shots of the real crowd's reaction moved to focus on one suspiciously gorgeous woman (who turns out to be future *Friends* star Courteney Cox) dancing excitedly in the front row. When the song moved into its final, instrumental bars, the still-grinning Bruce reached out for the woman, who just happened to be wearing the official *U.S.A.* tour T-shirt, thus inspiring a brief array of oh-my-God-this-can't-really-be-happening expressions to flow across her own shiny face until she's right there dancing with Bruce Springsteen in the Hollywood-enhanced spotlights.

And in 1984 that's what you called a state-of-the-art MTV music video. "I winced at that, too," Teller says. "It looked so goddamned stagey. I told Jon, 'That's so cheesy!' I could never watch *Friends* as a result." No matter, the clip was an immediate sensation. From July until

[6] According to pop music historian Stephen Pitalo's Golden Age of Music Video website, a large part of the problem with Stein's video came from a disagreement Bruce had with cinematographer Daniel Pearl about whether he should be in a gauzy light or the sheer white beams Pearl thought would accentuate the star's new musculature. Pearl talked Bruce into trying the harder light for a take or two, but Bruce didn't feel comfortable, so after just a few takes, he went back to the green room for a break, and then kept going to the parking lot, his car, and then home. "He didn't say a word to anybody," Pearl told Pitalo. "He's just out the door." They tried to make do with what they had.

February 1985, the *Born in the U.S.A.* album traded the top spot on the album chart with Prince and *Purple Rain*. And the LP's run, and Bruce's leap to the apex of mainstream culture, had only just begun.

Through the first leg of the American tour that summer, everything felt like business as usual. Granted, business was especially good. Shows sold out with lightning speed, often leading to multiple appearances at venues they had once struggled to fill. Already the audience had grown beyond the usual core of Springsteen zealots, due both to the broad appeal of "Dancing in the Dark" in radio and video formats. Bruce and Landau had also hired the industry's leading dance record remixer, Arthur Baker, to create an extended, heavily revised mix aimed at dance clubs[7] around the world. At the same time, Bruce acquiesced to requests for interviews with major celebrity media outlets including *People* magazine,[8] and the syndicated celebrity news TV program *Entertainment Tonight*, among others. They also worked with MTV to hatch the "Be a Roadie for Bruce" contest, the winner of which would be rewarded with a temporary job as a crew member (and thus be granted the opportunity to call the Boss "boss").

Bruce entered the 1984 cultural mainstream with unexpected force. In a decade of popular music increasingly dominated by women (Stevie Nicks, Debbie Harry, Madonna, Cyndi Lauper, among others) and men pushing the edges of male sexual identity (Michael Jackson, Prince, Boy George), Bruce's jeans and T-shirt, along with the old-school rock 'n' roll framework of his songs, shifted music back to familiar territory. When the celebrity-entertainment mags dropped by to kick Bruce's tires and take the aspiring idol out for a spin around the block, they came back as impressed by his offstage humility as they were by his onstage heroics. "The trappings of rock superstardom were astonishingly absent backstage," wrote *People*'s Chet Flippo in a cover story titled "Blue-Collar Troubadour." "No stretch limos for the rock stars; just unobtrusive

---

[7] Heavy on the synth drums and looped vocal tracks, and also with a new background chorus and other added elements.

[8] Full disclosure: also the professional home of the author from 1996 until 2000.

vans . . . there were no drugs and nothing stronger to drink than beer."
Certainly not where Flippo could see them, at any rate. Still, Bruce's
commitment to keeping his boots on the ground stayed firm. As he told
Rolling Stone's Kurt Loder (also the central face in MTV's thriving music
news broadcasts), the superstar treatment achieved nothing more than
separating the artist from the people he most needed to understand, and
vice versa. "The life of a rock band will last as long as you look down into
the audience and can see yourself, and [they] can look up at you and see
themselves," he said. "If the price of fame is that you have to be isolated
from the people you write for, then that's too fuckin' high a price to pay."

And yet Bruce's all-star physique, along with his ability to elevate his
concerts into something like the First Church of Rock (to quote *People*'s
Flippo) gave him the aura of a superhero: a larger-than-life figure keeping the world safe for truth, beauty, and the cleansing tide of rock 'n' roll.
Factor in the red, white, and blue imagery all over *Born in the U.S.A.* and
its songs about work, home, and family, and here rose the profile of an
American hero. Or, as Flippo put it to *People*'s forty million weekly readers, "He's a folk hero in his biker boots, tight jeans, kerchief headband,
and short-sleeved sport shirt with the sleeves rolled up to display his
newly pumped-up biceps."

In a presidential election year defined by the gauzy "Morning in
America" ads promoting the reelection of Ronald Reagan, the star-
spangled subtext to Bruce's popular image made him an irresistible
target for political maneuvering and manipulation. The first wavelet
came in *People* magazine's profile when Flippo described *Born in the
U.S.A.*'s title track as a proud anthem sung in the voice of a war-ravaged
Vietnam veteran who suffers "every raw deal imaginable but remains
a 'cool rocking Daddy in the U.S.A.'" How a sophisticated music
journalist like Flippo[9] could hear the rage written into that song and
come away thinking that the brutalized narrator's final roar amounted
to anything other than bitter irony is difficult to comprehend. But the
worst was yet to come.

[9] Best known for his work as a staff writer and editor for *Rolling Stone* during its peak in
the 1970s, and then for his series of well-received books on country music.

It began with a well-intentioned invitation from Max Weinberg. The drummer and his wife, Becky, were regular watchers of ABC-TV's weekly political talk show *This Week with David Brinkley*, mostly for the panel discussion segments that included ABC's liberal-ish newsman Sam Donaldson and the conservative pundit George Will. Curious to see what the hardcore pols would make of a rock 'n' roll concert, the drummer invited the show's entire panel to see Bruce and the band when the tour came to Largo, Maryland, a thirty-minute drive east of the capital. Will was the only panelist who showed up,[10] so when Weinberg took his guest backstage to see the show's inner workings, the conservative writer alone got to meet Bruce and take in the atmosphere. Will left the concert after the intermission but was still moved to devote his September 13 nationally syndicated column to Bruce and the event. The piece, titled "Bruce Springsteen, U.S.A.," dragooned the band in general—and Bruce in particular—into a political fantasy that said more about the author's electoral agenda than it did about his subject's beliefs and message. Starting with an approving nod to the absence of androgyny in Bruce's image,[11] Will compared his macho look to Robert De Niro's in the battle sequences of *The Deer Hunter*.[12] All of which clarified Will's vision of Bruce as a "wholesome cultural portent" whose own rags-to-riches story proved the conservative belief that no amount of socioeconomic privation could stand in the way of hard, honest, nonunionized work. That Bruce's extraordinary success was a result of otherworldly talents unavailable to virtually everyone else on the planet did not occur to Will. What did occur to him, however, was that uttering and repeating the words "Born in the U.S.A." amounted to an affirmation of patriotism and, thus, of Ronald Reagan and his administration. Will was so enamored of the idea that he repurposed it for the column's kicker: "There still is nothing quite like being born in the U.S.A."[13]

[10] Dressed in his customary bow tie and a double-breasted blazer.

[11] Unlike that prancing, heavily rouged, and tongue-lolling Prince, for instance.

[12] That feel-good war movie whose three main characters end up (a) crippled for life, (b) dead by suicide, and (c) leading a chorus of "God Bless America" in a bar.

[13] Given Will's observation that Bruce "is called the 'blue-collar troubadour' " referred directly, if without attribution, to *People* magazine's just-published story, it seems probable

Weinberg, to put it gently, felt chagrined. He hadn't known that Will intended to write about the concert, let alone transform Bruce into a character in Ayn Rand's libertarian *Atlas Shrugged*. And while Bruce never mentioned it to him one way or another, the drummer felt a distinct chill backstage when he got to the next show. "I was practically excommunicated by certain factions in our touring party," he says. "Blacklisted. Akin to being a traitor to some ideology. And while [Becky and I] did invite him to the show, it would be a stretch to say George Will was a friend of mine. I mean, I met him *that night*."

The situation grew even more complicated a week later, when Reagan made a campaign stop in Hammonton, New Jersey, and ingratiated himself to the southern Jersey crowd by declaring that "America's future rests in a thousand dreams inside your hearts; it rests in the message of hope in songs of a man so many young Americans admire: New Jersey's own Bruce Springsteen. And helping you make those dreams come true is what this job of mine is all about." Cue the balloons, cue the cheers, cue the presidential motorcade for the ride back to Air Force One and the next campaign stop. "He got his picture taken with the red, white, and blue balloons, and he mentioned me," Bruce says. "It was part of a shopping list of things that needed to be done for the six o'clock news. And I didn't want to be part of the shopping list, y'know?"

Heading to the next tour stop in Pittsburgh, Bruce and Landau agreed that he had to say something to deflect Reagan's attempt to claim spiritual kin. Five songs into the first set, Bruce stepped up to the microphone, acoustic guitar in hand, and noted that the president had mentioned him the other day. "I kind of got to wondering what his favorite album of mine must've been, you know," he said. "I don't think it was the *Nebraska* album. I don't think he's been listening to this one." Then came an intense reading of "Johnny 99," the tale of the unemployed auto plant worker who spirals into a bloody crime spree. Talking about the war memorials he'd seen in Washington and grown up among in Freehold, Bruce stopped short of mentioning Reagan by name but still drew a sharp

---

that Will lifted his interpretation of "Born in the U.S.A."-as-grand-affirmation from Chet Flippo, too.

line between the president's laissez-faire policies and his own progressive ideals. "It's a long walk from the government that's supposed to represent all the people to where it seems like . . . there's a lot of stuff being taken away from a lot of people that shouldn't have it taken away," he said. "Sometimes it's hard to remember that this place [the nation] belongs to us. That this is our hometown."

The Democratic nominee for president, former vice president Walter Mondale, took advantage of Reagan's political overstep by declaring that Bruce "may have been born to run, but he wasn't born yesterday." But when the Mondale campaign claimed falsely that Bruce had agreed to endorse its candidate, his handlers had to issue an official retraction. Bruce, for all his eagerness to impact American culture, still had no interest in diving into the partisan electoral fray. "I don't think people come to music for political advice," he says. "They come to be touched and moved and inspired, and if you've written about [political] things as a part of what you're doing—and you do it well—then you're moving and inspiring them with those things. But people aren't coming on an informational basis. I was attracted to Dylan because he sounded like he was telling the truth. I didn't sit there with a lyric sheet. It was just in the way it sounded."

TWENTY

SMILIN' KIND OF FUNNY, EVERYBODY HAPPY AT LAST

BY THE END OF 1984, Bruce's image—the close-cropped curls, strong jaw, concrete shoulders, and wood-hewn Fender Telecaster—had ascended into the international register of American icons. In the wake of all the magazine covers, the TV news stories, the endless loop of "Dancing in the Dark" and "Born in the U.S.A." videos on MTV, newspaper stories, and more, you didn't have to be able to identify a note of his music to grasp exactly who he was and what his profile signified. But most sensate people *had* heard the music, which was just as unavoidable as all the media coverage. So now Bruce was a brand, and when the Born in the U.S.A. tour reached Australia in late March 1985 for a monthlong swing—Bruce's first shows Down Under—the fame he had chased for the previous year turned to face him.

"The genie was out of the bottle," Garry Tallent says. When the band's plane arrived in Sydney, reporters from what seemed like every newspaper, television station, and radio outlet in the antipodes were waiting at the airport with notebooks, cameras, and skepticism in tow. "We arrived, and it was front-page news," Tallent continues. "And the photo captions were all glib: 'Bruce Springsteen and his burly minders.' And there was maybe one security guy with us. Suddenly you're at the position where someone wants to shoot you out of the sky."

Along with helping Bruce fend off the tabloid media, Jon Landau and friends had to scramble to keep up with an unprecedented ticket demand. In Brisbane a show scheduled for the eight-thousand-seat Chandler Velodrome had to be moved to the fifty-thousand-capacity QEII Sports Centre stadium. What would be Bruce's first stadium show flirted with disaster from the start. Rain poured from the sky, the sound system wasn't loud enough to fill the space, and the police's campaign to enforce a new no-alcohol policy slowed long lines to a crawl. Even Bruce seemed off his game in the cavernous setting, but by then things were spinning so fast they could only live, learn, and get onto the jet because the first-ever Japanese tour was about to begin, and now that country had erupted in ardor for America's rock 'n' roll laureate.

Everywhere they went in Japan, Bruce and the band were greeted by an eighties version of Beatlemania: fans waiting at the airport, paparazzi leaping out of doorways and hanging from balconies, mobs outside the hotel hoping to catch a glimpse through the upper-floor windows. Similar scenes would play out during much of the European tour that spring and then during a late-summer run through America's biggest stadiums (including six sold-out nights at Giants Stadium, just across the Hudson River from New York City, and a tour-concluding four nights at the Los Angeles Memorial Coliseum, from September 27 through October 2).

Even if it was a thrill to be on the receiving end of the sort of frenzy once directed at Elvis and the Beatles, Bruce was sophisticated enough to comprehend the dangers it posed. "Success at that level is a tricky business because a lot of distortion creeps in," he told Steve Pond in 1988. "There's the songs you're writing and things you're telling, and then there's what's happening to you, and that's another story . . . your success story is a bigger story than whatever you're trying to say on-stage."

For some critics, Bruce's reputation as rock 'n' roll's real working-class hero chafed against everything they knew about the verities of superstardom. He'd already been famous for a decade; surely he indulged the same appetites for champagne and deference that turned once-humble stars into cloistered divas. Apart from his globe-trotting, living-hero image, he worked with a vengeance to seem like a regular guy. At least one person on the Born in the U.S.A. tour recalls running into everyone's boss walking out of the hotel laundry room clutching a basket full of shirts and underpants to his chest. Which sounds positively heroic until you hear how Bruce's obsession with his Freehold street cred could turn ugly when he suspected that someone on his staff was subverting the regular-guy strictures.

Case in point: the night when a van driver strike forced the crew members charged with shepherding the touring party's luggage to the hotel to hire limos to transport the bags. It seemed like genius at the time: the price was almost exactly what it had been for the bus, and the bags got to the hotel only slightly late. Call it a win for the enterprising crew guys. Right up until a sleepless Bruce stepped out of the hotel lobby, caught sight of his guys unloading the tour's suitcases from shimmering limousines, and was moved to wonder, aloud, which fucking asshole had decided to use *his* money to haul luggage like that. Bruce stomped off, and when Landau came out to talk it over the next day, he simply asked the guys to try really hard not to do it again.

Then it wasn't long before another high-ranking member of the touring party observed to Bruce that it was maybe a little ironic for him to be such a diva about his just-plain-folks edict. Bruce didn't disagree, exactly. But as Landau and a few others had already figured out, his obsession with staying true to his roots flowed from the Randolph Street days of social isolation. "What occurs to me is that to Bruce, [being an average guy] is not a step down from being celebrated," Landau observes. "In his experience, it's a step *up* to be a part of the community. Rather than being isolated from it."

• • •

Throughout the tour, Bruce's song introductions and midshow stories focused on a subject he had rarely mentioned in a specific way: sex and romance. Mostly sex, though. Almost entirely sex, now that you mention it. Introducing "Glory Days," he reminisced about teenage encounters in the bedroom of his parents' house, conducted under the aural cover of balls banging around his pool table. (The occasional sweep of an arm did the trick.) Various tales setting up "Pink Cadillac" made its horndog lyrics all the more vivid, while the introduction to "I'm Goin' Down" traced the arc of a relationship in terms of a couple's sexual patterns. "[First] you're making love to 'em all the time, three or four times a day. Then you come back a little bit later, and, uh-oh . . . it's like 'Are you gonna make love to me tonight, or are we gonna wait for the full moon again,' y'know?" The giggly sex talk got started a few weeks after the tour's start in late June 1984 but took an abrupt leap in late October after a seven-night stand at the Los Angeles Sports Arena. It was not a coincidence.

"I knew people who knew a lot of actors, so I got to know Julianne," says Bruce's tour agent, Barry Bell. "I brought her to a show, introduced her to Bruce. I figured she'd be right for him because she was very down to earth. And the rest is history." A shadowy sort of history, considering what the future held in store. But given Bruce's steep arc into global fame, his blossoming romance with an up-and-coming model-turned-actress from the Pacific Northwest inevitably became the subject of intense interest for the world's media/celebrity industrial complex.

Born in Chicago in 1960 and raised in the waterfront suburb of Lake Oswego, Oregon, about ten minutes up the Willamette River from Portland, Julianne Phillips grew up with the tree-shaded comfort the Springsteens never enjoyed when Bruce was young. The sixth and final child born to Bill, a prosperous insurance executive, and his homemaker wife, Ann, Julianne went through school with the casual grace of a young woman thoroughly comfortable in her own skin. Fair skinned and blue eyed, with a lissome figure and classic schoolgirl features, Julianne floated through Lake Oswego High School, waving the pom-poms with the cheerleaders on Saturday night and cutting a fine figure in her dad's MG roadster on Macadam Boulevard to downtown Portland. A quick run through the two-year Brooks College in Long Beach, California, prefaced an early-eighties move to New York, where she joined the Elite modeling agency, soon earning top rates as a vision of fresh-scrubbed sensuality. Back in LA in 1983, Julianne rose quickly through the actress ranks, starting with a featured role in a video by Southern rockers .38 Special, which led to roles in TV movies.

All of which proved entirely beguiling to Bruce, who could also sense Julianne's warmth and lack of Hollywood pretense. That she also knew her way around his favorite rock 'n' roll classics was another bonus. After chatting for a while backstage, Bruce asked to see Julianne again, and when that date went well, they grew closer, then inseparable. "I knew they liked each other, but I didn't know how fast he was moving," Bell says. Very fast, as it turned out. Bruce took his new girlfriend home to meet his family and friends in New Jersey during his winter break, followed her back to Los Angeles and then went with her to meet the Phillipses when they visited Palm Springs, California, in February 1985. Bruce went to Australia alone in March, but Julianne met him in Japan when the tour got there three weeks later. It was all true love and lollipops in the land of the rising sun, and the short holiday they spent in Hawaii on the way back to the United States seemed to seal the deal. "She was just tough," he told Dave Marsh at the time. "She had confidence and resilience, and she wasn't afraid to face facts or their implications."

A day or two after they got home from Hawaii, Julianne called her mother in Lake Oswego and told her they'd better plan a wedding, and soon. And secretly, too. Because if the word leaked to the Bruce-frenzied press, the deluge would be immediate, intense, and unyielding. Both of Phillips's parents were thrilled, as one of Ann's bowling friends told a *People* magazine reporter a few weeks later. "Bruce was very quiet and subdued, didn't smoke or drink." But word did get out—the only thing that abhors a vacuum more than nature is an aroused celebrity media—and within hours, the Phillipses' suburban driveway became an encampment for the flocks of reporters who flooded Lake Oswego in hopes of getting a glimpse at the happy couple. Helicopter-borne photographers mounted aerial attacks, and it quickly got to the point where the absence of real news and photographs became a story all its own.[1]

The ceremony itself was miraculously untouched by the media's fanatic attention, although that feat required a level of cloak-and-daggery (decoy cars, fake schedules, back alley escapes, and more) unseen outside of a James Bond movie. When Bruce and Julianne stepped to the altar at Our Lady of the Lake Roman Catholic church a few ticks after midnight on May 13, they came with both sets of parents at their side, the E Street Band in the pews, and news reporters nowhere in sight. Bruce was attended by three best men, Clemons, Van Zandt, and Landau. The formal reception was held two days later in exurban Tualatin, Oregon, with helicopters churning the air, reporters pacing the road, and photographers hanging out of the trees down the lane. When it was all over, Bruce had a ring on his finger, a wife by his side, and a commitment to the domestic life he had avoided so assiduously for so long. It had taken him a long time to get there, but now he was determined to make it work.

If the video for "Dancing in the Dark" was the apotheosis of the airbrushed-for-your-safety Bruce, the video for *Born in the U.S.A.*'s title track went just as far in the opposite direction. Directed by independent filmmaker and writer John Sayles, the clip mixed concert footage (featuring a much more grizzled and steely Bruce) with lingering shots of factories, workers, and vintage home movies from what appeared to be working-class homes from the sixties and early seventies. The Sayles-directed video for the taut ballad "I'm on Fire" moved back toward the classically cinematic, ditching all visual references to Bruce the musician by casting him as a humble (but undeniably handsome) mechanic who has gained the flirtatious attention of a mostly unseen rich woman (voiced by Sayles's wife, the actress and coproducer Maggie Renzi) who

[1] By this point, it wasn't surprising that Bruce's wedding would be such enormous news—grist for another *People* magazine cover story and hundreds of front-page stories in newspapers all over the world. The *Chicago Tribune* thought it so significant that it devoted an editorial to praising the rocker's nuptials as yet another sign of his steadfast American values.

can entrust her shimmering white Thunderbird[2] to only one wrench jockey. Given a few simple lines of dialogue, Bruce looked surprisingly at ease. Which was no surprise to Sayles, who often casts nonprofessional actors in his films. "What you find is people who are storytellers have a feel for who the person is," he says. "If you give them things to do, and they understand the character, they can usually pull it off fairly comfortably." Bruce also played a character in Sayles's clip for "Glory Days," which wove together barroom performance scenes with sequences about a heavy equipment operator's nostalgia for his days on the baseball diamond, even as he revels in the comforts of his wife (portrayed by Julianne) and their pair of handsome sons. The final video for the album, "My Hometown," was a live concert performance.

The videos leaped into MTV's ceaseless rotation. All seven of the singles drawn from *Born in the U.S.A.* hit the *Billboard* Top 10, while the album was in the Top 10 for eighty-four straight weeks, moving enough copies to be the bestselling album of 1985, by which point it had gone platinum ten times over. At the same time, Bruce saw his ambition to be the voice of his moment become an inarguable fact. Certainly within the music community, where his agreement to participate in the multi-artist fund-raiser single being constructed by Michael Jackson, Lionel Richie, and Quincy Jones inspired a legion of reluctant rockers and/or serious-minded songwriters (who feared being roped in among a group of featherweight pop stars) to sign on too.[3] He'd raised

[2] Literally the same car driven by the goddess-like Suzanne Somers in the 1973 film *American Graffiti.*
[3] Despite Jones's famous warning that all performers attending the session must "check your egos at the door," it proved breathtaking to most that Bruce had piloted his own (rented) car to the studio, found his own parking space, and then walked into the event without an entourage in attendance. Richie, on the other hand, took the opportunity to observe loudly that if the A&M Studios exploded with so many fabulous stars inside, 1970s icon John Denver would be back on top of the charts, ha-ha. The jape became all the more amusing when you knew that Denver had actually asked to be included in the USA for Africa project, only to be turned away because he was no longer "cool." That line of reasoning doesn't explain the presence of Kenny Rogers or the guy from Huey Lewis and the News who wasn't Huey Lewis. Arguably, Denver had never been cool, even when he was a chart-topper in the seventies. But Denver's

attention and money through his nightly appeals for (and his own donations to) food banks, veterans' centers, and other local charities in the
cities the tour visited. And through his songs and words, Bruce had focused attention on the plight of ordinary working people. He had stood
on the biggest stages and made an even bigger noise than he had set out
to make.

Along the way, he had also become an international icon: a one-man
symbol of the United States of America, in all its spectacle, noise, and
supersized reach. And if the vast audiences all around the world hadn't
made that clear, Landau had also fielded a multimillion-dollar offer from
the Chrysler automobile company for Bruce to serve as the face of a massive new ad campaign. Not that Bruce would seriously consider that sort
of thing—he certainly didn't need the money, and now that he had the
world's attention, selling trucks was the last thing he had in mind. The
members of the E Street Band had certainly enjoyed their run at the top
of the mountain too. But even as they ran through the victory lap of sold-
out stadiums and noted the additional zeroes in their paychecks, success
came with a sense of unease.

"I felt that the end of the Born in the U.S.A. tour was the end of the
cohesion," Max Weinberg reflects. "I could tell things were changing. I
felt tremendous solidarity with the concept of the group pushing Bruce's
vision forward. But from January of '85 to October of '85, the end of the
Born in the U.S.A. tour, that's when I felt the dissolution happening. I
can remember being very depressed after the last concert we did at the LA
Coliseum on October 2 and saying to my wife, 'It's over.'"

It was a common feeling. "Me being a star, I didn't care that much
about it," Clarence Clemons said in 2011. "The one thing that mattered
the most to me was my relationship with Bruce. I felt there was some distance happening between Bruce and the band, and that Jon wanted it to
happen. Things were changing. Bruce was changing."

How could his installation in the grandest pantheon of celebrity
artists not alter Bruce's sense of himself and his place in the world? "He

---

charitable works exceeded Richie's by a vast degree, which made the snickering all the
more odious.

had the president of the USA quoting him. He had every form of recognition that you could have here and in Europe, Japan, and Australia,"
Landau says. "And when it was over, I think it was such a monumental,
life-changing event that he just wanted something different. I felt, at the
end of day, that [the *U.S.A.* era] was a great experience for both of us. But
I totally understood that we needed to settle into a mode that we could
now sustain for the rest of his life." And if that meant creating an entirely
new setting and sound for his music, that's just what had to happen.
Bruce had already broken up every band he'd been in. No surprise, then,
that his commitment to the E Street Band had its limits. Now that they'd
all seen their years of common struggle reach the astonishing heights of
Born in the U.S.A., what else could they do?

Not that the job was entirely finished. As with all of Bruce's marathon
shows, Born in the U.S.A. came with an encore: the long-dreamed-of
live album. Ten years and tens of millions of albums later, the stakes had
changed. Now the live collection would serve as a monument to the
sweep of Bruce's thirteen-year career as a recording artist, and the twenty-
plus years he'd spent onstage with the core of musicians he'd played and
lived with since they were all teenagers. Given the grandiosity of that
story and the wild intensity of popular demand, the set took on monumental proportions. More than a single, a double, or even a triple album,
this package stretched into a boxed set of five vinyl discs, or, for the latest audio technology, three compact discs. The five-disc/three-CD box
wasn't entirely unprecedented in rock 'n' roll: Bob Dylan had pioneered
the form with *Biograph*, the career-spanning collection released in the fall
of 1985. But this would be the first live rock 'n' roll album to get such
gilded treatment.

Given a collection of professional-quality live tapes dating back to
the Born to Run tour, Bruce, Landau, Chuck Plotkin, and engineer
Toby Scott sorted through the performances in search of a collection
that represented the arc of Bruce's musical and philosophical vision,
while also telling the story of the band's journey from bars to baseball
stadiums. They decided to limit themselves to the decade between the
intimate Born to Run shows in 1975 to the stadium leg of the Born
in the U.S.A. tour in 1985. With one ear tuned to the quality and

historical significance of the individual performances and the other to forming a cohesive narrative, the forty-track album they created journeyed from the hushed voice-and-piano reading of "Thunder Road" that opened his 1975 shows at Los Angeles's Roxy club to stadium-sized performances of "Born to Run" and a variety of *Born in the U.S.A.* songs[4] with one hundred thousand voices singing along. If "Thunder Road" set a dream in motion, the massive versions of "Born to Run" and "The Promised Land" made clear that the young man's fantasy of where he might go hadn't even come close to where life would actually take him. But a decade later, the man's own triumph was no longer big enough to sustain him. As Bruce called to the city-sized mobs of fans drawn to his shows night after night: "Remember that in the end, nobody wins unless everybody wins. *A-one-two!*"[5] And with that benediction came "Born to Run," the tale of one couple's bid for glory transformed into an anthem for the common man.

Readied for a November 1986 release, *Bruce Springsteen & the E Street Band Live/1975–85* presented a conundrum to industry analysts and the Columbia/CBS leadership alike. Dylan's *Biograph* had sold about 250,000 copies within a year of its release—which seemed like a bigger win when computed on a per-album basis, in which the sale of one box counted as the sale of five single albums (for example, 250,000 = 1.25 million = platinum-plus). So while CBS planned for Bruce's live box set to be a hot commodity in virtually every country in the world, initial estimations called for global sales of about 2 million (or, in industryspeak, 10 million) copies. Instead record store preorders in the United States alone added up to 1.5 million, with warnings that the retailers expected to have to restock their supplies within a week. International orders followed suit, and when the album hit the shelves on November 10, 1986, record buyers, store owners, and the Springsteen-hungry media approached the unveiling as a cultural event. Blocklong lines stretching

---

[4] No fewer than eight of *U.S.A.*'s twelve songs—which struck some listeners as overkill, particularly given the wealth of older and more offbeat songs that didn't make the cut.
[5] Although not heard on the album, this declaration of communal integration can be heard on the video made for the live "Born to Run" track.

to the shops' doors; mob scenes inside; joyous consumers carting their quarry home by the armload. Retailers and industrial observers supplied the superlatives: *Live/1975–85* was akin to a new Beatles album; it could be the album of the decade; it was a money-printing machine for everyone and anyone with a hand in its production, printing, distribution, and/or sale.[6]

How could any five-disc box of what was now classified as "heartland rock" live up to such superlatives? Debuting on the *Billboard* album chart at number one made for a nice start, and holding on to the top position through the holiday shopping season and well into January also helped reality transcend the hyperbole.[7] Sales were also enhanced by the success of the box's first single, a furious cover of Edwin Starr's Vietnam-era protest song "War," which peaked at number 8 on *Billboard*'s singles chart, stretching Bruce's streak of Top 10 singles to eight. The next single, "Fire," ended the streak in decisive form by stalling at number 46.

As it turned out, the record buyers who left that single on the shelves[8] weren't alone in their desire to take a break from all things Springsteen. "I just kind of felt Bruced out," Bruce told Jim Henke a few years later. "I was like, 'Whoa, enough of that.' You end up creating this sort of icon, and eventually it oppresses you . . . The whole image that had been created—and that I'm sure I promoted—it really always felt like, 'Hey, that's not me.' It was never me." Though, as he admitted in his next

[6] And yet there was plenty of room for fan discussion and dissent: along with the songs that didn't make the cut ("Incident on 57th Street"! "Jungleland"!), you could grumble about the editing choices (What happened to the entire middle part of the "Backstreets" they used [the Roxy, July 7, 1978]? Why did they censor Bruce's midsong rap during "Raise Your Hand" when he urged radio listeners to grab their volume knobs and "turn the motherfucker up as loud as it'll go"?) A big rap in the middle of "Fire," also taken from that same Roxy show, vanished as well. And so on and so forth.

[7] As of early 2012, *Bruce Springsteen & the E Street Band Live/1975–85* was credited with sales of more than thirteen million units. Whether that number is based on the mideighties calibration of one box = five vinyl albums is unclear, given the CD format's primacy. Decisions of this nature come out of the murky realm where accounting merges with shamanism. Or perhaps magical realism.

[8] Which did not include the fanatics who snapped up the single to play the live "Incident on 57th Street" on its B-side.

breath, that wasn't quite true, either. "It might be a little more of me than I think."

Temporarily relieved of the shifting burdens of art, fame, and commerce, Bruce turned his attention to the quieter challenges of domestic life with his new spouse. On one level, he and Julianne were a lot like any other pair of successful young professionals, juggling their relationship with their careers and the inner lives that had propelled them to the point where they had made themselves family. It's difficult even when you're not at the peak of one of the most high-profile careers in the world. Throw in a similarly motivated younger wife and a husband whose romantic/domestic commitment is counterbalanced by layers of doubt and psychological disquiet, and happily ever after becomes a tricky stretch of road. Were there conflicts? Of course there were conflicts: what couple doesn't have them? But when they got back to New Jersey, settling into Bruce's house in Rumson, he went right back to doing the things he always did, only now with his younger, movie-star wife on his arm. As far as friends and observers could tell, Julianne fit right in, as eager to get to know her husband's old neighbors in Freehold as she was to spend an evening with his more famous friends. When Bruce ran into his childhood best pal Bobby Duncan at his gym one day,[9] Julianne became an instant friend too, often tossing her mat next to where the golf course manager was stretching in order to chat and, Duncan says, be as warm and sweet as you would hope the wife of a childhood friend would turn out to be. "Juli was very down to earth and nice," Duncan says. "She was trying to get her acting career going at the time. But mostly she was outgoing and warm, and seemed like a really kind person."

And seemingly on board for whatever her husband wanted to do. A night at the Stone Pony? She was right there at the bar, checking out the band with Bruce and then edging away subtly when a crowd of fans

---

[9] Duncan, who hadn't seen Bruce in a decade or more, was getting the stern please-leave-Bruce-alone talk from gym owner Tony Dunphy, Bruce's trainer, when the star came running up, wrapped his old pal in a hug, and took him off to the locker room to reminisce for an hour.

enveloped him. And if it turned out that he had to escape the crush through a side door—always making sure to ask a friend to get Juli out safely to a quieter rendezvous point—she took it in stride. When engineer Toby Scott came out to Rumson to help build a recording studio in the guest apartment in the adjacent carriage house, they seemed as cheerfully settled as any pair of newlyweds. "We'd all have dinner in the house, Bruce, Juli, and I," Scott says. "They were very domestic. She liked to stay in, make popcorn, watch TV, and have some dinner. People kept asking if they had a problem, and I always said no. I thought Bruce and Juli were doing great." But when they went out for a pleasant dinner with Roy Bittan and his wife, the pianist went home with an uneasy feeling about what he'd seen. "It just wasn't like going out with the Julianne and Bruce that I knew," he says. "Juli was a lovely girl, but he just seemed like he was trying to be a different person. I think he was trying to develop a way of being on a social level. And Julianne wasn't anywhere on his train of thought."

To the extent that he could, Bruce tried to make it work. He'd made his vow, he knew he had to live by it. In every other relationship he'd had, the escape route was always there, as close as the front door and the highway outside. But that ring on his finger meant he'd surrendered his getaway keys forever. "The good thing about the [songs he'd started writing], was that I said you can *feel* like this and still make a go of it. Experience love or partnership, and also ambivalence, which is part of all human relationships," Bruce says. "The key is, how do you live with it and deal with it in your life. I was kinda coming to grips with it, my adolescent idea of romantic love, and coming to grips with the complexity of what I was finding out."

With his guitar in hand or notebook propped before him at the piano, Bruce followed the knotted strands of his married life, working to string them into words and music. Some songs had the gauzy sound of true love: "Rain and clouds and dark skies, well now they don't mean a thing / if you got a girl who loves you, and who wants to wear your ring," he sang in the lighter-than-air "All That Heaven Will Allow." The sweet "Two for the Road" described the highway as an escape made for two, while "When You Need Me" and the lean ballad "Tougher Than the

Rest"[10] cast romantic commitment in the rock-solid terms of faith, love, and commitment: "The road is dark, and it's a thin, thin line / But I want you to know I'll walk it for you anytime," he pledged in "Tougher."

But such gutsy proclamations don't amount to much in the dead of night, and thus came "Cautious Man," a spare, *Nebraska*-sounding ballad of the tightly wound Bill Horton ("a cautious man of the road") and his stumbling attempts to adjust to domestic life. His love is deep, and he doesn't question his wife's faithfulness, but a deep-seated turmoil, symbolized by the words *love* and *fear* he has tattooed on his knuckles,[11] unsteadies him. Late one night Bill rises from a nightmare, gets dressed, and slips out of the house to stand on the highway, where he has two epiphanies: the solitary road leads nowhere, and his urge to vanish into the nothingness will never cease. Returning to bed, he reaches for his wife and notices the glow of the moon in her hair, "filling their room with the beauty of God's fallen light." Bruce, who says most of the songs were not autobiographical, can't deny the significance of "Cautious Man." "That's one of the good ones. If there was some part of myself I was trying to explain, for better or worse, that song describes a good amount of it."

From there the majority of the new songs traced the fault lines in romantic commitment in general, and Bruce's marriage in particular. "Two Faces" described his restlessness in the terms of bipolarity, with the darker personality subverting his better nature at every turn. Even a bid for God's help can't banish the darker spirit: "he'll never say good-bye / two faces have I." The yearning "One Step Up" told a different version of the same story, describing a fraught romance as a series of blow-ups, reconciliations, and fantasies. And again, when the singer steps back from his anger, all he feels is his failure to live up to his own standards: "Somewhere along the line I slipped off track / I'm caught movin' one step up and two steps back." The one song that Bruce wrote specifically about his and Juli's wedding, "Walk Like a Man," was addressed to Doug Springsteen, recalling

---

[10] First written and recorded as a high-stepping rockabilly number.
[11] An image adapted from the 1955 film *The Night of the Hunter*, starring Robert Mitchum as a self-designated preacher who moonlights as a serial killer.

the years his son had yearned to follow his example. Fate and circumstance had pulled them apart, but the solidity of Doug and Adele's nearly forty-year marriage once again put Bruce in the position of the child straining to match his father's footsteps in the sand. "As I watch my bride come down the aisle / I pray for the strength to walk like a man."

In February 1987 Bruce called in Toby Scott to help him lay down some demo recordings in his new over-the-garage studio. Now equipped with a Kurzweil 250 synthesizer, which offered a variety of sampled horns, strings, various keyboards, and so on, along with a state-of-the-art drum machine and a bass guitar, Bruce built the tracks layer by layer, starting with a simple beat, adding hi-hats and other percussion accents, then cutting a two-bar stretch to loop through the song. The percussion established, Bruce took up a guitar or sat at the keyboard to play the basic chords, laid down a bass guitar track, and then went back to the Kurzweil to add other keyboard sounds, horn or string flourishes, additional guitar parts, and percussion. It took about three weeks to track the songs and add enough overdubs and effects to give them the rich sound of finished recordings. Listening to the final drafts, Bruce thrilled to how live and real his one-man-plus-engineer band sounded. "Man, this record's *done*," he said. What's more, the process had been easy, even *relaxing*. "It's the most fun record I've ever made," he said. Gesturing around the studio, his eyes lit up at the absence of other musicians, and the needs and expectations they always bring. "It's like, I don't have six other people throwing in their input. I can just do what *I* want and what *I* feel. And it sounds great. Why aren't these the masters? These *should* be the masters."

When Landau came down to listen to the new music a few days later, he said virtually the same thing: "Let's put it out like this!" But this time, hearing it come from a voice that had never actually been *in* the E Street Band, Bruce thought again. "Hold up, though," he said. "I've got a band." It was one thing to put out the *Nebraska* demos as solo recordings— everyone knew how distinctive those songs were and that their attempts to cut full-band hadn't worked. But these songs, on the other hand, were *band* songs. No reason why the band couldn't play them, except for that Bruce had beaten them to it. And maybe that wasn't the right thing to do.

"I probably oughta get the guys on this," he said. But he still couldn't stop thinking about how freeing the sessions had been. No disagreements, no arguments, no explanations required.

Whether Bruce's turn toward musical isolation stemmed from the intimate nature of the songs or the emotional stress that had inspired them (if his central relationship was in trouble, how could he confront the many relationships, needs, and opinions that would surely confront him when the band reconvened?) was less clear than the fact that he was raring to be a one-man band. So when Chuck Plotkin flew out to New Jersey to give it a listen, the coproducer's first reaction—after nearly bursting into tears when the procession of fractured love songs made him realize, "Oh God, that boy's in trouble"—was to suggest that at least a few of the songs might sound fuller with the actual E Street Band playing the parts. Bruce's eyes flashed. "He's pissed off. *Really* pissed," Plotkin says. "And I asked as easygoing as possible, 'I don't know if we can improve it at all, but one thing that *might* be interesting would be trying some of these tunes live with the band. Like, we might get a different feel that we like, or we don't.' But he does have a temper, and it's not hard for him to get pissed. It felt to me like he was maybe going to send me back to California 'til I got my mind right." Instead Bruce came up with a scheme that was intended to give every band member a shot at contributing to the album. However, it succeeded only in making most of them feel even more wounded than the Bruce-only album might have done.

They called the process "Beat the Demo." Bruce invited each musician individually to Rumson to come up with parts on his instrument that improved upon what Bruce and Scott had already recorded on their own. "And if they played it better, we used their part," explains Scott. "And if they didn't play it better, we used Bruce's original part. And that's tough because Bruce always prefers the demo."

The way Garry Tallent remembers his sessions, the new way of doing business made for a long afternoon of organized humiliation. "One day they give me a call and ask me to come in and play bass. I'm presented with an album's worth of material, and they're like, 'Play this, play this, play this!'" he says. "I'd never heard the songs before, but okay. I was like,

'Give me five minutes to come up with something!' But it was really, 'Okay, here's your chance.' And the album comes out, and I'm on one cut, maybe? Turns out they liked what they already had on the demo. So it was demeaning."

The other musicians either made their peace with the process or kept their feelings to themselves. Unsurprisingly, the individual players' aggravation correlated almost exactly with the amount of time they had been in the band. The original Asbury Park guys (Clemons, Federici, Tallent) were furious; the class of '74 (Bittan and Weinberg) took it with a grain of salt (Weinberg: "The point is that it's not the first solo record. They're *all* solo records"), while latecomer Lofgren was happy to do any recording with Bruce. "Though I certainly understand why the other guys were upset," the guitarist says. When the album was released, the vague credit to the E Street Band was little more than a gesture. The real story could be found in the individual credits, which revealed how sparse the band's contributions actually were. Weinberg adds drums or percussion to eight of the twelve songs, while Federici plays organs on four, Tallent adds bass to a solitary tune, and Clemons's saxophone doesn't appear anywhere. His sole credit is as a voice in the background chorus on "When You're Alone."

"My life had changed, I was married, experienced the ambivalence of relationships that had always been an undercurrent in my psychological life," Bruce says. "So I was writing about that, and I was looking for another path where I could be of value to both my own self, my inner life, and the fans. And we had such a huge impact at the time, I didn't want to take it for granted and take it down the road in the fashion we had been doing. I thought it was my responsibility to offer up something different to my fans and myself. Thought that was the deal you make with your fans, though it might not have been the deal I made with *all* of my fans, some of whom might have preferred something else."

TWENTY-ONE

I DIDN'T EVEN KNOW
THE LANGUAGE OF PARTNERSHIP

MIDWAY THROUGH THE ALBUM'S EDITING and mixing in the summer of 1987, Bruce came up with another song that seemed like a centerpiece for the work in progress. Built around the analogy of marriage as a carnival ride, it was bigger and glossier than the other songs he'd recorded that year. "Tunnel of Love" seemed a clear choice for a full-band treatment. But given the distinctive feel of the synth-driven tracks that Bruce and Scott had already created, Bruce stuck with the synthesizer-drum machine-and-many-handed-musician tactic for the album's crowning track. "I drew out a road map, programming drums and assembling the percussion," Scott says, "and then Bruce started to play through it" on his many instruments. "And he was like, 'Wow, this is great!' He'd never been freed up for his own creativity like that." Still, the clash of different styles and sounds pulled at Bruce's ear, guiding him to use four E Street Band members (Weinberg, Bittan, Lofgren, and Scialfa), along with the delighted screams of roller-coaster riders at the Point Pleasant Amusement Park.[1]

Now titled *Tunnel of Love*, the album arrived in record stores on October 9, 1987, with a cover portrait showing the thirty-eight-year-old, married artist dressed up like a cowboy romantic, his black suit and white button-up set off by a silver-tipped bolo tie and the gleaming silver buckle on his black leather belt. The music inside was striking both for Bruce's turn away from *Born in the U.S.A.*'s bombastics and for his clear-eyed portrayal of love's struggles—which seemed particularly striking given his careerlong avoidance of what he had dismissed, only three years earlier, as "married music."

Taken as a follow-up to *U.S.A.* the new record struck critics as a daring move against expectations. Noting Bruce's reputation for romanticizing his subjects, *Rolling Stone* critic Steve Pond began his celebratory review by declaring that on *Tunnel*, "he doesn't even romanticize romance." And while most critics also noted the dramatic shift away from Bruce's previous albums' full-volume blasts of celebration and fury, rock critic Jon Pareles of the *New York Times* described a recognizable parallel between the new record's fraught love songs and the earlier albums' stark analyses of opportunity and fair play in America: "[Now] he's confronting another illusion: the myth of love as perfect bliss and panacea."

Although Bruce had consciously stepped away from recapturing the mass audience he'd commanded in the mid-1980s, he didn't exactly oppose the thought of making a splash with the new record. So he, Landau, and everyone at Columbia/CBS were pleased to see *Tunnel* holding its

[1] Recorded by Scott and an assistant, who spent the majority of a summer's day recruiting and coaching the park's customers to please direct their reactions to the microphones they'd see jutting up from the ground at the coaster's final turn. The Schiffer family named in the song's credits were the park's owners and operators. This didn't mark the first use of ambient sound effects in Bruce's recording career. When the sound of crickets drifted through an open window into the basic track of "County Fair" several years earlier, Bruce asked Scott to take a recorder into the brush to capture the sound at closer range. The released version of the song (which emerged on the bonus disc of *The Essential Bruce Springsteen* in 2003) mixes the accidental crickets with the painstakingly recorded ones.

own in the market, claiming the throne of the bestselling album chart three weeks after its release, and selling more than three million copies in the United States within the first year. A trio of hit singles ("Brilliant Disguise," which hit number 5; "Tunnel of Love," number 9; "One Step Up," number 13) were all accompanied by popular video clips on MTV. But even the additional millions of albums sold in the foreign market weren't enough to hold back talk that America's biggest rock 'n' roll icon of the 1980s was already fading. Bruce's mind was elsewhere.

"I was always interested about how do I take this music and bring in adult concerns without losing its vitality, fun, and youthfulness. I'd thought about that since '77, with *Darkness*. So ten years later, it manifests itself in a different way. So I thought, okay, we're growing up together, me and my audience. And I took that idea seriously. So my usefulness as a thirty-eight-year-old is gonna be different than my usefulness as a twenty-seven-year old. And I was always looking for ways to be useful. That's what mattered to me, and excited me, and how I thought I'd be of good service and be entertaining."

Committed to mounting another world tour in 1988, Bruce couldn't decide whether he wanted to go out with the E Street Band or as a solo performer. He and Landau booked a series of midsized theaters (three thousand to five thousand capacity), thinking the smaller venues would be the right size for a solitary or near-solitary (if he wanted to add a small combo) performances. But Bruce thought about it again in the late fall, and called in his usual gang of musical compadres. "He convened all of us two days a week in New Jersey, and we started to play the *Tunnel* songs," Lofgren says. "He was exploring how he wanted to tour this time. One weekend I went in alone with acoustic instruments. Fortunately, by late '87, he decided he wanted to tour the album with the E Street Band and bring the horns along too."

When Bruce abandoned thoughts of touring solo, he opted for an onstage lineup that expanded the usual band with the five-piece Miami Horns, a regularly changing set of players that started as the horn section for Southside Johnny and the Asbury Jukes in the mid-1970s. (The "Miami" part was in tribute to Steve Van Zandt, the band's original producer and arranger.) A version of the section had toured with Bruce and the E Streeters on and off in 1976–77, and popped up at other gigs through the years.[2]

As Bruce imagined the tour ahead, other changes came to mind too. Determined to not replay the same ritual night after night and year after year, he made a list of his most-beloved stage songs—"Thunder Road," "The Promised Land," "Badlands," and so on—and put them on his do-not-play list. "I just felt I'd have to drop all the cornerstones of my set," he told journalists at the tour opener in Worcester, Massachusetts, on February 25, 1988. In the mood to toss everything in the air, Bruce had the set designed to move Weinberg's drums from the traditional back-middle spot to the rear left corner. Bittan's and Federici's keyboard rigs traded sides of the stage, while Clemons moved from Bruce's right to his left. In the Big Man's old place now stood Scialfa, who played acoustic guitar for most of the set while also taking many of Clemons's duties as the bandleader's onstage foil, dancing with him during some songs and joining him at the center stage for duets on others.

Along with the new stage placements came an array of other ideas, strategies, and strictures Bruce wanted his band members to follow. In a striking shift from every tour they had ever played, the set list for these shows would remain almost entirely consistent from night to night. When not participating in previously choreographed moves or theatrical bits between songs, the musicians were to stay on or near their designated spots onstage. Also, each band member had to meet with the tour's costumer in order to put together an approved set of of stage clothes that would match the elegant look Bruce wanted to match the more mature sound of his new music.

Between all that and the elaborately painted backdrop (a colorful blend of the Garden of Eden, cartoon lovers, and a juicy red rendition

---

[2] They're most famous now for serving in the Max Weinberg 7 on NBC's *Late Night with Conan O'Brien* from 1993 until the group became the *Tonight Show* band during O'Brien's brief 2009 tenure in the eleven thirty slot. Weinberg left the outfit when O'Brien moved to cable TV in 2010; the horns stayed with the show.

of the words *Tunnel of Love*) and the staged opening bit that involved a carnival ticket booth (manned by Bruce's assistant Terry Magovern), the highly structured, theatrical bent of the tour clattered all kinds of warning bells in the ears of the band members. "It was like a Broadway stage sort of thing," Tallent says. Weinberg took note of how carefully the tour name—Bruce Springsteen's Tunnel of Love Express Featuring the E Street Band—described Bruce's distance from the band. "[Earlier] he was one of us," the drummer says. "Now we were a completely separate entity." Covering Bruce's new solo songs also proved discomfiting for musicians accustomed to playing original parts they had developed for themselves. "I think some of us never felt comfortable with it," Bittan says. "The drum machine parts felt uncomfortable for Max, and the bass parts weren't in Garry's style."

The players also noticed a new caste system in the touring arrangements, in which Bruce and a few top management figures stayed in different hotels than the band did, and where the fancier parties along the way—the champagne-and-caviar affairs thrown by promoters and the record label bigwigs—no longer included the E Streeters. "We'd hear about it the next day," Tallent says. "Not even that you *wanted* to go, but you might, so you like to be asked. So Bruce would go, and the management and record company people. The publicity people would go. Anyone but the band. That was the vibe. Danny and I were completely fed up." Bruce remembers the tour differently, particularly when it came to the parties.

The Tunnel of Love Express tour was noticeably more subdued than any series of shows Bruce had ever played, divided between a tightly constructed first set built from the *Tunnel* songs and an unexpected assortment of B sides and rarities (including the *River*-era B sides "Roulette," "Be True," and a blistering cover of John Lee Hooker's "Boom Boom"), and a set-ending sweep of "War" and "Born in the U.S.A." A more spirited second half tossed in a few E Street favorites ("She's the One," an occasional "Backstreets" and "Rosalita") among a slew of new or obscure songs: a disused original called "Part Man/Part Monkey," the reclaimed throwaway "Light of Day," and a cover of Detroit R&B singer Gino Washington's 1963 minihit "Gino Is a Coward" rewritten into "I'm a Coward (When It Comes to Love)." The encores trended back to crowd favorites, with an emphasis on the radio hits, from "Hungry Heart" to "Glory Days" to "Dancing in the Dark." But the climactic "Born to Run" came in a subdued solo acoustic arrangement, less a call to action than a more mature man's realization (as Bruce said every night during his introduction) that "I thought I was writing about a guy and a girl who wanted to get in the car and run and keep on running. And I realized later that home really wasn't out there, but that it was buried deep inside of me someplace."

The shows had their joyous moments, to be sure. But on some nights Bruce came onstage looking agitated. On occasion he directed his anger at the audience, as when he was met by a celebratory crowd bouncing beach balls over one another's heads. Bruce concluded the opening song with a snarly edict: "Do me a favor and get rid of those fucking beach balls." When the tour reached Tacoma, Washington, in the first week of May, Bruce responded just as virulently when an unruly fan snuck onstage and interrupted his spoken-word introduction to "Spare Parts." Security guards had the guy in hand within seconds, but even after the intruder was gone, Bruce glared icily at the audience. "A short public announcement," he barked. "No one onstage but the fucking band, please." Looking over his shoulder back to where the guy had emerged from, Bruce shook his head. "I hate assholes like that."

Surprising bursts of anger from a man who always found his greatest joy while standing on a stage with a guitar in his hands and an audience at his feet. But he had his reasons. Days earlier, he and Julianne had separated.

Talking about his marriage to *Rolling Stone*'s Steve Pond earlier that spring, Bruce enthused about the sense of security he got from being in a committed relationship. Asked if he had found the elusive "place where we really want to go" he'd envisioned in "Born to Run," he nodded. "Sometimes I really do," he said. "You have to find the strength to sustain it and build on it and work for it . . . [but] gee, I've been married for three years, just about, and I feel like we'd just met." Was he saying that his marriage still had the magic of early love, or that the years to-gether still hadn't fostered the emotional intimacy married people are supposed to develop as a part of each other's lives? Bruce didn't seem to know. "There's a part of you that wants the stability and the home thing, and there's a part of you that isn't so sure . . . there's days when you're real close and days when you're real far away."

Both halves of the couple kept news of their breakup as quiet as pos-sible. No press releases, no leaks to friendly reporters, no public heart-to-hearts with *People* or Barbara Walters. Some sharp-eyed observers might have figured out that Bruce had taken off his wedding ring. Backstage crew and visitors noticed that Julianne, a fixture at earlier shows on the tour, was nowhere to be seen, even on the couple's third anniversary on May 13. What could be seen, however, was that the duets he performed with the increasingly prominent Patti Scialfa, particularly on "Tougher Than the Rest," had grown so steamy it seemed like the singers' romantic heat was, perhaps, a bit too realistic to be limited to the stage. But what might have seemed shocking to outsiders—is Bruce *really* fooling around with his backup singer?—was no surprise to anyone who had seen the Born in the U.S.A. tour from the inside. "What was obvious on the Tunnel tour was also obvious at an early point in the Born in the U.S.A. tour, let's just say that," says Dave Marsh. Even if the electricity between Bruce and Patti seemed obvious in 1984, the in-house gossip didn't travel beyond the touring party. When Julianne became a part of the scene in the fall of 1984, the crowd on the tour figured her for an outlier candidate for Bruce's affections. So when word broke that Bruce would be traveling with a serious girlfriend during the Far East swing in the spring of 1985, some tour members assumed they could book one less hotel room for the band. "I know I was surprised when he came to Japan with someone other than Patti," Marsh says.

Still, when he thought about settling into a serious romance, some-thing pushed him in a different direction. Certainly Julianne's beauty, warmth, and intelligence had magnetic properties all their own. And the prospect of taking up with his newest band member, weaving a ro-mance into the always-complex chemistry of the E Street Band while also stirring up a tabloid frenzy, couldn't have seemed appealing. So then came Julianne, the wedding, and three years of marriage that hardly anyone had guessed might be less than the openly affectionate romance most observers believed they were witnessing. When Julianne accompanied Bruce to the early shows on the Tunnel tour in late February and early March, they had impressed observers with how relaxed and happy they looked together. But something else was going on too.

Both members of the couple were, and remain, tight lipped about the inner workings of their marriage. Speaking to the writer Nick Dawidoff in the mid-1990s, Bruce said, "[Juli]'s one of the best people I've ever met. But we were pretty different, and I realized I didn't know how to be married." When asked now, Bruce has one question: "Did Juli speak to you at all?" Told that she basically hadn't, he speaks only about his ex-wife's strengths and his own weaknesses. "The emotions of mine that were uncovered by trying to have an adult life with a partner and make that work uncovered a lot of things I'd avoided and tried not to deal with previously," he says, and more or less leaves it at that. Julianne returns the favor. "I have always been incredibly private when it comes to my private life," she says. "The one and only thing that I *will* say is that that period was a time of incredible personal growth and introspection for me. And I will forever give that credit to Bruce." Which is remarkably gracious given how swiftly, and thoughtlessly, Bruce moved into the next stage of his life.

Once Bruce showed up backstage without his wedding ring, he and Patti stopped hiding their affections from the rest of the touring company. They cuddled backstage and shared seats on the jet from one show to the next. Given no official declaration about his separation from Julianne, it came as a shock to Tallent and his girlfriend when they stumbled across the couple smooching on the airplane. "My girlfriend's going, 'What's going on here?' and I had no idea what to say." But the news stayed hush-hush, more or less, through the end of the American tour on May 23 and through the first few dates on the European tour, until the company got to Rome in mid-June.

The sun was bright, the skies deep blue, and the hotel room's balcony all but irresistible when Bruce and Patti woke up on the morning of June

15 and stepped outside to take in the view. With the sun on their shoulders and new love in the air, they held each other as they gazed across the rooftops—not suspecting that an observant photographer, a professional in the land that invented the term *paparazzi*, was peering at them through his viewfinder. *Click-click-click.* Then they were lying together, drinks in hand, on a single patio recliner. *Clickity-click.* Those photos made headlines all across Europe and then in the United States, and on June 17 Jon Landau Management released a statement acknowledging that Bruce and Julianne had separated. A day after that, Bruce and Patti sealed the deal by strolling arm in arm through Paris, in full view of a procession of French reporters and photographers.

At the moment, and with memories of Bruce and Julianne's wedding still fresh in the public mind, photographic evidence of his marital two-timing struck at the roots of the moral righteousness he seemed to carry onto the stage. That his wholesome image was only the latest iteration in more than two decades of growth, change, and shape-shifting did not seem to matter. The vast majority of the popular culture media had come to know Bruce since he'd taken on his clean-cut working-class hero image. Having been branded as such, he was expected to behave accordingly. The first wave of headlines were as jagged as you might expect. Phillips's friends stood up for their justifiably wounded friend. But given Phillips's dignified response (essentially saying nothing in public, except for a career-focused interview in *Us* magazine in August, followed by more than twenty years of silence), and perhaps the foreshadowing in virtually all of the key songs on *Tunnel of Love*, the story fizzled quickly. As David Hinckley reported in the New York *Daily News*, many fans accepted Bruce's affair as a sign not of perfidy or hypocrisy but of mortality. And if the "It humanizes him" argument might have exuded the aroma of fan-boy rationalization, a closer look at the artist's work—going all the way back to the Castiles' Theiss-Springsteen B side "That's What You Get"—made clear that the conflicting calls to sin and grace had never relaxed their grip on his soul.

None of this justifies ill behavior, no matter toward whom it's directed. But it was (and remains) impossible to accuse Bruce of violating some code of ethics he'd prescribed for others in the text of his work, since the real struggle his characters waged almost always took place within themselves. Virtually every male character on *Tunnel of Love* and the B sides and outtakes recorded during the sessions has some kind of ungodly hound baying at his door. "When I look at my face I don't see / The man I wanted to be," he sang in the self-lacerating "One Step Up," in which the confused, unhappy husband makes eyes with a woman sitting across the bar. Like Bill Horton, whose marked hands labored to reconcile the divided forces of love and fear, Bruce could only raise his fists and hope that he wouldn't hurt anyone else as badly as himself.

"But of course I did," he says. "I didn't protect Juli. Some sort of public announcement would have been fair, but I felt over concerned about my own privacy. I handled it badly, and I still feel badly about it. It was cruel for people to find out the way they did."

Away from home, cut loose from whatever chains of anger or guilt he'd carried through the last months of his marriage, Bruce hit the stages of Europe with a renewed appetite for unrestrained rock 'n' roll. The last few weeks of the American tour had already traded out the romantic "Be True" for the man's-man blues "Boom Boom," with Clemons's saxophone blasts kicking down the doors that Bruce's guitar attacks hadn't already splintered. A steamy "Because the Night" brought the passion to the second set in the European tour's opening night in Turin, while U.S.A. tour highlights "Bobby Jean," "The River," and "Downbound Train" pounced back into the set during the next week or two. In Munich on July 17, Bruce called out for "Badlands" as an onstage audible, and was so thrilled by the arms-aloft response that he made it the opener for the band's next performance, with "Out in the Street" following in the second slot and another previously exiled favorite, "The Promised Land," turning up a few songs later. Which would seem like a conceptual retreat of sorts, but for the fact that the July 19 show was taking place in East Berlin, just beyond the wall that compelled so many nations to view one another as combatants.

Already aware that the people of Eastern Europe were shaking off the grip of the Soviet empire, Bruce and Landau imagined the impact that a big rock 'n' roll show might have on the freedom-starved Easterners. Landau asked the tour's promoter to see if the East German government would allow a free concert on its side of the Berlin Wall. The officials loved the idea, particularly given Bruce's proletarian, seemingly anti-capitalism reputation. With the show set for the Radrennbahn Wessensee park, the Communist politicians borrowed a play from Ronald Reagan by sweeping Bruce into their own political narrative. As the war between the socialist government of Nicaragua and American-funded rebels (the Contras) simmered, the East Germans dubbed the nationally broadcast show the Concert for Nicaragua. And while Bruce was no fan of the Reagan administration's covert war against the government of Nicaraguan president Daniel Ortega, he also wasn't going to sit still long enough to let the Soviets drape a red flag over his shoulders.

Set loose in front of 250,000 Berliners and far more East German TV viewers, Bruce and band marched onstage with something beyond the intricacies of romance on their mind. From "Badlands" to "Out in the Street" to "The Promised Land," "War," "Born in the U.S.A.," and the first full-band "Born to Run" since 1985, the show served as a testament to the basic right of freedom. To make his point—and refute the government's attempt to co-opt him—Bruce wrote (and then worked with his German driver to translate) a statement separating himself from any government or political system: "[I'm here] to play rock 'n' roll for East Berliners, in the hope that one day all walls will be torn down." Or that was the plan until word about Bruce's statement leaked and the panicked West German promoter begged him to change "walls" to the less offensive "barriers." Bruce made the change, but if he pulled that punch, the performance of Bob Dylan's "Chimes of Freedom" (in the Byrds' arrangement, with harmonies and jangling guitar leads) that came next made his liberation ideology entirely clear.

"I think it was recorded as the largest concert ever in Europe," Landau says. The show also underscored Bruce's just-announced commitment to share the stage with Sting, Peter Gabriel, rising folk star Tracy Chapman, and Nigerian singer Youssou N'Dour, among others, on the globe-trotting twenty-date Human Rights Now! tour designed to help raise money and attention for Amnesty International. Bruce's endorsement of the international rights organization came with a distinct political charge, given its connections to the world's left-leaning groups and governments. The far-flung stops on the six-week tour—which visited Africa, Europe, Asia, India, and South, Central, and North Americas—stirred less controversy around the world than it did at the headquarters of CBS, where company president Walter Yetnikoff flew into a rage when he heard that Bruce had signed on with Amnesty.

Now Yetnikoff admits that his reaction had more to do with the extremes of his newly sober consciousness than anything else, but the strong supporter of the Israeli government harbored (and still harbors) a beef with Amnesty over its denunciations of the Jewish state's human rights record. "So I called Landau and told him I was fucking pissed off, and he said, 'You better not start this political stuff with Bruce.'" Landau offered to bring Amnesty chief Jack Healey to CBS headquarters so that they could all talk it over, but by then Yetnikoff stopped taking the manager's calls. "Did I say I was right?" Yetnikoff says. "I was on my own *farkakta* ego trip. I wasn't right, and I probably picked the wrong fight. But I had a lot of problems then." Already on notice from CBS's board of directors, the hot-wired executive lost even more support when Bruce and Landau publicly distanced themselves from him. Yetnikoff was finally escorted down the CBS execu-plank in 1990.

For Bruce and the E Street Band, the Amnesty tour made for an invigorating change of pace. The musicians liked the spirit of comradeship that bonded all the performers and their bands—in distinct contrast to the distance Bruce kept from the group throughout the Tunnel tour—and the visits to cities, nations, and continents they had never seen before, let alone performed in, were peak experiences for everyone. "That was my favorite tour," Clarence Clemons said to me. "When we went to Africa, the whole audience was black. It was the first time I ever saw more than one black person at Bruce's concerts. The people were all dressed up in bright yellows and reds, the jacaranda trees were blooming in purple, and I was like, *Wow!* Purple trees and no white people! This must be heaven!"

Bruce was having his own set of revelations too, and not all of them came from his own new sense of the globe and its people. Given the opportunity to spend quality time with similarly creative and successful stars, Bruce grew particularly close to Sting, with whom he shared a working-class background and a similarly troubled relationship with his father. "Bruce and I figured a way out," Sting says. "But no matter how successful . . . you're always hungry, which is a good thing too. To be complacent or even happy, that's kind of a bovine concept, really. What's interesting is that we both strive to understand what this fucking thing is." Sting had cut his ties with the Police and scored back-to-back triumphs with *The Dream of the Blue Turtles* and . . . *Nothing Like the Sun*. Peter Gabriel had also scaled new creative and commercial heights since leaving Genesis in 1975. As the tour went on, and Bruce had a chance to watch Sting and his new band in action, the British musician could sense a growing fascination beaming his way. "Bruce would watch our band—Branford Marsalis and the amazing group of musicians—and it was obvious that Bruce was interested in doing that too, working with a different set of musicians."

What Bruce saw affirmed his realization that the time had come for him to reestablish his own independence. From the shadows of the past, from the relationships that had always defined him, from the sights, sounds, and riffs that had shored up his existence since he was a boy.

Even with the Amnesty shows in the fall, the 1988 Tunnel touring cycle was the shortest post-album run Bruce had taken since the five-month Born to Run tour in 1975. Back home in mid-October, the weather turned chilly. The December issue of *Esquire* magazine featured an essay designed to deconstruct Bruce's reputation on every conceivable level. Starting with a sardonic cover illustration portraying Bruce as a Catholic saint, anchored by a "Saint Boss" headline (subhead: "Has Fame Crucified Bruce Springsteen?"),[3] the seven-thousand-plus-word story meandered through author John Lombardi's lengthy disquisition on a

[3] Unprinted answer to its own question: not yet, but keep reading.

new-to-him phenomenon he called "mass hip"—for example, popular culture—and then turned to an ill-reported account of Bruce's life and career, culminating in his recounting of a concert marred by the fact that Lombardi's backstage pass wasn't powerful enough to get him into the band's bathroom facilities. Redirected to the public bathrooms on the concourse by a pair of security guards, the author gained his revenge by gathering quotes from fans sitting in what seems to be the least articulate section of the arena. The story ended, inexplicably, with the thoughts of celebrity sex therapist Dr. Ruth Westheimer. "Bruce is a national monument," she proclaimed. "This is what America's about!"

The story itself is less interesting than the vein of hostility it taps. The years of presenting himself as rock 'n' roll's last true believer, and being portrayed by the media as a paragon of moral and musical virtue, had elevated Bruce onto a platform too lofty to stand on. Love it or hate it, the music was beside the point. These were stories about image and public narrative. And while Bruce certainly contributed to, and benefited from, his superheroic aura, he also knew it was a trap. The food bank donations, the fund-raising for veterans, and the many tales of the dispossessed he'd written set a standard he couldn't meet. If he'd given x amount of money to the cause, why did he stop there? How could he criticize any other tycoon's selfishness when the size of Bruce's own fortune could make the Monopoly man's mustache droop? All this talk of faith and virtue from a guy caught on an Italian balcony not only without his pants but with a woman not his wife? And worse, how could Bruce stand up for the rights of working people when people who worked for Bruce said *he'd* violated their rights?

Wait. What?

In the midst of Lombardi's polemic came actual news. Two of Bruce's ex-employees, Doug Sutphin and Mike Batlan, had filed a lawsuit alleging, among other things, that Springsteen Inc. had violated federal labor laws governing the payment of overtime wages. Still, the actionable parts of the filing were less eye opening than the allegations about Bruce's penchant for fining employees who disappointed him—such as when Sutphin was dunned $100 for touching Nils Lofgren's guitar, while Batlan claimed he was docked more than $300 when a storm swept away one of

Bruce's canoes. Also, the litigants noted, house manager Obie Dziedzic had to cough up her own hard-earned cash for arriving late with Bruce's preshow soup and sandwich. *The withholding of the royal soup!* Not an actionable offense, to be sure, but Bruce's most precious fine would be exacted in the court of public opinion.

Batlan had resigned and Sutphin was shown the door after the U.S.A. tour, both walking out with six-figure severance packages that added up to about two years of their $50,000-plus salaries. Still, both departures had seemed friendly at the time, with, as Bruce recalled, "hugs and handshakes all around." Everyone went on with his life for the next two years, until Batlan and Sutphin filed their complaint in Monmouth County civil court. Whether they intended the case to go to court or hoped to compel Bruce to buy his way out of a publicity nightmare is unclear. Either way, it was difficult to ignore the emotional undergirding to the complaint, which dated back to Batlan's joining the crew in 1973, when Bruce and the band still earned $35 a week, and Mike Appel had to bounce checks to keep their vans running. The twenty-four-year-old Bruce talked in grand terms in those days, often declaring that everyone in his organization was part of the family, and that once he hit it big, he would make sure everyone else got dealt into his good fortune too. Whether such talk can or should be taken as legally binding fifteen years later is an interesting question.

Still, some members of Bruce's staff sympathized with Batlan's sense of injustice. For while Bruce had come home from the Born in the U.S.A. tour toting an astronomical sum of money, twelve-year veteran Batlan didn't have enough cash to make a down payment for a simple family home. When he went directly to Bruce to remind him of his age-old promise, the once openhanded boss shrugged him off. Or so Batlan said. But when ex-drummer Vini Lopez, who got the sack years before any serious money rolled in, was called to give a deposition about his own memories of Bruce's verbal assurances, he quickly refuted Batlan's claim. "Give me a fuckin' break," he says. "And don't ask me any questions [in court] 'cause I'll tell you the damn answers."

Settled eventually for an undisclosed amount rumored to be in the neighborhood of $325,000, the lawsuit left a bitter taste in Bruce's mouth. "I worked with these two people for a long time, and I thought I'd really done the right thing," he told David Hepworth in 1992. "Then about a year later, bang!" Continuing the thought with *Rolling Stone*'s Jim Henke that same year, Bruce noted that the majority of his crew members tended to stay with the organization for years, even decades. "But it only takes one disgruntled or unhappy person, and that's what everyone wants to hear. The drum starts getting beat . . . but outside of all that . . . if you spend a long time with someone and there's a very fundamental misunderstanding, well, you feel bad about it."

Sutphin's and Batlan's postlawsuit thoughts, feelings, and/or regrets were (and remain) impossible to know: as part of their $325,000 payoff, they signed away their right to ever utter a public syllable about the case, Bruce, or his related enterprises "*until the end of time*," as the legal documents were rumored to say.

With the rush of 1987's album, 1988's tour, and the supercharged early days of his romance with Patti behind him, Bruce once again found himself adrift. Once again, the day-to-day pleasures of ordinary life didn't register in his consciousness. And yet again, the same bony fingers tugged him back into the netherworld. "I'd made a lot of plans, but when we got home, I just kind of spun off for a while," Bruce told Henke. An attempt to settle into the Rumson house dissolved in the spectral presence of Julianne and other figments of the recent past. Bruce and Patti tried an apartment in New York, but the close quarters made the small-town boy feel cramped: not enough room to move, no car at his doorstep, and way too much traffic to navigate even if he did keep a car in the city. "I just got lost. That lasted for about a year," he said. "Somewhere between realization and actualization, I slipped between the cracks. I was in a lot of fear. And I was just holding out. I made life generally unpleasant. So at some point, Patti and I just said, 'Hell, let's go out to LA.'"

Settling into a new house near the top of the Hollywood Hills, Bruce girded himself for another shot at domestic life. "I knew it was going to be challenging for me because I had so much personal license," he says. "I didn't even know the language of a partnership. I didn't know basic behaviors, of, like, if you're out and gone, it's nice to call. I hadn't called anyone for twenty years. So a million little things were hard to adjust to. I'm sure it's like that for a lot of people. But I pursued it, so I suppose I was ready, as ready as you can be. I had pursued it since my early thirties, really." One thing that made it easier, he continues, was that Patti had also spent her entire adult life in the rock 'n' roll world. "She was an outsider also; the domestic thing was unusual for her too. So maybe that's why it worked. It was a little strange for the two of us, and we thought, 'How are we going to invent this for the two of us?'"

Eventually Bruce felt the southland breeze softening his impenetrable core. Perched above the city of illusion and reinvention, the bonds of the past no longer seemed quite so constricting.

"People always came west to re-find themselves or to re-create themselves in some fashion," he told David Hepworth. "Mostly in some distorted way, but the raw material is here." But when it became apparent to Bruce—and, perhaps more importantly, to Patti—that his psychic scars were not going to be burned off by the Southern California sun, he rededicated himself to psychotherapy. "I knew I'd had to spend eight hours a day with a guitar to learn how to play it," he told Jim Henke. "And now I had to put in that kind of time just to find my place again." Moving beyond the symptoms of his discomfort, Bruce dove in as deep as he could go. "I crashed into myself and saw a lot of myself as I really was. I questioned all my motivations. Why am I writing what I'm writing? Why am I saying what I'm saying? Am I bullshitting? Am I just trying to be the most popular guy in town? I questioned everything I'd ever done, and it was good."

Progress came slowly, but it came. Back in New Jersey for the summer of 1989, Bruce made the rounds of clubs, sitting in with whatever friends, acquaintances, or just-made friends happened to be onstage. The summer hijinks came to a climax on September 23, when Bruce celebrated his fortieth birthday at his friend Tim McLoone's Rum Runner bar just up the coast in Sea Bright. With a house full of friends and the entire E Street Band—including Steve Van Zandt—around him on the bandstand, Bruce faced his latest landmark birthday with far more aplomb than he had ten years earlier. He led the band through a long list of favorite oldies and rock 'n' roll oddities, and then led into a wild run at "Glory Days" by shaking his fist at the passing years. "I dedicate this song to, to, to *me!* I may be forty years old, but goddamn it, I'm still handsome!" Bruce hit the opening chords, Van Zandt and Lofgren followed, with Bittan and Federici joining in behind them, and they were all in lockstep, with Bruce leading the way back to the glories of the past and the natural yearning to re-create moments that can never be relived. "Oh, they'll pass you by," they all sang together. "In the wink of a young girl's eye . . . glory days."

TWENTY-TWO

GET THE HOSTILITY OUT NOW,
I CAN TAKE IT

ON OCTOBER 18, 1989, BRUCE sat down with his address book and a task he'd both feared and fantasized about for most of the decade: breaking up the E Street Band. "I think we got into a rut in our relationships, that had something to do with it also," he says. "Relationships got a little muddy, through codependence, or whatever. Probably that aggravated everyone a little bit. I needed to take a break, do some other things, probably play with some other musicians, which I hadn't done in a long time.

"So I called the guys up and talked to them as best I could. I never looked at it as the band being done or kaput or finished. But it was a call that said, 'I'm gonna do something else, and you're not gonna be a part of it for a while.' And that was very difficult for the guys and me." The suspicions that Max Weinberg and the others felt at that last show on the two-year, world-conquering Born in the U.S.A. tour turned out to be exactly right.

"I just didn't know where to take the band next," Bruce reflects. "It seemed like we'd reached an apex of what we were trying to do and say."

Some found it easier to accept than others. Tallent, for one, noticed that absence of finality in what Bruce had to say. "He never said he was breaking up the band," the bassist says. "He was like, 'Just so you know, for the next little while I'll be doing some other things, and you're free to do other things.' It was a courtesy call to let you know you were free to go down any pathways you found appealing. So it seemed like a very nice, gracious call." Lofgren, who had started his sideman career working with the always unpredictable Neil Young, didn't blink. "You gotta understand that this guy had spent his whole life playing with the same seven people," he says. "No matter how good they are, you want to play with other people, try some different things."

Weinberg had seen it coming. "You would have had to be completely blind not to notice there were major changes coming here," he says. But the news was still "unrelentingly depressing," if only because just a few weeks earlier Bruce had mentioned, in his usual offhand way, that he'd been writing new songs and expected to call the band together to start recording in January 1990. But then Weinberg opened *Rolling Stone* and learned that Bruce had already returned to the studio to record a rollicking "Viva Las Vegas" for an Elvis Presley tribute album with a studio full of high-end LA session players. On the phone, Bruce urged him not to take it personally. "It's just something I feel I've got to do artistically." Sensing the shock in the drummer's voice, Bruce did what he could to put him more at ease. "I know it's going to hurt," he said. "But someday you'll realize it was the right thing."

Clarence Clemons got the call in Japan, where he, along with Lofgren, was touring with Ringo Starr's first All Starr Band. As Clemons remembered, Bruce sounded so casual, he assumed he was being called back to E Street. "I picked up the phone and heard him say, 'Hey, Big Man!' I said, 'Hey, Boss!' And he said, 'Well, it's all over.' I said, 'Oh, uh, okay,' because I thought he meant the Ringo tour was over, and I had to come back home to go into the studio or start another tour." The sax player said he'd get home and check in as soon as possible, but then Bruce set him straight. "He said, 'Naw, naw, naw. I'm breaking up the band.'"

Bruce recalls talking to Clemons for a while. "I had the kid gloves on delivering what I knew would be very bad news." But Clemons was outside of himself by then, juggling his surprise and grief with a sudden urge to reduce his hotel room to ruins. So many years on the road, so much sacrifice, the thousands of hours spent waiting for Bruce to hear just the right sound from the recording studio speakers. "And I'm thinking, 'It's all for this? My whole life dedicated to this band, this situation, this man, and what he believes in, then I'm out of town and I get a fucking phone call?'" Fortunately, he was in the company of Ringo Starr, who had experienced his own traumatic breakup when the Beatles imploded in 1970. And it wasn't long before Clemons simply accepted the change for what it was:

"Something in the back of my psyche said, 'This is okay. He'll come back. Because anything so great cannot be destroyed altogether. Anything the goddess created can't be thrown away. It'll come back.'"

Just before Thanksgiving 1989, Bruce and Patti learned that she was carrying their first child. A son, Evan James, was born on the evening of July 24. Watching from the side, a surge of feeling burst against a part of himself Bruce had kept locked down since he was old enough to know how to protect himself. "I got close to a feeling of a real, pure, unconditional love with all the walls down," he told David Hepworth. "All of a sudden, what was happening was so immense that it just stomped all the fear away for a little while, and I remember feeling overwhelmed. But I also understood why you're so frightened. When that world of love comes rushing in, a world of fear comes in with it." It was a moment Bruce had imagined, described, and sang about for years. "My music over the last five years has dealt with those almost primitive issues. It's about somebody walking through that world of fear so that he can live in the world of love."

Bruce and Patti made their bond official at a backyard wedding the next spring, and their daughter, Jessica Rae, was born on December 30, 1991. "I had to change old attitudes and leave a lot of fears behind," Bruce told USA Today's Edna Gundersen in 1995. But he called having a family "the birth of my second life."

Not that he could shake off every lingering shadow. Living in Los

Angeles, Bruce and Patti were about an hourlong commuter plane ride from the house he'd bought his parents in Belmont, a pleasant suburb about ten minutes down Highway 101 from San Mateo. Bruce always reveled in his mother's company, but the prospect of seeing his father still set him on edge. "Doug was tough for him even when he was grown up," says Shelley Lazar, a tour staff veteran who became a close friend to both Bruce and Patti. "He'd be a little more tense than when he was at home. I'm not sure if it was intimidation as much as the respect he had for his father." In the early phases of a battle with emphysema, Doug's breathing became labored and his health lagged. "Bruce knew [Doug] was his dad, and that he wasn't feeling well."

The anger between father and son had largely faded, due both to the passage of time and other less expected developments. A stroke Doug suffered in 1979 had somehow rewired the part of his personality that made it all but impossible for him to share his emotions. "Now he couldn't hide anything," Pam Springsteen says. "You could mention any of his kids' names to him, and he'd burst into tears. You could see what meant the most to him. He was just a very real person. No pretense, no persona. And everyone loved him."

Doug's new openhearted countenance had a magnetic effect on the people who encountered him. "He was lovable," Pam says. "He drew people to him, especially women. Put him on a plane, and within seconds the stewardess was standing over him. And he'd be doing *nothing*. He was just warm and kind, and had a warmth in his voice." As Bruce once recounted to the writer Nick Dawidoff, he was settling in for a visit with his family backstage after a show in the late 1980s when his father held up his hand. He wanted his son to sit in his lap. Taken aback, Bruce stammered. *"Really?"* Doug nodded. So Bruce lowered himself, and all the years of hurt, anger, and misunderstanding, into his father's lap. It couldn't have been comfortable for either of them—physically, emotionally, and in every other conceivable way. But the awkwardness told its own story about an aging father and his grown son still struggling to express the love that had haunted them both for so long. Some scars never heal, and the strangeness of the scene hung thick in the room. But they still sat like that for quite some time.

The love between Springsteen men might come in unexpected ways, but to them, that only made it more meaningful. When Bruce held his own son in his lap a few years later, Patti noticed that her husband hadn't read a word of the picture book he held. Instead he'd hold up the book so he and Evan could both see it, and then, after a minute or two of silence, turn the page so they could look at the next picture.

Patti, puzzled, said. "You're not *reading* it to him!" Bruce shrugged. "This," he explained, "is how Springsteen men read." The toddler, meanwhile, twinkled happily. "Evan was loving it," Lazar says. "There was something nonverbal going on with them, and it was so touching."

About a month after making the fateful band telephone calls, Bruce dialed up Roy Bittan, the E Street Band keyboardist, and invited him out to dinner. Bittan had moved to Los Angeles a few months earlier, and they didn't live very far from each other, so it was easy to grab the keys and head out for a casual evening. The wheels in Bruce's internal songwriting machinery had been locked for a month or two, and he was on the prowl for some kind of inspiration. When they got back to Bittan's house, the topic turned to home recording and the multisynthesizer recording rig the pianist had set up in his garage. Bruce absolutely had to take a look and check out some of the tracks his old colleague had been recording. "I took him into my garage studio, fired it all up, and played him my demo of 'Roll of the Dice,'" Bittan recalls. "It seemed shocking to him."

At first Bruce marveled at the breadth of the sounds available on Bittan's synthesizer setup. Virtually everything he heard—the guitar sounds, the drums, the percussion, and more—had been simulated so well that you had to strain to believe that you *weren't* hearing the natural instruments. And as Bittan explains, he'd written "Roll of the Dice" with Bruce's style in mind. "It was an E Street Band track. It had the riff and everything. The glockenspiel, the tambo, the whole bit." Eager to hear more, Bruce listened to two or three of Bittan's other backing tracks. The pianist hadn't composed the melodies or lyrics, but the body of the songs were there, along with the central riffs and structure. Bruce liked what he heard. "Make me a cassette," he said. He took it home with him that same night.

At nine thirty the next morning, Bittan's phone rang. When he picked up, a familiar voice barked one word: *"Hit!"* Bittan recognized Bruce but had no idea what he was talking about. "I wrote a hit last night," Bruce proclaimed. Bittan laughed. "Well, that's nice," he said. Bruce explained that he'd spent the night writing to the instrumental tracks Bittan had handed him twelve hours earlier, and that the keyboardist should come over right that minute to take a listen. Bittan sped to Bruce's house. When he got there, his host played the cassette he'd taken home the previous evening, singing his just-composed lyrics and melodies over the top. "And I was like, 'Oh my God,'" Bittan says.

Bruce felt the same way. Bittan's songs had jump-started his own writing, and the keyboardist's skill at digital recording (yet another quantum leap in home recording) gave him a new sense of technical possibility. With a growing list of tunes to capture and more appearing every day, Bruce asked Bittan if he'd like to coproduce his next record. Bittan was up for that. "I'd gotten the breakup call too and was as devastated as anyone," he says. Given a shot at jumping back in without missing a beat, he wasn't going to say no. When news of the new creative union filtered back to the other ex–E Streeters, their responses were what you might call muted. "I didn't speak to the guys about it," Bittan says. "Max called me occasionally—we had a special relationship since we joined the band together. But I could tell in his voice that he was feeling emotions from my working with [Bruce]. Frankly, I had survivor's guilt. It's like the plane goes down, everybody dies except for the one guy who survives. I had to ask myself, 'Why me?'"

The question in Bruce's mind was closer to "What's next?" He summoned Landau from New York, ushered him into the studio, and played him two new tracks—"Roll of the Dice" and "Trouble in Paradise"—singing his lyrics over the recorded music. "He was incredibly excited about both of these songs, and I happened to love both of them," Landau says. "That got us both moving." As determined as he'd been to trade E Street for the unexplored horizons, Bruce wasn't entirely certain that he wanted to disassociate himself entirely from the people he had come to depend on. So the production team of Springsteen, Landau, and Plotkin stayed put, now with Bittan elevated to coproducer status. Anticipating the risk of familiar tropes, Bruce established a rule: Bittan had to leave the piano alone and stick to synthesizers and other electronic keyboards.

A series of home demos, made two-man-band-style with engineer Toby Scott and Bittan, got things rolling. A few weeks later they moved to Ocean Way Studios, then they ended up at Soundworks West, better known in its previous incarnation as Motown's Los Angeles studio. No longer bound to the E Street Band's skills and textures, Bruce followed his own musical history back to the soul belters who had first defined his sense of musical passion and performance. His writer's block cleared away, Bruce returned to cranking out more songs than he could possibly use. Most didn't survive the editing process, but of the ones that did stick, more than a few bore the mark of psychotherapy, while others had the determinedly upbeat, structured language of self-help books. "If I can find the guts to give you all my love / Then I'll be feelin' like a real man," Bruce declared in the evolved man's swagger of "Real Man." The tune's companion piece, "Man's Job," repeats the same clog-stepping sentiment: "Gettin' up the nerve is a man's man's job / Lovin' you's a man's job." Other songs took on more visceral themes—the sultry lust in "Cross My Heart" and "All or Nothin' at All"—but the conceptual thrust of the songs sounded curiously like post-therapy directives.

Feeling again that he'd hit a crucial, make-or-break moment in his career, Bruce slowed the recording to a crawl. The sessions dragged for months, a year, and then kept on going. Determined to stretch into the future while remaining true to the essential spirit that had always animated his music, Bruce and company blended the grit in his voice and guitar with the synth-and-drum-loop backdrop that had come to define nineties hip-hop and soul music. Hoping to add a little more human chemistry into the playing, Bruce, Bittan, and the others called in an all-star lineup of LA studio players: Sting's drummer Omar Hakim, Little Feat keyboardist Bill Payne, ex-Faces and longtime Rolling Stones keyboardist Ian McLagan, bassist and future *American Idol* star Randy Jackson, and, in an intriguing move, long-ago E Streeter David Sancious on keyboards. Ultimately, the LA studio whiz-turned-cofounder of the popular 1980s pop-rock band Toto, Jeff Porcaro, and Jackson became core band members, along with Bruce and Bittan. The small parade of guest vocalists was even more prominent, including Sam and Dave's Sam Moore, Righteous Brother Bobby Hatfield, and every songwriter's idol, Smokey Robinson. And yet the unifying spirit of the project remained elusive. "The atmosphere was occasionally a little glum, then lots of times it was very exciting," Landau says. "I think it was a very challenging spot for Bruce to be in. He was trying to make a rock album in this new world without E Street. I think he was taking a lot of time doing the work he was doing and thinking about the work to come." Coproducer Bittan puts it more succinctly: "He didn't have a real good vision of where he wanted to go. And the production really suffered as a result."

Taking a break to join Jackson Browne and Bonnie Raitt in a two-night benefit for the public interest law firm the Christic Institute at Los Angeles's Shrine Auditorium in mid-November 1990, Bruce broke a two-year live drought with sets that recast songs from throughout his career into the more intimate terms of a solo performance. Opening his first show with a plea for silence ("It's been a while since I did this, so if you feel moved to clap along, please don't"), he strapped on an acoustic guitar for a taut "Brilliant Disguise" that segued quickly into "Darkness on the Edge of Town" sped up to the point of twitchiness. "Tenth Avenue Freeze-Out" and "Thunder Road" played like memories from a long-lost youth, setting the stage for a surprise visit back to "Wild Billy's Circus Story," unheard onstage since the mid-seventies. Bruce also hearkened back to the old days with his song introductions, many of which were more personal and revealing than any he'd ever told in the spotlight. Along with affectionate stories about his costars and Patti, he told one or two of his Flannery O'Connor–like stories from his Freehold childhood, spoke openly about his therapy sessions, and told a sweet tale of watching Patti give birth to their baby son, Evan. "We go to the hospital, and I'm, you know, thinking, 'Okay, I don't wanna faint, that's my main concern.'" He paused, as if to reconsider how self-involved that sounded. "That's disgusting, right?"

He also premiered five new songs, including the comic blues plaint about modern media, "57 Channels (And Nothin' On)" and a rockabilly-style love song/letter to *Penthouse* magazine "Red Headed Woman," which vividly described the songwriter's enthusiasm for performing cunnilingus on his wife. The Bittan collaborations "Soul Driver" and "Real World," the former played on guitar and the latter on piano, sounded like vintage Bruce, their basic rock chord changes a solid platform for gut-deep vocals describing love as a standoff between better angels and the "snakes, frogs, and love in vain" lurking in the forest. Performed by a lone musician armed with only a guitar and an evolving sense of his own psyche, they came girded with heart and bone, the sound of a man only just starting to believe that he could trust himself to be the man he wanted to be.

Back in the studio in the winter of 1991, Bruce blew past the deadlines for the spring release they had imagined, not looking up until the middle of the summer, when he, Bittan, and coproducers Chuck Plotkin and Landau put their heads together to winnow the stacks of finished songs into something closer to an album-length collection. Bob Clearmountain came in to perform his rites of mixology, and after Bruce had tentatively named the project *Human Touch*—for a love-from-the-ashes duet sung with Patti—they declared a halt to the production process.

"All the assistants in the studio were going, 'You're done! Finally!' because it seemed like years since we'd started," Scott says. "And I said, 'We ain't done. We just stopped, but we still aren't done.'" A week later the engineer's telephone rang, and Bruce was on the other end. "He said, 'Hey, Tobe, don't we have a bunch of recording equipment around somewhere? Can we get it set up in the house next door?'" (Bruce had recently bought a small house next to his family's home, planning to use it as a combination guest house and temporary/portable recording studio.) Setting out to write a new single for the much-fussed-over studio album, he ended up writing an entirely new set of songs instead. "He was loose and happy," Plotkin says. "Having *Human Touch* out of the way eased up the constipation factor. And then—*Bam!*—he had a whole new album in a matter of days."

None of it sounded like it belonged in the uptown company of the songs Bruce had labored on for the last two-plus years. These tunes were raw and urgent, hand hammered structures built on three and four-chord footings, again addressing the harrowing journey through his own poisoned depths to the "little piece of the Lord's undying light" he'd seen at the birth of his child. Throughout, the lyrics tumbled out in a rush, sometimes overwhelmed by the wildness of their creation. "I took a piss in fortune's sweet kiss," Bruce shouts in "Better Days," while "Leap of Faith"'s meaty chorus pins its testimony to a vague urging to "get things goin'" by showing some guts. But what doesn't show up on the page—the fire in Bruce's voice, the rich gospel chorale behind him, and the joy in the melody—trumps everything else, just as it does in (eventual title track) "Lucky Town"'s windblown call to action; the rueful portrait-of-the-artist-as-recovering-celebrity "Local Hero"; and the everyday moral corruption traced in the murky folk-blues "The Big Muddy," which is built on open-ended, unresolved chords that underscore the shifting moral sands in the lyrics.

All of it rough, spontaneous, and ready to be recorded in the knock-about way the music had erupted from his muse. Once Scott finished setting up the new Thrill Hill studio in the Springsteens' guest house, he and Bruce worked in their usual two-man way, programming a drum track upon which Bruce stacked the guitars, keyboards, bass, vocals, and effects. Finished with the basic tracks in about two weeks, they took a short break and then relocated to A&M Studios in Hollywood. There drummer Gary Mallaber (the Steve Miller Band, and more) replaced the computerized drums, and a small group of other guests—keyboardist Ian McLagan, bassist Randy Jackson, Roy Bittan, and vocalists Patti, Lisa Lowell, and Soozie Tyrell—added their talents where needed. Clearmountain created a basic mix, and the album was done. "I think the entire process took four weeks," Scott says.

How could Bruce pivot from the yearslong pitched battle required for *Human Touch* to writing, recording, and finishing a whole other album in a single month? Easily, he told David Hepworth. "All that work on *Human Touch*," he explained, "was me trying to get to the place where I could make *Lucky Town* in three weeks."

Heading into 1992, more than four years since *Tunnel of Love*'s release and two years since the end of the E Street Band, Bruce had two new but very different albums waiting to be released. Ordinarily, Bruce would take measure of each set of songs, hold the individual tracks up to one another, consider how closely they reflected his feelings and the message he wanted to present, and send one set out into the world while locking the other into his increasingly crowded vault. When he played the nearly finished albums for Steve Van Zandt, his ex-bandmate and oldest friend first advised Bruce to trash all the *Human Touch* recordings and redo them with the E Street Band. "And he might have been right!" Bruce says. "But it just wasn't something I was in a mood to do at the time. In fact, it was exactly what I was in a mood to *not* do. But then I played him *Lucky Town*, and he said, 'Oh yeah, that's more like it.'" But Van Zandt still couldn't abide the chilliness he heard in the production of *Human Touch*. Bruce: "It was outside his self-interest to say that, 'cause he wasn't *in* the band at the time. But once again, he said, 'Look, this'll be good with the band, this'll be good the way they play.' And he was probably on the money with that." Landau disagreed. "Just the sheer time that went into *Human Touch*," he says. "I just think there's too much great stuff and blood, sweat, and tears with *Human Touch*. It just felt disorienting to me. Bruce quickly came to the conclusion that the best thing to do was to put them both out."

The move came with more than a few intangibles. Bruce was now a forty-two-year-old husband and father as distant from the dance-oriented pop of Paula Abdul as he was from the pop rock of Bryan Adams and the hardcore rock of Guns n' Roses. Even the great Seattle grunge bands— Nirvana, Alice in Chains, and so on—seemed to come from another, far more jaundiced, world. Meanwhile, Bruce had distanced himself from the diehard fans who would never quite forgive him for abandoning his homeland and the faithful band that had helped him fight his way from the Asbury Park boardwalk to the uppermost reaches of fame, wealth, and power. But no matter how many times the cultural wheels had spun since 1987, Bruce and Landau cast away their usual caution and told Columbia Records'[1] newish president Don Ienner that they wanted to release both albums. What's more, they wanted both of the records to be released on the same day. And not as a double album or with any discernible link. Simply two free-standing albums.

[1] By then part of Japan's media behemoth Sony.

The strategy had immediate precedent: Only months earlier, Guns n' Roses had issued two albums, *Use Your Illusion I* and *Use Your Illusion II* on the same day, and spurred eye-opening sales for both. In this spirit, Landau told Ienner, the finely honed *Human Touch* and rough-hewn *Lucky Town* would emerge together in the spring of 1992. While Ienner could identify the relative commercial positions the bands occupied (G n' R still approaching its commercial peak, while Bruce had purposefully stepped back from his mideighties height), his mind was less on potential sales than the significance of Bruce's work and respecting one of his leading artists' vision. "It would have been tough, and not right, to try to combine them into one," Ienner says. "They were so different from one another. And scrapping one, yet again in Bruce's life, was obviously not the answer, either. So the sense was, Guns n' Roses had just done it, so let's give it a shot."

Released on March 31, 1992, *Human Touch* and *Lucky Town* presented Bruce as two distinct visions of himself. On *Human Touch* he shimmered in gauzy light, the mature rocker as a Hollywood pirate, draped in silver jewelry, silky shirts, and, in less formal shots, a funkily perfect fedora. Meanwhile, the guy on *Lucky Town* boasted a half-week beard and a shirt blown apart by the velocity of the fat motorcycle parked in the dirt just yonder. So while both albums addressed the same up-and-down-and-up-again stretch of life, they reflected very different perspectives on the journey.

Led off by the title track and lead single, *Human Touch* came across like the studied work of a songwriter as fluent in swampy rock 'n' roll as he is in old-school soul and the beat-and-bass funk of urban spoken word. But the heart of the piece, the struggle to achieve an emotionally evolved adult life, is more talked about than experienced. The rocking "Gloria's Eyes" loses its punch in the production haze, while the lyrics step neatly around the hearts of the characters in the song. The same set of problems presents itself repeatedly on the album, although the better tunes still summon a charge. The ambitious boy's cautionary tale, "With Every Wish," floats gracefully over hand percussion and Mark Isham's muted trumpet riffs; "Cross My Heart" throws sparks into the sultry night; and "Roll of the Dice," for all its self-consciously Bruce-like swagger, still stirs the blood. And yet, both of the Christic show stand-outs, "Soul Driver" and "Real World," get steamrolled beneath a hurtling pace and perfectly aligned layers of drums and computerized percussion. Digital perfection, but not even a touch of the gospel, let alone rock 'n' roll.

Lucky Town, on the other hand, tears toward the listener on a plume of dirt and pebbles, its carburetor snarling like a can of wasps. From the leather-lunged declaration of independence in "Better Days" to the roar of life in "Living Proof" to the glimpses of hell in "Souls of the Departed," the music bristles with nerve endings, sparks of joy, geysers of contempt, whispers of love, and bald admissions of fear. Absent virtually all of the professional entertainer's mediating skills, the songs grab for the listener's lapels and refuse to unlock their grip: Listen to this *now*. But was the eruption of feeling too unfiltered, too rich in the murk of life, death, and misery, for listeners to absorb?

Although primed by weeks of speculation about the albums and how they would, or wouldn't, launch Bruce into his post–E Street, post–New Jersey, post-forty era, the dual albums made the lightest of waves. Critical reaction was generally upbeat, but many came pocked with mitigating points and complaints. Writing in *Rolling Stone,* Anthony DeCurtis noted the many similarities between Bruce's traditional sound and his supposedly relaunched LA-based sensibility. Worse, "Real Man" had a "slick, annoying repetitive keyboard riff" that put the critic in mind of Phil Collins. But while *Entertainment Weekly*'s David Browne took sour measure of the albums' "unfocused blur of clattering guitars and faceless rhythm sections," and dismissed most of the songs as "shockingly generic," *Time*'s Jay Cocks led by calling the records "wonderful," and concluded by saying "Springsteen's reborn and running again," more or less harmonizing with British rock magazine *Q*'s David Hepworth and the *Chicago Sun-Times*' Lloyd Sachs.

Commercially the albums started strongly, with *Human Touch* debuting at number 2 and *Lucky Town* just behind at number 3. But the spectacle of Bruce being batted about by the pop-metal Def Leppard (whose *Adrenalize* held the album chart's top spot the first week) and then by the kiddie rap act Kris Kross (who took the crown the next week)—along with both Bruce albums' relatively swift descent toward the floor of the Top 100—did not add up to the triumphant comeback Bruce, Landau, and Columbia hoped to achieve. "Sure, there were some disappointing sales," says Ienner. "But you did have two competing records out there. Some people were upset that the E Street Band wasn't there, and some people were upset that he'd left New Jersey. Music was changing dramatically at the time. But the thing is, if you added the sales of both albums together, you'd get exactly what you'd expect to sell on an album at that time." And, as Ienner points out, even with the other release as a direct competitor, both albums sold enough copies to each go platinum.

No matter, Bruce's campaign was to launch his new music, along with his post–E Street identity, as high into the firmament as possible. Obviously that meant hitting the road. And with the first leg of a multistage, perhaps multiyear, world tour set to start in Europe in June, he worked through the winter and spring, often in consort with Bittan, to pull together an eleven-piece band with the strength to play the old E Street songs and the versatility to find the pocket in all the soul, funk, gospel, folk, and rock 'n' roll he could throw in its direction. Just as, or perhaps even more important, the new musicians had to come at the music with the right feel: their own unique version of the tuned-in, turned-on, play-it-all-night spirit he discovered at the Upstage in Asbury Park nearly twenty-five years earlier.

Already certain that Bittan would serve as the band's sole keyboard player, requiring him to play both his and Danny Federici's parts at the same time, Bruce auditioned an array of drummers and bassists. He settled eventually on Zach Alford, a young New York drummer best known for his work with the B-52's on their smash 1989 Cosmic Thing tour, and bassist Tommy Sims, who at twenty-six had emerged as one of the most talented young pop musicians in the industry. He had an easier time finding a guitarist. Channel surfing sometime around the holidays, he'd come across a repeat of a 1986 Saturday Night Live episode that featured the alt-country band Lone Justice as the musical guest. The Maria McKee–fronted group included a British guitarist named Shane Fontayne, and his rough but melodic style rang in Bruce's ears. Fontayne had left McKee's band, but Lone Justice's manager, onetime *Darkness* engineer Jimmy Iovine, called Fontayne to relay Bruce's message.

"He said a friend of his wanted to know if I might want to go on the road with him," Fontayne says. "I said, 'Who's your friend?' And he said, 'Springsteen.'" Fontayne flew out to Los Angeles a few days later and reported to Bittan's Hollywood studio to audition. The guitarist found all the equipment he'd requested set up in a tight circle on the studio floor. Bruce came in with Bittan at his side, and with Alford on drums and another player on bass,[2] Bruce counted off a blues groove, and they started to play. During a break a couple of hours later, Bruce looked over at Bittan. "A lot of twang out there," he said, gesturing to Fontayne. The guitarist piped up, "Too much?" Bruce and Bittan answered in unison: "Nope."

They played the next night with another bassist, and then Fontayne went home to the East Coast. Fontayne was called back in late April for another go-round, this time with Sims on bass and Alford still on drums, after which Bruce came out of a control room conference with Landau and Bittan and waved for the players to gather round. "This is it, boys," he said, gesturing around the circle. "Welcome to the big show!"

"Bruce had an extreme consideration for everyone else," Alford says. "He treated everyone with respect and was way more down to earth than I expected anyone that famous to be."

With the band's five-piece core in place, Bruce fleshed out the R&B-gospel sound with a chorus of a half dozen singers, including Bobby King, a fixture in folk/blues revivalist Ry Cooder's band. The others were Cleopatra Kennedy, Gia Ciambotti, Carol Dennis, Angel Rogers, and Crystal Taliefero, a young singer-guitarist who would soon add saxophone to her arsenal. Patti, who took most of the tour off to tend to Evan and Jessie, guested on "Human Touch" and other songs when she could get out.

Rehearsals started on a soundstage at Hollywood Center Studios in late April, rolling through the first week of May. The operation shifted

[2] No offense to that guy, but the years have sapped a lot of memories.

to the Bottom Line in New York, where they gave a private show for two hundred Columbia/Sony executives and then headed uptown to the NBC studios in Rockefeller Center for Bruce's first-ever appearance on *Saturday Night Live.* Back at the Hollywood soundstage two weeks later, they worked through the first week of June to prepare for an open rehearsal to be held for a small invited audience and, more significantly, a live radio broadcast beamed across the country. Along with the usual questions and quandaries facing the start of every previous tour, now Bruce had to find a way to balance this new stage in his career with the twenty years of work that had propelled him to this point. Needing perspective, Bruce called Steve Van Zandt and asked him to come out to Los Angeles and lend his ear and wisdom.

After overseeing a single remix of "57 Channels"—adding new layers of percussion, music, voices, and looped sounds that gave the song a harder political edge[3]—Van Zandt played alongside the band for a few days. For a time, some members assumed that Bruce's old buddy was joining the group. "It looked like Bruce was thinking about bringing him out on the road with us," Fontayne says. "He was wondering, 'Should I? Shouldn't I?'"

Van Zandt doesn't remember it quite like that. "It was just kinda helping them understand the songs," he says. Still, Van Zandt does remember Bruce asking what he was up to for the next year or so. Bruce recalls the same thing, after a fashion. "Yeah, ya know, I might have played with the idea of bringing him along," he says. "Like, he was in the E Street Band, and now he can be in *this* band! But for some reason, it just didn't happen." Van Zandt left, but not before urging his friend to play more of the older songs his audience obviously wanted to hear. As ever, Van Zandt's words mattered: the first notes heard at the start of the widely broadcast open rehearsal were the opening bars of "Born in the U.S.A."[4]

---

[3] Particularly relevant after the April 29 rehearsal had been stopped by the rioting that tore through Los Angeles in the wake of the not-guilty verdicts handed down to the LA police officers who had been videotaped kicking and beating an unarmed African-American motorist named Rodney King.

[4] Note to wiseguys: yes, the actual show began with "Better Days." But we're talking about the *broadcast*.

Launching the world tour with a monthlong swing through Europe gave Bruce some breathing room, given how many of his most fervent fans could now be found outside the United States. Indeed, the European shows were well attended and riotously received, particularly when they played one of the six or so *Born in the U.S.A.* songs he got into the habit of tossing in to juice things up between the newer songs. The American leg kicked off with a record-breaking eleven-night stand at the Brendan Byrne Arena (also know as Meadowlands Arena) in the Meadowlands complex in East Rutherford, New Jersey. A chorus of boos greeted Bruce's reference to living in Los Angeles. "Get the hostility out now, I can take it," he responded, spurring a new wave of boos and cheers. "C'mon, you can do better than that!" As the mix turned more to cheers, he grinned. "Okay. Where was I?"

Triumphant homecoming aside, the five-month American tour didn't develop the momentum that Bruce and the E Streeters had taken for granted since the River tour in 1980. "Booking it was no problem," says Barry Bell, the Premier Talent agent who had booked literally every show Bruce had put on since 1977. "Selling it was something else." Now the tide ran in reverse. Cities that once required multiple shows to satisfy demand got by with one-nighters, not all of which sold out. "Most of the shows sold fine," Bell says. "But it was fast in some places and slower in markets where he was weaker." Hearing one of Bell's ticket sales reports that fall, Bruce shook his head. "Wow, it's just like 1978 all over again!"

He had it exactly right. Only this time the general audience's disinterest seemed less disturbing than the disapproval coming from so close to, and sometimes within, Bruce's inner circle. For Columbia president Ienner—who had danced to "Thunder Road" with his wife at their wedding—the new band's look got under his skin, particularly the guitarist with his pointy shoes, skin-tight pants, and thick mane of dark curls. "Shane just didn't look like he belonged on stage with Bruce," Ienner says. "He was a great player but looked a little strange up there, with his Beatle boots and hair. Steve [Van Zandt] was odd too. But that was *family* strange. I certainly got used to it after a few shows. But if you're used to seeing something, it's tough to get past it." Some members of Bruce's road crew felt like interlopers had swarmed their stage. They referred to the group as the Other Band, and when they could find a chink in a particular musician's performances, they made sure everyone else knew about it too.

If Bruce knew about any of that, he never let it get back to his musicians. He liked what he heard, for one thing. And if he felt things weren't working out—if technical bugs had dulled the band's punch, or the crowd simply wasn't connecting—he'd grit his teeth and dig deeper. "Nothing stood in his way," Alford says. "He just gave more and more of himself until the crowd were on their feet at the end. I never saw another artist do that. I'm not sure any other artist *could* do that. In the end he always gets them where he wants them to be: in a state of bliss."

Heading back for another run through Europe in the spring of 1993, the new machine had the smooth power of every seasoned band. Fontayne's slinky guitar solos contrasted nicely with Bruce's two-fisted attack, while Tommy Sims's bass had a pop that clicked together with Zach Alford's light-footed drumming. The back line of singers gilded everything they touched, while singer-multi-instrumentalist Crystal Taliefero became such an engaging onstage foil for Bruce it almost, if not quite, wasn't a shock to see her at center stage at the end of the set, blowing the saxophone solo in "Born to Run." But as the various E Street Band members came to visit their old boss's new stage, they spurred eruptions of cheers that revealed the distinction between an ordinary concert and the rock 'n' roll communions that Bruce and the E Streeters once held. Clarence Clemons kept his distance until the tour's penultimate stop, a benefit for hunger relief at the Brendan Byrne Arena. When he finally did show up in the midst of "Tenth Avenue Freeze-Out," striding out of the shadows just as Bruce got to the part about the Big Man joining the band, the ovation nearly blew Fontayne out of his boots. "I've never heard a reaction that intense before," he says.

Bruce certainly had. He'd been at the center of it for most of his adult life. And while the band members left their year on the road with assurances that they'd almost certainly be heading to Japan for another leg of the tour, with more to come after that, Fontayne hoped for the best while resolving to be satisfied with what he'd already experienced. "Everything that happened was top drawer. You didn't have to negotiate a contract, and no one had a chance to get unhappy because everything they did was so organized, and so sympathetic, and so perfectly done. You learned quickly that this was the organization you were working for, and there was nothing to worry about."

TWENTY-THREE

HOLY SHIT, I'M BACK

TAKING UP JONATHAN DEMME'S REQUEST for a song to go with his film about an AIDS-stricken gay man confronted with institutionalized prejudice, Bruce need only think back to his childhood. Everything he needed to know already resided in his memory. The kids who giggled at his clothes. The distance between the schoolyard games and his solitary place against the fence. He knew that contempt, and its ashen taste never left his tongue. "That's all anybody's asking for: basically some acceptance and to not be left alone," he said to the gay community magazine the *Advocate* in 1996. The words and the music had always been in the back of his mind. And he had other, more immediate feelings to draw from too. A gay friend falling to a cancerous sarcoma. The daughter of close friends, an effervescent woman just moving into adulthood, losing her hair, her health, and then her life in a fight against another deadly strain of cancer.

So came "Streets of Philadelphia," and with Toby Scott in his new studio next door to the Rumson house, Bruce experimented with a hard-rock arrangement. Then he slowed it down into a slower rock rhythm. Shifting back toward the contemporary feel Bruce tried to achieve during the *Human Touch* sessions, the piece evolved into a spare urban ballad. Built on a gently funky drum loop, with synthesizer and organ chords and a background chorus of "lah-lah-lah-lahs," the mournful lyric is as simply stated as the few notes that comprise the melody. If the chords rise for the song's bridge, neither they, nor the song's narrator, are headed anywhere heavenly: "Ain't no angel gonna greet me," he sings blankly. "It's just you and I, my friend."

Released the day before Christmas 1993, Demme's film *Philadelphia*, which starred Tom Hanks as an AIDS-infected lawyer who sues his firm after being fired for suffering from such a stigmatized illness, became a critical and commercial smash—and, in the eyes of gay activists, a crucial step in the campaign to combat prejudice. Although the voting members of the Motion Picture Academy of Arts and Sciences bypassed the film in its Best Picture and Best Director categories, *Philadelphia* earned nominations for five Academy Awards, including two separate nods for Best Original Song: both "Streets of Philadelphia" and Neil Young's contribution to the film, the equally moving "Philadelphia." The film eventually won Hanks his first Best Actor trophy. And when they opened the Original Song envelope, the winner was . . . Bruce Springsteen. The lifelong movie buff accepted his trophy with a brief speech, thanked the movie people for "inviting me to your party," and then carted it home to his parents. When he placed the Oscar on the kitchen table in front of Doug Springsteen, his father wept with pride. Then he repeated the phrase he'd first said when his son called to say he'd signed a contract with Columbia Records: "I'm never going to tell anybody what to do ever again."

Columbia president Don Ienner, on the other hand, got paid for telling people what to do. Or, in the case of Jon Landau and Bruce Springsteen, convincing them to cooperate when his instincts told him he had a product that could live up to the company's full-court promotion treatment. So when the airplay for "Streets of Philadelphia" spiked after the Academy Awards, he met with Landau to talk about releasing Bruce's

Oscar-winning song as a single. Ten years earlier, the answer would have been obvious. By the mid-nineties, however, the structure of the pop music industry had fractured into subcategories that rarely overlapped with one another. "[The song] didn't fit anything on the radio at the time," Ienner says. "That video of Bruce walking down the street[1] wasn't exactly like anything on MTV then." When Landau worried about the single falling through the cracks ("This record can't come and go to number ninety-nine on the charts!"), Ienner admitted that he had no guarantees. "But wouldn't it be a horrible shame if we didn't try?" he countered. "If we just made it *not* get to where it needed to get because we're scared it won't chart?" That argument made an impact on Landau.

The manager gave his go-ahead, and though the category-defying song waded against the currents of radio formats, beats-per-minute restrictions, and the offbeat look of its video, Ienner and his sales force kept working. "It was up, it was down, it was going to be a hit, it wasn't going to be a hit," he says. "It was just *wild*." Their work paid off: upon its February 1994 release, "Streets of Philadelphia" blew up into a worldwide smash, crowning the charts in eight countries, peaking at number 9 on *Billboard*'s Hot 100 singles list, and selling more than a half million copies in the United States alone.

With "Streets of Philadelphia" on the charts, Bruce returned to his studio in Los Angeles.[2] Armed with a stack of premade drum loop CDs, he passed most of the year working on a new collection of synthesizer-based songs. Working with occasional help from Zach Alford, Shane Fontayne, and especially Tommy Sims (who coproduced a few of the songs), Bruce's burst of experimental work went much further than what he had done earlier in the decade. Much of what emerged, Toby Scott remembers, shared an undulating, trancelike sound unified by what he describes

---

[1] On the tumbledown streets of south Philadelphia, singing live (amid the ambient sounds of the city, barking dogs and all) to the camera-and-microphone rig driving alongside him.

[2] Actually the temporary home studio Toby Scott put together in a rented home in Bel Air, made necessary when the powerful January 17, 1994, Northridge earthquake did enough structural damage to the Springsteen home to send the family to the guest house Bruce had been using for the Thrill Hill West studios.

as "a pulsating underbeat." Most of the twenty or twenty-five songs they finished have never been heard or even named in public. The two exceptions, an early version of "Secret Garden" found on an extended CD single released in late 1995, and "Missing," which became a part of the soundtrack to the 1995 Sean Penn–directed movie *The Crossing Guard*, allow for a fragment of insight: the insistent percussion, drifting veils of synthesizer, a *chukka-chukka* rhythm guitar filtered through a wah-wah effect, and, as the song builds to a close, a metallic guitar solo spidering up through the layers.

The 1994 sessions ran into the week before Christmas, when Bruce, Patti, and the kids went back to New Jersey to spend the holidays with their families. Scott went back to his place in Whitefish, Montana, where he was still musing on the snow-heavy mountains on January 5 when a ringing telephone produced Landau's voice. "Tobe!" he crowed. "Y'know all that stuff we were working on? Well, we're done. We're moving on to something else." That's when Scott started taking notes. "Look, I've got the E Street Band coming to New York on Monday. The guys are all ready, so I need you to find a studio, get us in there, and get back here to record."

When Landau rang off, Scott looked at the calendar on his desk. It was Thursday. He had until Monday. Four days. He got out his book of New York recording studios and started dialing.

The plan started with Bruce's suspicion that the synth-driven album he'd spent most of 1994 creating could push his core audience beyond the brink of its connection to him. "I felt like I needed to reconnect around the basics, around our history," he says in retrospect. Putting out a greatest-hits album—an ace that he and Landau had kept up their sleeves since the *Born in the U.S.A.* era—was an obvious plan. But the prospect of reuniting the E Street Band to record some new material[3] only took shape as the project launched. "Really, the band for me at that time was a way of restabilizing," Bruce explains. "Of letting people know that I

[3] The industry standard for greatest-hits packages in the 1990s, largely to inspire serious fans who already owned the original albums to buy the compilation too.

honored their feelings, and these things that mattered a great deal to them also mattered to me. It was just a way of staying in touch."

Which felt particularly important to a veteran artist who couldn't abide the prospect of being dismissed as a figure from yesteryear. "You're having a conversation with your audience," he says. "If you lose the thread of that conversation, you lose your audience. And when people say so-and-so don't make any good records anymore, or people talk about favorite bands from whom they haven't bought any records of in the past fifteen years, I always feel that the reason is they lost the thread of that conversation and the desire to make that conversation keep growing." With the success of "Streets of Philadelphia" shoring up his currency, the external timing seemed as good as it would ever be. So more than six years after the E Street Band's last scheduled gig, and eleven years since they last entered a studio as a unit, Bruce sat down to write a song or two for the band to record.

When Clemons got the call at his house in San Francisco, he flew back to New York so quickly he didn't have time to cancel the birthday party his friends had planned for one of the city's largest, flashiest nightclubs. "I'm sure there are some people *still* walking around San Francisco looking for that party," he said to me in 2011. More than fifteen years later, his face still lit up at the thought. "I was so ready to go."

But while the other band members felt just as excited to play with Bruce, their enthusiasm came with equal amounts of confusion, hurt, and resentment. All had struggled to build their own careers in the post–E Street era. Some found it easier than others at first, but a half dozen years later, they had all adjusted to the new reality. Clemons recorded and played with his own band; Max Weinberg was leading the band on NBC's *Late Night with Conan O'Brien*; Roy Bittan produced artists and played sessions in Los Angeles, while Garry Tallent did the same in Nashville. Danny Federici pursued a career in jazz, and Nils Lofgren went back to his own career, playing with Ringo Starr on two of his world tours and writing music for TV series. The fact that this invitation had come with such clearly stated limits—don't expect it to stretch into a full-length new album or a tour or anything like that, they were told—didn't help.

"The wound was still open," Bittan says. "And so here you are: you get a call to come in. And like always, it's abrupt. *'Come tomorrow.'* Or maybe we had some notice. But the question was, well, what for? What are we doing? And as usual, our thing is that we don't ask, we just do. And are happy to do it." Only now the prospect of coming back together came with something like post-traumatic stress disorder. Even Weinberg, by then a fixture on network television, still reeled from the band's dismissal. "I've never gotten over the breakup," he says.[4] Still, he could sympathize with the emotional complexities Bruce faced. "I think it was a very distasteful thing for Bruce to have to do. And sometimes when you have to do things that are hard like that, it gets the better of you. So [the reunion] wasn't a pleasant occurrence, just the whole way it was done."

Watching from the control room, coproducer Chuck Plotkin knew exactly where, and how large, the unacknowledged elephant in the room stood. "They're trying to figure out what happened here," he says. "*'Did we get bad all of the sudden?'* Everyone's trying to figure out what Bruce is thinking. But the E Street Band is not the most socially comfortable group of people on the face of the earth. And I learned a tremendous amount from Bruce about the power of *not* talking."

Bruce's attempt to write a song that captured the essence of the E Street Band's history had none of the lion-hearted fraternity he'd written into "No Surrender" a decade earlier. Instead "Blood Brothers" describes onetime Kings of the Mountain reduced by time and experience into ordinary stiffs, so consumed by daily tasks that long-ago proclamations of faith and friendship ring as hollow as "a fool's joke." Speaking directly about the series of telephone calls he'd just made to his erstwhile band and friends, Bruce sounds doubtful, at best, about what lay ahead. Why had he decided to reunite the band? Why did it even matter? Not exactly a stirring call to arms. What it was, he says, was honest. "It captured the feelings of the moment. I still had ambivalent feelings about the band at that time."

---

[4] He says this in the fall of 2011, more than a dozen years after Bruce reconvened the band for good (albeit in his off-and-on-when-it-feels-right-to-me way) and months before the start of the long touring cycle Bruce had all but guaranteed would begin in 2012.

Still, to observers, and to the cameras of Ernie Fritz, the filmmaker Jon Landau Management had hired to shoot the first day of recording for publicity and historical purposes,[5] it looked like it could have been a scene from the *River* sessions. With Landau, Plotkin, and Scott at their usual stations in the control room and Bruce at the center of the studio floor describing a new song to the E Street Band,[6] all of whom sat scribbling chord changes, riffs, and feels, it could have been a return to the source of modern American rock 'n' roll.

So then they took up their instruments, waited for Bruce to count to four and then tiptoed into "Blood Brothers"'s first verse, led by acoustic guitar and piano. They picked it up a notch when the organ and brushed drums came in to greet the light guitar stings Lofgren added, and then leaned hard into the final verse to hurl the song across the finish line. And maybe it was all a little *too* hard. When the next takes still didn't work, Bruce came back with a completely different version of the song, rewritten into an electric, minor-key rocker with a shouted backwoods melody and lyrics that spent more time on hard, dirty roads than in the blood oaths of young rock 'n' rollers. When that didn't work, they moved on. As ever, Bruce had more than a few new songs to try out.

Next came the semi-apocalyptic love song "Waiting on the End of the World" and the spookily erotic "Secret Garden." Then came a heart-wringing soul crooner called "Back in Your Arms," a nearly note-for-note cover of the Los Angeles folk-punk band the Havalinas' "High Hopes"; a weak-kneed party song called "Without You"; and a fresh go at the wonderful 1982 outtake "This Hard Land." As filmmaker Ernie Fritz recorded it all for posterity, he noticed how carefully all these long-bonded friends addressed one another. "If these guys were pissed, they weren't showing it," he says. "Everyone was on their best behavior. It was more like, 'Hey! It's nice to see ya!' Period. They were all walking on eggshells but happy to be doing so."

Eventually Bruce came up with an arrangement of "Blood Brothers" that suited both him and Landau; a return to the original structure,

[5] Landau soon decided to keep Fritz and his crew around through the end of the sessions.
[6] Minus Scialfa, who wasn't scheduled to turn up until the vocal sessions later.

only hushed to the point where, except for Clemon's gentle sax licks, the band's contributions barely peek from behind Bruce's own guitar, harmonica, and whispery voice. With the recording sessions completed by mid-January, the gang returned to their lives until February 21, when they reconvened in New York to shoot a live video (for the cameras of *Philadelphia* director Jonathan Demme) for the hits package's lead single, "Murder Incorporated."[7] Set up on the cozy stage at the Tramps nightclub in New York, the band crowded together to run through a half dozen live takes for the cameras and then rewarded the crowd's patience by playing a rough but spirited miniset of thirteen E Street favorites, including "Darkness on the Edge of Town," "Prove It All Night," "Thunder Road," and "Badlands," all worked out in the space of a short break between Demme's video shoots.

Although the *Greatest Hits* album came out at the end of February 1995, the not-quite-reunited band went on hiatus for the month of March. Bruce celebrated the start of the break by winning three Grammy Awards (Best Rock Song, Best Male Rock Vocal Performance, and Song of the Year) for "Streets of Philadelphia." Then he returned to New York to reunite with the E Streeters to prepare for a long day of work on the fifth, which began with a group performance of "Murder Incorporated" on David Letterman's *Late Show*, followed by a move to the Sony Music Studios soundstage, where they prepared to tape the E Street Band's first rehearsed concert since the end of the Amnesty International tour in October 1988. It would also be the last engagement planned for the minireunion, and with no hints that anything else might come in the future backstage nerves ran more raw than usual. No one mentioned it, of course. Not until Bruce and the band started their walk from the dressing rooms to the stage and the already cheering mob on the other side.

Somewhere in midstroll, Bruce noticed the pattern on Federici's shirt and concluded that he didn't like it. So like any bandleader would do, he turned to his keyboardist and asked him to run back and grab

---

[7] Another also-ran from the 1982 *Born in the U.S.A.* sessions, finally released as Bruce's tribute to the nameless fan who had attended dozens of shows during the eighties holding up the same "Murder, Inc." sign.

a new one. Federici's face went abruptly red. "No!" he barked. "I love this shirt! I'm *wearing* this shirt! So what are you gonna do: *fire* me?" Bruce stiffened and snarled right back, which was when everyone else, including Nils Lofgren, figured the time had come to be somewhere else, anywhere else, and right away. "Look, there was justifiable tension," Lofgren says. "But no one had a gun, no one's throwing fists. It was a philosophical argument." Which, as they all knew, had nearly nothing to do with Federici's shirt. "It *was* a silly shirt," Tallent says. "We all knew the parameters of what to wear. So I think he changed, but everyone was on edge."

The *Greatest Hits* album, a single disc collection featuring fourteen songs that were either hit singles (such as "Hungry Heart" and "Dancing in the Dark") or nonhits that had taken on the career-defining weight of a hit ("Thunder Road," "The River"), plus one outtake ("Murder Incorporated"), a rerecorded outtake ("This Hard Land"), and the two new E Street songs ("Blood Brothers" and "Secret Garden"), received only middling reviews.[8] Yet it topped album charts in a dozen countries, selling more than ten million copies. Invited to play a significant role in the opening festivities of the Cleveland-based Rock and Roll Hall of Fame in September, Bruce gathered the band (with Steve Van Zandt on board) to perform a few of their own songs while also serving as the backup band to Chuck Berry and Jerry Lee Lewis. They gathered at Cleveland's Municipal Stadium, where the problems began when Lewis heard that the show would open with Bruce and the band playing with Berry, whom "the Killer" considered a bitter rival. "So Jerry Lee Lewis was in a very bad mood," Landau says. "He had taken offense to something and was very tense." For whatever reasons, the sour energy took root in the E Street Band. "That was one of the only bad shows I've ever done with anybody, let alone the E Street Band," Van Zandt says. "Nobody was into it, and it was just so weird. I didn't get the feeling Bruce wanted to be there, and

---

[8] Which seems odd, considering the amount of adoration so many of the same writers had larded upon the work in its original release. But the critics had their reasons. Some complained that the absence of pre–"Born to Run" songs distorted the collection's use as a historical overview, while it didn't quite work as a greatest hits either, given that some of Bruce's biggest *Born in the U.S.A.*–era hits had been rejected too.

it was all uncomfortable. Everyone felt like 'What am I doing here?' And even now I'm not sure why. Too soon, I guess."

Back home in Los Angeles, Bruce pulled out his motorcycle and headed off for one of his regular trips into the desert. "It takes about thirty minutes to get to the foothills of the San Gabriels. Once you're there, you go up the hills, and the views are incredible," he says. "If you have a couple of days, you can go over them and down the eastern side of the foothills and ride all those roads down through there, which are still relatively empty. I got to know people just in different little rest stops and restaurants, and would occasionally go to visit."

When longtime pal and motorcycle buddy Matty Delia came to visit with his brother Tony, they all mounted up and took off together. "We were at some old motel, some four-corner desert town on the California border, just sitting around and met some guy. We ended up talking about his brother, who died in a motorcycle accident." That tragedy, like so many of the similar stories Bruce heard or intuited, was far from random. At night came the dusty armadas of migrant workers on the hunt for jobs, and not so far in the distance, the nickel-and-dime drug runners. An entire sub-rosa economy whirring away on the wrong end of the law, powered largely by people compelled to do whatever it took to get by. "The stories were just floating around, just in the air," recalls Bruce. "Clashing cultures and people trying to fit in, accommodating and conforming to these norms."

In Los Angeles the culture of desperation became all too visible. In the jerry-rigged camps beneath the bridges and in the faces of Hispanic families lined up for day labor. As if nothing had changed since John Steinbeck walked among the Dust Bowl migrants in the 1930s. Something about the Mexican immigrants pursuing their lives in the face of racial, cultural, and economic discrimination touched Bruce the deepest. "He talked about stuff he'd read and people he'd met," says producer Chuck Plotkin. Once again, the stories of outsiders resonated with those awful memories of childhood isolation. "The main thing he said was, 'They're all me. It's all me.'"

The first tendrils of the new work emerged in January, when Bruce sat down to write some songs for the E Street Band to record for the *Greatest Hits* project. Combining his own experiences with stories gleaned from the pages of the *Los Angeles Times* and from a book about the history of the American underclass, Bruce located "The Ghost of Tom Joad," a portrait of modern poverty that transformed Steinbeck's *The Grapes of Wrath* character into a guiding spirit for all displaced and ill-treated people. The ex-con turned laboring family man in "Straight Time" lives on eggshells, only just resisting the pull of easy money. The narrator of "Highway 29" falls to temptation until his existence shatters, while the drifter in "The New Timer" grieves the murder of a friend until his own blood grows poisonous.

As with the songs that became *Nebraska*, a sense of gloom infuses everything. But given the thirteen years of home, family, and professional psychiatry, the darkness couldn't keep hope entirely at bay. With a small acoustic band (Gary Mallaber on drums, Marty Rifkin on pedal steel guitar, Federici manning the keyboards, and Tallent on bass) adding color, and an implicit sense of community, the glimmers of humanity never quite fade away. Murderous hands are stilled; love defies the least humane strictures of the law; even a battered dream of the promised land carries on. "For what are we / Without hope in our hearts."

If Bruce wasn't ready to lead his own band through a new rock 'n' roll album and tour in 1995, he did find a way to air out his noisier impulses thanks to Joe Grushecky and his Pittsburgh-based band, the Iron City Houserockers. Friendly since Grushecky's band had worked with ex-Columbia exec Steve Popovich and Steve Van Zandt in the late seventies and early 1980s, the two singer-songwriter-guitarist-bandleaders stayed in touch even after the Houserockers broke up in the mideighties and Grushecky worked his day job as a special education teacher in Pittsburgh. Grushecky spent the next decade raising his family, but he continued writing songs and playing the club circuit. The two musicians' paths would cross occasionally, and when they did, Bruce always made sure to check in. Grushecky's songs—with their East Coast bar band sound, girded with tough-minded observations on the day-to-day life of working people—shared a lot of Bruce's own impulses, and he enjoyed the other writer's sensibility. Still, Grushecky's career continued to ebb in the nineties, and by the early weeks of 1995, the now solo artist (playing several nights a week in an unpopular Mexican restaurant) figured he'd reached the end of his rope. Tempted to pack it in entirely, Grushecky instead followed his wife's advice and reached out to his famous friend from New Jersey. Bruce returned the call a day or two later and invited Grushecky to come to Los Angeles and bang around some songs. "I borrowed some money from my dad to get out there," Grushecky says.

After hearing a dozen of Grushecky's new compositions, Bruce told him to try again. "He said, 'Well, you can do a lot better,'" Grushecky recalls. But when Bruce heard a rough draft of "Homestead," a song about the Pennsylvania mine that employed almost every man in Grushecky's hometown, Bruce's eyes lit up. He helped finish the lyrics, cowrote another song (the Native American story "Dark and Bloody Ground"), and then told Grushecky that he wanted to help make the album in his own New Jersey studio, starting as soon as possible. "That record became *American Babylon*, which he graciously produced for us," Grushecky says. In fact, Bruce got so caught up in the project that he volunteered to join the revived Houserockers as a lead guitarist and backup singer for the six-stop tour Grushecky had booked to launch the album for its October release. "That's pretty wild when you think about it," Grushecky says. "He's playing bars with these guys from Pittsburgh."

Released on November 21, 1995, *The Ghost of Tom Joad* presented a tonic for critics unsettled by *Human Touch*. The album earned Bruce a renewed chorus of good reviews, many informed by their authors' own expertise in cultural, literary, and political history. Which was entirely appropriate, since, as the bibliography in the album's liner notes made clear, the songs on *Joad* came with specific sources and references ranging from Depression-era literature, movies, and news stories published in the *Los Angeles Times*. "At a time of increasing income disparity—when the right distracts with immigrant-bashing—Springsteen, rock and roll's populist, offers an eloquent reminder of what economically dispossessed angry white men and desperate brown border crossers share," David Corn wrote in the political journal the *Nation*. "Where else in popular mega-culture are the nightmares of the American and immigrant poor recognized and granted sympathy?" Indeed, *The Ghost of Tom Joad* contains some of Bruce's most gripping lyrics: slashing portrayals of economic injustice in "The Ghost of Tom Joad" and "Youngstown"; miniaturized portraits of racism in "Galveston Bay" and "The Line"; and the small but symbolic lives and deaths traced in "Sinaloa Cowboys," "The New Timer," and "Balboa Park."

Perhaps it isn't surprising that *The Ghost of Tom Joad* also stands as the least musical album Bruce had ever made. Even *Nebraska*, set entirely to Bruce's guitar, harmonica, and percussion, built its desolate vision on songs with distinctive rhythms, chord changes, and melodies. On *Joad*, even the five (of twelve) tunes featuring the other musicians hardly register as musical constructions. The players brush their instruments lightly. Bruce half whispers most of the songs, accentuating their intimacy but at the same time raising a barrier for listeners. If you wanted to grasp these stories, you had to find a quiet place, shut the door, and *focus*. Preferably with the lyrics within reach. Certainly, Bruce can't help but uncork a few memorable melodies when he's got his guitar in hand. But the *Joad* songs that bear his musical touch[9] wield it as subtly as possible. In the context of the album, the approach makes sense. Drawn to a kind of postgrad version of Woody Guthrie's folk journalism/commentary, Bruce focused his muse on socially charged storytelling. Anything that stood between the character's voice and the listener's ear was obviously in the way. And even if the album's sales suffered as a result,[10] the risks made sense to an artist whose whims had mined so much gold in the past two decades.

With more than two and a half years gone since the last show of the

[9] Particularly the title track and "Youngstown," both of which became showstoppers in subsequent full-band arrangements.

[10] *Joad* peaked at number 11 on the Top 200, his first album to miss the Top 5 since *The Wild, the Innocent and the E Street Shuffle* in 1973.

'92–'93 Human Touch–Lucky Town tour, Bruce geared up for another world tour, this time as a solo act. Just himself, a few guitars, harmonicas, possibly a piano, and maybe a nice rug on the floor. As new experiences went, this one wasn't entirely unprecedented. The pair of solo sets he'd performed at the Christic Institute benefits in 1990 set a model for how he could present his work, including the stadium-shaking anthems, in arrangements that drew power from the empty space once inhabited by the roar of a rock 'n' roll band.

And as with the album that launched it, the Joad tour came with an entirely new set of aesthetics and expectations. Booked into theaters seating two thousand to five thousand—tiny halls compared to the arenas and stadiums he had played for most of the previous twenty years—Bruce stepped onto the stage in loose-fitting trousers and earth-toned work shirts, his goatee and long, tightly swept-back hair describing the profile of a passionate, if stern, academic. Unconcerned with showmanship, he came out each night bearing orders for the audience to respect his, and the music's, need for peace and quiet. No singing along, in other words. No clapping along, either. If anyone felt moved by what they heard, they should keep their appreciation to themselves until the song's final notes had rung. Which sounds a lot more off-putting than it actually was, since Bruce's appeals tended to be funny and self-deprecating, begging the audience to not make him wreck his good-guy image as he'd been forced to do in Los Angeles when a chatty crowd required him to speak harshly to supermodels, confiscate cell phones, and so on.

The unsmiling image Bruce presented for *Joad* could never quite eclipse the joy he felt performing to the fans he saw gazing up at him every night. No matter the seriousness of his new material—and the older songs that told different versions of the same stories ("Darkness on the Edge of Town," "Born in the U.S.A.," among others)—he also found room for the likes of "No Surrender," "This Hard Land," and even rarities such as "Does This Bus Stop at 82nd Street?" and "Blinded by the Light." As the tour went on, Bruce also made a point of lightening the mood with one or two of his new, darkly comic tunes, such as the sleazy pickup ballad "It's the Little Things That Count" and the infomercial satire "Sell It and They Will Come."

The Tom Joad solo tour ran from late 1995 into the spring of 1997, stretching through two American and European legs and jaunts through Japan and Australia. Bruce collected a Grammy in the Best Contemporary Folk Album category along the way, but no other show was quite as emotionally charged as the evening he spent playing in the gymnasium at the St. Rose of Lima elementary school in Freehold. He had few pleasant memories of the place—mostly from the CYO dances the Castiles played on Friday nights in 1965. Even so, he'd been singing about the school, one way or another, for his entire adult life. Now the institution was celebrating its seventy-fifth anniversary with an increasingly Hispanic population, and when its administration asked him to play a show to benefit the school's scholarship fund, Bruce couldn't refuse.

Set for November 8, 1996, the show created a bigger buzz in Freehold than President Bill Clinton's visit had done two months earlier. Anticipating a rush of out-of-towners, the organizers set strict guidelines for ticket sales, requiring every attendee to present some form of identification or other proof of Freehold residency to pass the school's door. When the night arrived, the crowd jammed inside the auditorium greeted Bruce just like they used to when they saw him walking down the street to the park. Even the *"Brooooce!"* calls sounded familiar enough to ignite a boyish smile. And the feeling was mutual. So many of Bruce's old friends and neighbors had long ago come to see him in the bars, or made the trek to catch the big shows up at the Meadowlands Arena or Giants Stadium and marvel at the hero he'd become. But here in the old neighborhood, he went right back to being one of them: an overgrown kid who managed to get out for the night.

After opening with "The River," Bruce paused to absorb his unlikely setting. "I wouldn't have believed it myself if I wasn't standing here now," he said with a chuckle. "Right under the cross, too." Everyone laughed, and he described a friend's reaction to hearing that he'd be playing his old Catholic school. "He said, 'Oh! Revenge, eh?' But I said no, no, no." He paused for a beat. "Well, maybe just a *little*."

Bruce wasn't kidding, as St. Rose's Father Gerald McCarron would soon learn. But Bruce also had serious—and often quite moving—memories and observations to share, including a tender dedication of "The Ghost of Tom Joad" to a nun, Sister Charles Marie, whom he remembered teaching him about empathy and kindness. He spoke at length about the Vinyards, remembering Tex (who had died in 1988) and the crucial help he and Marion gave to the Castiles, and dedicating "This Hard Land" to her. He also talked lovingly to Adele, capping it with a rare airing of what he liked to call his "mother lover's song," "The Wish."

And yet the warm memories took him only so far. For no journey back to the cradle of his youth would be complete without a glimpse back into the cauldron of "Adam Raised a Cain" or the gleeful rebellion fueling "Growin' Up." Back in the seat of his Catholic education, hoisted up onto a stage with a large wooden cross over his head, Bruce couldn't resist pushing the church's boundaries of acceptability until he could hear them splinter. He made a brief gesture while introducing "Highway 29," noting that the sort of insight reflected in its final verse "usually comes after you fuck up pretty badly." He'd glanced apologetically at St. Rose's head priest just then, but he wasn't all that sorry, as Father McCarron, and some un-suspecting congregants learned when Bruce got around to his tribute to Patti, "Red Headed Woman."

"I'm gonna move on now, to a great song about a great subject," he announced. "*Cunny-lingus.*" He let that hang in the air for a beat. "I know, I know. You're sayin', 'Bruce, how can you stand up in your Catholic school and sing a song about *cunny-lingus?* But I talked to Father McCarron, and I said, 'Father, can I sing a song about cunny-lingus in your school?' He said [*speaking stonily*], 'I'm not sure.' So I took that for a yes."

"That's when the priest walked out, I'm pretty sure," says Freehold native Kevin Coyne. "I don't know if he stormed out or stalked out. But he definitely left. That's for sure."

If Bruce saw, he didn't care. "Because I'm talking about *marital sex* here. That's right, *marital* sex. And as we know, the doctrine on that is that the Pope says, 'I can't, but you go right ahead.' So anyway, as we speak, there's probably some folks practicing cunny-lingus right here in my hometown. Well, uh, I hope so. You *do* need practicing because it takes a while to get that, uh, down. Pun intended."

Lest anyone get the idea that he had come to ridicule the church, humiliate its leader, and leave his neighbors in the ashes, Bruce had written an original song for the evening; an alternately sharp and loving ballad for the town and people he could never bring himself to abandon completely. Titled "In Freehold," the song recalled his youth, from Randolph Street to St. Rose of Lima, from escorting Doug home from the pool hall to picking up his first guitar, his first kiss, the Vinyards, the tragedy of his father's life, and the small-mindedness that made Freehold "a bit of a redneck town" to outsiders and outcasts. "He nailed it with that one," says former musician-turned-mayor Mike Wilson. He also offered more recent memories: walking the streets with his kids, taking them on a fire engine ride (he didn't mention that he had single-handedly paid for the city's new rescue vehicle), and, he had to confess, being happy to be on the streets that raised him. "Well, I left and swore I'd never walk these streets again, Jack / Tonight all I can say is, 'Holy shit, I'm back.'"

It was true. After eight years of living in Los Angeles, Bruce and Patti had packed up their kids, including their youngest, Sam Ryan, born in 1994, and made a family home in Colts Neck, a quiet, partly rural town about ten minutes from the Monmouth County court building at the center of downtown Freehold.

TWENTY-FOUR

HOPE, DREAMS, AND REDEDICATION

BRUCE AND PATTI MOVED THEIR family back to New Jersey in 1996, setting up in a farmhouse on a pastoral spread of land just east of Freehold. Moving so close to his hometown had not been an accident, Bruce told me. "My oldest boy was going into first grade, and we just decided we didn't want to raise the kids in LA. Patti and I wanted the children to have more of a normal upbringing." In Colts Neck, he says, "We lived in a nice neighborhood, and [the kids] went to good schools, but outside of that they grew up around dry cleaners, hunters, people who did all sorts of things. So, really, the intent was to create as regular a life for the kids as possible, and we liked it. We have a family that is huge, and everybody really gets along. It's truly a miracle, you know."

Back on his home turf, Bruce took on the paradoxical roles of ordinary neighbor, dad, old friend, and local legend. Stranger still, his easygoing commitment to being the former only added more of an otherworldly glow to the latter. The more normal he behaved, the more extraordinary it seemed.

You didn't hear about it so much if you didn't live in central New Jersey. But from the Springsteen epicenters around Freehold and Asbury Park, the stories have the ring of folk legends. There he is on Main Street on Freehold's weekly Cruise Night, his son perched on his shoulders as they watch the vintage hot rods parade past. See that guy in the Range Rover with the car seats in back? That's Bruce Springsteen dropping his kids off at school. An hour later he's in sweats in the Gold's Gym at the mall, straining through his weight room regimen while his trainer barks encouragement. By midafternoon, he'd be back at school, arriving early enough to sit on the hill above the playground to watch the kids running and swinging through recess. "That's my boy down there," he boasted, pointing out his eldest to a friend. He'd never seemed more proud. Possibly because the boy wasn't lost on the outskirts of the games; he was right there in the middle, laughing and playing with everyone else.

Bruce also couldn't resist an invitation to take a seat at the center of a party. So when he pulled over on Route 97 to check out a Harley-Davidson with a For Sale sign on it, Bruce introduced himself to the owner when he came out, talked about the bike, spent a little while trading road trip stories, and when the guy mentioned that he and his buddies were grilling and drinking beers out back, Bruce came right back to have a few. He shook hands all around and ended up staying for two hours, working through a few Budweisers and a plate of ribs before he realized how late it had become. In the summers you'd find him stretched out on the sand at Manasquan Beach or standing on the Asbury Park boardwalk—just outside Madam Marie's little fortune-reading shack. He didn't wear disguises or come with a posse or even a single bodyguard. He simply lived the adult version of the life he always led on the streets and boardwalks.

Since the mid-1980s, Bruce's chief recording engineer, Toby Scott, had spent his out-of-the-studio periods listening to, cataloging, and converting to digital files the enormity of recorded music his boss had compiled over the years. Rehearsal tapes, live tapes, the teetering skyscrapers of studio outtakes, rejects, and early versions of subsequently rewritten tunes. A Herculean job, given the wildly prolific habits Bruce had lived by for so long. "We had at least three hundred fifty unused songs by the time we got to 1997," Scott says. And not all of them had been judged substandard. More than a few, in fact, had been dismissed in favor of songs whose main strengths derived from what they added to their albums' narratives rather than their own singular charms. "Listen to 'Roulette,' that's a great little piece," Jon Landau says of the early *River* outtake. "Bruce and I would hear that and look at each other in shock, both of us saying, 'It wasn't *my* idea to leave that off the album!' We had our reasons at the time, and every decision represented a choice."

With so many songs in the backlog, and so many of them at least as good as the tunes that had already found their way onto his albums, Bruce took a long listen to his musical history, hearing the sound of his own development: from the solitary folksinger following John Hammond's instructions in mid-1972 to the grandiose visions of *Born to Run* up through *Born in the U.S.A.* and beyond—right up through the early-nineties sessions, the cast-off 1994 album, and more. Bruce was particularly struck by the *The Wild, the Innocent & the E Street Shuffle* outtakes, from the songs' many cantilevered sections to the hell-bent way that Vini Lopez, Clarence Clemons, David Sancious, Garry Tallent, and Danny Federici played them. When an instrumental studio take of "Thundercrack" came up, his jaw dropped. "Oh geez, *listen* to that!" he said to Scott.

The original plan for the compilation album was to stick with the original rough mixes of the songs. But as Bruce's enthusiasm for the project grew in 1998, so did his ambitions for how the material should be presented. What began as a simple collection of old roughs became a full-on production effort, with three sets of engineers and mixers working in three separate studios. Scott worked in the semipermanent studio Bruce had set up in the eighteenth-century farmhouse that stood on the edge of his land, a mobile recording unit parked nearby; and they had Bob Clearmountain's Mix This! studios in Los Angeles, which could send and receive files via an ISDN telephone line. Bruce oversaw all of the operations, checking in every afternoon to hear the day's work and either approve it or tell them how he wanted the songs revised. And when he heard a tune's original take lacking a certain something—a horn section, a background vocal, or even a lead vocal—he took the tape into a recording studio and opened the tracks for improvements.

They did the most dramatic work on "Thundercrack," which had only a patchy lead vocal and no backing vocals from 1973. Intent on re-creating the track as it would have sounded in the old days, Bruce called Lopez and invited him over for dinner and then a reunion session with himself, Federici, and Clemons, where they all sang the parts they had performed onstage so many years earlier. "I just did my parts that I used to do. And he was amazed that I still knew all that shit," Lopez says. "But I don't forget that kind of stuff. So we did the vocals, and it was fun. I can still hit those high notes." Bruce summoned his 1973 voice to fill in the lead vocal, and when they were done, it sounded just about perfect. The only song they rerecorded completely turned out to be "The Promise," which Bruce decided to add very late in the album's progress.

Although they had a wide variety of recordings and arrangements of the song to choose from, nothing they had on hand seemed to do the trick. And when Bruce heard how convoluted a process they'd have to weather in order to prepare the original tapes to work with the modern technology, he shook his head and took a seat at the studio's piano. He played through the chords once or twice and then looked up at Scott. "Toby, turn the thing on." Two takes later he stood up. "Okay, that's good. Put it on the record."[1]

Named *Tracks*, to play off the recording studio term for individual songs while also referring to Bruce's liner-note description of it as "an alternate path to some of the destinations I traveled to on my records," the album turned into a sixty-six-song behemoth: a four-disc boxed set with a richly illustrated booklet of lyrics and song credits. Sort of, but not quite in chronological order, the discs divided Bruce's twenty-five-year recording career into four eras.

The first disc begins with "Mary Queen of Arkansas" and three other

[1] The song would turn up as a bonus track on the single-disc boildown of the box set *18 Tracks*.

solo performances from his studio audition for John Hammond; stops briefly at Max's Kansas City for a live acoustic number; and then skips ahead to a handful of studio takes of live favorites ("Santa Ana," "Seaside Bar Song," "Zero and Blind Terry," and "Thundercrack") recorded during the *The Wild, the Innocent & the E Street Shuffle* sessions in mid-1973. It ends with a pair of outtakes from *Born to Run* ("Linda Let Me Be the One" and "So Young and in Love"), and a scattering of leftovers from the *Darkness on the Edge of Town* sessions in 1977 and 1978.

The second disc starts with a long look at the *The River* sessions of 1979 and 1980[2] and then dips into the voluminous *Born in the U.S.A.* outtake collection. *U.S.A.* material makes up the rest of disc two and all but disc three's last four songs, which come from the *Tunnel of Love* era. The fourth disc essays his solo era in the 1990s, with one leftover ("Back in Your Arms") from the "Blood Brothers" sessions with the E Street Band.

Released in the fall of 1998, *Tracks* didn't become the hit that the live box set had been a dozen years earlier, although it did cast a spell on listeners and fans who recalled again how powerful Bruce's music sounded in the hands of the E Street Band. No surprise, perhaps, that his own full-body submersion into his lost works infused Bruce with a new appreciation for his old musical companions. "I remember it was Rosh Hashanah [in September 1998], and he asked me to come over," Max Weinberg says. "I was on my way to my mother's house, and he said he'd been working on the *Tracks* thing and had fallen in love with the E Street Band all over again." When Weinberg came over to listen, they compared memories of the songs until Bruce mused lightly about the future. "He sort of felt me out about touring. I told him I had a bit of a time-scheduling complication,[3] but I'd love to." The musing didn't end there.

Later in the fall Bruce called Roy Bittan to gauge his interest in a reunion tour. Bittan, while riding high on his coproduction of and playing on alt-country singer-songwriter Lucinda Williams's breakthrough album, *Car Wheels on a Gravel Road*, was more than interested. "It was a

---

[2] With one callback to the 1977 *Darkness* sessions and a preview of the 1982 *Born in the U.S.A.* sessions, for some thematic reason I can't figure out.

[3] Given his full-time job as Conan O'Brien's *Late Night* bandleader.

great band, headed by an amazing singer-songwriter-performer," the pia-nist says. "Dylan and Elvis, all in one. And how often do you see some-thing like that?" Bruce had other questions too. What did Bittan think of bringing Steve Van Zandt back into the fold?

Well, everyone knew Steve belonged in the band. And as Bittan knew, the doubt in Bruce's voice came from somewhere far deeper than his concern that Steve and Nils Lofgren would get in each other's way. "He always has ambivalence. He was maybe fearful about putting it back together and taking a step back instead of forward," Bittan says. "I think that he had a lot of concerns."

"I just wasn't sure, you know," Bruce says. "I was worried it would be a nostalgic exercise, and I wouldn't be comfortable with it." He was even less comfortable with the emotional currents that would surely run through every step of a full-scale reunion. According to Landau, "We'd had conver-sations about doing a band tour, and Bruce suggested booking ten shows, because he was unsure of the chemistry. I said that is something we *can't* do, because if we announce we're doing ten or fifteen shows, then our true fans become a factor, and what are we saying to them? What are we saying to the band members?" Bruce couldn't argue with that.

When he made his first call to Clarence Clemons, he made certain to appeal to the Big Man's sense of majesty. "He called and said, 'Big Man! I need you!'" Clemons told me in 2011. "I expected it. It had to happen. He took that other band out there, and it sucked compared to what I was used to. I thought I brought something to Bruce that he didn't have, or really didn't have 'til I came. I don't mean to blow my horn, but it was just how it was, the way it was supposed to be."

Still, Bruce's ongoing insecurities seemed to play out in the calls made to band members by one of the accountants in his financial man-ager's office, where such contracts were often negotiated. At least two of them—Garry Tallent and Danny Federici—hadn't heard directly from Bruce, so the first they heard of the proposed reunion came in the form of a telephone call from an accountant who seemed to be reading a script that began by emphasizing how gracious Bruce was being in including the E Street Band in his new tour. It ended with a lowball offer that, ac-cording to several members of the band, bumped them back to what they earned during The River tours in 1980 and 1981. The musicians' pay had increased significantly during the Born in the U.S.A. tours, and ebbed on the Tunnel of Love tours only in accordance with the smaller scale of the shows and the brevity of the itinerary. Tallent, for one, felt more than a little slighted. "After all that time, to get a call from the accountant telling us we should be *thankful* we were being allowed to do this? I was insulted," he says. "I said, 'Thanks, but no thanks.'" Tallent called Weinberg, who had already gotten the same call from Federici. What the hell was *this* supposed to mean? they both wanted to know. What are we supposed to *do* about it? Weinberg suggested keeping calm and seeing what happened next. "I agreed with them that it seemed incompatible with the status of the band, the abilities of the band, and the reunion factor," he says. "But on the other hand, that's what managers do. They have a constituency of one, their client, so they're out for the best deal for their client, if they can get away with it. And I don't blame anyone for trying."

Neither did Bruce, as Tallent discovered the next day. "Bruce called, and I guess he was driving in a convertible, I don't know. There was all this wind, and I could barely understand what he was saying, but he was definitely laughing, going 'Ha-ha-ha, that's right! Stick it to 'em! That's how it's supposed to work! Go for it!' Something like that. I didn't quite understand it, but I took it to mean, okay, he has no problems with me negotiating. So we did, and obviously it worked out." But even after the band convened for rehearsals in February 1999, Bruce's doubts remained.

"So now we've got the band rehearsing, so it was done. We were doing this, unless he really . . ." Landau doesn't finish the sentence, if only because the nightmare scenario he had imagined seemed to be taking shape when a rattled Bruce called after the first few days. The old connections weren't there, he fretted. Something important was missing—some spark or electric current or *something*—so maybe this was all a huge mistake, and . . .

"So," Landau continues, "I said to him, 'Look, I think it's going to work out; that you're going to make the connections. Because the way I look at it is that you'll be performing Bruce Springsteen songs with Bruce Springsteen's band to Bruce Springsteen's audience." His client still wasn't sure. Not until they decided to end one rehearsal by giving a handful of fans a sneak peek. "We let fifty people in that were hanging out in the front of the theater in Asbury, and then, boom, everything became electric suddenly," Bruce recalls. "And I never worried about it again."

Once Bruce's nerves settled, the company of his oldest and closest collaborators eased a trace of the grief that had been growing in him since 1997, when it became clear that Doug Springsteen would soon lose his yearslong struggles with emphysema and a weakened heart. (Doug had undergone a quadruple-bypass operation several years earlier.) "He was sick, we knew it was coming," Bruce says. "The medicine that was helping one part of him was hurting some other part of him. Eventually there's no window of tolerance, and you just run out of time." And while Bruce never quite felt as if he had breached the walls around his father's spirit, there was no escaping the warmth in the old man's eyes and in the grasp of his weathered hands. "One generation before that, he would have probably died like his parents did, in their sixties. But he lived to see all the grandkids. They knew him, and that's very important."

Doug's ailing heart ebbed to silence on April 26, 1998, and his grieving family moved quickly from there, transporting his body back home to Freehold, where he was laid out in Freeman Funeral Home for a late-night viewing for family and friends. At the funeral at St. Rose of Lima, only a small clutch of family and local friends filled the pews. When the eulogies began they heard glimpses of a warm-spirited son, husband, father, and cousin, and a quiet but friendly friend and classmate who never had a harsh word for anyone. This was the man who emerged whenever the fog lifted enough to grant him a precious few hours or days of clear vision. "Dougie, you're sleeping at last, the struggle and horrors past," his cousin Glenn Cashion said in his eulogy. "Wearing a captain's headdress and a smile, sleeping at last." Cashion concluded with one last thought: "He loved warmly, he was warmly loved."

"It rained for many, many days after my father died," Bruce says. "It truly rained for weeks. I didn't want to be inside, for some reason. I spent a lot of time outside. I sort of made my way through it, but that was difficult. A big loss."

•   •   •

The tour rehearsals dovetailed nicely with the mid-March festivities for the Rock and Roll Hall of Fame, into which Bruce would be inducted in his first qualifying year.[4] No surprise there—Bruce had not only helped launch the organization's Cleveland edifice in that star-packed (if star-crossed) stadium show in 1995 and been a regular at the annual ceremony's climactic jam sessions, but he'd also spent his entire career being the vision of mainstream rock 'n' roll's most satisfying character: the outsider/rebel with the ambition to bend the mainstream to his will, the vision to balance art and commercialism, and the common sense to do it from within the confines of a major record label, selling one hundred million albums and filling every significant concert venue, repeatedly, all over the world. As with Elvis Presley, Chuck Berry, the Beatles, the Rolling Stones, and Bob Dylan, Bruce's ascension was a foregone conclusion.

Inducted by U2 lead singer Bono—whose band rivaled Bruce's masterful balance of art, protest, and big-league commerce, and whose persona straddled grandiosity and humility—Bruce delivered a funny but heartfelt tribute to all the major totems in his life and work: his mother, of course, for buying him the Kent guitar they both knew she couldn't afford; his father for giving him so much to write about; Tex and Marion Vinyard for giving him and the other Castiles a place to play rock 'n' roll; Tinker West for helping him turn pro; and Mike Appel for launching him into the big leagues. Then came Landau, of course, and every member of the E Street Band, including David Sancious, Vini Lopez, and Ernest "Boom" Carter, the latter two of whom took up Bruce's invitation to attend the festivities as his guests. When the time came for Bruce to take up his guitar and perform the traditional miniset of greatest hits, the revived E Street Band came with two weeks of rehearsals at its back. When Bruce caught Lofgren's eye in midsong, their faces broke into silly grins. He was even more giddy clowning with Clemons during "Tenth Avenue Freeze-Out," and when Bruce found a moment to shout "C'mon, Steve!" at Van Zandt, his once-and-future consigliere took on a beatific shine: the look of a man who had finally reclaimed the musical job he was born to do.

[4] Exactly twenty-five years since the 1973 release of *Greetings from Asbury Park, N.J.*, since the '99 festivities marked the induction of the 1998 class.

Heading straight to Europe to launch the tour, Bruce and the band started out with a pair of riotous arena shows in Barcelona, Spain, on April 9 and 10, and then made straight for Munich en route to what would be a three-month journey through most of the major cities on the continent and in the British Isles. After more than a decade's absence, the Bruce and E Street lineup sparked joyous receptions everywhere they played. Particularly when they got to the night's climactic song, which Bruce introduced by promising that this reunion was not a onetime deal. "This is the rededication of our band, the rebirth of our band," he proclaimed at the end of each night. "We're here to serve you, so . . . we're gonna leave you tonight with a new song. This is called 'Land of Hope and Dreams.'"

An avalanche of drums resolving into a soul-shaking gospel stomp. A chiming, two-chord guitar riff and then an airy organ line, joined quickly by an entirely different piano melody and then an even sharper melodic riff from Van Zandt's mandolin. Then Bruce, his voice taut with conviction: "Grab your ticket and your suitcase / Thunder's rolling down this track / Well, you don't know where you're going now, but you know you won't be back . . ." Then a prime Clarence Clemons saxophone solo and a chorus that describes both the essence of faith and the heart of the place Bruce's songs had yearned for, questioned the existence of, and kept right on chasing. Written for the tour and adapted in part from Woody Guthrie's "This Train Is Bound for Glory" with a touch of "Mystery Train" and the DNA of too many gospel songs to count, "Hope and Dreams" takes up the theme of faith as a force as sure and mighty as a steam engine. Only, in direct contrast to Guthrie's vision, Bruce's train opens its doors to everyone in sight: saints, sinners, losers, winners, whores, and gamblers, the powerful and the forsaken, the good, the bad, and the truly egregious. All welcome where "Dreams will not be thwarted / [and] faith is rewarded."

To launch the American tour in mid-July, Bruce and the band started with an unprecedented fifteen-night stand in the Meadowlands basketball arena, then called Continental Airlines Arena. All 308,000 tickets had sold out within twenty-four hours, and the homeland fans flooded the arena like pilgrims returning to a Mecca that had been barred for more than a decade. From the moment the houselights snapped off each night, the emotional energy in the air made Bruce's comic proselytizing seem something less than ridiculous. Because even when he put his full Jimmy Swaggart into claiming that he'd come "to *resuscitate* you, *regenerate* you, *reconfiscate* you, *reindoctrinate* you, *resexualate* you, *rededicate* you, *reliberate* you with the power and the *promise* . . . with the *majesty*, the *mystery*, and the *ministry* of rock 'n' roll!" the twenty thousand faces turned up to see him let loose a roar from so deep in their chests it didn't seem anything like a joke.

The tour rumbled through sixteen cities in the next four months, playing multiple shows in most of them (including six nights in Philadelphia, five in Boston, and four in Los Angeles) until taking a break from the end of November until the end of February 2000. Then they launched another four-month run, climaxing in ten sold-out shows at New York's Madison Square Garden. And as Bruce swooned over how far the individual band members' musicianship had come in ten years, the years had also worked a treat in the musicians' abilities to withstand, and even enjoy, the quirks they each brought into the group. "The respect for one another and ability to appreciate the uniqueness of each player was better than it ever was," says Tallent. "I'd look around the stage and be in awe. Everyone had grown up, everyone was playing great, everyone was a complete professional."

As the tour completed its first year and kept rolling, Bruce began coming in to the afternoon sound check with new songs to work through. "American Skin," sometimes known as "41 Shots," turned up first at the preshow warmup at the Raleigh Arena in North Carolina, went through one rough runthrough, then vanished until April 29, when Bruce reintroduced it along with "Further On (Up the Road)," a raw-throated highway song he'd worked out that winter. "Another Thin Line" and "Code of Silence," written with Joe Grushecky, came next. Bruce held them back until they got to the tour's penultimate stop in Atlanta in early June. On the stand's second night, June 4, they opened the show with "Further On," shifted back to more familiar terrain for the next five songs, and then without introduction launched into the quiet but insistent keyboard opening to the song now called "American Skin (41 Shots)."

It started in darkness, with the frontline players—Clemons, Lofgren, Bruce, Van Zandt, and Patti—standing still with feet planted, staring out into the hall. When the descending chord sequence cycled back to its beginning, Clemons leaned forward. "Forty-one shots," he sang. Lofgren repeated the words, followed by Van Zandt and Patti. When Bruce stepped forward, they sang it together four times, leading into an opening verse that traced the outlines of a shooting. The bullets in the air, the victim bleeding on the floor, someone kneeling above the body, praying he'll survive. The lyrics in the chorus made clear which shooting Bruce had in mind.

Is it a gun? Is it a knife? / Is it a wallet? / This is your life . . .

Anyone familiar with contemporary New York controversies knew what was on Bruce's mind. In early February 1999 four New York Police Department officers, all dressed in plain clothes and searching for a rapist said to be wandering the Bronx, called out to a twenty-two-year-old African immigrant named Amadou Diallo as he stepped into the doorway of his apartment building. A recent immigrant still learning the nation's language, Diallo responded to the officers' shouts as he'd been trained to do in Guinea, by reaching into his pocket for his identification cards. One or more of the officers mistook the wallet for a gun, and all four opened fire with their automatic pistols. In a split second, they got off forty-one rounds. Nineteen of the bullets hit Diallo, wounding him mortally.

The outrage began immediately. Diallo, an observant Muslim, possessed neither a gun nor a criminal record. Meanwhile, the police officers who had killed him had colorful pasts. All members of the NYPD's aggressive Street Crimes Unit, three had already been involved in shootings while on duty,[5] and one of them was still being investigated for his role in a fatal shooting. In the wake of other police shootings, and pretty

[5] A particularly striking detail, the *New York Times* pointed out, given that 90-plus percent of all NYPD officers serve entire careers without unholstering their guns, let alone shooting at anyone.

much exactly at the point where many citizens had lost their enthusiasm for Mayor Rudy Giuliani's campaign to hose street crime, civil disobedience, and decadence in general into the East River, a broad consortium of neighborhood and political activists flew into action. Protests began in New York and then spread to Washington, DC, where the US Attorneys' Office launched a federal investigation of the Diallo shooting. At the same time, voices from the Giuliani administration and the police force (and the officers' union representatives) shot back vehemently.

Working against this backdrop, Bruce wrote "American Skin." The song's first verse describes the Diallo shooting from the perspective of a police officer praying for the innocent man's life and recalling the stab of panic that caused him to mistake the leather wallet for a deadly weapon. The next verse visits a mother reminding her young son how to walk the streets so the police won't mistake him for a threat: ". . . never, ever run away / And promise Mama you'll keep your hands in sight." If there's an indictment in the song, it's aimed at the racial, social, and political divisions that feed into the fear, confusion, and violence that overwhelms the forces of humanity and community. The most striking line in its chorus—"You can get killed just for living / In your American skin"—addresses society in all its racial, political, and class-based divisions. At which point the forty-one shots and the Diallo case recede into a metaphor for the social disconnection that spawns so much of the world's violence. No one is spared, including the song's author. "Got my boots caked in this mud," Bruce sings. "We're baptized in these waters / And in each other's blood."

Premiered with no advance notice and no immediate follow-through from Landau Management (such as a statement of purpose or a printed set of lyrics), word of Bruce's fiery new song moved onto the newswires ("New Springsteen Song Laments Bronx Shooting"), to the nascent Internet sites and chat boards, where off-the-cuff analyses, criticisms, and defenses of the song soon blew up into a mainstream media storm. Less than four days after the song's debut, Microsoft's online journal, *Slate*, published a blog entry by political writer Timothy Noah, proposing that Bruce had written the song intending to help Hillary Clinton defeat Rudy Giuliani in the 2000 US Senate race. That Giuliani had withdrawn from the race in mid-May struck Noah as a minor point, since he guessed (correctly, as it turns out) that Bruce had written the song months earlier. If Noah's speculation about Bruce's Hillarymania was a bit far-fetched,[6] he did grasp one important fact: with the exception of the Three Mile Island–inspired "Roulette" from 1979, "American Skin" was the first Springsteen song to refer to specific events still playing out in the headlines. In this, Bruce crossed a bridge he'd avoided in the twenty years since he began to explore the larger socioeconomic factors that control the fates of the working class and the poor. That he tended to pursue larger issues through character-driven stories made it easy to avoid specific controversies. "When you deal with politics and pop music, they're always going to be thrown together, and they're always going to be uncomfortable bedfellows," Bruce says. "Popular music is always going to be something people take home, don't read the instructions, and just use. That's the way it is; that's okay." He shrugs. "Maybe you *should* have to read the instructions."

The president of the NYPD's union, Patrick Lynch, followed one bombast with another, by calling for officers to not work security at any of the Madison Square Garden shows, even if they needed the extra money. "I consider it an outrage that [Springsteen] would be trying to fatten his wallet by reopening the wounds of this tragic case," Lynch said. Both Mayor Giuliani and his police commissioner, Howard Safir, also released statements criticizing Bruce and "American Skin," with Giuliani complaining about the "people trying to create the impression that the police officers are guilty," while Safir asserted that the city's officers had a right to dislike Bruce Springsteen if they so chose. "I personally don't particularly care for [his] music or his songs," Safir added. Never mind that "American Skin" made no such assertion about the police, just as no one had ordered NYPD officers to purchase Bruce Springsteen albums. But neither Giuliani nor Safir could hold a roman candle to Bob

---

[6] Speaking now, Noah hastens to say that the piece was a blog entry, and thus closer to a random thought than the carefully researched and considered analyses he publishes in other venues. Noah also notes that he's a longtime Springsteen fan and hadn't intended to condemn him. "I don't see anything wrong with achieving a political end with a song," Noah says. "I think political engagement is a good thing."

Lucente, leader of the New York chapter of the Fraternal Order of Police, who dismissed Bruce as a "floating fag" and a "dirtbag" for criticizing the NYPD.[7]

"I think Stevie ran in with a newspaper—Steve is always the bearer of news—saying, 'Hey man, did you see this? Look at what they're calling you on the front page!'" Bruce says. Van Zandt handed him the day's *New York Post*, its front page filled with a headline, "10th Avenue Cop-Out," about the controversy. "I said, '*What?* It was kind of, 'Wait a minute! This guy hasn't even *heard* this song!'" That "American Skin" didn't criticize the NYPD or anyone in the force didn't matter.

When Bruce and company rolled into Madison Square Garden on June 12 to start their two-and-a-half-week residency, Bruce opened the show by premiering another song, "Code of Silence," that seemed to throw down another gauntlet. For while the lyrics never specify if the conflict at hand looms between lovers, family members, or civic institutions, controversy enthusiasts couldn't help but interpret it as another layer of protest or contempt. "American Skin" found a spot with the show's heaviest songs at the heart of the set, and with Diallo's family looking on (when they called Landau's office, Bruce made sure they got preferential treatment), the song became the gravitational center of the performance, a pivot between the gloom of "Point Blank" and the resolute optimism of "The Promised Land." The crowd reaction sounded more like acclaim than disapproval, although as the *New York Times'* Jon Pareles wrote, it would have been difficult to hear the difference between boos and the perpetual rain of "*Bruuuuuce!*" cheers called out by fans. At least one observer shared his thoughts by planting himself at the foot of the stage with both middle fingers extended toward the man at the center microphone.

Pareles published his review of "American Skin" and the rest of the first Madison Square Garden show two days later, including the song's full lyrics. Meanwhile, on the day's editorial pages, a piece by the *Times'* libertarian columnist John Tierney attacked the song, and Bruce, repeating

---

[7] Lucente apologized almost instantly when his words hit the media, although he never explained the meaning or derivation of the term *floating fag*.

the inaccurate charge that the song was a slam against New York's police. To establish his contempt, Tierney began by ridiculing the repetition of the words "Forty-one shots" at the start of the song ("he is firmly on record against the extra bullets"). Next, he unspooled the traitor-to-his-class argument ("Springsteen . . . doesn't have to hitchhike on Route 9 anymore") on the way to asserting that the onetime spokesman for the American working class had become a "limousine liberal" fixated on "conventional liberal causes, like homelessness and AIDS." While it was surprising to think that Tierney considered the destitute and certain terminally ill people as abstract symbols in political clichés, the writer says he figured that the anti-NYPD outcry spurred by protesters was doing exactly that to Diallo. "To me, the [song's] emphasis on the forty-one shots did play to the antipolice mob mentality that existed at the time," Tierney writes in an e-mail. "That was the rallying cry of those trying to exploit the tragedy for their own political reasons. And Springsteen's choice of those lyrics . . . struck me as another example of Springsteen pleasing the Central Park West audience instead of the Asbury Park one."

Tierney, who carries no brief for authoritarian police or mayors, is welcome to his opinions on the herding instincts of New York liberals. But his disquisition on "American Skin" takes enough liberties with Bruce's lyrical intent to make his analysis seem questionable, while his assertions that Bruce's wealth somehow disqualified him from publicly empathizing with the less powerful seemed more like a political tactic than anything else. What bothered Bruce about it, along with the bitter protests of Giuliani, Safir, and others, was how detached from reality they were.

"That's what we ran into: willful distortion," he says. "You don't want to be naive and say it's shocking, because it's not shocking. I understand how the world works. But still, I don't get it. It's not that somebody got the story wrong. It's the willful distortion of what you're trying to say. That was the problem I had, not just with 'American Skin,' but you can take that all the way back to Reagan and 'Born in the U.S.A.' *The willful distortion of what you're trying to say.*"

TWENTY-FIVE

THE COUNTRY WE CARRY IN OUR HEARTS IS WAITING

FOR BRUCE, THAT TUESDAY BEGAN much like it did for every other American lucky enough not to be in the buildings or on one of the doomed airplanes. He was at the kitchen table, ploughing through a bowl of cereal and berries when someone ran in and told him to turn on the TV. An airplane had just crashed into the World Trade Center's north tower. The second airplane hit the south tower a few moments later. By the end of the afternoon, the terrorist attacks of September 11, 2001, had toppled the skyscrapers, smashed through a wing of the Pentagon, sent another jet hurtling into a Pennsylvania field, and sent the nation hurtling into something approaching chaos. Bruce drove to the Rumson–Sea Bright Bridge, which crosses the Shrewsbury River near the edge of the ocean, and gazed at the Manhattan skyline in the northern distance. "It all didn't really hit home 'til I took a ride across the bridge, and there was nothing where the towers used to be," he told writer Robert Hilburn.

Taking another look from the Sea Bright beach a few days later, Bruce was just pulling out of a parking space when a man cruising by unrolled his window. "We need you, man!" he called.

"I knew what he was talking about," Bruce said to NBC's Matt Lauer a year later. "I think one of the things folks wanted to see in those early days was . . . the faces of people who were familiar to them, and people who mattered to them . . . We've worked hard for my music to play a very central and . . . purposeful place in my audience's life. [So] it was a small wake-up call."

When the leaders of the nation's four major television networks joined forces with director Joel Gallen and actor George Clooney to plan a national telethon to aid the families of the attack's victims, Jon Landau got a call from Jimmy Iovine, the engineer-turned-industry powerhouse,[1] then helping to recruit music acts. When Landau mentioned that Bruce already had a song on hand that addressed the grief and determination they hoped to tap, Gallen gave him the opening slot on the telecast that would be viewed on all four American networks and the majority of major US cable channels, along with cable outlets from all over the world.

The September 21 broadcast began with a live glimpse of New York Harbor, a tugboat moving with the Statue of Liberty in the foreground and the emptiness marking the missing towers in the rear. The image darkened and then faded up on the candle-bedecked soundstage where Bruce stood, guitar in hand, harmonica rack around his neck, and a seven-member chorale[2] standing behind. There was no spoken introduction, no name written across the bottom of the screen. Bruce strummed a chord progression, issued a quick dedication—"This is a prayer for our fallen brothers and sisters"—and then leaned into the opening verse of "My City of Ruins," a melancholy gospel-style ballad he'd written a year earlier, thinking about the fall of Asbury Park. But in the days after

[1] Iovine founded Interscope Records in the early 1990s; by 2001, he was the chairman of Interscope-Geffen-A+M.
[2] Consisting of Steve Van Zandt, Clarence Clemons, Patti, and longtime friends Lisa Lowell and Soozie Tyrell, and original Bruce Springsteen Band singer Delores Holmes and her daughter Layonne.

the attacks on New York City, when the nation felt as bereft as the forsaken town Bruce describes, where the church pews are as empty as the storefronts, its residents as lost as their own sense of hope. When the song's narrator speaks to a missing lover, his description of the emptiness in their bed sounded far too familiar to those left to mourn a loved one. "Tell me how to begin again," he sang. "My city's in ruins."

But as with the gospel and (not coincidentally) so many of his own songs, the darkest moments of night foreshadow the dawn. "Now, with these hands, with these hands, with these hands . . ." The choir joined in softly and then with growing urgency as Bruce's voice and guitar gained power. Then he lifted his voice even higher, imploring the skies for some sign of hope.

> *I pray for the strength, Lord; I pray for the faith, Lord; We pray for the lost, Lord; We pray for the strength, Lord . . .*

The singers swayed to the music, their raised hands locked together, their voices expressing the grief in the air and the most American of ideals: that no tragedy can undo a person, or a community, determined to climb back to their feet, roll up their sleeves, and rebuild. And with that vision, proffered in a rare moment of posttraumatic national solidarity, Bruce's voice set the tone for the evening and, for many viewers, nodded toward the path from devastation to redemption.

Bruce's journey from rock star to cultural symbol had been increasingly vivid since the start of the reunion tour. On the posters promoting the tour-ending Madison Square Garden concerts, and then on the cover of the *Live in New York City* CD drawn from the final two shows (released in 2001), the central image captures a silhouette of Bruce and Clarence Clemons onstage: Bruce holding his Fender Telecaster; Clemons, his saxophone. Something about the red sky behind them lends an industrial look; rock 'n' roll machinery powered by molten hearts. Bruce's name marches across the top, with the E Street Band just below, more for design than informational purposes. The cover image alone, Bruce's wide stance, the hunch over his guitar, and Clemons's shoulders thrown back, had become a recognized symbol. For a certain kind of barroom-sprouted rock 'n' roll, to be sure. But also for a set of ideas and beliefs. You didn't have to like his music to respect Bruce's commitment to his craft or admire the egalitarian ideals he had both pursued and written songs about for so many years. That so many of those songs described, celebrated, or mourned the absence of basic American values gave Bruce another kind of gravitas. More than any other contemporary artist, he had made himself synonymous with the cause of the common man; a fellow traveler on the same path trod by Woody Guthrie, John Steinbeck, Mark Twain, and Pete Seeger.

Still, Bruce had resisted the lure of explicit partisanship. Apart from occasional onstage comments (for instance, telling his Tempe, Arizona, audience on November 5, 1980, that the election of Ronald Reagan the previous night struck him as "pretty frightening") and his obvious dismay at Reagan's 1984 attempt to claim spiritual kinship, his public activism during that decade was limited largely to supporting the causes of Vietnam veterans and community food banks. But while Bruce's role in Steve Van Zandt's "Sun City" showed his willingness to take on hotly controversial issues, he'd downplayed partisanship in favor of a populist, vaguely anticorporate, proworker message that could come as easily from political conservatives with an ear for the common man. "I think Bruce was presenting and inhabiting an alternate patriotic vein than the one that was dominant in the country at the time," says Eric Alterman, a political analyst and author of many books and articles for the *Nation*, MSNBC, and the *Jewish Daily Forward*, among others. "He became sort of the president of an imaginary America—the *other* America, so the rest of the world could admire the country the way they wanted to, without having to accept the fact that Reagan or George Bush spoke for America."

Bruce became increasingly explicit about his politics in the 1990s, appearing at the fund-raisers for the left-wing Christic Institute in 1990, and then serving as a central face for the opposition to California's Proposition 187, a 1994 ballot measure intended to bar illegal immigrants from hospitals, schools, and other social services.[3] His biggest hit single of the decade, "Streets of Philadelphia," made Bruce the first heterosexual rock star to give voice to a gay person's inner feelings. The "American Skin" brouhaha, meanwhile, didn't make much of a ripple outside New York City, where most citizens who didn't have an immediate connection to the NYPD or City Hall saw it more as another chapter in the psychodrama of the Giuliani administration than an indication that one of New York's and New Jersey's most long-standing local heroes had revealed himself as a cop-hating radical.

So while Bruce's sensibility flowed largely from New Deal liberalism, his working-class idealism came with bedrock principles on the virtues of work, family, faith, and community. None of which would be considered partisan had the collapse of American liberalism in the late 1970s and 1980s not included a large-scale redefinition of mainstream values as being conservative. That Bruce neither accepted nor acknowledged the politicization of traditional values could be seen in his own work ethic and the symbolic communities he formed with the E Street Band and the fans who bought his records and attended his shows. And even when his songs decried ruling-class greed and the fraying of the social safety net, they still came bristling with flags, work, veterans, faith, and the rock-solid foundation of home and family. "He does not attempt to hide his politics," Christopher Borick and David Rosenwasser wrote in "Springsteen's Right Side: A Liberal Icon's Conservatism," a paper presented at Monmouth University's Bruce Springsteen symposium in 2009. "He's got a Democratic ideology, a Republican vocabulary, and a Populist delivery system."

Just as he'd synthesized gospel, rock 'n' roll, rhythm and blues, folk, jazz, and carnival music into a sound that echoed the clamor of the nation, Bruce's particular magic came from his ability to trace the

---

[3] Prop 187 won handily at the voting box but never took effect due to a series of appeals, restraining orders, a lower-court ruling that the law was unconstitutional, and then the election of a Democratic governor, Gray Davis, who in 1999 dropped the state's appeal of the lower court's ruling.

connections that hold the world together, even when it seems on the verge of flying apart.

For weeks the church bells in central New Jersey rang steadily, each heralding another funeral. Firefighters and police officers, bankers, stockbrokers, insurance executives. Also secretaries, support staff, the passengers on the airplanes bound for San Francisco and Los Angeles. The local newspapers ran thick with obituaries. Intent on acknowledging the lives of all three thousand–plus victims, the *New York Times* launched "Portraits of Grief," a series of mini-profiles describing each person as their family and friends knew them. The rabid Giants fan, the committed gardener, the prize-winning tango dancer, and so on. Bruce read them all and found it stunning when his name started turning up. The memorial service for Jeremy Glick, one of the passengers who attempted to liberate United Flight 93 from the hijackers, ended with a high-volume sing-along to "Born in the U.S.A." New Jersey native Thomas Bowden was remembered as being "deeply, openly, and emotionally loyal to Bruce Springsteen." The profile of insurance executive Jim Berger came under the heading "A Fan of the Boss," noting, along with his love for his sons and the New York Yankees, a penchant for singing "Thunder Road" to anyone who would, or couldn't avoid being made to, listen. "Every time you rode in Jim's car, Bruce was on, whether you liked it or not," his wife, Suzanne, said.

Bruce wrote down the names of his fans' survivors and often reached out to them. He called on the telephone, usually unannounced, to pay his respects and, if it seemed appropriate, learn more about the lives of the lost. Whether he considered the calls a tribute to the dead, a generosity to their survivors, or part of his method to create an even larger tribute seemed unclear, even to Bruce.[4] But for Stacey Farrelly, whose husband, Joe, served as a New York Fire Department captain, hearing the voice, and the concern, of a man her husband had admired felt like a small blessing. "After I got off the phone with him, the world just felt a little

---

[4] He still shies away from discussing the calls seemingly out of respect for the survivors and his desire to not be portrayed as a saint or, conversely, a kind of pop-culture carrion.

smaller," she told *Time*'s Josh Tyrangiel a few months later. "I got through Joe's memorial and a good month and a half on that call."

Looking back a few months later, Bruce was careful to point out that he hadn't set out to make an album about September 11. He'd been working on new songs for several months before the tragedy, already thinking of making a new record with the band. When the writing came more slowly than he'd hoped (he suffered a crisis of confidence, having not made a real rock 'n' roll album since *Lucky Town* in late 1991), Bruce teamed up again with Pittsburgh bar rocker Joe Grushecky, cowriting "Another Thin Line," "Code of Silence," and another half dozen songs before the horrors of 9/11 consumed his thoughts. With the ruins of the World Trade Center still smoldering in New York, mourning banners strung across so many New Jersey streets,[5] and President George W. Bush already setting the stage for a war with Afghanistan's terrorist-supporting Taliban government, Bruce's muse clicked back into gear. "Into the Fire," a blues-and-gospel tune that evoked both the sadness of the rescue workers' deaths and the spiritual beauty of their sacrifice, came just after the attacks and had been his first choice for the *America: A Tribute to Heroes* telethon until he realized it needed more work and adapted "My City of Ruins" instead. "You're Missing," a metronomic ballad adapted from the 1994 outtake "Missing," arrived soon after.

Other songs came on their heels, and after laying down a few demos with Toby Scott, Bruce moved into the recording process. After nearly thirty years of coproducing his own albums, twenty-five years with various combinations of Landau, Scott, Chuck Plotkin, and Steve Van Zandt, it seemed like a good time for him to both find a new producer and step back from his own position in the control room. A series of recommendations led to Brendan O'Brien, an Atlanta-based producer-mixer-multi-instrumentalist known for his work with Pearl Jam, Paul Westerberg, Stone Temple Pilots, and many others. Bruce invited O'Brien up to listen to demos in his own New Jersey studio, and they got to work immediately.

"He played 'You're Missing,'" O'Brien says, "and I remember saying,

[5] Monmouth County lost more than 150 citizens on September 11.

'Your bridge is actually your chorus; you should top the chorus and rear-range it. I can play it for you on the piano right now.'" Bruce listened to O'Brien's revisions and then picked up his guitar to record a new demo of the song. He seemed impressed at the time. But as O'Brien found out later, in an interview that Bruce gave to *Rolling Stone*, his prospective client was less than thrilled. "I'd immediately set to messing with his songs, and he didn't like it. In fact, he was pissed off." No matter, Bruce liked what he heard enough to offer O'Brien the job.

When the sessions started in O'Brien's Atlanta studio, Bruce kept his focus on being the artist while his new producer handled everything else. Starting with the band's four-piece rhythm section—Bruce, Garry Tallent, Max Weinberg, and Roy Bittan—O'Brien led them quickly through the recording of a basic track for "Into the Fire." Leaving so many other parts for overdubs certainly marked a departure in the band's recording style. But it also allowed O'Brien, Bruce, and the core band to produce a dense foundation upon which the soloists and vocalists could later overdub their parts. If the overdub process lost some of the excitement of the live, in-studio feel that Bruce and the band had used for so long, it would also gain clarity and precision. "There were a lot of guys, and a lot of personalities," O'Brien says. "I wasn't sure how close they were anymore; it was all very hush-hush." Nevertheless, the sessions ran quickly and productively. Clemons, Federici, Lofgren, and Patti came down to put on their parts while O'Brien brought in a string section, and when they listened to the playbacks, Bruce marveled at how different yet perfectly right the re-formed E Street Band sounded in O'Brien's studio. "The band sounded like the band, but not like I'd heard them before, and that was what I was looking for," Bruce told *Uncut* magazine's Adam Sweeting. "I wanted it to be like, *this* is the way we sound right *now*."

The band members liked what they heard too. Mostly. "The tracks sounded cool immediately and were experimental. We spent time trying to get different sounds," Tallent says. "People came in to do their parts individually, so there wasn't a lot of camaraderie. But it was all efficient. The record's a bit murkier than something I'd have produced, and it's a departure. But it's still Bruce and the E Street Band." Van Zandt, Bittan, Weinberg, and Clemons felt the same way. "Brendan's style has a sensibility that's a bit different," says Van Zandt. "The tracks are good. They really are. And Bruce was a lot more relaxed than he used to be. But he was very involved."

"I don't remember ever talking to Bruce about giving the album a 9/11 theme," O'Brien says. "When he was around, we just worked and figured it out as we went on." Indeed, only a few songs addressed the September 11 terrorist attacks in specific terms. "Into the Fire" and "The Rising" evoked the crumbling World Trade Center—witnessing the horror of the moment and finding inspiration, even transcendence, in the courage of the fire fighters, rescue workers, and the many who risked everything to help other victims. "Nothing Man," "You're Missing," "Mary's Place," and "Empty Sky" gave voice to the survivors trying to build new lives or maintain a connection to what they lost beyond the poison-belching wreckage. The identity of the attackers and any analysis of their motives and morals are unexplored. Instead the songs stay in the personal realm, sketching a modern variation of *Romeo and Juliet* in the divide between the Western world and the Middle East in "Worlds Apart," and the deadly temptations encountered by a suicide bomber and a grief-stricken spouse in "Paradise." Other songs—"Lonesome Day," "Further On (Up the Road)," "Countin' On a Miracle," "The Fuse"—underscored the personal connections that make life worth living, and how their absence can push someone to believe that a particular ideology or conflict can reduce the value of another human life until it seems worthless.

With the album, titled *The Rising*, finished and ready for a late-July 2002 release, Bruce and Landau set to laying the groundwork to make sure it got the attention they felt it deserved. That it was Bruce's first record with the E Street Band since *Born in the U.S.A.* would have been big enough news on its own. But as Bruce's response to 9/11—and arguably the first major work of popular art to address the meaning and ongoing impact of the terrorist attacks—*The Rising* carried even more cultural significance. It certainly had intense meaning for Bruce. Speaking at an advance listening party with the Columbia/Sony executives, he made certain they knew how far he was willing to go to get the new record across to the largest possible audience. "It ain't business," he said. "It's personal." As Columbia president Don Ienner recalls, the phrase became a rallying cry for the company. "The next day we had T-shirts printed up with 'The Rising' on it, and his quote 'It Ain't Business, It's Personal,'" he says. "It was one of those galvanizing moments of Bruce with the company. We didn't give a shit about radio, or anything. We just went out on it."

Bruce led the charge, diving headlong into the highest-profile sales campaign he'd ever signed on for, prefacing his new album's release with a series of in-depth interviews in major magazines and newspapers around the world. Then he sat for a multipart interview with ABC-TV's Ted Koppel which aired several times on his late-night news show, *Nightline*, during the week the new album came out. *The Rising*'s actual release date, Tuesday, July 30, kicked off like a kind of national holiday, starting with NBC's *Today* show broadcasting from Asbury Park. With hosts Matt Lauer and Katie Couric stationed on the boardwalk and reporters filing reports from other locations in town, the two-hour news program revolved around Convention Hall, where Bruce and the band performed a handful of *Rising* songs, along with an oldie or two, for an audience of 2,500 contest winners. The publicity tour continued the next day when Bruce and the band performed two songs on David Letterman's *Late Show*.[6] The Rising concert tour opened with a single show at the Continental Airlines Arena on August 7. An instant sellout—as any single show would be, given that they had sold out a fifteen-date run at the same venue in 1999—the crazed atmosphere around the arena served as the exclamation point to weeks of album publicity that were now paying off handsomely. First-week sales of *The Rising* rose above a half million copies, propelling it instantly to the top slot on

---

[6] "The Rising" was broadcast on July 31, while "Lonesome Day" turned up on the show the next night.

Billboard's Top 200 albums list. It stayed there for three weeks, fast on its way to selling better than any of Bruce's albums since *Tunnel of Love* in 1987.

Weighing in at fifteen songs and nearly seventy-five minutes long, *The Rising* hit the ground with the weight of a monument. Back on the cover of *Time*, an unshaven Bruce peered past a red, white, and blue headline, "Reborn in the USA: How Bruce Springsteen Reached Out to 9/11 Survivors and Turned America's Anguish Into Art." Writing in *USA Today*, Edna Gundersen dismissed the post-9/11 anthems produced by country musician Toby Keith and Paul McCartney as "flag-waving bombast," before asserting that "it took populist rocker Bruce Springsteen to get it right." So right, in fact, that *New York Times* film critic A. O. Scott, writing in the online magazine *Slate*, declared him "the poet laureate of 9/11." Traditionally conservative publications, including the *National Review* and the *New York Post* (the latter of which played a lead role in sparking the "American Skin" controversy) published rave reviews.[7] Not every critic fell head over heels, particularly when they stepped past the album's emotional ballast to point out that it might have gained power by losing a song or two—"Let's Be Friends (Skin to Skin)" and "Further On (Up the Road)" being prime candidates—and what the *Village Voice*'s Keith Harris called the "eternal vagueness" of the lyrics.[8] Nevertheless, the album and its creator had already been cast in triumph. And as the rocket-fast first legs of the 2002 Rising tour (forty-six shows in forty-six American cities, and then seven shows in seven European cities, leaving many markets sorely underserved) led into a long march through 2003 that concluded with thirty-three stadium shows, including ten nights at Giants Stadium and ending with three nights at Shea Stadium in Queens. While the E Street reunion tour of 1999–2000 succeeded in part due to

[7] Although the *NR*'s critic, Stanley Kurtz, wagged a finger at the absence of stars and stripes, explicitly patriotic statements, or support of the war in Afghanistan. "Something fundamental is missing," he complained.

[8] "You can wander through *The Rising* for countless stanzas without tripping over a single concrete object," Harris wrote. And he's got a point, although stripping away details in favor of a universality was a considered decision on Bruce's part.

the nostalgia of fans eager to hear the old songs, the 2002–2003 shows drew their power from Bruce's most recent work. A segment of the crowd came to hear *The Rising* songs in the same way that *Born in the U.S.A.* drew so many unfamiliar faces in the mid-1980s. By the end of the final encore at Shea Stadium on October 4, 2003, the Rising tour was even more successful than the reunion tour had been, grossing more than $221 million in 120 concerts.

When Bruce sat in front of his TV and saw the bombs pounding the streets of Baghdad, Iraq, in March 2003, when the troops flooded over the border and the United States of America was at war, one thought echoed. "I knew that after we invaded Iraq I was going to be involved in the [2004] election," he told *Rolling Stone* publisher Jann Wenner. "I felt we had been misled. I felt [the George W. Bush administration] had been fundamentally dishonest and had frightened and manipulated the American people into war . . . And I don't think it has made America safer."

Once Bruce would have spun his anger into music, perhaps into a small-scale narrative such as "Seeds," which deconstructed and then reconstructed Reagan-era economics into the story of an unemployed itinerant oil worker forced to spend a frigid night with his family in the cramped shelter of his car. But as 2003 marched into the presidential election of 2004, he felt compelled to expand his influence beyond the limits of rock 'n' roll music. "Sitting on the sidelines would be a betrayal of the ideas I'd written about for a long time," he told Wenner. "Not getting involved, just sort of maintaining my silence or being coy about it in some way . . . wasn't going to work this time out. I felt that it was a very clear historical moment."

It had all been sown in the panicked weeks following September 11. And while the quick mobilization of American forces against Afghanistan's Taliban government made sense in light of its cooperative relationship with the Al Qaeda terrorists, the creation and passage of the Patriot Act, which strengthened government powers (particularly regarding law enforcement) at the expense of civil liberties, infuriated Bruce. When the Bush administration's military ambitions shifted away from Afghanistan, which had aided America's attackers, to Iraq, which had not,[9] the specter of the attacks all but silenced debate and made dissent seem akin to sedition. With his teenage son exactly the age Bruce had been when young men from Freehold were first being shipped to combat in Vietnam, his decision had already been made. If George W. Bush's administration could leverage 9/11 into a wide array of unrelated points on the neoconservative's to-do list, he could take whatever authority he'd earned with *The Rising* and push in the opposite direction. Most of the stadium shows in the summer of 2003 paused in mid-encore while Bruce made a speech ("my public service message," he calls them) urging the audience to pay close attention to what their government might be doing in the name of national security. "Playing with the truth during wartime has been a part of both Democratic and Republican administrations in the past," he said. "Demanding accountability from our leaders and taking our time to search out the truth . . . that's the American way."

When Senator John Kerry claimed the Democratic Party's presidential nomination in the summer of 2004, he'd already known Bruce for nearly twenty-five years, and known of him even longer than that. A richly decorated Vietnam veteran who had returned from duty a vehement opponent of the war, Kerry met Bruce when he played the Vietnam vets benefit in Los Angeles in 1981, and kept a framed, autographed copy of the concert poster in his offices as he ascended from lieutenant governor of Massachusetts to the US Senate. When Kerry got back in touch with Bruce during the summer of 2004, the musician didn't hesitate to throw his support to the Democratic candidate. It was a bridge he hadn't set out to cross, certainly not when his music and his career loomed over every other aspect of his life. But with three children at home, other priorities loomed. "Well, it's your flesh-and-blood connection to the future; this is what's going to matter when I'm gone," he says. "Their presence sets off a whole series of new realizations that affect you all along the spectrum,

[9] Despite strong Bush administration assurances to the contrary, which turned out to be just as accurate as the administration's guarantees that Saddam Hussein's government possessed weapons of mass destruction, which is to say, not at all.

including political." However Bruce had made his decision, the candidate was delighted to have him on board. "There's an authenticity about Bruce that's just incontrovertible," Kerry says. "I think it's because he is so true to who he is, and people know it."

Bruce also signed up (with the E Street Band in tow) to headline the Vote for Change tour put together by the political group MoveOn .org. The series of large-scale benefits starred pop and rock stars (Bruce, R.E.M., John Legend, John Mellencamp, the Dixie Chicks, Pearl Jam, and others) equally determined to change the nation's direction. As they all knew, or were soon to learn, celebrities shouldn't expect to transition into political advocacy without taking fire from a variety of fronts. Even Ted Koppel, who had devoted so much time on *Nightline* to the release of *The Rising*, didn't hold back his skepticism when Bruce came back two years later to talk about the presidential campaign. "Who the hell is Bruce Springsteen to tell anybody how to vote?" Koppel asked pointedly. Some fans, Bruce admitted, marched up to him on the street to explain why they wouldn't be coming to see him this time around. But Bruce didn't care. "It's an emergency intervention," he told *USA Today*'s Elysa Gardner. "We need to get an administration that is more attentive to the needs of all its citizens, that has a saner foreign policy, that is more attentive to environmental concerns."

The Vote for Change tour ended in mid-October, and when the presidential campaign entered its final week at the end of the month, Bruce went out on the road again, playing warm-up for Kerry at a series of rallies heading into election day on November 2. He came out Woody Guthrie–Pete Seeger style, carrying an acoustic guitar and a pair of songs—"The Promised Land" and "No Surrender"—that spoke to the electoral battle to come and the visions that fueled it. When Kerry and Bruce came to Madison, Wisconsin, on October 28, the amassed crowd filled the Capitol Square and flowed down the streets. "The future is now, and it's time to let your passions loose," Bruce told the crowd. "The country we carry in our hearts is waiting." When the candidate reached the stage, he was astonished. "It was huge," Kerry recalls. "Just stunning, people lined the street, there must have been one hundred ten thousand people out there, and it was electric. A beautiful fall afternoon, near the end of the campaign. There was just an energy and a magic to that particular rally and appearance."

A thrilling afternoon at the end of a heated campaign that would end, for Bruce, in heartbreak, as optimistic early returns turned darker as election night went on. Kerry conceded the election to Bush late the next morning. "Patti peeled me off the wall after a couple of weeks," Bruce said to NBC's Matt Lauer. "I was disappointed like everyone else, y'know?" The next day in Atlanta, Brendan O'Brien's telephone rang, and Bruce's craggy voice greeted him. "I'm ready to get back to work," he said. "I'll play you some songs, tell me what you think, and we'll take it from there."

When he reemerged a few months later, Bruce came in the cowboy boots and black suits of America's ghost-swept frontiers. He'd set his course back to the lonesome houses and the sad-eyed souls living within. Titled *Devils & Dust*, the new album collected a dozen stark, character-driven songs, much like the ones that had filled his acoustic solo projects *Nebraska* and *The Ghost of Tom Joad*. The songs didn't represent a new burst of creativity as much as a thoughtful sifting of Bruce's old notebooks and recorded archives. The title track, a whispered monologue by a soldier clutching a gun in some unnamed but sandy battle zone, dated back to 2003. And that was the newest song on the album. "All the Way Home" had been composed in 1991, while many of the others were recorded originally during the *Joad* sessions in 1995.

O'Brien counseled Bruce to add more texture to this set. "I said, 'You can do it one of two ways,'" the producer says, recalling his first hearing of Bruce's tentative lineup. " 'Either just like this, as per *Nebraska*, which not a lot of people would connect to, or else another way.'" They chose the latter route, punching up the songs with new instruments and vocals, giving the disparate material a unified sound. The songs focused most intently on relationships: what holds them together, what tears them apart, what survives their collapse, and what doesn't. Far more melodic and musically feisty than Bruce's earlier folk albums, the songs on *Devils & Dust* also range far beyond traditional song structures. The verses ramble with the needs of the narrative, abandoning the mathematics of meter. Few of the songs boast anything like a traditional chorus. Most strikingly, the verses of "Matamoros Banks" describe the drowning death of a Mexican immigrant in reverse order, starting with his body floating up from the river bottom and ending with the moment he leaves his lover behind, bidding her to meet him by the same river that would claim him.

Released in late April, *Devils & Dust* established the sales pattern that Bruce's nonrock albums would follow in the digital/iTunes–defined world. Buoyed by loyal fans eager to pick up any new Springsteen album the moment it became available, *Devils* debuted at the top of the *Billboard* album chart and then fell into a downward drift eased—and sometimes reversed—according to media coverage and tour schedules. *Devils* earned gold status (five hundred thousand units) within weeks and then settled into a slower pace toward platinum. Bruce's sales certainly benefited from his bottomless appetite for the road. Starting with the marathon reunion tour in 1999–2000, he mounted an even longer charge to promote *The Rising* in 2002 and 2003, pausing for only a year before taking the band on the Vote for Change jaunt in the fall of 2004. After that, only a few months passed before Bruce set out on a global Devils & Dust tour, playing in seventy-two cities across the United States and Europe.

Unlike the austere *Tom Joad* shows a decade earlier, the *Devils* shows featured a stage crammed with instruments, the acoustic guitars joined by piano, pump organ, banjo, and several varieties of keyboards and synthesizers. Just beyond the edge of the stage, a hidden collaborator, Alan Fitzgerald, played tape loops and added other textures. Bruce changed instruments according to his whims, at one point performing "I'm on Fire" on the banjo, and finding new sounds in his keyboards, synthesizers, and sound processors. The most striking example came at the end of the show, when he sat at the pump organ to play the electronic punk duo Suicide's "Dream Baby Dream." Slowing down the original's pace to give the song a rich, hypnotic flow, Bruce sang the chant-like lyrics in his sweetest Orbisonian croon, evoking the romanticism that flowered on "Born to Run"—as if the years and the mileage had never come and gone, as if he still believed that a simple pattern of chords and a few romantic phrases could light up the night and alter the course of a life. "Come on and open up your heart," he sang. "Come on and dream on, baby, dream."

And so Bruce kept moving and dreaming. Dreaming about the horizon, and yet wide awake to the sawtooth realities of daily life and the arc of his own life—what he'd felt, what he'd heard, and played along the way about the folk music he'd played back when he went to his older cousin Frank Bruno to help tune his guitar and maybe learn a few chords. Frank had switched from accordion when the folk revival hit in the early 1960s and thus pointed his pimply cousin to the plainspoken music's wonders and possibilities. Three chords and the truth, and it's only the last part that's complicated. That fed into Bruce's Bob Dylan fixation a few years later, and the Woody Guthrie passion that came in his early thirties. But those early songs, the ones about work and slavery and the outsized characters who wielded the axes, hammers, picks, and guns that built America's identity, if not the nation itself, never left Bruce's imagination.

Invited in 1997 to contribute a song to a tribute album for the great activist folkie Pete Seeger, Bruce signed on happily, forming a backing band the old-fashioned way: he hired the guys who had just performed at his birthday party. The Gotham Playboys were a New York–based zydeco-Cajun outfit that included Patti's musical partner, Soozie Tyrell, on fiddle and vocals, along with keyboard-accordion player Charlie Giordano among its members. They could play anything with equal dollops of charm and skill, so of course they'd be perfect. Summoned for a day's worth of sessions in early November 1997, the band followed Bruce's lead through a half dozen folk songs Seeger had played (if not written) during his career.

Working in one of the restored farmhouses nestled around Bruce and Patti's farm, the band came in cold, which was exactly how he wanted them. "The feeling I got was that we weren't going for perfection but for energy and spontaneity. That was the approach," Giordano says. "This was going to be fun." When the musicians walked in and uncased their instruments, they ran through the usual technical chores: tuning, miking, balancing, and so on. But when Bruce slung on his guitar, that was the end of the preparing. He called out the name of a song, counted it down, and *boom*, off they went. If you couldn't figure out the key by looking at the chords his fingers formed on the neck of his guitar, that was your problem. "Just focus, listen, and look, and don't think," Giordano says. And, of course, that was exactly what Bruce wanted.

"It's fascinating to record a song when musicians don't know it," he told *USA Today*'s Edna Gundersen. "If people learn their parts too well, they consciously perform rather than flat-out play. When you just launch into it, it breaks down another barrier between you and the audience. One less layer of formality." Bruce could take a little more time when the situation called for it; as in the hushed version of the civil rights anthem "We Shall Overcome" that he eventually chose to contribute to the Seeger tribute album. But mostly his aesthetic could be summarized in the instructions he gave upon hearing a rough-and-ready intro to one of the songs: "That's good!" Then he waved his hands to make them stop. "If it gets any better than that, it'll be *worse*."

Years passed, but Bruce always remembered the day's spontaneity most fondly, and when he sat with Jon Landau to spin through their archives with an ear toward a *Tracks* follow-up, he heard it again and decided on the spot to get the gang back together and give it another go. They reconvened on March 19, 2005—this time with Frank Bruno's son, Frank Jr., on board as a rhythm guitarist—and knocked out another handful of tunes. Ten months later Bruce called the band back for a final recording date in January 2006, after which they had more than enough tracks for a full-length album. Released three months later, *We Shall Overcome: The Seeger Sessions*[10] got Bruce itching to hit the road and give his new band a whirl around the globe. Landau booked a fifty-six-show tour that began with an emotional appearance at the first New Orleans Jazz and Heritage Festival since Hurricane Katrina had all but drowned

---

[10] The album was completed without the help of the decade's regular producer, Brendan O'Brien, largely because off-the-cuff recordings of folk songs were something other than his thing. "He knew I wasn't going to like it, and he didn't want to hear about it from me," O'Brien says. "He was absolutely correct. I just said, 'Dude, thumbs up to you. Don't worry about me.'"

the city in September 2005. From there they headed off for a long swing through Europe and then returned to the United States for a few months of shows at concert halls and, in larger eastern cities, a small scattering of arenas. Then it was back to Europe for a final go-round before the holiday season. Also, Bruce had another batch of rock 'n' roll songs he wanted to play for Brendan O'Brien. Two months later, he went back to Atlanta to work on the next E Street Band album.

Watching as it happened, and then in the weeks that followed, Bruce couldn't get the flood of New Orleans out of his mind. The city's role in the birth of jazz, along with its rich mix of cultural and ethnic traditions (African, Cajun, Caribbean, Hispanic, French, and more), would be more than enough to make it an indispensable cultural resource. And even that should have been dwarfed by the simple fact that the lives of a half million Americans were in immediate danger. For Bruce, the motivations mattered less than the simple fact that the government had neglected to help citizens who needed it desperately. "When you see the devastation and realize the kind of support the city will need to get back on its feet, there's no way to make sense of someone pushing for more tax cuts for the [top] one percent of the population," he told *USA Today*'s Edna Gundersen. "It's insanity and a subversion of everything America is supposed to be about."

Bruce rolled out a series of compositions that spun what he saw as the essential themes and failures of the Bush administration into terms intimate enough to describe a broken romance. "The best of my music that has social implications functions like that," Bruce explains. "They reach for your heart first, they speak to your soul, then they get in your bloodstream, move through the rest of your body and into your mind." The approach comes through in every note of "Livin' in the Future," the deceptively upbeat rocker that fell across his guitar in late 2003. Seemingly a rueful response to a Dear John letter, the song begins with its narrator reminiscing about his ex, from the moment he first saw her strutting his way, boot heels snapping like "the barrel of a pistol spinnin' round." So alluring, so dangerous, and far too seductive to not fall for, no matter the obvious warnings. Consider the hint of blood in her mouth as they kiss. From there, the seas rise, the earth gives way, the forces of liberty and justice head for the exits. Did he mention that they met on Election Day? Beneath skies as gray as gunpowder? Now his faith is ruined, the thunder sounds like righteousness crumbling into fragments. What remains? Try denial: "We're livin' in the future, and none of this has happened yet."

Sonically, Bruce came at the tracks in an expansive mood, working with O'Brien to sculpt the songs into the sort of intricate productions he hadn't attempted since he and Mike Appel spent six months hand tooling "Born to Run" into a rock 'n' roll symphony. "He was really ready to bust it out that time," O'Brien says. "It's always my thinking that if you can present a tough lyric with a brightness to it, it keeps it from getting too one-dimensional. And he was letting it go. Let 'em all be filled with candy and sugar. And I was only too happy to oblige."

Released in the fall of 2007, *Magic* and its accompanying one-hundred-stop tour played out at the same time as the American presidential election. Although Bush was nearing the end of his political career, his philosophies and policies loomed over the process. Looking among the candidates for someone who seemed to come from the country Bruce grew up imagining he lived in, he settled on Illinois senator Barack Obama. Clearly, Obama's liberal-realist policies matched Bruce's fire-cured optimism. But after reading Obama's prepolitical memoir, *Dreams from My Father*, he was even more impressed by the senator's history. The symbolic impact of electing the nation's first African-American president only made it feel that much more crucial. "He's a unique figure in history," Bruce told the UK *Observer*'s Mark Hagen. "The fundamental American-ness of his story and the fact that he represents . . . an image and a view of the country that felt like it was so long missing in action . . . that's fabulous."

When the rough-and-tumble campaign for the Democratic nomination turned particularly bruising during the Pennsylvania primary in April,[11] Bruce posted his strongly worded endorsement of Obama on his official website. "*He has the depth, the reflectiveness, and the resilience to be*

---

[11] Based in part on Obama's connection to a fairly radical African-American minister named Jeremiah Wright.

our next President," he wrote. "*He speaks to the America I've envisioned in my music for the past 35 years, a generous nation with a citizenry willing to tackle nuanced and complex problems, a country that's interested in its collective destiny and in the potential of its gathered spirit. A place where* [quoting now from the *Magic* song "Long Walk Home"] ' . . . *nobody crowds you, and nobody goes it alone*.'"

Released without the knowledge of the Obama campaign, the endorsement caught the candidate by surprise. "We were on the campaign RV in Pennsylvania, and he came back and said 'Bruce Springsteen just endorsed me!'" campaign chief David Axelrod remembers. Obama sat down, handed his BlackBerry to him, and kind of beamed. "I'm not usually impressed by celebrity endorsements, but I just read this thing," the candidate said. "And I *like* the guy. I've got a bunch of his music on my iPod. I *really* like him."

Obama got Bruce on the phone by that afternoon, and when the general campaign began in the fall, the musician played starring roles at benefits and last-week campaign stops. After Obama won the election in November, he invited Bruce to perform at the We Are One concert held two days before his inauguration, where Bruce stood on the steps of the Lincoln Memorial to sing "The Rising" with a gospel choir and then joined with Pete Seeger for a sing-along of "This Land Is Your Land." When Bruce got tapped for a Kennedy Center Honor in 2009, the president of the United States watched the proceedings from the presidential box with the musician seated just beyond First Lady Michelle Obama, who sat at her husband's side. Still within reach of any presidential whisper, which Obama delivered multiple times that evening.

"I think [the president] sees Springsteen as a kind of poet of the American dream," Axelrod says. "A poet who brings life to everyday hopes, aspirations, and challenges people face in a distinctive and wonderful way."

TWENTY-SIX

THAT'S A BIG SHARK, MAN

SITTING ON THE BALCONY OF his beachside thirtieth-floor penthouse on Singer Island, Florida, Clarence Clemons took in the morning sun as he considered the future of the E Street Band. He'd be ready, he was sure. It was a Wednesday in early March 2011, somewhere between the end of Clemons's morning physical therapy session and the start of the one that would fill the latter half of his afternoon. A couple of months past his sixty-ninth birthday, the regal saxophonist had suffered a chain of physical betrayals. Knees gone bad, hips shot, spine scraping so painfully that he had to have portions of it fused just to stay on his feet. He said repeatedly in interviews that he felt more bionic than human. So many organic parts traded out for artificial replacements, some functioning better than others. For the last few years, Clemons had required a golf cart to get from dressing room to stage. "I've been going through hell, man," he told me with a shrug. "Having to climb those steps to get up to the show—it's amazing pain just to get *to* the steps. But I don't care what happens. I'm gonna *make* it happen. This is what I do; this is who I am."

His eyes narrowed, and he nodded at the water below. "See that?" Not at first, but then he pointed out the five-foot mud shark slicing its way through the breakers. It looked like a warhead, colorless, fast, and razor finned. Even thirty floors up, it cast a chill. Clemons chuckled. They come past all the time, he said. Vast migrations, all sifting the waves for something, or possibly someone, to eat. "Oh yeah, people get chomped," he said. "Not as often as you'd think, though." The thing came closer, slid even with the balcony, and continued on its way. "That's a big shark, man," he said.

The beast slithered off and Clemons began to talk about Danny Federici. They had always been partners in crime, going all the way back to that wild house they shared with Vini Lopez during the $35-a-week days of 1973. Back then they had to combine their talents to fend off starvation: Lopez could catch fish, Clemons could clean and cook them, and Federici made pasta. So many miles, so many nights on the road, so many great shows, so many surprise twists. For instance, the girl Federici met in Houston in 1974, who offered to drive the organist and his sax-playing friend the 250 miles to the next day's gig in Dallas so they could sightsee and have a few laughs. Who knew that she had stolen that car? Or that she had just gotten out of jail? Or that her dad was a cop? "I *knew* something was fucked up," Clemons said, laughing. "Something was *always* going to fuck up."

Oh, but put the man at the business end of a Hammond B3. "Danny's sound was so important to the sound of the band," Clemons said. "I always thought Bruce wrote tunes according to what he knew he had in his hands, bandwise. He could anticipate how a song would sound." The trick was realizing that Federici would never play the same part in precisely the same way. If Bruce, or anyone, pressed him to repeat a performance, he'd shrug. "If you asked him to play something twice in recording, he'd say, 'I probably can't remember,'" Roy Bittan says. "But he'd come up with something else that was totally organic and very natural and beautiful." Nils Lofgren, the creator of a million intricate song charts, could only marvel at his colleague's ability to play from the opposite direction. "Danny was a stream-of-consciousness player," he says. "Half the time he couldn't tell you the chords to a song, but he could weave with extreme technical precision. He could play the hell out of it, with soulfulness and technical facility."

On his balcony, Clemons had tears in his eyes. "We'd been very close, ever since we lived together in that house. He was on my side of the stage, so we had our own thing going on over there. Always talking about the girls in the front row: '*the white vest to my right!*' So it was particularly tough for me."

In November 2005, Federici found some bumps on his back, went to a dermatologist, and learned he had a cancerous melanoma. The treatment knocked the disease into remission for a while, but it came back with a vengeance just as the Magic tour got rolling in the fall of 2007. He made all the rehearsals, manned the keyboards at the big *Today* show album launch, and then set out with everyone else on the first leg of the world tour, a six-week swing through media centers and the American East and Midwest. When they learned in early November that Federici would have to leave the tour to focus on battling his cancer, Bruce called on Charlie Giordano, the keyboard-accordionist from the *Seeger Sessions* band, to fill in. After spending a week poring through Bruce's catalog, often with Federici's help, Giordano joined the tour to watch the organist do his thing. "I watched three shows, and Danny was so kind to me and ready to help in any way," he says, "in spite of his being in tremendous pain, and also the sadness."

When they got to the final bows at the end of the first leg of the Magic tour, Bruce made straight for Federici, threw his arm across his shoulder, and steered him to center stage. With Bruce on one shoulder and Steve Van Zandt on the other, the one E Street resident who could claim to being in the band longer than Bruce (given that he and Lopez had hired Bruce to be their guitar player-front man in Child) smiled into the spotlight and leaned into his friend's hug. Federici shouted something into Bruce's ear, and they both laughed. Speaking in the tongues of the Jersey Shore, of musicians, of boyhood friends.

Bruce and the band took six days off, then flew overseas for a three-week trip across Europe. When the opening strums of "Radio Nowhere" kicked on the lights in Milan, Italy, on November 26, Giordano sat in Federici's place. He stayed there through the foreign swing and into the second American leg. A dozen songs into the set in Indianapolis on March 20, 2008, Giordano slid off the bench and left the stage.

"We got a treat for ya tonight!" Bruce declared as Federici, smiling broadly beneath a dark slouch cap, slid onto the bench and threw himself into "The Promised Land" with the ease of a man who had never left. "Spirit in the Night" came next, and then Federici took up his accordion and stepped forward. "Before we went on, I asked him what he wanted to play," Bruce said a few weeks later. "He said 'Sandy.' He wanted to strap on the accordion and revisit the boardwalk of our youth during the summer nights when we'd walk along the boards with all the time in the world . . . He wanted to play once more the song that is of course about the end of something wonderful and the beginning of something unknown and new." Federici's cancer had metastasized into his brain. The next time Bruce played the song was at the April 21 memorial service in Red Bank.

Bruce and the band cancelled three shows after Federici's death and then traveled to Tampa to honor their April 22 booking. The show began with a filmed tribute to their vanished organist. When it ended, a single white spotlight shone on the riderless Hammond B3, holding for a long moment until the first notes of "Backstreets" grew into the full cacophony of innocent love, time, and the cruel verities of life. The show became a kind of public wake, a succession of musical tributes and funny stories from back in the band's wildest days. Federici's sweet, cockeyed spirit hung over the next few nights too, with more memory-freighted oldies ("Does This Bus Stop at 82nd Street?," "Spirit in the Night," "Blinded by the Light," and "Wild Billy's Circus Story"), more stories, and a growing sense that Danny had taken something big with him.

"The thing I've been proudest about for a long time was that unlike many other bands, our band members lived," Bruce said to the *Observer*'s Mark Hagen. "And that was something that was a group effort. Something we did together, the surviving part. People did watch the other person. And it was a testament to the life force that I think was at the core of our music. Nobody gave up on you. That lasted a long time."

The inevitable cracks in the E Street foundation snaked into view a

year earlier. For more than twenty years Bruce had leaned on the broad
shoulders of Terry Magovern, an ex-navy man, club owner, and (mostly)
gentle behemoth who had served as his longtime assistant, bodyguard,
and buffer against and connection to the real world. Magovern went all
the way back to the prehistoric Jersey Shore days too,[1] knew exactly who
was who and why they mattered, and kept his arms crossed and his heart
open to those who needed it. "He was a lifeguard," Bruce says. "That's not
a job you pick. It's who you are internally." Once an explosives expert in
the Navy SEALS, Magovern also trained to rescue American astronauts
in case their water landings went awry. "He was always busy saving someone," Bruce wrote on his website. "That was his blessing and his tragedy."
His body weakened by cancer and cardiac problems, his spirit sapped by
the death of his fiancée, Joan Dancy, whom he'd nursed through amyo-
trophic lateral sclerosis, Magovern died in his sleep, inspiring Bruce to
make his just-written and -recorded tribute "Terry's Song" a last-second
addition to *Magic*. "A bad attitude," Bruce sang, "is bigger than death."

A year later Bruce wrote "The Last Carnival" for Federici, revisiting
the rolling home of Wild Billy nearly forty years since he'd signed on to a
lifetime of flash, daring, and illusion. Imagining them both as a team of
daredevils—trapeze artists, high-wire walkers, lion tamers—Bruce climbs
alone onto the steaming train, pausing for one last glance into the gloom
rising in the fields behind.

*Sundown, sundown / Empty are the fairgrounds / Where are you now, my
handsome Billy?*

The next day, clouds smeared the Florida skies, and Clemons stayed in
his kitchen. He had an industrial-strength stool back there and enough

[1] His first run-in with Bruce came in 1972, when Bruce, playing with Van Zandt's Sundance Blues Band, played Magovern's Captain's Garter club in Neptune, New Jersey.
They drew a decent crowd, earned a great response, and went to the club owner thinking he'd be delighted to book them regularly. Instead Magovern fired them. For all the
crowd's size and enthusiasm, they didn't buy enough drinks. And, Magovern said, in case
they hadn't noticed, selling drinks was what he did for a living.

wingspan to reach into the refrigerator on his right and then adjust the temperature on the stove in front of him. He had some oxtail soup going, and a nice bottle of red a friend had recently shipped from his winery in Italy. "I'm not really supposed to drink these days," he said. "But if *you* want some . . ." He produced two glasses and suggested letting it breathe for a few minutes.

Clemons spoke at length, recalling the many moments when he and Bruce stood together—the brilliant white boy and his dark-skinned shaman—basking in and amplifying each other's glow. "In the old days, we'd do these crazy dances, slide across the stage. So spontaneous, so magical. Like that time when he slid into my arms and kissed me. That was sudden, out of nowhere, and became a big thing." But the tectonic plates shifted, and relationships changed. When Bruce turned in other directions for inspiration, Clemons resented it, even when he understood why it had to happen. "It's like being married to someone. You have certain expectations of someone because you love them so much. But then these things happen, and he probably doesn't even notice. So I felt like I put out all this for the situation and didn't get much back." Clemons felt that way for most of the nineties. Then the telephone rang in 1998 and it all came rushing back.

"Bruce is so passionate about what he believes, that if you're around him, you have to feel it. It'll become part of your passion," he said. "I believed in him like I believe in God. That kind of feeling. He was always so straight and dedicated to what he believes, you became a believer simply by being around him. People see him and think, 'This is how it's supposed to be, this is how it's supposed to happen.' You dedicate your life to something. And Bruce represents that."

On the threshold of his sixtieth birthday, after achieving virtually everything he ever imagined achieving and then some, Bruce felt free to follow his instincts. "I'd gotten to an age where you're less caught up into being fooled into believing that you have something to protect," he says. "So you're more relaxed about who you are. You're as serious as ever about it, but it doesn't feel ephemeral anymore. It doesn't feel like something that's going to disappear or vanish." When a burst of new songs came at the end of the *Magic* sessions, he called the band back to put down some more basic tracks, and then visited more studios around the country during the tour's off days. Expanding on the dense, Brian Wilson–esque production style of the earlier album, the new songs came cloaked in strings, bells, and other sonic fancies. But if the studio sparkle played counterpoint to the dystopian visions on *Magic*, the new songs came out as upbeat or whimsical: meditations on supermarkets, cowboy legends, and the joys and complexities of long-standing love. Some of the songs had undeniable charms. "What Love Can Do" is all sharp angles and minor chords, its lovers finding their connection on the rim of an apocalypse where "our memory lay corrupted and our city lay dry." "Surprise, Surprise" jangles like prime sixties pop, with a melody so hummable that even the seasoned popsmith Mike Appel pronounced himself impressed. "That's surprisingly melodic," he told Bruce. "I didn't think you had it in ya!" His former client laughed happily. "See?" he said.

"Queen of the Supermarket" imagined a pure form of beauty in the aisles of the neighborhood Whole Foods.[2] Elsewhere, the gnarly blues heart of "Good Eye" vanishes beneath layers of studio silk. The midtempo "Working on a Dream"[3] trudges the same path trod by all those other determined Springsteenian laborers, only this time it doesn't lead anywhere beyond the formless dream cited in the title.

Still, the Danny Federici tribute, "The Last Carnival,"[4] brimmed with enough love and sorrow to sting the eyes. And the real masterpiece in the collection, recorded by Bruce alone in his home studio, turned out to

---

[2] Despite being one of the most underappreciated, even hated, songs in Bruce's catalog, "Queen" is actually really cool, particularly when you consider the creative process Bruce described to Mark Hagen: "I hadn't been in one in a while, and I thought this place is spectacular . . . it's a fantasy land! . . . The subtext in here is so heavy! It's like, 'Do people really want to shop in this store or do they just want to screw on the floor!?' They're sort of shameless; the bounty in them is overflowing." And thus the vision of loveliness stacking cans in the aisle, "something wonderful and rare," and the smile powerful enough that it "blows this whole fuckin' thing apart." Love ballads don't get much quirkier than that, but set to an airy piano riff, with the glockenspiel ringing, a light scrim of strings, and Bruce's Big Voice sailing at the top of its range, the whole thing feels delightfully alive and real.

[3] Premiered at the rallies for Barack Obama during the fall of 2008.

[4] Featuring Danny's son Jason on his old man's accordion.

be "The Wrestler," the elegiac theme he wrote for the low-budget film of the same name. Starring the brilliant but mercurial Mickey Rourke, the portrait of a broken-down professional wrestler risking his life to reclaim former glories felt remarkably familiar. Following its character through the same crumbling East Coast towns Bruce had always known, the film played in his eyes as a kind of nightmare vision of who he might have become if the anger had consumed him and left him alone and fuming in a barely rented mobile home, broke and deaf, the Telecaster long lost to the pawn shop. That wasn't Bruce's fate. But he knew what might have led him there, and how easy it would have been to slam that aluminum door and feel right at home. Another variation on the archetype portrayed by John Wayne in the emotionally fraught western *The Searchers*. The story of the young rocker so determined to make a home and family through his music that he couldn't sit still long enough to make those things part of his real life. "These things that have comforted me I drive away / This place that is my home I cannot stay / My only faith's in the broken bones and bruises I display . . ."

Titled *Working on a Dream*, and wrapped in a gauzy, airbrushed painting of Bruce standing with the ocean behind and heavenly sky (half scattered stars, half summery clouds, all dreamy) above, the new album floated into the marketplace on January 27, 2009. Released just sixteen months since *Magic* in September 2007, *Working* set an instant mark as the quickest follow-up album Bruce had made with the E Streeters since *The Wild, the Innocent & the E Street Shuffle* emerged in November 1973, ten months after the January release of *Greetings from Asbury Park*. While the album was greeted with respectful, if muted, reviews,[5] the weeks surrounding its release featured some of Bruce's most spectacular promotional appearances.

He started with the Golden Globes, where "The Wrestler" won the Best Original Song–Motion Picture Award. Next, Bruce made his

---

[5] Ann Powers, writing in the *Los Angeles Times*, summed it up nicely: "Only a great artist could make an album that's at once so stirring and slight. This is the Boss, after all; he can wring meaning out of a dish towel."

star-spangled appearance at Barack Obama's inauguration festivities on January 18, then pivoted immediately into rehearsals for his appearance at another unimaginably huge, nation-binding event. Which is to say, the halftime show of Super Bowl XLIII. "I wasn't sure I expected it to mean something," Bruce says. "I thought it would be just, okay, we've got a record coming out. You're looking for new ways to have your music heard. Also, they'd been asking me to do it for ten years."

Why wouldn't Bruce play the Super Bowl for all those years? Pop stars (from Michael Jackson to Britney Spears to Shania Twain) had in recent years turned the halftime shows into gigantic promotional stunts for their next albums and tours. Serious-minded rock 'n' rollers, on the other hand, took it to the people over the radio and in the concert halls. At least, that's how it worked until the radio industry collapsed into tiny, computer-programmed shards. For most of the mainstream rock stations in the United States, even the most worshiped artists had been reduced to the sum of their original hits. No matter how prolific you were, or how celebrated your new work, you had little chance of introducing listeners to anything new. By the mid-'00s the terrain had shifted enough to push Paul McCartney to make the pilgrimage to the big game in 2005. The Rolling Stones followed in 2006, then came Prince in 2007. And when Jon Landau saw fellow stripped-down rockers Tom Petty and the Heartbreakers playing the halftime of the 2008 Super Bowl, he had a small revelation. "I just thought, 'That could be *us*,'" Landau says. He picked up his telephone and dialed Bruce, who also happened to be sitting in front of his living room TV. "He had the same reaction." Landau called the National Football League executives charged with planning the Super Bowl broadcast, and it wasn't long before they had a deal. Bruce and the E Street Band would star in the 2009 halftime show.

Despite the many, many thousands of concerts Bruce had performed over the years, the twelve-minute Super Bowl appearance was the first to be scripted with graphic storyboards. Still, Bruce's shows had long included light cues and even skits that required particular performers to be in particular places at precise times, so it wouldn't be too much of a stretch for him or anyone in the band. The one requirement Landau had lain down to the producers, in consideration for his man's oft-stated standards, was this: no fireworks. Looking over the storyboards a few months later, only one detail furrowed Bruce's forehead. "Where's the fireworks?" he demanded. Told that Landau had ruled them out, Bruce gazed at his partner incredulously. "How are you gonna do the Super Bowl without any fireworks? Are you *crazy*?" When game time approached in Tampa, Bruce fired up the E Streeters by telling them to think about the one hundred million pairs of eyes that would be locked on them during the show. "I said, 'Look, today's a day when we get to do what we've always wanted to do. We're gonna play for *everybody*.'"

Designed as a kind of comic book version of the history and spirit of Bruce Springsteen and the E Street Band, the halftime show began with Bruce and Clemons evoking the *Born to Run* cover by standing back to back against a sheer white backdrop, their instantly recognizable profiles augmented by the outlines of their lofted saxophone and Telecaster guitar. They separated with the opening chords of "Tenth Avenue Freeze-Out," Bruce jogging to center stage and hurling his Tele to hardworking guitar tech Kevin Buell,[6] then bolting to the front to lead the band's best-known creation myth. A quick four-count announced the start of "Born to Run," minus its second verse, but with its "everlasting . . . kiss" emphasized with a burst of rocket fire. The berobed Joyce Garrett Singers jogged out to bring some gospel to a sliver of "Working on a Dream," which gave way to a goofier than usual "Glory Days," with lyrics adjusted for the occasion

---

[6] Bruce took up the practice of tossing his guitars at Buell during the 1999–2000 reunion tour. What began as gentle heaves from not far away grew eventually into long-distance, often sky-high hurls, some better thrown than others. Long since resigned to do his part in a now beloved bit of stage theater, Buell is still not fond of the ritual. Electric guitars are both heavy and unwieldy, with a lot of sharp edges and moving parts. If they come at you neck first, you're in trouble. If the tosser doesn't take care in aiming, or if he's the kind of guy who might occasionally *try* to catch you off guard, you're also in trouble: snapped fingers, forearm bruises, and so forth. If you look carefully at the Super Bowl video, you'll see Buell, who came into the show with a broken finger, trip on an uneven seam in the stage and nearly crash into the percussion setup before coming up with the guitar. Later, Bruce called it the best catch of the entire game. "I don't try to screw him up," he says. "I try to make it *exciting*." Asked if he's ever let a guitar crash to the ground, Buell shakes his head. "I'd say there were a few wild pitches, but no passed balls." Bruce responds by changing the terms of the discussion. "There may have been a few that glanced off of him, y'know. But he's pretty good with it."

("I had a friend who's a big football player . . . He could throw that Hail Mary right by ya . . ."), and a zebra-striped referee sprinting out to throw a delay of game flag when the show threatened to run long. Another hail of rockets swept the band off the stage, and a private plane carried Bruce back to New Jersey in time for him to light a bonfire in his backyard and contemplate the stars until close to dawn, the pulse of the one hundred million viewers still tingling in his fingertips. "It wasn't what I expected," he says. "I wasn't sure I expected it to mean something. But it had a little strange sacrament to it. For weeks afterward, everybody came up and told me what they thought. The guy handling the baggage on the airlines, this person, that person, the nine-year-old kid on the street. 'Hey, didn't you . . . ' You know? It was quite wonderful and meant quite a bit to all of us."

Clemons nearly didn't make it to the game. In early October 2008 he entered a New York City hospital and in two weeks weathered two knee replacement surgeries. The recovery process was excruciating. The pain, Clemons told Don Reo, his close friend and cowriter of his memoir, *Big Man*, was beyond anything he'd ever known. "They haven't made a drug that can touch this pain," he said. "I feel like I'm made of pain." Almost entirely convinced that he could never be in shape for the halftime show, Clemons worked with trainers through the holidays and then into January. And when the lights came on in Tempa that evening, one hundred million Americans, and God only knows how many other viewers around the world, saw him standing tall, moving with the music as he blasted his trademark solos, and moving easily to punctuate Bruce's "Tenth Avenue" proclamation that Scooter and the Big Man were about to tear the Super Bowl in half with a mighty high five. "There's something about being onstage," Clemons said. "I call it the healing floor. I do all this shit, then I sit back later and wonder, how the hell did I do that? It revives you."

Clemons made it onto the Working on a Dream tour, albeit with the golf cart and elevator, and a stool to lean on when he didn't have an active role in the song at hand. As on the Magic tour, Clemons's hobbled condition altered his presence. No longer able to stalk and then rush into the spotlight, he hung back in his shades, fedora, and floor-length black duster, dark and inscrutable until the moment the spotlight put the gleam on his sax and he pinned his shoulders back. "I'll be seventy years old soon," Clemons said that afternoon on his balcony. "So you have to find different parts of your body to make it happen."

Bruce, on the other hand, made like Peter Pan with his gym-solid shoulders and chest, his impressively trim waistline, and the jumping, strutting, piano-dancing performances that seemed every bit as electric as they had been in the nineties, the eighties, and the seventies too. This time out, however, his new material didn't light up the arenas like the tunes from *Magic* and especially *The Rising* had done. So while Bruce had long built his shows around his newest songs,[7] mixing in the older stuff to underscore certain themes or to allow the new material to reveal new dimensions in songs whose meanings had once seemed chained to other eras or messages. True to form, the Working on a Dream tour's April 1 opener in San Jose, California, featured half a dozen songs from the new album, with a nearly ten-minute "Outlaw Pete" tapped as the night's second song and each of the show's five-to-six-song minisets built around *Working* tracks. When the tour got to Philadelphia on April 28, the set was down to four new songs, which ebbed to two when they opened the European swing on May 30. When the tour ended in Buffalo six months later, only the album's title song remained in the set. "It was a record that just wasn't as popular as a lot of our other records," Landau says. "On the Magic tour, he was doing seven or eight *Magic* songs a night. And on the Working tour [the new songs] weren't making a connection to the live audience that we would like them to make. Not for a lack of trying, though."

Sensing the lag in his audience's enthusiasm, Bruce went back to his catalog for rarely played songs, many inspired by the handmade signs audience members brought to inspire a last-second call for "New York City Serenade," "I'm on Fire," and so on. That Bruce even acknowledged the signs represented a philosophical shift. The signs had first appeared nine

---

[7] Including the 1999–2000 reunion tour shows, which often kicked off with the just-released *Tracks* song "My Love Will Not Let You Down," and made set pieces from songs never played by the E Street Band, including "Youngstown," "Murder Incorporated," "If I Should Fall Behind," and the instant classic "Land of Hope and Dreams."

years earlier during the reunion tour, when a concerted effort by hard-line fans (rallied for the first time by Internet fan sites) tried to compel Bruce to play "Rosalita," the one beloved classic he had made a point of not performing on the tour.

Back then the "fuckin' signs," as he called them, aggravated him so much that the one time he did play "Rosalita," at the end of the fifteen-night stand in the Continental Airlines Arena, it was because he *didn't* see any "Rosalita" signs in the crowd. Bruce did a 180 on the signs during the Magic tour in 2008, and made a ritual of calling for them to be passed forward to the stage, where he could sift through the requests and pull out the ones he liked. He became particularly fond of the requests for obscure and/or just plain odd non–E Street oldies, which led to a recurring feature he called Stump the Band. Anything could happen, given the right sign. One night, ZZ Top's "I'm Bad, I'm Nationwide." The next, ? and the Mysterians' "96 Tears." Or maybe the Troggs' "Wild Thing," the Kinks' "You Really Got Me." Or how about a "Hava Nagila"–"Blinded by the Light" medley?

When the tour went into its final leg in the fall of 2009, Bruce began a series of full-album shows, during which he and the band would perform one of his most beloved albums from start to finish. Starting with a complete *Born to Run* in Chicago, they repeated the performance at Giants Stadium, following at the same venue with shows featuring *Darkness on the Edge of Town* and *Born in the U.S.A.* When they got back to New York after a short sweep of Midwestern and East Coast arenas (which included several *Born to Run* shows), they lit up their Madison Square Garden shows with song-by-song re-creations of *The Wild, the Innocent & the E Street Shuffle* (with Richard Blackwell playing his original conga part from "New York City Serenade") and then a full playing of the two-disc *The River*. A few more *Born to Run* shows followed, but Bruce saved the tour's last concert—an arena show in Buffalo—for the full performance of his debut record, *Greetings from Asbury Park, N.J.* With Mike Appel along in the airplane and then backstage, Bruce pulled his ex-manager into the preshow band circle and called out to every person in the ring— Clemons, Tallent, Appel, and Van Zandt, and the absent Federici and Vini Lopez—who had helped him get into that first recording studio and then so far beyond. Onstage Bruce dedicated the show to his ex-manager. "*This* is the miracle," he said. "This is the record that took everything from *waaay* below zero to, uh, to *one*." He reminisced about John Hammond and the audition he'd earned thanks only to Appel's insistence. "So tonight I'd like to dedicate this to the man who got me through the door. Mike Appel's here tonight. Mike, this is for you." That tumbling guitar riff kicked off "Blinded by the Light," and off they went, back to his tentative first steps in the big-time music industry and on the road that had led them so far.

When they got to "Growin' Up," and the spot in the middle where the music had always hushed in order for Bruce to tell one of his shaggy dog tales about the birth of the band, he put on his dreamiest voice and began with what has to be the archetypical opening line of every band story he'd ever told.

"There I was . . . it was a stormy, stormy night in Asbury Park, New Jersey . . ."

The audience roared happily.

"A Nor'easter was blowing in, rattling all the lampposts and washing Kingsley Avenue clean. And me and Steve were in a little club down the south end of town. When suddenly the door lifted open and blew off down the street. And a large shadow of a man stepped in. I looked. King Curtis? King Curtis has come out of my dreams and landed right here! No! Jr. Walker! He walked to the stage and—"

Clemons, his eyes hard and face blank, stepped to Bruce's microphone and spoke in his most sinister baritone.

"I wanna play witchoo."

Bruce cracked up.

"What could I say? I said, sure! And he put the saxophone to his mouth, and I heard . . ."

Clemons played a pretty little riff.

"Something as coooool as a river."

Clemons let loose a snarling run up the blues scale.

"Then I heard a force of nature coming out. And at the end of the night, we just looked at each other and went—"

The two men faced each other, gazed into each other's eyes for a long moment, and then nodded slowly in perfect unison. Clemons turned to face the crowd, put his saxophone to his mouth, and hunkered down low enough for Bruce—Telecaster against his waist—to lean against his shoulder in the iconic *Born to Run* pose.

"So we got in the car, a *loooong* Cadillac. Drove through the woods at the outskirts of town. And we got very sleepy. And we fell into this long, long, long, long dream. An' when we woke up . . ."

Bruce paused, the crowd straining to hear what would come next.

"We were in fuckin' Buffalo, New York."

An avalanche of drums, and the song burst into its final verse, pushing Bruce right into that old parked car with the keys to the universe dangling from its ignition.

Three weeks later Bruce reconvened the surviving members of the 1978-era band—Bittan, Clemons, Tallent, Van Zandt, and Weinberg, with Giordano subbing for Federici—to perform all of *Darkness on the Edge of Town* in Asbury Park's beachside Paramount Theater. The house dark and empty, save for documentarian Thom Zimny and his film crew, Bruce and the band played the songs without regard for their future audience, their eyes on one another, their bodies given over to the rhythm and the music. Shot by Zimny with virtually all of the color washed out of the shot, Bruce and the band seemed lost to time. Still squaring off to fight their way off the boardwalk, out of town, and onto the western highway. As if they hadn't already been there and back a hundred times. As if the years had done nothing to shake their bond or weaken their belief in the music.

The *Darkness* box set, released in 2010, came five years after the multidisc commemoration of *Born to Run*'s thirtieth anniversary. Both included a remastered version of the original album, along with bonus CDs and documentaries directed by Thom Zimny, Bruce's go-to documentarian since 2000. The *BTR* package included a full-length video of the notorious Hammersmith Odeon show from 1975, while the *Darkness* box included a 1978 show filmed in Houston and, to the endless joy of Van Zandt, a two-disc set of the sixties-pop-inspired songs Bruce had written and recorded, only to toss aside. "Thank God he finally put 'em out!" Van Zandt says. "That's his highest evolution, and he takes it completely for granted."[8] As if to show he still had it in him, Bruce took the bones of "Save My Love," an unused song seen in a filmed 1976 rehearsal Zimny included in his documentary film about *Darkness*, finished the lyrics, and got the *Darkness*-era band (plus Giordano) into his home studio to record it like they used to do: all in the same studio at the same time, playing it exactly as they had when they were skinny, frizzy-haired kids on a hot summer afternoon, making a big noise in Bruce's basement rec room.

With no tour planned for 2011, Bruce made a few talk show appearances,[9] then in early December got the *Darkness* band together to play a handful of the unearthed songs in the Carousel House just off the Asbury Park boardwalk. Playing for a small invited crowd and Zimny's cameras (which would capture the performance for an edited Internet broadcast a few days later), the band—enhanced by the Miami Horns and violinist David Lindley, who had played on some of the original sessions—seemed a bit stiff. Blame the winter chill in the unheated Carousel House, the year of not playing together, the crowding of the cameras. But also note the flatness of Bruce's performance. And when he throws it to Clemons for his big solo in "Gotta Get That Feeling," moving right over to cheer him on and maybe bump shoulders, Bruce finds him on his stool, his eyes hidden behind thick glasses, and his entire being focused on hitting notes he once played while stalking the stage like a colossus.

Back in his Florida penthouse, Clemons was in his living room, rolling the shades up after previewing his documentary, *Who Do I Think I Am?*, about the spiritual evolution he experienced traveling through Asia,

---

[8] Van Zandt continues: "My favorite song ever is 'The Little Things (My Baby Does).' Why? Because it's *perfect*. Everything is right about it. You hear how the guitar and piano answer the vocals, and the level for once is pretty close to right. And the whole arrangement, the sensibility, is the greatest thing ever."

[9] Including a visit to Jimmy Fallon's iteration of NBC's *Late Night*, where Bruce performed "Save My Love" with Bittan, Van Zandt, and the show's house band, the Roots, and also participated in a remarkable skit during which he donned his old *Born to Run*–era clothes (and curly brown wig) to perform Willow Smith's lighter-than-fairy-floss hit "Whip My Hair" with ace Neil Young impersonator Fallon accompanying him on acoustic guitar and yearning high tenor vocals.

where no one knew or cared about his fame and achievements in the Western world. Now it was about to be screened at a couple of festivals. He had a lot going on. Clemons played some sessions with pop sensation Lady Gaga a few weeks earlier and found the experience thrilling.

"When I asked her what she wanted, she just said, 'Just be Clarence Clemons. Play what you want, be who you are. I'm gonna drop the needle, and you go.'" The memory opened a smile. "So that's what I did, and she loved it. That was very cool. Something I hadn't experienced in a long time, not since Bruce's first albums. Sit down to play, and just play. It reminded me of why I love being a musician and doing what I do." Now she wanted him to be in her videos and accompany her to *American Idol* for her performance on the series's season finale.

He had one foot in ecstasy and the other planted in irritation. Bruce is in the Rock and Roll Hall of Fame, and deservedly so. But what about the E Street Band? Didn't they have something to do with that big, and always distinctive, noise that made Bruce so beloved? "What the fuck are we, chopped liver? I've gotta go to jail because of the band but still don't end up in the Hall of Fame." The Big Man was clearly pissed, but then he shrugged and his smile returned. "The thing is, now they have a saxophone of mine in the Hall of Fame. My manager at the time told me it'd be a good idea to let 'em have that. But *I'm* still not in there. My fuckin' *saxophone* is in there, but I'm not. And I'm the one who fuckin' *played* it. So my sax is in the Hall of Fame, my ass is on the cover of *Born to Run*, and here we are. Oh man!"

Victoria Clemons called the paramedics at about three o'clock on the morning of June 12. Clemons had suffered a serious stroke. The surgeons did what they could to seal the blood leak in his brain, to mend the artery and relieve whatever swelling or damage it created. When Bruce got the news in France, where he and Patti were celebrating their twentieth wedding anniversary, he flew immediately to Palm Beach, with Patti and the rest of the band in close pursuit. The official diagnosis made clear that Clemons was seriously ill, with significant paralysis on his right side. Still, the next hours and days seemed promising. By Tuesday, reports had him conscious and in stable condition. "Miracles are happening!" one unidentified friend told the *Backstreets* fanzine website. Friends and family got another message: get here fast.

Clemons's condition grew worse; then his brain function collapsed entirely. Realizing that his body no longer contained his soul, the Clemons family chose Saturday, June 18, to allow his body to take its leave. When the machines switched off, Bruce brought his guitar to the room and sat close for the next three hours, singing and playing with the Clemons family, giving witness to his friend's departure and, perhaps, on some level, easing his journey. "I'll miss my friend, his sax, the force of nature his sound was, his glory, his foolishness, his accomplishments, his face, his hands, his humor, his skin, his noise, his confusion, his power, his peace . . ." Bruce said in his eulogy.

> But his love and his story, the story that he gave me, that he whispered in my ear, that he allowed me to tell . . . and that he gave to you . . . is gonna carry on. I'm no mystic, but the undertow, the mystery and power of Clarence and my friendship, leads me to believe we must have stood together in other, older times, along other rivers, in other cities, in other fields, doing our modest version of God's work . . . work that's still unfinished. So I won't say good-bye to my brother. I'll simply say, "See you in the next life, further on up the road, where we will once again pick up that work, and get it done."

TWENTY-SEVEN

THE NEXT STAND OF TREES

A FEW TICKS AFTER TWELVE NOON on March 15, 2012, Roland Swenson, the executive director of the South by Southwest indie music festival in Austin, Texas, got the day's festivities started with a worshipful introduction of the keynote speaker. Uncompromising artistry, he said. Wild energy, unwavering commitment to righteousness and the determination to "give it all he's got, without hesitation, every time he steps on the stage." And with that, Bruce Springsteen came clomping out to the lectern, pulled a few wrinkled yellow legal sheets out of his jeans pocket, and gazed across the convention hall crowd.

"How can we be up this early in the fucking morning?" That was his hello. "How important can this speech be if we're giving it at noon? Every decent musician in town is asleep. Or they will be before I'm done with this thing, I guarantee you."

It wasn't a sleepy kind of speech. Leaning crookedly against the podium and kicking his right foot against the stage floor, Bruce channeled his scrawled notes about music and life into the jazzy rhythms of a beat poet. "Doo-wop!" he chanted. "The most sensual music ever made! The sound of raw sex. Of silk stockings rustling against leather upholstery, the sound of bras popping open all across the USA. Of wonderful lies being whispered into Tabu-perfumed ears. The sound of smeared lipstick, un-tucked shirts, running mascara, tears on your pillow, secrets whispered in the still of the night, the high school bleachers in the dark at the YMCA canteen. The soundtrack for your incredibly wonderful, blue-balled, limp-your-ass walk back home after the dance. Oh! It hurt so good."

Ignore the temptation to draw lines, make rules, and dismiss anyone offering another way of doing things, he said. "Purity of human expres-sion and experience is not confined to guitars, to tubes, to turntables, to microchips. There is no right way, no pure way, of doing it. There's just doing it." Talking directly to the musicians in the audience, the ones still sleeping off whatever SXSW hijinks they'd been up to the previous night and all the others in the world, Bruce projected his own internal experi-ence into a universal code of being.

> Don't take yourself too seriously. Take yourself as seriously as death itself. Don't worry. Worry your ass off. Have iron-clad confidence, but doubt. It keeps you awake and alert. Believe you are the baddest ass in town—and [that] you suck! It keeps you honest. Be able to keep two completely contradictory ideals alive and well inside of your heart and head at all times. If it doesn't drive you crazy, it will make you strong. And when you walk on stage tonight to bring the noise, treat it like it's all we have—and then remember it's only rock 'n' roll.

Nine hours later at Austin's Moody Theater, Bruce delivered the same speech in musical terms. Starting with an acoustic, chorale-of-singers cover of Woody Guthrie's "I Ain't Got No Home," the nearly three-hour show moved easily from the folk-rock-soul of his just-released (and cur-rently chart-topping) album, *Wrecking Ball,* to the boardwalk R&B of "The E Street Shuffle," to the dust-and-grease visions of "The Promised Land" and "Badlands" and beyond. Rage Against the Machine's Tom Morello, the very image of thrash-and-scream musical anarchy, added vocals and guitar screams to the live arrangement of "The Ghost of Tom Joad," and the pair of *Wrecking Ball* songs he played on. Then the encores ranged even further, with collaborations with reggae hero Jimmy Cliff ("The Harder They Come," "Time Will Tell," and "Many Rivers to Cross"); old-school British Invasion with the Animals' Eric Burdon ("We Gotta Get Out of This Place")[1]; then a stage-filling "This Land Is Your Land" sing-along, with all of the above, the night's first two artists (the Low Anthem and Alejandro Escovedo), Garland Jeffreys, and members of reigning indie-rock heroes the Arcade Fire.

Bruce's apparent mission, to establish his credentials and ongoing artistic vitality with the younger generation(s), proved enormously successful. From the festival's Austin Convention Center headquarters, up to the beer-stained clubs on Austin's Sixth Street, and out to the weird old roadhouses on the far side of the freeway, the roughnecks agreed with the city punks who agreed with the geek bloggers: the man could put on a show. "One of the most stirring and inspiring shows in SXSW history," Dennis Shin wrote on PopMatters. Josh Modell, writing in the Onion A.V. Club, described his reaction like this: "I'd never seen Springsteen live before, though of course I'd heard the stories about him and the E Street Band . . . it was, as expected, an incredible experience."

Fifteen months earlier, in late 2010, Bruce called Ron Aniello, a producer-arranger who Toby Scott and Brendan O'Brien had recommended (and who had worked on Patti's record, *Play It as It Lays*), asking if he could help finish some tracks he'd been working on. As Aniello remembers, the thirty or forty unfinished tracks sounded like nothing Bruce had ever done. "It's stunning, really. Like Aaron Copland, the American landscape style. Soft and deep and open sky. There's definitely a story going, but it's different. Just gentle and beautiful, gorgeous, and so disarming." Aniello wrote a symphonic arrangement for one of the songs and worked with

---

[1] Bruce had rhapsodized over Burdon and the Animals at his keynote speech, only to learn that Burdon himself was in Austin that very day. Invited to perform at the show, Burdon popped by the sound check, spent fifteen minutes with the band, and then nailed the song during the encore. "He's still got that hard-ass sound," Bruce told me the next day.

Bruce for the next few months creating similar treatments for a handful of the other tracks. They worked steadily until Valentine's Day 2011, when Bruce interrupted one of Aniello's work sessions to play him a song he'd written while running errands that afternoon. Bruce picked up an acoustic guitar, Aniello set up a microphone, and three and a half minutes later they had a rough demo for "Easy Money," a front-porch-style three-chord stomper sung in the voice of a stickup man who finds inspiration in Wall Street traders and bankers. Bruce came with another new song the next morning, and when they played back the rough demo for "We Take Care of Our Own" a few minutes later, he looked up at Aniello. "This day is gonna change your life," he said.

Jon Landau drove down from New York to take a listen. First came the ten orchestrated songs and then the two demos they made in the last few days. The newer songs changed the expression on the manager's face. "Rock 'n' roll is back!" said Landau when "Easy Money" finished playing. Bruce and Landau went off to talk, and when they returned ninety minutes later, Bruce greeted Aniello with a hug. Now they were definitely making a full album. "And you're the producer," Landau said. Wondering aloud how they would find a union between the orchestrated songs and the snarly rock 'n' roll, Landau shook off Aniello's question. "Forget it. Bruce will write a new record. It starts with 'Easy Money.'" Bruce came into the studio armed with new songs every morning for the next two weeks. "I thought, 'This is what it's like to work with a genius,'" says Aniello, who soon suspected that he would never be able to keep up. "I thought, 'He's killing me. He's going to need *three* producers.'" Bruce insisted it was no big deal. "I'm a craftsman," he told Aniello. "You give me the shovel, and I keep digging until I find what we're after."

Eight months later, Bruce drove a visitor up the dirt road to the recording studio that serves as the center of his musical world. It was late October. The album was all but finished, with only a final mix left to do. According to Landau, this afternoon would mark the first time Bruce played the new music to someone outside his immediate circle. This prospect was both exciting for the artist and, it was said, nerve wracking. Climbing out of his Jeep, Bruce did seem more pensive than he'd been earlier that day, but coming off of a sleepless night[2] plus a long afternoon of talking, he was also pretty bushed. Still, he pushed through the door while explaining how the wood-and-glass building—the first real studio he'd ever owned—had been constructed under Patti's aegis. The entry area leads directly onto the studio floor, which is open and airy, with the control board at one end and a music-store-sized collection of instruments—digital and vintage keyboards, basses, a drum set, scattered percussion instruments, walls hung with black cords, microphones, effects pedals, and a big array of electric, acoustic, and pedal-steel guitars[3] stationed throughout. The sitting area back by the front door has a couch, a few comfy chairs, and a coffee table centered by a new boxed edition of Robert Frank's *The Americans*, the collection of stark photographs that inspired so much of *Darkness on the Edge of Town*.

Bruce led the way to the control board, introduced Rob, one of his engineers, and gestured to the two other chairs at the desk, both set with a neat stack of typed lyrics in front of them. When Rob had the first song cued up, Bruce turned to his guest. "One thing I have to apologize for in advance: musicians like to hear their music loud." The pile-driver-and-siren opening to "We Take Care of Our Own" thundered from the speakers, and Bruce sat back in his chair and nodded along to the backbeat.

---

[2] Bruce had spent the previous evening watching the St. Louis Cardinals pull out an improbable eleventh-inning win over the favored Texas Rangers in the World Series. Too thrilled to sleep, Bruce had been up for hours afterward, toasting the underdogs. Asked if some portion of his joy came from watching a team so closely allied to (former owner) George W. Bush crumble, Bruce grinned. "Exactly," he said.

[3] For a guy whose life has revolved around guitars, Bruce has almost no interest in collectible or exotic instruments. "I was never a guitar aficionado," he says. "I'm not an audio freak. I don't pay much attention to equipment. My goal is very simple: to play something that worked and to hear something that I liked." Beyond the one legendary Telecaster-Esquire mutt, all of his guitars are interchangeable. Most of his electrics come in as stock reissues of 1950s era Telecasters (with some Mustangs and other models thrown in), only to be stripped apart and rebuilt by guitar tech Kevin Buell, who does God only knows what to the wiring and electronics, and then goes at the body and neck to make it look and feel like a lovingly worn-in axe. If there's one exception beyond the Esquire/Telecaster to the interchangeable-guitars rule, it's the acoustic sunburst Gibson J-45 Toby Scott gave him for Christmas in 1987.

He gazed into the middle distance, occasionally tilting his head and then launching forward to adjust a knob. Other times he leaned back in his chair and closed his eyes. But just when it seemed Bruce had dozed off, he bolted up to push another knob a fraction of an inch. When the songs ended, Bruce accepted compliments with a grin and led the way back to his car for the drive home.

Bruce talked a lot about the new album over the next few days. Almost every subject led back to some aspect of the songs and their production, as if he'd taken every experience and thought he'd had in the last year or two and invested it into words, chords, beats, and melodies. Earlier that summer, Landau described the record as a summary, or perhaps a modern iteration, of themes Bruce had explored throughout his career. "I'm always looking for new ways to tell the story that I'm interested in," Bruce says. "The point is, you come back and keep coming back until people hear you. That's the point. You have to find new ways to tell it, you have to find deeper and different levels in it." As an artist fixated on the intimate stories of ordinary folks whose labors make wealthier mens' dreams come true, the early twenty-first century offered nothing but inspiration. "People went for the easy money," he said over pizza in Freehold. "Tore the whole thing down. Didn't care about you or themselves, really." He talked about the America he'd been raised to believe in, the one he described in one song as a place where "Nobody crowds ya / Nobody goes it alone."[4] "And if you throw that away, or spit on that, you're throwing *all* of this away." He gestured past the walls to the country beyond. "And if you do that, that should be addressed, and there should be some outrage."

The songs did not stint on outrage. The drums on "We Take Care of Our Own" led the charge against the ones who looked the other way when New Orleans drowned, whose good hearts had hardened into stone. "Easy Money" described the financiers in the terms of a petty thief with a .38 tucked in his waistband. "Jack of All Trades" and "Death to My Hometown" told the story from the workers' perspective, while "Rocky Ground" and "We Are Alive" spun today's struggles into an entire history

[4] "Long Walk Home," from *Magic*, 2007.

of bad times. And the confusion and heartbreak didn't begin or end in the political or socioeconomic tides. The death of Clarence Clemons, four months into the process, left Bruce as wrung out as a ghost, forced to contemplate a future without the man whose spirit had somehow made his own burn brighter and loom larger. No surprise, perhaps, that the funereal "This Depression" brooded on a helplessness that sounded more psychological than economic. "I haven't always been strong, but never felt so weak," the narrator intones, "All of my prayers, gone for nothing."

The music spun into a distinctively new kind of rhythmic folk-and-funk, as redolent of his ancestor Ann Garrity's Ireland as of cyberspace, of Harlem's gospel churches as of the Jersey Shore and Preservation Hall in New Orleans. When a familiar saxophone blared from the studio speakers the day before in the midst of the new recording of "Land of Hope and Dreams," Bruce cuffed his visitor and shouted over the music. "C's last solo!" Asked later when Clemons had recorded his part, Bruce added a little more detail. "That was a combination of some things he recorded, you know. He played it live often, so we were able to use some of that. And that meant a lot to me, this sort of, *'Yeah! That's the song, that's the solo.'*" What anyone would think of it—or of the entire album, for that matter—was still unclear. "It's going to be interesting," he said, goosing his Jeep down a dark country road a few miles outside Red Bank. "It's very different, and I know it's a lot to take in during one listen, but I wanted to give you an idea of what I've got my hands in next. It connects to *The River*, and *Tom Joad*, and *Darkness*. Thematically it connects to a lot of my music in my past. But now we're headed to the next stand of trees."

Four months later, Bruce and the E Street Band—Steve Van Zandt, Garry Tallent, Roy Bittan, Max Weinberg, Nils Lofgren, and Patti Scialfa, with Charles Giordano on organ, Soozie Tyrell on fiddle, a five-piece horn section, singers Cindy Mizelle, Curtis King, and Michelle Moore, and Everett Bradley on percussion and vocals—have set up on the stage of the bomb shelter–like Expo Theater in the middle of Fort Monmouth, a disused military base near Tinton Falls, New Jersey. The day's rehearsal started late due to the designer who came to fit the musicians for the coming Grammy Awards, so Bruce took a seat in the house to wait. He talked a bit about Jake Clemons, a nephew of Clarence who would share saxophone duties with Jersey Shore veteran Eddie Manion.[5] At first it wasn't clear how visible a presence Jake would have beyond the horn line's place at the left rear of the stage. But when it became clear that his intonation and feel for the instrument, along with his bushy-haired charisma, were every bit as striking as his uncle's, Bruce felt a kind of inevitability taking hold. "Another great sax player from the same family?" he said. "What are the odds?"[6]

Dressed in a white T-shirt, black trousers, and black boots, Bruce started the session by striding to the center of the stage, announcing "Okay, everyone man your stations!" into his microphone, and accepting one of his blond Telecasters from Kevin Buell. When the musicians and singers were in place, he counted off "We Take Care of Our Own," the ending of which segued into "Wrecking Ball," which erupted into "Badlands" and then "Death to My Hometown." Some songs went more smoothly than others. Nils Lofgren dropped a few vocal cues, Max Weinberg forgot a key drum fill—earning a swivel of Bruce's head and a loud gale of teasing laughter. When the horn section sat mutely during what was supposed to be a charted riff, Bruce shot Manion a look and laughed again. "Gotta figure that spot out, gents!" he called after the song ended. Bruce constructs his shows in modular fashion, with minisuites of songs blending into distinct moods or themes that feed into the larger thrust of the show. The rehearsal broke between each setlet, and as they got back to it, stage moves started to emerge. Lofgren did a few of his spins; Bruce jumped on his monitors to lock in with Weinberg, and then did a few jumps to emphasize shifts in rhythm and mood. By the end of the second

---

[5] Manion led trombonist Clark Gayton, trumpeters Curt Ramm and Barry Danielian, and another young saxophonist whose last name seemed oddly familiar.

[6] As Jake described it a few weeks later, the story is nearly as fairy tale–like as his uncle's door-smashing entrance into the band. Born into a musical family (his father was also a performing musician, his chops honed as a Marine Corps band director), Jake traced his obsession for the sax to the night he saw his uncle perform on the Tunnel of Love tour in 1988. A fine guitarist and songwriter in his own right, Jake came with years of experience as a bandleader and journeyman saxophonist. Nearly as imposing as Clarence, with his own kind of magnetism, Jake filled his uncle's place in the band by being his own soft-spoken self.

setlet, he was drenched in sweat. "Very good! Great! Terrific!" he called into the microphone. "Yeah, yeah, yeah!"

When the afternoon ended, Landau huddled with Bruce onstage, prompting quick revisions to the harmonies and piano riff on "We Take Care of Our Own." Bruce fairly skipped offstage, but when he returned a half hour later, his face was blank and his body seemed to droop. "Same time, same place tomorrow," he said to me. But his voice sounded empty. An hour later, Landau called to explain. In his dressing room, Bruce had learned that a close friend, just forty years old, had unexpectedly died. Bruce was devastated, and feeling far too vulnerable to have a guest at the next day's rehearsal. He would get in touch the next afternoon. Bruce did exactly that, apologizing for the change in plans, saying he'd come by in a half hour. Why he felt more comfortable being interviewed than having an observer at rehearsal is as intriguing as it is hard to figure. But true to his word, Bruce walked into the hotel bar on schedule, ready to tell more stories about his life, work, and glorious career.

After the interview ended, he sipped his beer and talked about the friend he had just lost. He'd come from a tough background and, like Bruce, hadn't had the benefit of a good education. But he'd worked his way up to owning a business and settling into the life of husband and father. Bruce had lived his own version of that life, too, and hoped to give his friend a helping hand on his way to a better life. But now that the darkest kind of fate had stepped up, all Bruce, or anyone else, could do was try to absorb the blow. In the silence that followed, he did not look like a cultural icon or even a rock 'n' roll star. He looked like one of his own characters. Strong but sad and a little crumpled around the edges.

Bruce has wrestled with his moods, and a psyche genetically prone to extremes, for most of his adult life. Decades of psychotherapy helped reveal and cast light on some of his most primal traumas and conflicts, but his raw moods, and occasional descents into full-blown depression, never quite went away. "You go through periods of being good, then something stimulates it," he says. "The clock, some memory. You never know. The mind wants to link all your feelings to a cause. I'm feeling *that* because I'm doing *this*, or because *that* happened."

Eventually Bruce realized that his worst moods had nothing to do with what was actually taking place in his life. Awful, stressful things could happen—conflicts, stress, disappointments, death—and he'd be unflappable. Then things would be peaceful and easy and he'd find himself on his knees. "You're going along fine, and then boom, it hits you. Things that just come from way down in the well. Completely noncausal, but it's part of your DNA, part of the way your body cycles."

Not long after the end of the Rising tour in 2003 Bruce started taking antidepressants. Within days he felt like a shroud had been lifted from his shoulders. "It was like, get me this stuff *now*, and keep it coming," he recalls. Almost always a prolific writer, now Bruce not only composed and recorded a flood of material but also released it. *Devils & Dust*, the multidisc *Born to Run* box set, *We Shall Overcome (The Seeger Sessions)*, *Live in Dublin* (a double live set with the Seeger Sessions band), *Magic*, the *Magic Tour Highlights* video/music EP, and then *Working on a Dream*, along with four world tours, emerged between 2005 and 2009, making those years the most productive in his career, by far.

And yet Bruce knows his particular brain chemistry will never leave him completely in the clear. "You manage it, you learn and evolve, but another recognition you gotta have is that these are the cards you were dealt," he says. "These things are never going to be out of your life. You gotta be constantly vigilant and realistic about these things."

The release of the new album, titled *Wrecking Ball*, kicked up a satisfying fuss in early March 2012, greeted with reviews that were mostly positive, if not quite the tsunami of veneration that swept his earliest albums to such lasting heights.[7] The lead single, "We Take Care of Our Own," inspired more talk than anything Bruce had released since "The Rising." The band's show-opening appearance at the Grammy Awards made more

---

[7] A surprising number of the bad reviews, particularly those of Jon Caramanica in the *New York Times* and Jesse Cataldo in *Slant* magazine, asserted that "We Take Care of Our Own" was intended as a "jingoistic" (as both Cataldo and Caramanica called it) celebration of the American spirit rather than the bitter criticism of those who had violated it that it actually was. Given the fury in the song's verses, and the striking references to the botched rescue of post-Katrina New Orleans, the critics may have benefited from giving the songs a closer listen.

news, while the debut of the new, Clarence-less E Street Band—in a special concert at Harlem's soul music palace, the Apollo Theater, simulcast by SiriusXM Satellite Radio—extended the group's reputation into another decade. Meanwhile, *Wrecking Ball* shot to the top of the charts in fifteen countries, including the United States.

The afternoon of the official tour opener in Atlanta on March 18, Bruce led the band through portions of a few songs, focusing mostly on the transitions from one tune to the next. Between songs, he looked around the stage for a moment, and then stepped to his microphone and summoned one of his crew members with Mighty Oz–ian volume. "Light man, come forth! I have an idea." The guy ran in from his board at the center of the arena floor and took note of Bruce's direction, retreating as Bruce counted off the relevant part of the song, looking for the stage lights to follow the new cue. When it didn't happen, he held up a hand and called again into the mike, "C'mon, I just wanna entertain my fuckin' self up here!" Another count-off. The band fired up, the lights did not, and when Bruce stopped the music, he wasn't kidding at all. "Okay, I want someone to come down *now* to fuckin' explain this." He stalked to the front of the stage and hunkered down on his haunches, counting the seconds until a man with a clipboard sprinted up to explain the lapse.[8] Hardly the worst meltdown in rock 'n' roll history, but disconcerting nonetheless. The Bruce in your head, given shape by so many books, magazine profiles, tales of regular-guy benevolence, and his own musical meditations on right and wrong, doesn't do that kind of thing.

Except of course he does. He can be selfless and selfish in equal measures. If you're in crisis, he'll drop everything to help make it right and then stay at your side until it is. But on another day, he's just as liable to not care that you promised to pick up the kid at school in fifteen minutes. "Not my problem. I need you here." "When you're in your kitchen, you know there's a stove and a pot to boil water in," longtime engineer Toby Scott says. "For Bruce, the studio is his kitchen, and I'm part of the furniture. So he needs to know I'll be there, ready to work, when he's

---

[8] In a nutshell: the effect Bruce wanted depended on one of the venue's own spotlight operators, and he wouldn't report for the show for another couple of hours.

ready to go." Most often Bruce is more even-keeled than he seemed in Atlanta. But not all the time, and woe to anyone who can't read his mood.
Particularly in a high-stress performance situation. Not just because he's
more than a little narcissistic, but also because Bruce is so committed to
the idea that music, particularly his music, really does have the power
to change lives. To be in the position to possibly do that is both a high
privilege and nearly impossible burden. "Tonight I'm the custodian of all
those people's feelings and memories," he said in Atlanta. "That's my responsibility. There are so many things I have to honor. This has been the
most complicated stretch of the band's life, this past year or so. And the E
Street Band is a purpose-based organization, you know."

The arena house lights went dark just after eight o'clock and the band
came out in darkness, each member finding his or her place in the murky
light. When the floor lights came up behind him, the backlit Bruce rose
bigger than life, holding for a moment before the pounding intro to "We
Take Care of Our Own" hoisted the arena crowd to their feet and kept
them up there, marveling at the sight of a man whose black boots seemed
as rooted in American history as in their own record collections and pop
culture memories.

The concrete walls shook even harder two and a half hours later when
Bruce and his extra large E Street Band draped the entire hall in the
gospel vision of thundering to the promised land with a load of saints,
sinners, losers, winners, whores, gamblers, and sweet souls. Then came
"Born to Run," with the house lights on full, connecting the front of
the stage to the back of the hall, everyone up and dancing to the sound
of their own adolescent rebellion; then "Dancing in the Dark"; then the
immigrant Irish folk rock of "American Land"; and finally, "Tenth Avenue Freeze-Out," the story of Scooter and the Big Man, of Bruce and
the E Street Band, of rock 'n' roll and everyone who ever heard their own
thoughts, dreams, and heartbreak coming through the front of a radio.
It's probably trite to point out that tears flowed across faces that night.
Maybe it had less to do with Bruce (and his light cues) than the memories of vanished times, friends, lovers, and strong, agile hearts. Or maybe
some fragile vision of what life could still bring. Or perhaps it really did
come down to that guy up there, the guitar-wielding, boot-stomping

sixty-two-year-old as proof that Thunder Road is still out there, still leading the way to the place we really want to go.

Focus on that, and everything else makes sense. Which is why tour director George Travis[9] makes certain that every new crew member, or a down-in-the-dumps veteran, walks with him to the back of the arena in midshow. Standing there, he tells them all the same thing: that between them and Bruce stand x thousand people. Among them, a small but important segment will go home with something that will be with them for their entire lives. It could be the buddies who experience something together. It could be the guy who chose this night and place to propose to his girlfriend. Being a part of this with Bruce makes you a part of what made that happen, Travis tells them. "And I want all the guys who work with me to take that into account," he says. "That's what makes their job, no matter what it is, important."

He's describing the same feeling that inspired Tinker West to open his surfboard factory to the quartet of hairy boardwalk freaks in 1969, and then invest his time and money in building them a sound system and driving them up and down the Eastern Seaboard and all the way across the United States. That compelled Mike Appel and Jim Cretecos to drop everything and stake their lives on this skinny New Jersey kid; that inspired those Columbia executives to grab their bosses by the lapels and insist they keep him on the label's roster. That sent an emotionally reeling Jon Landau to his typewriter to risk his own reputation by designating a virtual unknown the living future of rock 'n' roll. When he hears the word *apostle* used to describe the first generations of Bruce's supporters Jon Landau grins. "You know what that makes me, don't you?" he jokes. "I'm Paul."

Landau has made a life, career, and thriving industry out of Bruce and his music. Known widely as one of the best, and toughest, managers in popular music, the former critic is both a fierce defender of his main

[9] Whose ability to keep the show running smoothly in very unsmooth circumstances, along with his preternatural ability to produce, say, twenty-five cups of hot coffee and pieces of pie, all on china with nice silverware, at two in the morning in response to someone else's spontaneous joke, have long made him legendary throughout the music industry.

client's life and work, and also a canny packager of his music work and its ancillary products. His understanding of, and advocacy for, Bruce's creative vision helped ease the artist's resistance to large halls, hit singles, promotion, stadiums, and the superstardom he secretly craved, while still encouraging the less commercial instincts that created *Nebraska, The Ghost of Tom Joad,* and more experimental works. As the music industry grew, evolved, fell apart, and became something else entirely, Landau (with partner Barbara Carr contributing ideas, projects, and occasional tough-cop exterior) kept the Springsteen industry in high cotton, using Bruce's peerless legacy to keep interest in his new work at a far higher level than most artists of his generation can summon. Bruce's own abilities, personality, and unceasing creative drive gave the manager plenty to work with, just as Landau's planning and strict negotiating enhanced the musician's image and kept it afloat, and sometimes at the fore of the cultural mainstream. The screwups along the way, particularly an ill-considered deal to allow the corporate imperialist Walmart to market a greatest-hits collection under its own imprint, were most notable for their rarity.

"If Jon is not the best manager in my time in the business, he's certainly tied for it," says Danny Goldberg, who has run record labels and managed the careers of Nirvana, Tom Morello, Bonnie Raitt, and many others. "But there's no question in my mind that if Jon hadn't existed, then Bruce would have found somebody else and . . . still would have been Bruce Springsteen." Landau says he sees it like that too. "My life has been so incredibly benefited by our friendship and working relationship, I couldn't adequately put that into words," he says. "I think when the dust is settled, to me he's a great man. He's done great things, he has a great heart and a great mind, and having a chance to make my contribution to the overall project, the thrill of a lifetime." [10]

It's hard to imagine Landau leaving, or being asked to leave, Bruce's organization. But others have cycled in and out, some leaving for new jobs and opportunities made possible by their association with him.

---

[10] "I sure use the word 'great' a lot when I'm talking about Bruce, don't I?" he adds a bit sheepishly.

Others stuck around for decades with no intention of going anywhere. Engineer Toby Scott is well past the thirty-year mark, while George Travis has nearly thirty-five years under his belt, and some of his staffers have been around even longer than that. The E Street Band tells the same story: with Steve Van Zandt back in the fold, no member has left voluntarily since David Sancious and "Boom" Carter quit in 1974. Many of the longtime employees who left for reasons beyond their own describe the departure in the terms of a romantic breakup, or even a death. The lighting designer Marc Brickman says his 1984 departure (a subject that still makes everyone involved visibly uncomfortable) as being far more emotionally devastating than any of his actual divorces. Chuck Plotkin, who mixed and then coproduced Bruce's music for nearly twenty-five years, left under more collegial circumstances, but he still gets teary eyed when he talks about the day Bruce told him he needed to work with new producers for a while. "I miss it," Plotkin says. "I miss him. There were hours and hours, days, weeks, months, years when we spent time together, and I miss that, and it's sad. And there is the dimension of the work: the meaningfulness of the work. And I miss being involved in something as meaningful to me as that."

Bruce was back in Freehold, standing on the sidewalk in front of the small but well-tended house his aunt Dora Kirby has lived in for more than fifty years. On this patch of McLean Street, he was fifty yards from the spot where the door of 87 Randolph Street once stood, and within sight of the corner where young Virginia Springsteen's tricycle veered onto the macadam that spring afternoon in 1927. When he walked around to the kitchen door, he knuckled the screen door as he opened it. "Hey, kid!" he said when his aunt appeared. Then it was kisses and hugs and introductions, and he headed out to run some errands. Dora led the way into her cozy living room, pointing out the spinet piano her nephew ran to as a boy, reaching over his head until his little fingers could press the keys. "He's just an ordinary person that has a beautiful talent and loves his music," she said. "He's just a nice, ordinary boy to me."

And yet so extraordinary too. Given the histories of the Springsteen and Zerilli families, the long pattern of work and sacrifice, of ill health, psychic demons, and death, the one boy's radiant spirit changed the meaning of his ancestors' lives and labors. Nearly four centuries since Caspar Springsteen's ship set sail from Holland, it found purchase on the golden shore of the American land. Ann Garrity's Irish beech tree bore magical fruit. Anthony Zerilli's investment hit a bigger jackpot than he could have imagined.

"So is that God's gift to us? Is it a gift, or were we chosen?"

Bruce's aunt Eda, sitting in her living room not far from Dora's place on McLean Street, traded her customary smile for the solemn cast of a woman trying to account for the wisdom of the ages. For the death of the little girl on the tricycle, the fractured lives of her parents, the husband she lost to World War II, the burdens she and her sisters shouldered for so many decades. Now she's ninety and, according to what her doctor told her yesterday, might not be celebrating her ninety-first birthday. Eda is remarkably cheerful given the circumstances but in moments like these, it's hard not to search for some overarching wisdom in it all. "Why is a person chosen? Are you chosen in this world to do good for other people? Bruce is gifted, but was he chosen? I don't know. I just know that he has a big responsibility. God gave it to him, and he has to live up to that. When the band gets done, the audience is so happy. If they were sad when they went there, when they're done they're so happy. We're happy too. And that's a big responsibility."

Particularly in a world where pain and loss never quite go away. The Springsteen-Zerilli clan suffered another blow in 2008 when a cousin named Lenny Sullivan, who had worked as one of Bruce's assistant tour managers for ten years, overdosed on amphetamines and heroin in the midst of the Magic tour, dying in a Kansas City, Missouri, hotel room. "When my nephew died, I had no idea," Eda says. "I always want to fix things, and if I had any inkling, no way would I have let that boy die. I worked with young people; had I known he was on drugs . . ." She shook her head. "But I was not so knowledgeable, and I have no idea why I was so stupid."

So close to the unquenchable black hole, the strangely blessed life of the other nephew. "Bruce was chosen, but did it come through Douglas's side? Was it Douglas? Was it the mother and father who were so heartbroken? What made Adele able to do what she did? I don't know if I could've done it." [11]

Adele Springsteen had no choice but to wake up every morning and do what was needed to keep her family alive, healthy, and growing. The years of labor turned to decades, life became an ordinary blur, and then a very extraordinary blur. She lost her husband, gained a legion of grandchildren, and as she neared her tenth decade of life and recognized the shadow of her own mortality, Adele felt entirely blessed. "I think with all the problems we had in our lives, God has rewarded me. I thank God for that; I could cry over it. It's terrible to brag. But I can brag because I'm the mother, right? It's hard to believe he's my son."

A small but bustling factory town. A tree-lined neighborhood of humble but well-tended homes. The church on this corner, the sub shop here, the gas station there, the high school around this corner. It's a warm summer afternoon in 1968, and in this yard behind 68 South Street, a little girl sat with her big brother on the lawn, both of them watching the butterflies and, every so often, tossing a ball from hand to hand. Pam Springsteen was six years old, Bruce was eighteen, a month or two from turning nineteen. His dark hair hung thick across his shoulders, but she knew nothing of hippies and straights, of wars between generations or anything like that. Bruce told her stories when she was bored and fixed her snacks when she was hungry. He tied her shoes and picked her up, he played her songs on his guitar and put it down when she wanted to go outside to play.

After a while, he picked up the ball and started tossing it up into the air, catching it and throwing it a little higher, then a little higher than that. "Then he said, 'I can throw this ball up into the sky so far it will never come down,'" Pam says. "I said, '*Do it! Do it!*'"

Bruce stood up, planted his feet in the grass, took a deep breath, and tilted his head to gaze toward the fluffy clouds drifting across the blue. He took another deep breath, reared back until the knuckles of his throwing hand nearly touched the grass, and then, with a mighty heave, sent the

[11] Although, of course, she did, even after her first husband died in World War II before he could lay eyes on the son she named Frank Bruno Jr.

ball skyward. "It goes up and up and up," Pam says. "I'm looking and looking." It kept climbing. From where Pam was sitting, and then standing, the white ball grew smaller and smaller. "I saw it going up, and I waited and waited." Bruce watched with her for a little while, then went back into the kitchen, leaving Pam to stand alone, eyes wide and searching the depths of the clear blue sky. She has no explanation for what Bruce did; whether he'd performed some kind of trick, conducted real magic, or somehow found the power to hurl an ordinary baseball into the outer reaches of the earth's atmosphere. All she knows for sure is what she saw. Or, more accurately, what she didn't see.

The ball never came down.

A NOTE ON SOURCES

I **READ, ANNOTATED, AND DERIVED VITAL** information from thousands of books and newspaper, magazine, and website articles during the course of my research. The sources of specific quotes and anecdotes are cited in the text.

The reporting process began informally in 1978 with Dave Marsh's jaw-dropping cover story in *Rolling Stone* (the original copy I bought that summer still sits in my desk drawer), then hit a new level with the release of Dave's *Born to Run: The Bruce Springsteen Story*, still one of the key texts in understanding the higher possibilities of rock 'n' roll in general and Bruce Springsteen in particular. *Glory Days*, Dave's 1987 account of Bruce's journey to and through the *Born in the U.S.A.* era, describes the superstar experience in its every detail.

I also consulted regularly with June Skinner Sawyers's terrific compendium of interviews, reviews, and analyses, *Racing in the Street: The Bruce Springsteen Reader*. Same deal with *Bruce Springsteen: The Rolling Stone Files*, Anders Martensson and Jorgen Johansson's *Local Heroes: The Asbury Park Music Scene*, Eric Alterman's *It Ain't No Sin to Be Glad You're Alive*, Jim Cullen's *Born in the U.S.A.: Bruce Springsteen in the American Tradition*, the lovely memoir *John Hammond On Record*, Daniel Wolff's *4th of July, Asbury Park*, Kevin Coyne's *Marching Home*, the terrific photos in Lynn Goldsmith's *Springsteen Access All Areas*, Fred Goodman's *The Mansion on the Hill*, Marc Eliot and Mike Appel's *Down Thunder Road*,

Jon Landau's *It's Too Late to Stop Now,* and the essays and lyrics in Bruce
Springsteen's own *Songs.*

The online world overflows with Springsteen sites, databases,
chat boards, and more. Of these, Christopher Phillips and company's
backstreets.com is the most reliable source for breaking news, set lists,
and detailed concert/event reports, while also including the most above-
board ticket traders' board I've ever encountered—face value only, folks.
Brucebase (http://brucebase.wikispaces.com/) has the most detailed account of Bruce's day-to-day musical activities from 1956 to yesterday,
along with vintage photos, posters, sound, and video clips. Their pursuit
of more and better information continues to this minute, which should
qualify them for a medal of some sort. The official site, brucespring
steen.net, has all kinds of fun, useful information, along with official
videos and a very helpful lyric search function. I am also a more or less
daily visitor to Blogness on the Edge of Town (http://blogs.wickedlocal
.com/springsteen/#axzzlIBr8bJIl), which combines solid reporting with
thought-provoking essays and just the right amount of wise-assery. Paolo
Calvi's database (http://www.brucespringsteen.it/) has an extremely thorough collection of lyrics (often including early, unrecorded versions).
I also found a small mountain of archival news stories, interviews, and
reviews stored on http://www.greasylake.org/home.php.

Of the thousands of interviews Bruce has given over the years, many
of which are quoted and noted in the text of this book, I am particularly grateful for the work of Joan Pikula at the *Asbury Park Press*; Greg
Mitchell and Peter Knobler at *Creem*; Jerry Gilbert from *Sounds*; the unknown reporter who spoke to Bruce after his March 24, 1974, show at
the Celebrity Theater in Phoenix (personal to him: if you're reading this,
please get in touch and I'll credit you appropriately in the next edition of
this book); Paul Williams at *Crawdaddy*; John Rockwell at the *New York
Times*; and Maureen Orth and Jay Cocks at *Newsweek* and *Time*, respectively. Also, James R. Petersen at *Playboy*; Eve Zibart at the *Washington
Post*; Robert Hilburn at the *Los Angeles Times*; Bill Flanagan at *Musician*; Fred Schruers, Kurt Loder, Steve Pond, Joe Levy, and Jim Henke,
all writing for *Rolling Stone*; Neil Strauss and Nick Dawidoff, writing
for the *New York Times* and the *New York Times Magazine*; Will Percy at

DoubleTake; Adam Sweeting at *Uncut*; Ted Koppel, then at *ABC Night-line*; Andrew Tyler at the *New Musical Express*; and David Hepworth, then writing for *Q* (David now edits *The Word*, which in 2010 published an early version of material that is now part of this book).

I'm also grateful for the work of filmmaker Bary Rebo, who started working on a documentary about a struggling young Jersey Shore rocker in 1971. He shot concerts, rehearsals, recording sessions, and more before moving on in 1980. Trust me on this: the footage is spectacular, and surprisingly voluminous. Some of Barry's work can be seen in the probing, insightful documentaries Thom Zimny created for the *Born to Run* and *Darkness* box sets. Thom has also made several indispensable concert films for Bruce, all vital in their own way, but none more beautiful than his film of Bruce and the band playing the entire *Darkness on the Edge of Town* album, shot at Asbury Park's Paramount Theater in 2009.

Thanks also to the scores of fans who have shot, and continue to shoot, telephone-cam video of so many memorable concert moments over the last decade or two.

ACKNOWLEDGMENTS

THE IDEA FOR THIS BOOK first took form in a telephone conversation with my then editor, Zachary Schisgal, in mid-2009. Zach has jumped the fence into literary agency since then, but his enthusiasm and trust lie at the headwaters of this project. Matthew Benjamin, who assumed editing duties when he got to Simon & Schuster, has been rock solid throughout. I also owe thanks to Touchstone publisher Stacy Creamer, Kiele Raymond, and the only book publicist I'll ever want or need, Jessica Roth. Thanks also to Simon Lipskar, Dan Conaway, Joe Volpe, Stephen Barr, and everyone else at Writers House.

A legion of friends and colleagues helped inspire, guide, encourage, and in some cases provide editing notes for this book. Big thanks from me to you: Dave Marsh, Claudia Nelson and Rory Dolan, Katherine Schulten and Mike Dulchin, Christie Beeman and Peter Weber, Brendan and Christe White, Amy Abrams, Tim Goodman, Bill Goodykoontz, Ryan White, Kasey Anderson, Tim Riley, George Kalogerakis, Glenn Cashion, Tad Ames, James Parker, Geoff Kloske, Bob Spitz, Jim Brunberg, David Leaf, Cutler Durkee, Lanny Jones, Jamie Katz, Jack Ohman, Don Hamilton, and my main man in the music blogosphere, Sal Nunziato (http://burnwoodtonite.blogspot.com/).

Freehold native, historian, and journalist Kevin Coyne was enormously generous with his time, knowledge, and insights into the history of his hometown and Monmouth County. He's been an invaluable resource, and charming company at Sweet Lew's and Vincente's and on the sidelines of the Freehold Little League baseball diamond.

Enormous thanks also for the friendship and expertise of Jersey Shore music experts Bob Crane, Stan Goldstein (who leads highly informative tours), Billy Smith (connections, details, and photos), and Carl Beams (music, music, music). And a special thanks to Jim Harre, who personifies the public-spiritedness of serious Bruce fans everywhere. I'm also grateful for the help of Christopher Phillips, editor of *Backstreets* magazine (a special shout-out to *Backstreets'* founding editor and publisher, Charles R. Cross). I'm also very grateful to Albee "Albany Al" Tellone for his warmth, vivid memory, and generous but honest perspective on everything from the Upstage and the Cutthroat Monopoly days to the early misadventures of the E Street Band. In a world of conflicting memories and interpretations, the one provider of fact and detail that nobody ever questioned was Albee.

I got to spend a lot of time in Freehold during the course of this project, and am grateful for the help and generosity of ex-Castiles George Theiss, Frank Marziotti, and Vinny Maniello (RIP). Thanks also to Bobby Duncan; Bill Starsinic; Richard Blackwell; David Blackwell; Joe Curcio; Barney, Peggy, and Mike DiBenedetto; Norman Luck; Bill Burlew; Lou Carotenuto; Carl Steinberg; Mike Wilson; Jimmy Mavroleon; Father Fred Coleman; Bernadette Rogoff and all her colleagues at the Monmouth County Historical Association; and Ed Johnson and Joe Sapia at the *Asbury Park Press*. And last but never least, the great New Jerseyite turned Californian Victor "Igor" Wasylczenko.

In Asbury Park, Vini Lopez and Carl "Tinker" West served as my welcoming committee at the Adriatic and pointed me in all the right directions. Thanks also to Patti Lasala at the Asbury Park Public Library, Howard Grant, Todd Sherman, and Earth's John Graham and Mike Burke.

Richie Yorkowitz opened the doors at the Upstage, and Geoff Potter, Joe Petillo, Bobby Spillane, Jim Fainer, and Jim Phillips provided the facts and stories. I'm also grateful to Bill Alexander, Greg Dickinson, Barbara Dinkins, Harvey Cherlin, Doug Albitz, Bobby Feigenbaum, Norman Seldin, Rick DeSarno, Lance Larson, Tim Feeney, Joe Prinzo (I knew how hard you were trying), Tom Cohen, Karen Cassidy, and Paul Smith.

Special thanks to Tony Pallagrosi, the great Sonny Kenn, Virginia's own Robbin Thompson, and the boys from Sunny Jim: Bo Ross, Tom Dickinson, and Tom Cron. Thanks also to Jack Roig, Dorothea (Fifi Vavavoom) Killian, Marilyn "Landlordess" Rocky, and an extra-special thanks to Eileen Chapman, who has been part of the Asbury Park scene for decades and now brings her expertise to the Bruce Springsteen Special Collection in its new home at Monmouth University.

Also vital resources along the way: Barry Rebo, Oregon's own Diane Lozito, Debbie Schwartz Colligan, Pam Bracken, Frank Stefanko, Eric Meola, Joy Hannan, Lynn Goldsmith, Jack Ponti, Robyn Tannenbaum, and Shelley Lazar. Mad props to Joyce Hyser, who was appropriately dubious at first, then became a crucial supporter. Thanks also to Julianne Phillips, whose strength and kindness can be measured in everything she doesn't say.

Thanks also to Mike Appel, Stephen Appel, Bob Spitz, David Benjamin, Jim Guercio, Greg Mitchell, Peter Parcher, Peter Golden, Mike Tannen, and Sam McKeith, whose contributions to Bruce's career should never be forgotten. Also unforgettable—the Columbia/CBS/Sony executives and staffers who helped make it all possible. Many, many thanks to Clive Davis, Walter Yetnikoff, Al Teller, Bruce Lundvall, Don Ienner, Peter Philbin (especially), Michael Pillot, Ron Oberman, Ron McCarrell, Steve Popovich (RIP), Glen Brunman, Paul Rappaport, Dick Wingate, Charles Koppelman, and Greg Linn.

Visions, words, and more: Ernie Fritz, Lawrence Kirsch, Peter Cunningham, Rocco Coviello, Mary Evans, Cliff Breining, John Sayles, Bob Leafe, Brent Wojahn, Ross W. Hamilton and Pam Springsteen, Maureen Orth, Jay Cocks, and Jim Henke. I'm also deeply grateful to Danny Goldberg, Don Mischer, Jackson Browne, Joe Grushecky, former US representative John Hall (D–NY), John Sayles, John Fogerty, Sting, Tom Morello, and Detroit's Wayne Kramer, who is still kicking out the jams. For observations from the campaign trail and beyond: David Axelrod, US senator John Kerry, Timothy Noah, John Tierney, and Eric Alterman. I was eager to talk to Bruce's biggest fan from the conservative side of the aisle, New Jersey governor Chris Christie, but he (or his staffers) couldn't squeeze it in. Next time, I hope.

Thanks also for the vital assistance of Craig Williams, who not only transcribed but listened deeply and came back with insights and connections I had failed to think/connect myself.

Let's give it up for the E Street Band, all of whom gave multiple interviews, e-mailed, traded texts, and more. Vini Lopez started things, in more ways than one. I am also very grateful for the time, memories, and insights of Garry Tallent, Max Weinberg, Roy Bittan, Steven Van Zandt, and Nils Lofgren. Patti Scialfa stayed out of it for the most part, but was welcoming all the same. Charles Giordano from the Sessions Band and E Street; Jake Clemons; and two key players from Bruce's Los Angeles era in the early 1990s, Shayne Fontayne and Zack Alford. Last but never least comes Clarence Clemons, whose generosity began with the effort he took to schedule our talks, then burned even brighter as he welcomed me into his home, shared his stories and unvarnished reflections, then made lunch and poured the wine. His death just a few weeks later was, and remains, a painful loss.

I had been working on the book for eighteen months before I heard the voice of Jon Landau, who called from out of the blue to ask if I had time to talk. Um, yes. This was never an "authorized" book in the technical sense. (I had no contractual relationship with Bruce, Thrill Hill Productions, or Jon Landau Management; they had no control over what I would eventually write.) But from that day forward Jon has been nothing but enthusiastic, helpful, and respectful of my independence. Thanks, Jon.

Major thanks also go to Jon's management partner Barbara Carr, the incredible Alison Oscar, Mary MacDonald and Kelly Kilbride at Thrill Hill, and Marilyn Laverty at Shorefire, all of whom were helpful and friendly throughout. Especially Ali.

Filmmaker/documentarian Thom Zimny was generous with his time, help, and inspiration, and even threw in the next generation of Zimny filmmakers (Hunter Zimny) for good measure. Thanks also to Kurt Ossenfort for the space to work. Tour director George Travis shared his stories and backstage areas with great charm and generosity. So did guitar tech and all-around cool guy Kevin Buell. Thanks also to

Jerry Fox, Jr., who opened doors all across the country. Big thanks also to staffers past and present, including Barry Bell, Rick Seguso, Bobby Chirmside, Marc Brickman, Obie Dziedzic, and a few others who know who they are.

Bruce's studio collaborators, the producers, engineers, mixers, and remixers who helped hone his music were to a man eager to talk it all over, often in intricate detail. Here Mike Appel steps up again, and while he sweetly declined to speak on the record, so does Jimmy Cretecos. Jon Landau did his part here too, along with the open-hearted, passionate Chuck Plotkin and techno whiz and walking music encyclopedia Toby Scott, both of whom spent hours and hours describing precise details of Bruce's recording work. Thanks also to Neil Dorfsman, Bob Clearmountain, Arthur Baker, Brendan O'Brien, and Ron Aniello.

The members of the extended Springsteen family opened their homes, hearts, and personal archives. Pam Springsteen shared her stories, photographs, and handmade videos in Los Angeles. Adele Springsteen invited me into her home and shared all her most precious memories and artifacts, with the help and often conspiratorial glee of her older daughter, Virginia Springsteen Shave. Thanks also to the other Zerilli sisters, Dora Kirby (RIP) and Eda Urbalis. Dora passed away while this book was in its final stages, but I left her quotes in the present tense because I'm convinced she'd find a way to come back and, as her nephew once warned on a different matter, "bop you on the friggin' bean" if I left her out of the party. Big thanks also to Glenn Cashion, who tied together the larger family story; Frank Bruno; and among the more distant relatives, Robert F. Zerilli in New York City and Anne Springs Close in South Carolina, the latter for her genealogy of the Springsteen/Springs family.

Bruce Springsteen made it clear that the only thing I owed him was an honest account of his life. He welcomed me into his world, spoke at great length on more than a few occasions, and worked overtime to make sure I had all the tools I'd need to do my job. Thanks for that, Bruce. And for everything else, too.

The final word goes to my kids, Anna, Teddy, and Max, whose music, light, and laughs give me all the hope I need. Thanks for sharing it all with me (and Mom too), and I can't wait to see what's next.

Oh wait. The real final word, and maybe the biggest thanks of all, go to my wife, Sarah Carlin Ames, for making it possible for me to go all in on this one, come what may. And for thinking up the title, too.

INDEX

A Note on the Author

Peter Ames Carlin was born in Syracuse, NY, in 1963. He is the author of *Catch A Wave: The Rise, Fall and Redemption of the Beach Boys' Brian Wilson* and *Paul McCartney: A Life*. He lives with his wife and three children in Portland, Oregon.